Professional Certificate in Marketing

STUDY TEXT

Stakeholder Marketing

Valid for assessments up to September 2015

The Chartered
Institute of Marketing

BPP
LEARNING MEDIA

First edition July 2012

ISBN 9781 4453 9144 1
e-ISBN 9781 4453 7617 2

British Library Cataloguing-in-Publication Data
A catalogue record for this book
is available from the British Library

Published by

BPP Learning Media Ltd
Aldine House, Aldine Place
142-144 Uxbridge Road
London W12 8AA

www.bpp.com/learningmedia

Printed in the United Kingdom by Polestar Wheatons

Hennock Road
Marsh Barton Industrial Estate
Exeter, Devon
EX2 8RP

Your learning materials, published by BPP Learning
Media Ltd, are printed on paper obtained from
traceable sustainable sources.

We are grateful to The Chartered Institute of Marketing for
permission to reproduce in this text the unit syllabus.

Lead Author: Bob Hogg

The Chartered
Institute of Marketing

Contents

1 Studying for The Chartered Institute of Marketing (CIM) qualifications

There are a few key points to remember as you study for your CIM qualification:

(a) You are studying for a **professional** qualification. This means that you are required to use professional language and adopt a business approach in your work.

(b) You are expected to show that you have 'read widely'. Make sure that you read the quality press (and don't skip the business pages), read *Marketing*, *The Marketer*, *Research* and *Marketing Week* avidly.

(c) Become aware of the marketing initiatives you come across on a daily basis: for example, when you go shopping look around and think about why the store layout is as it is; consider the messages, channel choice and timings of ads when you are watching TV. It is surprising how much you will learn just by taking an interest in the marketing world around you.

(d) Get to know the way CIM writes its exam papers and assignments. It uses a specific approach (the Magic Formula) which is to ensure a consistent approach when designing assessment materials. Make sure you are fully aware of this as it will help you interpret what the examiner is looking for (a full description of the Magic Formula appears later).

(e) Learn how to use Harvard referencing. This is explained in detail in our CIM Professional Certificate Assessment Workbook.

(f) Ensure that you read very carefully all assessment details sent to you from CIM. There are strict deadlines to meet, as well as paperwork to complete for any assignment or project you do. You also need to make sure you have your CIM membership card with you at the exam. Failing to meet any assessment entry deadlines or completing written work on time will mean that you will have to wait for the next round of assessment dates and will need to pay the relevant assessment fees again.

2 The Professional Certificate Syllabus

The Professional Certificate in Marketing is aimed at anyone who is employed in a supporting marketing role such as Marketing Co-ordinator or Executive. You may also be a manager with a senior role within a small or medium-sized company where marketing only forms part of a wider work remit. Or you may be looking to move into your first marketing role or to specialise.

The aim of the qualification is to provide a strong foundation of marketing knowledge. You will develop the breadth of knowledge of marketing theory but also appreciate issues faced within the organisation as CIM qualifications concentrate on applied marketing within real work places.

The complete Professional Certificate qualification contains four units:

- Unit 1 Marketing Essentials
- Unit 2 Assessing the Marketing Environment
- Unit 3 Marketing Information and Research
- Unit 4 Stakeholder Marketing

CIM stipulates that each module should take 40 guided learning hours to complete. Guided learning hours refer to time in class, using distance learning materials and completing any work set by your tutor. Guided learning hours do not include the time it will take you to complete the necessary reading for your studies.

The syllabus as provided by CIM can be found below with reference to the coverage within this Study Text.

Unit characteristics – Stakeholder Marketing

The focus of this unit is to recognise the nature and scope of an organisation's diverse range of stakeholders (of which customers are part) and their relative importance to the marketing process and the market-oriented organisation.

The unit considers how to manage stakeholder relationships effectively, in terms of utilising a marketing mix that influences and satisfies stakeholder needs in line with the organisation's business and marketing objectives.

There is a particular emphasis on developing approaches to communicating effectively with stakeholders based upon their relative importance and interest in the organisation, coordinated for maximum influence and effect.

On completion, students should be able to demonstrate a thorough understanding of the importance and status of different stakeholder groups and the priorities for managing an effective marketing and communications mix to aid relationship development.

Overarching learning outcomes

By the end of this unit, students should be able to:

- Assess the relative importance of organisational stakeholders on the marketing function, and the impact they have on the organisation's marketing activities

- Explain the importance of relationship marketing in the context of the organisation's stakeholders in achieving stakeholder interest, involvement, commitment and loyalty

- Explain how the marketing mix can be effectively co-ordinated to support internal and external stakeholder relationships

- Explain how to co-ordinate the communications mix to communicate effectively with the organisation's stakeholders in line with budget and time requirements

- Evaluate key methods for measuring the success of marketing mix and communications activities.

The Chartered
Institute of Marketing

SECTION 1 – The importance of stakeholders in the marketing process (weighting 15%)

		Covered in chapter(s)
1.1	Assess the different categories of relationships that exist between organisations: ■ One-to-one relationships ■ Relationship channels ■ Relationship networks	1
1.2	Assess the relative importance of the different stakeholder groups and consider the nature of stakeholder **relationships** and their influence and impact on the organisation: ■ Stakeholder maps/matrices – Johnson and Scholes power/interest matrix, Freeman participant stakeholders ■ Partners who support your agenda ■ Allies who will provide support and encouragement ■ Passive supporters ■ Fence-sitters whose allegiance is not clear ■ Loose cannons ■ Opponents ■ 'Voiceless'	1, 2
1.3	Explain the nature of the interactions between the organisation and its different stakeholders groups: ■ Partners – little interaction, but should not be ignored ■ Allies – 'light touch' in terms of frequency of contact ■ Passive supporters – build rapport and relationship ■ Fence-sitters – assess value that can be derived before deciding on level and type of interaction ■ Opponents – structured approach eg, formal meetings ■ Voiceless – 'light touch' in event of coalition being formed	1
1.4	Explain the significance of the range of pressure groups as key stakeholders interested in the organisation and their potential impacts upon market oriented organisations: ■ Sectional pressure groups, eg, Marketing Society, Law Society, TUC, Chambers of Commerce ■ Causal pressure groups, eg, welfare NSPCC, Fair Trade and environmental Countryside Alliance, Greenpeace ■ Impacts – change in strategy, development of new products and services, process change, negative publicity, decrease in share price.	2
1.5	Specify the role of marketing in managing these pressure groups effectively: ■ Planned marketing communications eg, PR and advertising, brochures, encouraging interaction and dialogue ■ Product messages – design, technical features, production process durability and distribution ■ Service messages derived from interactions with pressure groups ■ Proactive management of unplanned messages such as news stories, Blogs – Hainsworth and Meng issue lifecycle model.	2, 6

| 1.6 | Evaluate the different options to developing a Relationship Management (RM) approach within a market oriented organisation:

■ Transactional
■ Long term mutually beneficial relationship with a defined customer:
   – group
   – partnerships
   – strategic alliances
   – e-relationships
   – networks
   – customisation
   – internal customer relationships | 3 |

SECTION 2 – Stakeholder relationship marketing (weighting 20%)

		Covered in chapter(s)
2.1	Explain the position and importance of key stakeholders in the market oriented organisation and establish relationship priorities for the organisation: ■ Stakeholder maps/matrices ■ For stakeholders with little power/interest in project/programme – minimal effort ■ For stakeholders with interest but little power – keep informed and nurture ■ For stakeholders with little interest but high power – maintain relationships ■ Key players – high level of interaction in developing and maintaining relationships ■ Classic market relationships ■ Special market relationships ie, high income/high profile partners ■ Green/mega/nano relationships (Gummesson 2003)	1, 3
2.2	Explain the concept of relationship marketing and its approach in developing customer retention, encouraging customer loyalty, stakeholder interest and engagement both internally and externally: ■ Relationship lifecycle model ■ RM ladder of loyalty	4, 5
2.3	Explain how relationship marketing is based on trust, commitment and cooperation and the importance of this concept not only to customers but the broader stakeholder audience: ■ Service encounter ■ Collaboration ■ Transparency ■ Creation of value	5
2.4	Explain how relationship marketing can contribute to both long-term and short-term customer retention: ■ Improve customer experience and develop brand loyalty ■ Superior service levels ■ Develop stakeholders as advocates ■ Profile strategies – sponsorship, use of celebrities versus advertising	5

The Chartered
Institute of Marketing

SECTION 3 – Utilising the marketing mix to support stakeholder relationships (weighting 25%)

		Covered in chapter(s)
3.1	Explain how a coordinated marketing mix can be used to meet the needs of an organisation's broader stakeholder audience: ■ Product development eg, ethical clothing ranges, smoothies for children ■ Renewable resources ■ Price-value versus supply ■ Place – direct distribution, e-distribution ■ Promotion – bluetooth, compliance with regulation eg football clubs sponsored by alcohol companies removing sponsorship on children's replica kits, not advertising foods high in fat, sugar and salt (HFSS), products in children's programmes ■ People – recruitment, working conditions, equal opportunities ■ Process – recycling, alternative power sources, fair trade ■ Physical environment (décor, corporate image, livery, etc)	6
3.2	Analyse the behaviour and opinions of the decision making units in order to design and co-ordinate a marketing mix that is responsive to stakeholders' needs and adds value to them: ■ Involvement theory ■ Perceived risk – cost/value ■ Attitudes ■ Group influence and opinion leadership ■ Organisational buying behaviour – stakeholder ■ Personal buying behaviour and influence	7
3.3	Explain the dependencies of people, place and process in supporting relationship marketing approaches: ■ Employee satisfaction versus customer satisfaction ■ Reichheld Service Profit Cycle ■ Customer and stakeholder management ■ Product development ■ Place	6
3.4	Explain the methods available for measuring the success of a coordinated marketing mix aimed at multiple stakeholders: ■ Inquiry tests ■ Recall tests ■ Recognition tests ■ Sales ■ Tracking studies ■ Financial analysis ■ Media evaluation ■ Stakeholder satisfaction surveys	7

SECTION 4 – Communicating with stakeholders (weighting 40%)

		Covered in chapter(s)
4.1	Evaluate the extensive range of marketing communications mix tools and explain how they can be co-coordinated to contribute towards developing long-term sustainable stakeholder relationships: ■ Advertising ■ Public Relations ■ New media ■ Sponsorship and hospitality ■ Personal selling ■ Direct marketing ■ Sales promotion	8

4.2	Identify and evaluate the range of tools available to support the communications relating to internal customer loyalty, ie, employee support, engagement and retention within the organisation:
	
	■ Email
	■ Intranet
	■ Training – staff enrichment programmes
	■ Support – technical, management
	■ Flexible working
	   – Secondments
	   – Gap years
	■ Team meetings
		9

4.3	Explain the challenges in communicating with stakeholders in international markets: ■ Adaptation versus standardisation ■ Culture – influence of religion, cultural norms and protocols ■ Language and symbols ■ Availability of technology ■ Ensuring consistency of key messages ■ Availability of media	10
4.4	Identify and evaluate the continuously evolving impact of new technologies and their contribution to economic and environmental sustainability on stakeholder relationships: ■ Tele kits ■ Virtual conferencing ■ SMS ■ Voice over internet protocol (VOIP) ■ Economic – reduction in overheads ■ Environmental – CSR, carbon footprint	10
4.5	Explain approaches to managing budget resource for tactical communication activities: ■ Marginal analysis ■ Arbitrary ■ Affordable ■ Objective and task ■ Percentage of sales ■ Competitive parity ■ Share of Voice (SOV) ■ Centralised or decentralised management	11

The Chartered Institute of Marketing

4.6	Explain the methods available for measuring the success of coordinated marketing communications activities:	11
	▪ Media exposure measurement ▪ Campaign measurement ▪ Increased sales ▪ Response rates ▪ Conversion rates ▪ Order values ▪ Repeat orders	

3 Assessment

The unit covered by this Study Text (Unit 4 Stakeholder Marketing) is assessed using a work-based project. In order to help you focus specifically on your assessment we have also written a Professional Certificate in Marketing Assessment Workbook which is available either through your usual book retailer or our website www.bpp.com/learningmedia.

4 The Magic Formula

The Magic Formula is a tool used by CIM to help both examiners write exam and assignment questions, and you, to more easily interpret what you are being asked to write about. It is useful for helping you to check that you are using an appropriate balance between theory and practice for your particular level of qualification.

Contrary to the title, there is nothing mystical about the Magic Formula and simply by knowing it (or even mentioning it in an assessment) will not automatically secure a pass. What it does do, however, is to help you to check that you are presenting your answers in an appropriate format, including enough marketing theory and applying it to a real marketing context or issue.

The Magic Formula for the Professional Certificate in Marketing is shown below:

Figure A   The Magic Formula for the Professional Certificate in Marketing

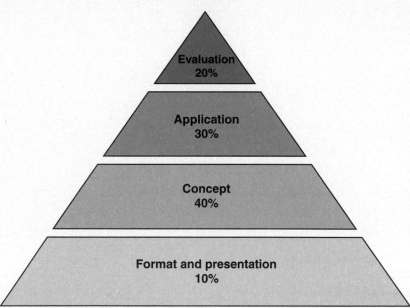

You can see from the pyramid that for the Professional Certificate marks are awarded in the following proportions:

- **Presentation and format – 10%**

    You are expected to present your work professionally which means that assignments and projects should **always** be typed. Even in an exam situation attention should be paid to making your work look as visually appealing as possible. CIM will also stipulate the format that you should present your work in. The assessment formats you will be given will be varied and can include things like reports to write, slides to prepare, emails, memos, formal letters, press releases, discussion documents, briefing papers, agendas and newsletters.

The Chartered
Institute of Marketing

- **Concept – 40%**

  Concept refers to your ability to state, recall and describe marketing theory. The definition of marketing is a core CIM syllabus topic. If we take this as an example, you would be expected to recognise, recall and write this definition to a word-perfect standard to gain the full marks for concept. Understanding marketing concepts is the main area where marks will be given within your assessment at the Professional Certificate level.

- **Application – 30%**

  Application-based marks are given for your ability to apply marketing theories to real life marketing situations. For example, a question may ask you to discuss the definition of marketing and how it is applied within your own organisation. Here you are not only using the definition but are applying it in order to consider the market orientation of the company.

- **Evaluation – 20%**

  Evaluation is the ability to asses the value or worth of something, sometimes through careful consideration of related advantages and disadvantages, or weighing up of alternatives. Results from your evaluation should enable you to discuss the importance of an issue using evidence to support your opinions.

  For example, if you were asked to evaluate whether or not your organisation adopts a marketing approach you should provide reasons and specific examples of why you think they might take this approach, as well as considering why they may not take this approach, before coming to a final conclusion.

5 A guide to the features of the Study Text

Each of the chapter features (see below) will help you to break down the content into manageable chunks and ensure that you are developing the skills required for a professional qualification.

Chapter feature	Relevance and how you should use it
Introduction	Shows why topics need to be studied and is a route guide through the chapter
Syllabus reference	Outlines the syllabus learning outcomes covered in the chapter
Chapter topic list	Study the list, each numbered topic denotes a numbered section in the chapter
Key Term	Highlights the core vocabulary you need to learn
Activity	An application-based activity for you to complete
The Real World	A short case study to illustrate marketing practice
Exam tip/Assessment tip	Key advice based on the assessment
Chapter roundups	Use this to review what you have learnt
Quick quiz	Use this to check your learning
Further reading	Further reading will give you a wider perspective on the subjects you're covering

6 Additional resources

To help you pass the entire Professional Certificate in Marketing we have created a complete study package. The **Professional Certificate Assessment Workbook** covers all four units for the Professional Certificate level. Practice questions and answers, tips on tackling assignments and work-based projects are included to help you succeed in your assessments.

Our A6 set of spiral-bound **Passcards** are handy revision cards, ideal to reinforce key topics for the Marketing Essentials and Assessing the Marketing Environment exams.

7 Your personal study plan

Preparing a Study Plan (and sticking to it) is one of the key elements to learning success.

CIM has stipulated that there should be a minimum of 40 guided learning hours spent on each unit. Guided learning hours will include time spent in lesson, working on fully prepared distance learning materials, formal workshops and work set by your tutor. We also know that to be successful, students should spend **at least** an additional 60 hours conducting self study. This means that for the entire qualification with four units you should spend 160 hours working in a tutor-guided manner and at least an additional 240 hours completing recommended reading, working on assignments, and revising for exams. This Study Text will help you to organise this 60-hour portion of self study time.

Now think about the exact amount of time you have (don't forget you will still need some leisure time!) and complete the following tables to help you keep to a schedule.

	Date	Duration in weeks
Course start		
Course finish		Total weeks of course:
Project received	Submission date	Total weeks to complete

Content chapter coverage plan

Chapter	To be completed by	Considered in relation to the assignment?
1 Stakeholders		
2 The wider stakeholder environment		
3 Organisational relationships		
4 Relationship marketing		
5 Value-creating relationship strategies		
6 The stakeholder marketing mix		
7 Planning and evaluating the stakeholder mix		
8 Stakeholder communications		
9 Internal stakeholder communications		
10 International and technology-based communications		
11 Managing marketing communications activity		

CHAPTER 1

Stakeholders

Introduction

This chapter explores the concept of stakeholders, which you may already have covered at a very simple level for the Introductory Certificate, and which you may also have studied for Unit 2: *Assessing the Marketing Environment*.

Stakeholders are, broadly, individuals or groups who have a legitimate 'stake' or 'interest' in an organisation and its activities: they may depend on the organisation to fulfil their own goals and needs, or they may contribute in some way to the fulfilment of the purposes and goals of the organisation. In sections 1-3 of this chapter, we survey the stakeholder environment, and consider the nature of the 'stake' a group may have in the organisation and its marketing activities.

In section 4, we go on to consider why stakeholders are important and how, in particular, they impact on the activities of a market-oriented organisation. Why should marketing professionals consider stakeholders – particularly those not closely connected with the organisation – as an audience for marketing messages and a target of marketing activity? We will pursue this theme further in Chapter 2.

In section 5, we survey each of the major stakeholder groups, and suggest a framework for thinking about them, in terms of their potential influence on the organisation, their interest in its activities, their potential to expose the organisation to risk, and their potential to contribute to its goals.

Finally, in sections 6 and 7, we set out an important framework for your own analysis of stakeholder groups, as a basis for deciding which groups need to be managed by the organisation, and how they might best be managed. This is a key component of the syllabus and is likely to form part of your work-based assignment.

This chapter focuses mainly on the more immediate or connected stakeholders of an organisation: those with contractual or close relationship ties to it. We will discuss the wider stakeholder environment – and the wider impacts of marketing – in Chapter 2.

Topic list

What are stakeholders?	1
Stakeholder interests	2
Stakeholder influence	3
Why are stakeholders important?	4
Key stakeholder groups	5
Stakeholder analysis	6
Stakeholder mapping	7

Syllabus references

1.1	Assess the different categories of relationships that exist between organisations: ■ One-to-one relationships ■ Relationship channels ■ Relationship networks
1.2	Assess the relative importance of the different stakeholder groups and consider the nature of stakeholder relationships and their influence and impact on the organisation: ■ Stakeholder maps/matrices – Johnson and Scholes power/interest matrix, Freeman participant stakeholders ■ Partners who support your agenda ■ Allies who will provide support and encouragement ■ Passive supporters ■ Fence sitters whose allegiance is not clear ■ Loose cannons ■ Opponents ■ 'Voiceless'
1.3	Explain the nature of the interactions between the organisation and its different stakeholders groups: ■ Partners – little interaction, but should not be ignored ■ Allies – 'light touch' in terms of frequency of contact ■ Passive supporters – build rapport and relationship ■ Fence sitters – assess value that can be derived before deciding on level and type of interaction ■ Opponents – structured approach eg, formal meetings ■ Voiceless – 'light touch' in event of coalition being formed
2.1	Explain the position and importance of key stakeholders in the market oriented organisation and establish relationship priorities for the organisation: ■ Stakeholder maps/matrices ■ For stakeholders with little power/interest in project/programme – minimal effort ■ For stakeholders with interest but little power – keep informed and nurture ■ For stakeholders with little interest but high power – maintain relationships ■ Key players – high level of interaction in developing and maintaining relationships ■ Classic market relationships ■ Special market relationships ie, high income/high profile partners ■ Green/mega/nano relationships (Gummesson 2003)

1 What are stakeholders?

'**Stakeholders** are those individuals or groups who depend on the organisation to fulfil their own goals and on whom, in turn, the organisation depends.' (Johnson & Scholes, 2005, p179)

'Stakeholders are individuals and/or groups who are affected by or affect the performance of the organisation in which they have an interest. Typically they would include employees, managers, creditors, suppliers, shareholders (if appropriate) and society at large.' (Worthington & Britton, 2006, p220)

'A **stakeholder** of a company is an individual or group that either is harmed by, or benefits from, the company *or* whose rights can be violated, or have to be respected, by the company. Other groups, besides shareholders, who typically would be considered stakeholders are communities associated with the company, employees, customers of the company's products, and suppliers.' (Jobber, 2007, p201)

Error! Bookmark not defined. It is important for marketers to appreciate that the organisation they work for does not operate in isolation from other organisations and other people. Many of these others will be affected by or will have some effect on the organisation's objectives. Collectively such people and organisations are known as "stakeholders."

1.1 Stakeholders in what?

With these definitions in mind, we can consider stakeholders to be people and organisations who have a say in the following:

- What you are to do
- What resources you have
- What you should achieve.

They are affected by, and feel they have a right to benefit or be pleased by, what your organisation does.

It is important to remember that if an organisation tries to implement strategies which are in conflict with the interests of powerful stakeholders, those strategies are highly likely to fail. This does mean, however, that if powerful stakeholders agree with what we are trying to do it will greatly improve our chances of success.

With that in mind, it is important for an organisation to identify its stakeholders and their power to affect the decisions and outcomes. Within this process it is worth noting that stakeholder values may not be immediately apparent, and it is important to distinguish between desired, stated and lived values.

Much the same as in real life, when mapping stakeholders you should always consider that individuals might be members of more than one stakeholder group. For instance, an employee, who is a trade union member, may also be active in the local community. This would place that person in three different groups – which you might consider to have completely different values. It would be silly to think that the groups did not communicate with each other and form alliances or that the same person could be treated in different ways depending on which group you choose to include them in.

1.1.1 Process and outcome stakeholders

The distinction between process stakeholders and outcome stakeholders is often made in project contexts, and this may also be a useful way of ensuring that you think comprehensively about who may have a stake.

■ Outcome stakeholders have an interest in the **outcomes** of a strategy, project or decision. So, for example, customers have an interest in the outcomes of marketing decisions: sales promotions, price rises, new products and so on.

■ Process stakeholders have an interest in the **process** by which outcomes are reached. Customers are less likely to have an interest in how the marketing decisions are reached, but managers and departments in the organisation *will* have such an interest: they will have expectations and concerns around whether their viewpoint is taken into account, whether information is shared, who is responsible and accountable for the decision, whether clear goals and plans have been agreed, how progress is going to be monitored and measured – and so on. Other external parties may also be concerned that the processes of marketing are legal, fair and ethical (for example, that large marketing organisations have not colluded in setting prices, or that privacy has not been breached in gathering customer data).

1.2 Categories of stakeholders

There are three broad categories of stakeholder in an organisation, as you may remember from your earlier studies.

■ **Internal** stakeholders, who are members of the organisation. Key examples include the directors, managers and employees of a company – or the members of a club or association, or the volunteer workers in a charity. They may also include other functions of the organisation (eg marketing, production or finance) which have a stake in marketing activity, and/or separate units of the organisation (eg regional or product divisions) which have a stake in its plans.

■ **Connected** stakeholders (or primary stakeholders), who have an economic or contractual relationship with the organisation. Key examples include the shareholders in a business; the customers of a business or beneficiaries of a charity; distributors and intermediaries; suppliers of goods and services; and financiers/funders of the organisation.

■ **External** stakeholders (or secondary stakeholders), who are not directly connected to the organisation, but who have an interest in its activities, or are impacted by them in some way. Examples include the government, pressure and interest groups (including professional bodies and trade unions), the news media, the local community and wider society.

Here is a quick visual snapshot of the total stakeholder environment: Figure 1.1.

Figure 1.1   Stakeholders in the marketing organisation

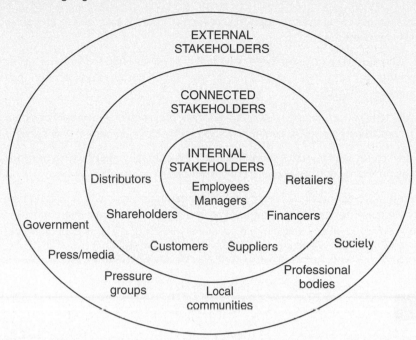

While it is useful to categorise stakeholders in this way, it would be a mistake to think of them as entirely separate groups. Customers are also members of the wider community, and may be shareholders in the company and/or members of a consumer or environmental protection group, for example. Employees of the organisation may also be customers, shareholders and perhaps members of a trade union which can bring influence to bear on their behalf with the management of the organisation. So there are always areas in which membership and interests intertwine.

The key point of stakeholder theory is that an organisation affects its environment and is affected by its environment. The boundaries of the organisation are highly permeable: influence flows from internal stakeholders outwards (eg through marketing) and from external stakeholders inwards (eg if a major customer pressures sales staff to represent its interests within the organisation, or more generally if a marketing-oriented organisation seeks to listen to its customers and meet their needs).

BT is one of the UK's largest companies. It operates in over 170 countries worldwide and provides telecommunications services to domestic and business customers.

Shareholders – BT shareholders include private individuals as well as large institutional investors, such as pension funds and banks. Shareholders are important to BT as they put money into the business and in return have a direct interest in seeing the company becoming more profitable.

Customers – In order to attract and keep customers, BT must offer products and services demanded by both businesses and consumers. This requires the company to continually invest in the development of new services as customers demand change.

Employees – Employees are an important asset of BT and the company runs training programmes to improve the skills of its employees as well as providing attractive rewards and good career prospects.

The wider community – Companies have an impact on the communities in which they operate, both positively (for example, in creating jobs) and negatively (for example, with pollution or other environmental disturbance). BT demonstrates social responsibility through environmental initiatives and community building. It is also supporting various national community projects in connection with its involvement with the London 2012 Olympic Games.

ACTIVITY 1.1

It is worth bearing in mind that organisations in the public and not-for-profit and voluntary sectors have similar stakeholder groups to private sector commercial firms – even if their 'customers' are more difficult to define. Consider the cases of:

- A local council which provides services and amenities to the surrounding area.
- A charitable organisation which raises funds and volunteer support for environmental 'clean up' activities nationwide.

Who are the customers of these organisations? To what other stakeholder groups will they need to address marketing messages?

1.3 Stakeholders in marketing

As we noted earlier, each function, unit and project of an organisation may be said to have stakeholders, whose needs and influence may need to be taken into account. For any given marketing activity or decision, it should be possible to identify relevant stakeholder groups.

- The **owners or sponsor** of the project or activity, who puts authority behind it, initiates it and sets its objectives (for example, the marketing manager or director).

- **Customers**, **users or beneficiaries** of the activity or its outputs: for example, internal departments who receive marketing advice or input, and external customers at whom products/services are targeted.

- The various **target audiences** of marketing messages: the customer base, consumer or industrial markets, the press, the recruitment and financial markets and so on.

- **Other functions** of the organisation, who may share marketing's overall aims (profitable and competitive business) – but may have differing goals, priorities, technology, culture and timescales.

- **Suppliers** of goods and services used by marketing (eg advertising agencies and media, research consultants, intermediaries) – and suppliers of goods and services to the organisation in general, since they also contribute to the products and services it offers to its customers.

- External **collaborators**, **partners or allies** eg in joint promotions, sponsorship or knowledge-sharing networks.

- **Secondary stakeholders** impacted by marketing: for example, communities affected by the environmental and economic impacts of marketing plans (eg waste packaging or price changes) or interest groups concerned with the environment, trading practices, consumer rights, advertising standards and so on.

For your own employing organisation, or an organisation of your choice which you know well:

- Identify its major stakeholders from the examples given above
- Categorise them as internal, connected or external stakeholders
- Identify the major internal stakeholders of the marketing function.

Where possible, and where they are sufficiently significant, identify particular, named stakeholders (eg individual managers, major customers/suppliers, organisational functions or departments).

We will consider each of these stakeholders, and the relationships the marketing organisation may wish to develop with them, as we proceed through the syllabus.

1.4 The nature of the 'stake'

We suggested earlier that the 'stake' or interest of a stakeholder group might arise from a number of sources. It is important to think about what the nature of the stake is, to decide:

- Whether the stakeholder's interest is legitimate, and therefore entitled to consideration and response
- How important the stakeholder is: how much power it has to influence, support or constrain plans and activities; what contributions it may make (if its goals coincide with those of the organisation); and what risks it may pose (if its goals conflict with those of the organisation)
- What kind of response may be required to satisfy the stakeholder, in order to gain or maintain its support – or minimise its resistance – to marketing plans.

We will look at each of these elements in detail when we come to analyse the various stakeholder groups, but some broad types of stake that you might use when analysing stakeholder groups include the following.

Table 1.1   Nature of stakes

Nature of stake	Comment
Market or contractual relationships	Employees, suppliers, distributors and intermediaries, customers and clients have formal economic or legal relations with the organisation. They directly participate in the organisation's activity, as part of the value creation system. Mutual rights, obligations and interdependencies apply, often protected by law (for example, on the fulfilment of contracts for the sale of goods, or fair terms and conditions for employees).
Participation and contribution	Stakeholders participate in an organisation's activity, and in the creation of value for the customer. Suppliers, for example, may contribute quality materials, efficient delivery, reliable availability and perhaps ideas for on-going product improvements – all of which may add value to the total offering to the end consumer. Different organisational functions may contribute to marketing (eg by supplying information on product features or allocating marketing budgets). Other stakeholders may participate less directly: for example, advisory bodies (such as the Health & Safety Executive) may help the organisation to develop best practice and compliance with regulations.

Nature of stake	Comment
Influence	Stakeholder groups may influence a marketing organisation in various ways. Some, like managers and regulatory bodies, have direct authority to shape decisions. Others, like major customers or suppliers, may be actively consulted or involved. Others may exercise indirect forms of influence, by: ■ Supporting or resisting plans – or mobilising others to do so ■ Providing information or skills which shape marketing decisions ■ Imposing constraints (eg limiting the budget) ■ Imposing or threatening sanctions if concerns are not met (eg withdrawing custom or co-operation). Stakeholders get their power from various sources, and we will discuss this in more detail below.

ACTIVITY 1.3

For each of the stakeholders you identified in Activity 1.2, identify the nature of their stake in the organisation and/or its marketing activity.

2 Stakeholder interests

2.1 Multiple interests

As we noted earlier, stakeholder groups are not discrete or separate: individuals may be members of more than one group – and may therefore bring a range of different interests and sources of influence to a given organisation or issue. Peck *et al* (1999) cite several examples from stakeholder literature to make the point that some parties or individuals will have multiple stakes in an organisation.

■ Some employees may also be shareholders and/or customers of the organisation that employs them, and perhaps also influencers in other ways (eg as opinion leaders in their communities or as members of a trade union)

■ Partners or allies in a business network may be each other's customers, suppliers – and even competitors.

Gummesson (1996, cited in Peck *et al*, *op cit*, p24) concludes that: 'However desirable it would be for the sake of orderliness and simplicity, there is no single dimension along which a relationship can be organised. Relationships partly overlap.'

2.2 Conflicting interests

One of the key points of stakeholder theory is that, inevitably, the interests of different stakeholder groups do not always coincide!

Johnson & Scholes (2005) note that: 'Since the expectations of stakeholder groups will differ, it is quite normal for conflict to exist regarding the importance or desirability of many aspects of strategy. In most situations, a compromise will need to be reached between expectations that cannot all be achieved simultaneously.'

The Chartered
Institute of Marketing

Tesco prides itself in bringing affordable food from around the world to its customers. But this involves transporting the food across the globe and these 'food miles' are a concern for many environmental groups.

Here is an extract from a speech by Sir Terry Leahy, the then Chief Executive of Tesco in January 2007:

'We must also face up to the debate about food miles. That will mean a whole series of actions to reduce the carbon footprint of our distribution system and I will speak of those a little later because it is important to remember that food miles are not just about air miles. However, we cannot avoid the fact that transporting a product by air results in far higher carbon emissions than any other form of transport.

We are not willing to avoid the hard fact that there is a conflict between the issue of carbon emissions and the needs of some of the poorest people on earth whose lives are improved by the ability to sell in our markets products which are brought here by air.

There is a strong international development case for trading with developing countries. So, the question is: should we shun Fairtrade horticulture from East Africa to save CO_2, or champion it as an important contribution to alleviating poverty?

To try to resolve that conflict, we will seek to reduce our reliance on air transport overall by restricting it to less than 1 per cent of our products, with a bias to the poor countries.'

The full speech is on the Tesco website at http://www.tesco.com/climatechange/speech.asp

The following are just a few examples of conflicting needs and expectations of key stakeholder groups.

- In order to maximise profits (in the interests of shareholders and investors), the organisation may downsize or limit pay levels (affecting employee interests); pressure suppliers to lower their prices, or pay them late to improve cash flow (affecting supplier interests); use low-cost suppliers which may cause a decline in quality standards (affecting customer interests); or cut corners on controlling the environmental impacts of production (affecting the interests of local communities and environmental groups).

- Marketing may aim to make strong, attractive and high-profile promises to customers about product features, quality and delivery dates. This often conflicts with the agenda of the finance function (to manage or reduce costs) and the production/operations function (which may feel the promises are unrealistic!).

- Professional bodies such as the CIM set codes of professional ethics and technical standards – but individual members may be under pressure within an organisation or business network to 'cut corners' or behave unethically (eg not reporting irregularities, or not maintaining impartiality in awarding contracts).

▶ **Assessment tip**

A work-based assignment option will almost certainly ask you to analyse the interests (and influence) of different stakeholder groups, and one of the outcomes of such an analysis will be to identify where different stakeholder interests conflict. This may be important for further tasks (such as planning a co-ordinated marketing mix for stakeholders), because it highlights the need for: (a) the prioritising of stakeholders (because the interests of some will be more important than those of others); and (b) trade-offs between different interests, in order to achieve acceptable outcomes for as many key stakeholders as possible.

We will explore the implications further as we go through the book – but don't be tempted to skip past these introductory concepts. We are giving you tools which can be applied in your work-based assignment, and theoretical models which you can use to underpin your points and justify your proposals.

2.3 Dovetailing interests

On the bright side, stakeholder interests may also coincide or overlap, creating situations in which stakeholder groups may seek (or be willing) to support and collaborate with each other, to achieve **mutual gains**. (This is sometimes called a win-win situation: by working together, both parties achieve something they want.)

A dovetailing of interests may even create **positive synergy**: an effect whereby parties working together are able to achieve *more* than if they worked alone. (This is sometimes expressed by the equation $2 + 2 = 5$.)

For example, a marketing-oriented organisation believes that by satisfying its customers, it can also survive, grow and maintain profitability – which is in the interests of shareholders, managers and employees, and also fulfils the needs of local communities, and society at large, for economic activity and employment.

ACTIVITY 1.4

From your knowledge of the business environment, or a particular organisation, what other examples can you come up with regarding the way in which the interests of different stakeholder groups may coincide?

Synergy may be achieved by planning and managing activities in such a way as to dovetail the interests of key stakeholders (to create win-win situations), and by emphasising shared interests in communications with key stakeholders (to gain support and/or minimise opposition). Much of the rest of the syllabus focuses on how these two things can be accomplished through the disciplines of relationship marketing, which we introduce in Chapter 4.

3 Stakeholder influence

3.1 Sources of stakeholder influence

As we noted earlier, stakeholders may have power to influence the organisation in various ways. French and Raven (1958) classify the sources of power as follows. (We have added some notes as to how each type of power might apply to stakeholders.)

- **Legitimate power**: legal/rational, formally conferred authority.

  This is often associated with a formal position or role: the marketing manager, for example, has influence over marketing decisions by virtue of delegated authority, while government and regulatory bodies have power given to them by the state to control organisational activities. Power may also be legitimised by law, contract terms, agreed standards or the ruling of a higher authority. Any of these might be appealed to in order to reinforce a stakeholder's claims or interests: for example, the statutory rights of employees (to health and safety or equal opportunity, say), or the rights of consumers to have basic product quality/safety expectations met.

- **Expert power**: the power of expertise or knowledge which is recognised and valued by the organisation (or marketing function).

  This influence may be used by stakeholders such as professional marketing staff, experts in other functional areas (engineers, HR or legal advisers, accountants), specialist service providers (such as advertising agencies) and advisory bodies.

- **Resource power**: control over resources that are scare and/or valued by the organisation (or marketing function).

  In the broadest sense, this is the power of customers to withhold valued business from the marketing organisation; the power of suppliers to control access to critical supplies; and the power of managers to control employee behaviour through the reward system.

- **Referent power**: power emanating from an attractive and inspiring personality, image, or leadership quality.

 The Chartered Institute of Marketing

This may be exercised by a charismatic leader of the organisation; a supplier, distributor or competitor with a strong brand or reputation in an industry; or the opinion leadership of pressure groups, for example.

- **Coercive power**: the power to threaten sanctions, punishments or negative consequences.

    This may be exercised through the aggressive use of competitive leverage by a dominant supplier or customer (an accusation currently being levelled at large UK supermarket chains, for example) or by threats of strike action by employees, say.

3.2 Analysing stakeholder power

Johnson & Scholes (2005) set out some more specific ways in which power can be exercised in stakeholder relationships – and how you can tell when a stakeholder has power: 'indicators of power' are the visible signs that stakeholders have been able to exploit one or more of the sources of power.

Table 1.2   Sources and indicators of power for internal stakeholders

Within organisations	
Sources of power	*Indicators of power*
Hierarchy (formal power) eg formal authority for decision making	**Status** eg seniority, job grade or reputation
Influence (informal power) eg charismatic leadership	**Claim on resources** eg size of budget or staff allocation
Control of key resources eg information, rewards	**Representation** eg members in powerful positions
Possession of knowledge and skills eg marketing or IT specialists	**Symbols of power** eg titles, office space, privileges, support services
Control of the human environment eg influencing, negotiating skills	
Involvement in implementing plans eg exercising initiative/commitment to shape outcomes	

Table 1.3 Sources and indicators of power for external stakeholders

External stakeholders	
Sources of power	*Indicators of power*
Control of key resources eg materials, labour, money, support	**Status** eg speed with which company responds to concerns/demands
Involvement in implementing plans eg suppliers, distribution outlets, agents	**Resource dependencies** eg size of shareholding or loan; proportion of business tied up with one customer/supplier; ease with which supplier/financier/customer could switch (or be switched)
Possession of knowledge and skills eg consultants, agencies, partners	**Negotiating arrangements** eg preparedness of the organisation to consult/negotiate on decisions
Internal links eg relationships with influencers within the organisation, formal representation of interests (eg by trade unions)	**Symbols of power** eg hospitality offered, level of person in the organisation who deals with the stakeholder, amount of communication

ACTIVITY 1.5

Using the following template (adapted from Johnson & Scholes 2005, p187), assess the relative power of two functions or divisions and two external stakeholders of your organisation, from those you identified in Activity 1.2.

- For each stakeholder, assess the extent to which it shows each indicator or power: mark the appropriate column H (high), M (medium), L (low) or 0 (None).

- Give 3 points to each H, 2 points to each M and 1 point for each L, and add up the total power score for each stakeholder.

Internal stakeholders

Indicator	Stakeholder 1:		Stakeholder 2:	
	H/M/L/O	*Points*	*H/M/L/O*	*Points*
Status	☐		☐	
Claim on resources	☐		☐	
Representation	☐		☐	
Symbols	☐	_____	☐	_____

Total power score:

External stakeholders

Indicator	Stakeholder 1:		Stakeholder 2:	
	H/M/L/O	*Points*	*H/M/L/O*	*Points*
Status	☐		☐	
Resource dependence	☐		☐	
Negotiating arrangements	☐		☐	
Symbols	☐	_____	☐	_____

Total power score:

4 Why are stakeholders important?

4.1 Stakeholders and the marketing-oriented firm

As you may remember from your studies for Unit 1: *Marketing Essentials,* a marketing-oriented firm is one which operates according to the belief that 'achieving organisational goals depends on determining the needs and wants of target markets and delivering the desired satisfactions more effectively and efficiently than competitors' (Kotler, 2002).

Note that Kotler's definition does not just focus on the needs and wants of 'customers', but of '**target markets**'. It is possible to see a range of stakeholder groups as targets for marketing activities and as audiences for marketing messages, as we will see in later chapters.

The important point is that the marketing-oriented firm recognises that its reason for existence and activity lies outside itself, in the market. It cannot simply do or produce whatever it likes and then push the results on people (a selling orientation); or do or produce whatever it is good at and assume that people will respond positively (a production or product orientation). It has to analyse the complex needs and drivers of the **people who keep it in business**, and attempt to satisfy them, profitably and competitively – and those people include not just customers, but other stakeholder groups as well. It also needs the input of **internal and external contributors** in order to deliver customer satisfaction – and these contributors are also stakeholder groups.

4.2 The stakeholder view of the firm

▶ **Key term**

The **stakeholder view of the firm** is that many groups have a stake in what an organisation does, and therefore have a legitimate claim to have their interests considered.

The stakeholder view hinges on the concept of natural justice. It is argued that modern corporations are so **powerful** (socially, economically and politically) that they are able to ride over the rights of others. For example, they may use their purchasing power or market dominance to impose unequal contracts on suppliers, customers and employees – and on a wider scale, they may damage communities by polluting the environment, closing a facility (causing local unemployment) or putting prices beyond the reach of ordinary consumers.

Meanwhile, corporations exist within society and are **dependent** on it for the resources they use, either directly (eg by contracting for supplies and labour and competing for capital and customers) and indirectly (eg by benefiting from government expenditure on communications infrastructure, essential services and skills training).

Henry Mintzberg (1983) suggests that viewing organisations as existing only for the benefit of their owners (shareholders) is inadequate.

- In practice, organisations are rarely controlled effectively by shareholders. Most shareholders are passive investors.

- Organisations benefit from the contributions of various stakeholders, who therefore have a legitimate claim to have their interests considered.

- Business activities have impacts on stakeholders, including wider social consequences (eg for employment, business sustainability and environmental impacts). Firms effectively produce two kinds of outputs: goods and services – and social consequences. They rarely bear, or even account for, the total social cost of their activities (often called 'external costs or 'externalities'), but they owe it to wider stakeholders to minimise those costs, or to put something back.

There are, however, two approaches to stakeholder theory for business organisations.

Table 1.4   Approaches to stakeholder theory

Strong view	Weak view
Each stakeholder in the business has a legitimate claim on management's attention, and management's job is to balance stakeholder demands.	Satisfying key or 'active' stakeholders, such as customers, suppliers and employees *is* a good thing – but only because it enables the business to satisfy its primary purpose, the long-term growth in the wealth of its owners (shareholders).

Although stakeholder management is an increasingly fashionable discipline, and corporations are increasingly taking account of the wider stakeholder environment (as we will see in Chapter 2), you should be aware that there are arguments against the strong stakeholder view.

- Managers who are accountable to everyone are, in fact, accountable to no one
- People may have interests – but this does not necessarily give them rights
- The legitimate purpose of a business is to create shareholder wealth
- Not all stakeholder demands *can* be legitimately balanced: as we have seen, they may be genuinely conflicting.

In practical terms, this has led to a recognition that stakeholder groups must be **prioritised**: some stakeholders are more important than others, and the resources of the organisation should be focused on balancing their interests first. We will discuss this further when we come to the topic of stakeholder management.

4.3 Stakeholder impact on marketing

This is really the subject of this whole book, and we look specifically at the importance and value of relationships with stakeholders in Chapter 4. However, to give you an overview:

- Stakeholders may seek deliberately to **influence marketing decisions** that affect them. They may have the power to do this directly (as in the case of a marketing manager, or a regulatory body) or indirectly (as in the case of consumer response or pressure group campaign).

- Stakeholders – beyond the immediate market of potential customers – may be seen as **markets** in their own right. They may be the target of marketing activity and messages intended to secure their interest, support and engagement in some kind of exchange or co-operation with the organisation. (This is the basis of trade promotions, supplier relations, public relations, media relations and corporate affairs activity, for example.)

- Stakeholders may **contribute** to marketing activity, both formally (eg suppliers of marketing services, media who carry advertising, or suppliers and distributors who are part of the process of adding customer value) and informally (eg by giving positive 'word of mouth' promotion, recommendations and endorsements, say).

- Stakeholders may **undermine or oppose** marketing activity, if their interests are threatened or damaged (eg by boycotting products, withdrawing their labour or business, spreading negative 'word of mouth' or mobilising public opinion – or even government action – against the organisation).

- Stakeholders basically **sustain marketing activity**: they represent the pool from which the organisation draws customers, contacts, suppliers and employees. If the conduct of the organisation damages or alienates them, it is effectively 'shooting itself in the foot' for sustainable future business activity.

Lush

Lush Fresh Handmade Cosmetics Ltd (Lush) is a privately owned, UK based company.

The company invents its own products and fragrances, which are handmade using vegetarian ingredients sourced from organisations not involved in animal testing. Lush's approach to marketing is also distinctive in that it does not adopt many of the standard methods. Instead it relies wholly on in-store advertising, word of mouth recommendations and PR.

As part of its ethical culture, 2% of the profits from Lush are donated to charity. It uses Fairtrade sources where possible and has some product lines whose entire proceeds are donated to charity (including the Dorset Wildlife Trust and the Sumatran Orangutan Society). It has made a concerted effort to find alternatives to palm oil, a common ingredient in cosmetics but one that is associated with the destruction of rainforests, especially in South East Asia. In 2010, Lush announced that it had found an alternative, using a combination of oils, and promoted its discovery to encourage other soap manufacturers to make the switch.

(Siegle, 2010)

Lush is also regularly listed in The Sunday Times 100 Best Companies to Work for.

R is a large high-class hotel situated in a thriving city. It is part of a worldwide hotel group owned by a large number of shareholders. The majority of the shares are held by individuals, each holding a small number, and the rest are owned by financial institutions. The hotel provides full amenities, including a heated swimming pool, as well as the normal facilities of bars, restaurants and good-quality accommodation. There are many other hotels in the city, which all compete with R. The city in which R is situated is old and attracts many foreign visitors, particularly in its summer season.

- Identify the main stakeholders with whom relationships need to be established and maintained by the management of R.

- Explain why it is important that relationships are developed and maintained with each of these stakeholders.

5 Key stakeholder groups

In this section, we will survey some of the major stakeholder groups, and give you some ideas for analysing the nature of their stake or interest (what they want from the marketing organisation), and the nature of their influence and potential contribution (why the marketing organisation would want to take their interests into account, or develop relationships with them).

Note that stakeholders' influence is *not* just about power to get their needs met: stakeholders also make a positive contribution to the organisation's needs and objectives. (This is often what gives them influence: they have the power to give, or withhold, something the organisation wants.) Stakeholder management is ideally a mutual exchange of benefits: a classic marketing process!

▸ **Assessment tip**

The tables given here are intended to be a useful starting point for your own work-based analysis of stakeholders, but please be aware that they are only a general framework: they cannot be comprehensive – and not all elements will be relevant to particular organisations. (Also, of course, any analysis you present in an assignment must be your own work!)

5.1 Internal stakeholders

Some of the key factors in internal stakeholder groups can be summarised as follows.

Table 1.5 Factors to consider about internal stakeholders

Stakeholder	Interests, needs or drivers	Influence and contribution
Managers	■ The organisation's survival and growth ■ Fulfilment of task goals and accountabilities ■ Fulfilment of personal goals (reward, career, development etc)	■ Formal authority over planning, organisation and control ■ As leaders, shape the commitment, loyalty and motivation of staff ■ Project corporate image to the outside world ■ Interpersonal influence on decisions through politics, networking, influencing skills
Employees (and/or volunteer workers and/or members)	■ The organisation's survival and growth, for continued employment/prosperity ■ Fulfilment of personal goals (security, rewards and benefits, job satisfaction, responsibility, status, opportunity for development) ■ Sense of belonging and being valued ■ Support, information and empowerment to fulfil task goals ■ Healthy and safe working environment ■ Equitable treatment (equal pay, non-discrimination, employment protection)	■ Key resource: ultimate source of all added value (especially in service provision) ■ Scarce resource: impact on bottom line, competitive edge in times of skill shortage ■ Negative power: threat of withdrawn or restricted labour ■ Potential for added value through committed, skilled, motivated performance (eg enhanced productivity, service, innovation, flexibility)

The internal stakeholder environment will be explored in detail in Chapter 9.

THE REAL WORLD

Vodafone, the mobile telephone company, makes strong commitments to its employees on its website:

'Like any successful business, we want to employ talented, committed people who can help provide what our customers demand: the best communications solutions and the very best customer service.'

It goes on to list the areas that the company is committed to, including:

■ Engaging and motivating employees through regular one-to-one meetings

■ Mentoring and support programmes for employees

■ Offering attractive pay and benefits

■ Provision of training and development to people at all levels of the company

■ Ensuring safe, attractive environments for employees to work in

■ Encouraging employees to work both flexibly and remotely (and providing them with the communications technology to help them do so)

■ Promoting diversity at Vodafone because 'we know it contributes to innovation and creativity and because a diverse workforce better represents our customer base. '

You can read the full statement here:
http://www.vodafone.com/content/index/uk_corporate_responsibility/employing.html

---

The Chartered
Institute of Marketing

5.2 Connected stakeholders

Table 1.6   Factors to consider about connected stakeholders

Stakeholder	Interests, needs or drivers	Influence and contribution
Shareholders	<ul><li>Return on investment: growth/consistency in dividend payments, growth in share price and net asset value</li><li>Influence through participation in general meetings and election of officials</li><li>Good corporate governance: transparency, accountability, directors protecting interests</li></ul>	<ul><li>Owners of the company</li><li>Equity finance to fund activity (preferable to long-term debt finance: no interest costs, doesn't have to be paid back)</li><li>Voting power at company meetings</li><li>Negative power to sell shares (withdraw financial support)</li><li>Influence on perceptions of financial markets and media (investor/consumer confidence)</li></ul>
Customers	<ul><li>Satisfaction of a complex range of expectations and motives for purchase (competitive price or value for money, quality, enjoyable or efficient purchase experience, reliable supply, constructive business relationships): NB different for consumer/industrial buyers and market segments</li></ul>	<ul><li>Target and ultimate *rasion d'être* of all business activity</li><li>Influence on (target of) marketing strategies: product/market, segmentation and targeting, marketing and promotional mix etc.</li><li>Source of short- and potentially long-term sales revenue</li><li>Source of feedback information for improvement and product development</li><li>Source of positive or negative word-of-mouth, viral promotion and referrals, complaints to regulatory bodies</li><li>Negative power to switch or withdraw custom and support competitors</li></ul>
Financial institutions/ lenders	<ul><li>Financial strength of the company, quality of company management and quality of assets available for security (all relevant to the security of loans)</li><li>Return on investment (eg via interest payments)</li><li>Mutually beneficial on-going business relationship</li></ul>	<ul><li>Short- and long-term loan finance to maintain and develop operations</li><li>Added-value services: eg international payments, insurances</li><li>Negative power to withhold, restrict or withdraw loans or credit facilities</li></ul>
Suppliers (including logistics/transport providers and marketing services agencies)	<ul><li>Clear specifications, for fewer disputes and errors</li><li>Efficient order processing, expediting and relationship management</li><li>Fair procedures for awarding orders, evaluating tenders</li><li>Support for sustainability (eg of small or medium enterprises and local suppliers)</li><li>Ethical dealings</li><li>Timely and complete payment of debts</li><li>Opportunities for reasonable profit taking</li><li>Opportunities for development (and gain sharing) through longer-term relationship</li></ul>	<ul><li>Often, fairly high influence by virtue of supplying scarce or hard-to-source materials or components ("Resource Power")</li><li>In the above case, supplier relationship development is a priority (Kraljic, 1983)</li><li>Some suppliers are vital strategic partners (eg advertising agencies or market research companies)</li><li>Less important items can be sourced with a lesser RM approach</li></ul>

Stakeholder	Interests, needs or drivers	Influence and contribution
Intermediaries	<ul><li>Ethical and efficient trading procedures and systems</li><li>Sales support: reliable supply quality/added value, promotional and point-of-sale support</li><li>Earnings (eg through discount margins, fees or commissions)</li><li>Not being undercut or made redundant by direct marketing to consumers</li><li>Mutually beneficial on-going business relationships</li></ul>	<ul><li>Help to promote, sell and distribute goods/services</li><li>Part of total customer 'value delivery system': may offer competitive advantage (eg wide availability, customer service, retail brand)</li><li>Potential for collaborative promotion</li><li>Source of information on sales, customer buying patterns, success of promotions (eg via EPOS systems)</li><li>Negative power to withhold payment or services, or aid competitors (eg with exclusive distribution deals)</li></ul>

5.3 External stakeholders

External stakeholder groups are likely to have quite diverse objectives and to have a varying ability to persuade the organisation to try and meet them. Strategies for communicating with them will therefore vary, according to their location (local, national or international), areas of interests (single issue or broad range of concerns), current and potential contribution/impact (and therefore importance to the organisation) and so on.

We will analyse elements of this wider stakeholder environment separately, in Chapter 2.

6 Stakeholder analysis

6.1 A stakeholder audit

> ▶ **Key term**
>
> A **stakeholder audit** is a systematic process of identifying stakeholders and assessing the effectiveness of current organisational strategies in relation to them.

A stakeholder audit is like a 'snapshot' of the state of the organisation's stakeholder relationships at a given moment. It may be accomplished, in the first instance, by informal brainstorming or discussion, followed up (if necessary) by more systematic research, using individual or focus group interviews or surveys.

The topics of a basic **stakeholder audit** might include:

- Identification of the main stakeholders in the organisation
- The needs/interests/concerns of each stakeholder
- The power/influence and potential impact on the organisation (positive or negative) of each stakeholder
- Current organisational strategies or thinking in relation to each stakeholder group
- Any problems or issues (perhaps reflected in particular incidents) arising from the handling of stakeholders, or a particular stakeholder.

We will propose some further techniques for analysis in Chapter 3, when we have looked in more detail at the concept of organisational relationships.

The Chartered Institute of Marketing

Obviously, if asked to carry out an audit, you should stick to any specific brief given in your assignment. The specimen assignment, for example, required you to:

'Undertake an audit of the stakeholders to:

- Identify the major stakeholders in your organisation
- Explain their level of influence and impact on relationship marketing.'

6.2 Prioritising stakeholder interests

We have already said that not all stakeholder needs and expectations can be met simultaneously – and because some stakeholders are more influential than others, it would not be worthwhile for the organisation to try.

The stakeholder view argues that it is important for the legitimate interests of stakeholder groups to be taken into account, but debate still rages about how many such interests are really relevant and which are more important than others.

- On the soft side, Campbell (1997) argues that organisations need to gain the loyalty of all 'active' stakeholders – shareholders, customers, employees and suppliers – because this is essential to the organisation's ability to compete in the markets for finance, customers, labour and materials/services.

- On the hard side, other authors (eg Argenti, 1997; Barry, 2008) argue that for businesses, the interests of the owners (shareholders) should clearly come first: decisions should be evaluated *not* primarily for their ability to balance the competing needs of stakeholder groups, but for their effect on profits.

Boddy (2005) concludes that: 'The overall message is that it is important to the long-run success of organisations to embrace stakeholder expectations, but that the degree of priority they give to each is unequal and changing.'

The most common method of prioritising stakeholder relationships is **stakeholder mapping**. This is an essential component of this syllabus, so we will look at it separately later in this chapter.

6.3 Stakeholder marketing

Once key stakeholders have been identified, it is possible to plan a management strategy for each. Key issues might include:

- **Goal analysis**. What are the goals, drivers or desired outcomes of these stakeholders? What fears or issues might your plans raise for them? Where might they support you – and where might they oppose you?

- **Desired outcomes**. What do you want or need from these stakeholders? What levels of support do you want from them? What role(s) would you want them to play in your project or plans?

- **Stakeholder marketing**. What methods of communication will be most effective for these stakeholders? Who influences their opinions? What messages will you need to convey to them? How can you sell the benefits (to them) of what you are proposing or doing? How can you tailor marketing plans to appeal to their needs and interests?

- **Issues management**. How will you identify and manage potential issues and problems, where stakeholders' goals may differ from yours? How will you gain stakeholders' early involvement, and collaborate with them in minimising or managing the impacts?

- **Danger signals**. What kinds of behaviour or responses might indicate resistance or lack of commitment/support from your key stakeholders?

What danger signals might indicate relationship problems for marketing, in regard to:

(a)   The production function?

(b)   Customers?

7 Stakeholder mapping

7.1 Mendelow's power/interest matrix

Mendelow (1985) developed a simple matrix to plot two factors for each stakeholder:

■   How **interested** it is in influencing the organisation to get its needs met or interests protected (or in opposing or supporting a particular decision); and

■   Whether it has the **power** to do so.

On the basis of these two factors, the matrix recommends the most appropriate type of relationship to establish with each 'quadrant' of stakeholder group: Figure 1.2.

▶ **Assessment tip**

If an assignment asks you to explain or assess the 'level of influence and impact' of a stakeholder, you might want to use a combination of diagnostic tools, such as:

■   A **power analysis**, with explanation of the source and indicators of power

■   A **power/interest matrix**, which adds the element of how likely a stakeholder is to *use* its power. You may need to justify *why* interest is low or high, depending on the perceived impact of the organisation on the stakeholder's interests or rights. You might also want to identify whether the stakeholder is *for* the organisation or decision, or *against* it.

Some such form of analysis is almost certain to be part of the assignment, so make sure you understand – and can use – both tools.

Figure 1.2   Mendelow's power/interest matrix

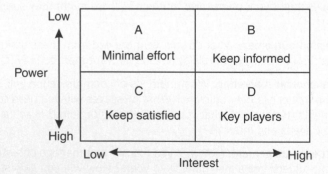

Working through each of the segments in turn:

■   Stakeholders in **Quadrant A** have *neither* interest in influencing the organisation/decision (because it doesn't impact on them greatly) *nor* the power to do so. They are a low-priority group: it will not be worth taking their goals into account, and they are likely simply to accept outcomes as they are.

Small investors, or large suppliers with whom the organisation only does a small volume of business, may be in this category, as may local communities in relation to particular decisions with low immediate

impacts. In relation to a marketing decision, other functions not directly affected by the decision may also be included here.

The appropriate approach is to devote minimal effort to them – although they will need to be monitored in case their status changes.

- Stakeholders in **Quadrant B** are more important because of their high interest in influencing the organisation/decision. They may have low power to do anything about it, but unless they feel they are being kept 'in the loop' and understand the need for a strategy or decision, their concerns may lead them to seek additional power by lobbying or banding together against it.

  For the organisation as a whole, community, small supplier and employee groups may be in this category, in relation to decisions which impact significantly on their interests. For a marketing decision, small customers and staff affected by the changes may also come into this category.

  The appropriate approach is to keep them informed, and monitor and manage any issues that may arise.

- Stakeholders in Quadrant C are important because of their high power. They currently have little interest in using that power to influence the organisation, but if they become impacted, dissatisfied or concerned, their interest may be aroused and their power mobilised.

  A large institutional shareholder may be in this category, as may government agencies and regulatory bodies (in relation to organisations which are currently broadly compliant). For a marketing decision, senior managers in other departments, not currently significantly affected by the decision, may also fall into this category.

  The appropriate approach is to keep such stakeholders satisfied, by ensuring that their needs are met and any concerns they may have are anticipated and addressed before they become 'issues' – without irritating them with excessive communication, which they may not see the need for.

- Stakeholders in **Quadrant D** are known as 'key players': they have high power and are highly motivated to use it in their own interests.

  Major customers, key suppliers and intermediaries, internal senior managers and strategic external allies/partners may be in this category.

  The appropriate strategy is to manage the relationship closely. This may include early involvement, consultation and negotiation, so that the key players' goals can be integrated with the marketing organisation's goals as far as possible. Plans must at least be *acceptable* to key players – and ideally, they can be encouraged to co-operate with the organisation, to mutual benefit.

In order to plan stakeholder management strategies in more detail, it may also be helpful to identify, on your matrix, which stakeholders are likely to be opposed to the organisation or particular plan (marked with a minus sign [-]) and which are likely to be supportive of it (marked with a plus sign [+]). This enables you to plan, for example, to engage the interest, or add to the power, of supporters – and to minimise the interest, or undermine the power, of opponents.

ACTIVITY 1.8

Draw up a blank power/interest matrix, and place each of the stakeholders you identified in Activity 1.5 in the appropriate quadrant. For each, add a [+] or [-], according to whether they are supporters or opponents.

7.2 The participant stakeholder framework

The traditional view of stakeholder influence is that 'the views and initiatives of stakeholders could be dealt with as externalities to the strategic analysis and planning process: as data to help management shape

decisions, or as legal and social constraints to limit them. We have been reluctant, though, to admit the idea that some of these outside stakeholders might seek and earn active roles with management to make decisions. The move today is from stakeholder influence to **stakeholder participation**.' (Dill, 1975).

Egan (1994) divides stakeholders in a change into nine distinct groups, in relation to a leader or agent of change (eg the marketing organisation).

Table 1.7   Stakeholder groups

Stakeholder	Position
Partners	Support the change agent
Allies	Will support the change agent, given encouragement
Fellow travellers	Passive supporters, who are committed to the agenda or need for change, but not to the change agent in particular
Bedfellows	Those who support the agenda or need for change, but do not know or trust the change agent
Fence sitters	Those whose allegiances are not yet clear
Loose cannons	Those who may vote either way on agendas in which they have no direct stake
Opponents	Those who oppose the agenda, but not the change agent in particular
Adversaries	Those who oppose the change agent and the agenda
The voiceless	'Silent' stakeholders who are affected by the agenda, but lack advocates or power to influence decisions

Like Mendelow's matrix, Egan's model argues that different stakeholder groups should be managed differently.

- **Supporters** (in various groups) must be encouraged and kept 'on side':

    - **Partners** may require little interaction, but the organisation cannot afford to be complacent: if dissatisfied, they may downgrade to less committed support

    - **Allies** require some encouragement, but infrequent contact (a 'light touch') is usually all that is required to maintain support

    - **Passive supporters** (fellow travellers and bedfellows) require more intense rapport- and relationship-building contacts in order to mobilise commitment to the change agent

- **Fence sitters** may or may not have the potential to become valuable supporters or harmful opponents. The change agent will need to assess what value can be added from their allegiance, and this will determine the level and type of interaction invested in the attempt.

- **Opponents** need to be 'converted': persuaded of the merits of the agenda and have their reasons for resistance addressed. This will often require a formal, structured approach to persuasion eg using a meeting or series of meetings for negotiation and conflict resolution.

- **Adversaries** may be too costly and difficult to 'win over': they may have to be marginalised or discredited, to reduce their potential to use their influence to mobilise opposition to the plan.

- The needs of the **voiceless** must also receive attention, despite their relative powerlessness, since they may be co-opted by opponents or adversaries to join the resistance coalition. Again a 'light touch', low-frequency-contact approach is all that is necessary to monitor stakeholders' responses and allow them to feel heard.

We will see how these stakeholder communication strategies are implemented in practice in Chapter 8.

The Chartered Institute of Marketing

In addition to the various frameworks discussed so far, you might like to consider a more creative format for stakeholder analysis: a **stakeholder mind map**. This would be particularly useful as a way of capturing ideas from an interview or group discussion about stakeholder issues, as it is highly flexible (allowing information of all sorts to be added as the picture emerges) and visually accessible (encouraging shared understanding and participation).

As an example, consider the following map of a **district general hospital** and its stakeholders in a decision to implement internal re-organisation. The map includes information on internal and external stakeholders, their concerns/interests, potential areas of conflict and direct relationships (or information channels) between individuals and groups.

Figure 1.3   Stakeholder mind map

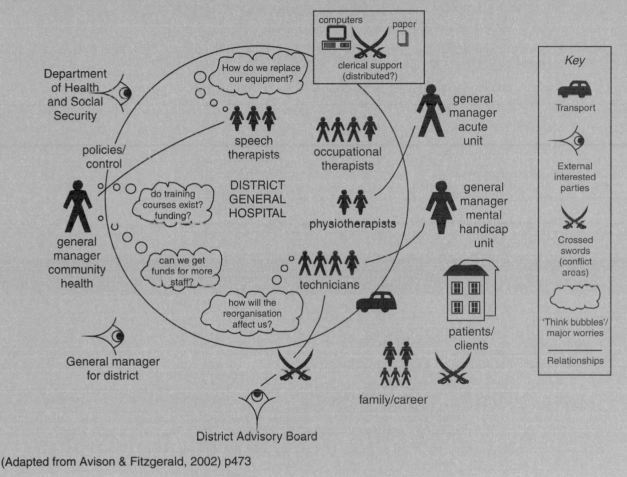

(Adapted from Avison & Fitzgerald, 2002) p473

- Definition of stakeholders

- Internal, connected and external (secondary) stakeholder groups

- Different types of 'stake' in the firm: contractual/legal, participation/contribution, influence and interests

- Multiple, conflicting and coinciding stakeholder interests: the need for trade-offs and the potential for value-adding collaboration and synergy

- Different sources of stakeholder power and influence: legitimacy, resources, expertise, reference, coercion

- Indicators of power, used for power analysis

- The marketing orientation: organisations prosper by satisfying the needs of the market (including customers and other stakeholders)

- The stakeholder theory of the firm: stakeholder needs should be taken into account (although there is debate about which ones, and how far)

- Stakeholder auditing

- Stakeholder prioritising

- Stakeholder marketing

- Mendelow's power/interest matrix

- Egan's stakeholders in change

FURTHER READING

Case studies

United Biscuits http://www.unitedbiscuits.com
Marks & Spencer http://www.marksandspencer.com
Virgin Group http://www.virgin.com

Stakeholders and stakeholder mapping

Johnson G, et al (2005) *Exploring Corporate Strategy: Text and Cases*. 7th edition. Harlow, Pearson Education. Chapter 4: section 4.3. (Illustrations 4.3a [Stakeholder mapping at Tallman GmBH] and 4.3b [Assessment of power at Tallman GmbH]).

REFERENCES

Argenti, J. (1997) Stakeholders: the case against, in *Long Range Planning*, Vol30(3), pp442-445.

Avison and Fitzgerald (2002) *Information Systems Development: Methodologies, Techniques and Tools*. 3rd edition, Maidenhead, Berks McGraw Hill Education.

Barry, B. (2008) *The stakeholder fallacy*, http://www.thefreemanonline.org/features/the-stakeholder-fallacy [Accessed 17 May 2008].

Boddy, D. (2005) *Management: An Introduction*. 3rd edition. Harlow, Essex, FT Prentice Hall.

The Chartered Institute of Marketing

Campbell, A. (1997) Stakeholders: the case in favour, in *Long Range Planning*, Vol30(3), pp 446-449.

Christopher, M. (2005) *Logistics and Supply Chain Management*. 3rd edition. London, FT Pitman.

Dill, W.R. (1975) Public participation in corporate planning, in *Long Range Planning*, pp57-63.

Egan, G. (1994) *Working the Shadow Side: A Guide to Positive Behind-the-Scenes Management*. SF: Jossey-Bass.

French, J. and Raven, B. (1958) The bases of social power in *Studies in Social Power*, Cartright D (ed). MI: Institute for Social Research, Ann Arbor.

Gummesson, E. (1996) Towards a theoretical framework of relationship marketing, in *Proceedings of the International Conference on Relationship Marketing*, Berlin, pp5-18.

Herzberg, F.W. (1966) *Work and the Nature of Man*. NY, Staples.

Jobber, D. (2007) *Principles and Practice of Marketing*. 5th edition. Maidenhead, Berks, McGraw Hill Education.

Johnson, G. *et al* (2005) *Exploring Corporate Strategy: Text and Cases*. 7th edition. Harlow, Essex, Pearson Education.

Kotler, P. (2002*) Marketing Management*, 11th edition. US Imports and PHIPES.

Mendelow, A. (1985) Stakeholder Analysis for Strategic Planning & Implementation in *Strategic Planning & Management Handbook*, King & Cleland (eds). Van Nostrand Reinhold, NY.

Mintzberg, H. (1983) *Power In and Around Organisations*. New Jersey, Prentice Hall.

Peck, H.L. *et al* (1999) *Relationship Marketing: Strategy and Implementation*. Oxford, Elsevier Butterworth-Heinemann.

Siegle, L. (2010) *Mo Constantine's innovation: Finding an alternative to palm oil. Guardian.* http://www.guardian.co.uk/environment/2010/may/30/lucy-siegle-innovator-lush-cosmetics-war-palm-oil [Accessed May 2012]

Worthington, I. & Britton, C. (2006) *The Business Environment*. 5th edition. Harlow, Essex, Pearson Education.

QUICK QUIZ

1   Distinguish between process and outcome stakeholders.

2   Distinguish between connected and external stakeholders.

3   Give an example of conflicting stakeholder interests.

4   List French and Raven's five sources of power.

5   What are the indicators of power of an external stakeholder?

6   Distinguish between the strong and weak versions of the stakeholder theory of the firm.

7   What are (a) the interests, needs or drivers and (b) the influence and contribution of shareholders?

8   What is a stakeholder audit?

9   Explain the quadrants of the power/interest matrix.

10   Who are 'fence sitters' and 'the voiceless' and how should they be managed?

Activity 1.1

Local authority. The customers are the people who receive the services or use the amenities, especially if they also pay for them (for example, through local tax charges). Other stakeholder audiences include employees, suppliers and subcontractors, local business and not-for-profit organisations (who may benefit from or compete with local government initiatives for funds and provision of services), the press (especially local media) and local interest and lobbying groups.

Charity. The customers are, arguably, the beneficiaries of the services: in this case, local communities and environmental groups. However, key stakeholder audiences will include current and potential funders and volunteers (without whom the charity's activities would cease). Others will include the press and government, whom the charity will attempt to persuade of the importance of local environment issues, and other pressure groups, who may support them in this attempt.

Activity 1.2

Your own knowledge and research. Note that this is likely to be useful practice (and possibly preparatory data) for your assessment, where you will almost certainly be asked to identify key stakeholders (prior to analysing them in detail, which we will follow up a bit later in the chapter).

Activity 1.3

This depends on the particular stakeholders you identified in Activity 1.2. You should be able to identify examples from the table. If in doubt, you can review your answers further when you have worked through section 5 of the chapter.

Activity 1.4

Some additional examples (by no means exhaustive) are as follows.

- By offering **employees** the satisfactions of rewards, security, job satisfaction and personal growth, an **organisation** and its shareholders may benefit from greater commitment and loyalty (Herzberg, 1966 and many others) in terms of: customer focus and quality, initiative and innovation, constructive communication, lower costs of disputes and employee turnover, and so on. This can be seen most clearly in the example of training and development, which is desired by, and has benefits for, employees – but is also highly beneficial for the performance of the organisation.

- Responsible and ethical policies on marketing, trading, labour management and the environment benefit the **directly affected stakeholders** (customers, suppliers, employees, community), and dovetail with the objectives of **pressure and interest groups** (eg consumer and fair trade groups, supplier groups, trade unions and environmental groups). In turn, however, this also benefits the **marketing organisation**, by protecting its reputation, heading off opposition, establishing positive public relations, attracting staff and external partners – and so on.

- In a buyer-supplier relationship, negotiation has traditionally been used to enlarge the gains of one party at the expense of the other (eg buyers trying to force suppliers' prices down). However, modern writers on supply chain management (eg Christopher, 2005) argue that it is possible for **buyers** and their key **suppliers** to work together to create value gains (eg by improving product quality or delivery/availability, or making it harder for new competitors to enter the market), so that when it comes to negotiating for a *share* of the value, *both* parties come out ahead. In other words, you 'enlarge the pie' before slicing it up!

The Chartered Institute of Marketing

- **Different organisations within an industry** (and even from different industries) may form partnerships or alliances, or plan collaborative promotions, with the aim of mutual gain. There are many examples of this, including: credit card companies teaming with brands, charities or loyalty schemes (eg earning 'air miles'); joint sales promotions (eg offering competition prizes from one brand to promote another); corporate associations with charities; and so on.

Activity 1.5

Your own assessment.

Activity 1.6

The main stakeholders in the hotel business can be identified as follows.

(a) **Hotel employees**. It is important for the hotel management to develop and maintain positive working relationships with its employees for a number of reasons. At a basic level, there are legal obligations inherent in the employment relationship, so that the hotel will need to pursue 'employee relations' in various forms (such as consultation and involvement, within the EU framework, for example). More broadly, the hotel management needs to pursue constructive relations with staff in the interests of securing their commitment, loyalty and input, to support a high (and competitive) level of service to customers. Service levels are a key differentiating factor for hotels, and only committed and informed staff will be able to deliver appropriate customer care. While staff turnover is traditionally high in hotel and catering, R will benefit from staff continuity through relationship-building, because of its emphasis on high quality service and group branding.

(b) **Hotel group shareholders**. Shareholders have an ultimate say in the strategic management of the group and the employment of its management – as well as providing its share capital and financial market credibility. Hotel management has legal obligations to pursue shareholder relations in the sense of reporting requirements and the referral of decisions to shareholders at statutory meetings. This may be sufficient for many of the small individual shareholders. The larger institutional shareholders, however, have greater individual power to give or withhold support from the hotel's management: they represent an important 'public' which must be co-opted to support its strategic initiatives.

(c) **Other sources of finance**. Banks, for example, are another important stakeholder as they provide long- and short-term loan finance for the hotels. Expansion plans (new facilities, new hotel premises) will need backing. The banks' ability to deny credit if they are not satisfied with the relationship could hamper development of both the worldwide group and the individual hotel R. If cash flow problems develop, the bank's willingness to help will be needed if the hotel is to stay in business at all.

(d) **Suppliers**. The hotel 'product' is a complex bundle of product/service elements, many of which are supported and/or provided (on a contracted basis) by external suppliers. Suppliers help to ensure the smooth running of the hotels through provision of goods such as food and domestic consumables, and services such as equipment maintenance, cleaning and security. Relationships with suppliers must be maintained (eg by supplier relationship management, a good payment record and collaborative improvement planning) so that these goods and services continue to be provided. Consistency (and therefore continuity) of supply will be particularly important for a hotel with a high-quality brand to maintain. Supplier loyalty, partnership and perhaps exclusivity will also be helpful in maintaining competitive advantage, as a core resource.

(e) **Hotel customers**. Customers are the *raison d'être* of the hotel, and the source of its continued competitive survival. As we will see in Chapter 4, it is more cost-effective to retain customers (by building mutually satisfying long-term relationships with them) than to win new ones, particularly in highly competitive markets. It will therefore be important for R not only to provide one-off excellent experiences for customers, but relationships with them: loyalty incentives and rewards, on-going contacts (perhaps a newsletter, special offers to returning guests and so on), and personalised service at

all points of contact ('valued guest'). This should be possible not only for those who stay at the hotel, but for community users of its swimming pool (perhaps by 'winter membership' to stimulate out-of-season custom) and other facilities.

Activity 1.7

Production function: reduction in information flows (eg about production schedules or product changes); conflict between representatives of the functions; spoken criticism, complaints or innuendos; competition for budget allocations

Customers: reduced sales and sales revenue; product returns/refunds; complaints or poor feedback; switching to competing brands; poor word of mouth (eg showing up in online web logs or discussion boards).

Activity 1.8

Depends on your identified stakeholders, and analysis of their power in Activity 1.5. We give a completed example in Chapter 2.

QUICK QUIZ ANSWERS

1   Outcome stakeholders have an interest in the results of decisions, projects or processes: process stakeholders have an interest in the process by which they are arrived at.

2   Connected stakeholders have a direct legal or commercial connection with the organisation. External stakeholders do not: they are interested in the organisation's activities by virtue of their potential to impact on their interests or rights.

3   An example of conflicting stakeholder interests is shareholders' desire to maximise profits (and therefore returns on their investment), while this may work against the interests of customers (eg higher prices, lower quality).

4   The sources of power are: legitimate power, resource/reward power, expert power, referent power and coercion.

5   Indicators of power for an external stakeholder are: status, resource dependencies, negotiating arrangements and symbols.

6   The strong stakeholder view argues that all stakeholders have a legitimate claim on management's attention, and stakeholder demands should be balanced. The weak stakeholder view argues that stakeholder demands should only be met insofar as that enables the business to satisfy its primary purpose: long-term growth in shareholder wealth.

7   See the table in section 5.2 for a full answer.

8   Stakeholder audit is a systematic process of identifying stakeholders and assessing the effectiveness of current organisational strategies in relation to them.

9   See section 7.1 for a full answer.

10   Fence sitters are stakeholders whose allegiance is not yet clear: if their allegiance is considered valuable, effort should be made to persuade and engage them. The voiceless are stakeholders who lack advocates or power to influence decisions: a light degree of contact should be maintained to monitor their responses and allow them to feel heard.

The Chartered
Institute of Marketing

CHAPTER 2

The wider stakeholder environment

Introduction

Following on from Chapter 1, this chapter explores the wider external or secondary stakeholder environment in more detail. As we have seen, the strong stakeholder view argues that these stakeholders – even if they are not 'active participants' in the marketing organisation and its activities – should nevertheless be given consideration, because their interests and rights are affected by the marketing organisation and its activities.

The topic of Corporate Social Responsibility (CSR) is an important underlying strand in stakeholder marketing, which may be the focus of a work-based assignment. CRM (Customer Relationship Management) provides a rationale for marketing to external stakeholders. It has also become an important expectation of customers, suppliers and employees, and will therefore be an element in marketing to them.

In section 1, we explore the nature of the external stakeholder environment and analyse the interests and influence of some major external stakeholder groups. This should enable you to complete a power/interest matrix and stakeholder analysis for the full range of stakeholders.

In section 2, we explain some of the key values of corporate social responsibility, marketing ethics and sustainability, and consider *why* organisations should be concerned to apply those values to marketing. In section 3, we look at some of the specific marketing approaches that have developed in response to the pressure (and fashion) for social responsibility.

Finally, in sections 4 and 5, we return to the syllabus-highlighted topic of pressure groups, examining in more detail their nature and impact, and the role of marketing in managing them.

Topic list

The wider stakeholder environment (1)

Marketing ethics and CSR (2)

The role of marketing in CSR (3)

Pressure groups (4)

Marketing's role in managing pressure groups (5)

1.2	Assess the relative importance of the different stakeholder groups and consider the nature of stakeholder **relationships** and their influence and impact on the organisation:
	■ Stakeholder maps/matrices – Johnson and Scholes power/interest matrix, Freeman participant stakeholders
	■ Partners who support your agenda
	■ Allies who will provide support and encouragement
	■ Passive supporters
	■ Fence sitters whose allegiance is not clear
	■ Loose cannons
	■ Opponents
	■ 'Voiceless'
1.4	Explain the significance of the range of pressure groups as key stakeholders interested in the organisation and their potential impacts upon market oriented organisations:
	■ Sectional pressure groups, eg, Marketing Society, Law Society, TUC, Chambers of Commerce
	■ Causal pressure groups, eg, welfare NSPCC, Fair Trade and environmental Countryside Alliance, Greenpeace
	■ Impacts – change in strategy, development of new products and services, process change, negative publicity, decrease in share price.
1.5	Specify the role of marketing in managing these pressure groups effectively:
	■ Planned marketing communications eg, PR and advertising, brochures, encouraging interaction and dialogue
	■ Product messages – design, technical features, production process durability and distribution
	■ Service messages derived from interactions with pressure groups
	■ Proactive management of unplanned messages such as news stories, Blogs – Hainsworth and Meng issue lifecycle model.

1 The wider stakeholder environment

As we discussed in Chapter 1, the view of what constitutes a legitimate stakeholder has broadened from a focus on groups involved directly with the organisation, or participating actively in its operations, to a wider range of groups who are affected by an organisation's behaviour and outputs.

R Edward Freeman, a professor at the Darden School of Business at the University of Virginia, is one of the proponents of stakeholder theory. You can hear him summarise his approach to the wider stakeholder environment in this short YouTube video: http://www.youtube.com/watch?v=bIRUaLcvPe8

1.1 External stakeholder groups

External stakeholders are likely to have quite diverse objectives and a varying ability to ensure that the company meets them.

1.1.1 Stakeholders in public and voluntary sector organisations

Public sector organisations (such as state schools, health services, government authorities and the armed forces) are particularly likely to have a wide and diverse range of external stakeholders, because:

The Chartered Institute of Marketing

- They are owned and funded by the state on behalf of all its citizens (taxpayers): they do not have a single primary stakeholder equivalent to business owners or shareholders in the private sector

- They are designed to ensure that a range of essential services are provided, and citizens' rights protected, across a broad spectrum: they do not focus their objectives on market demand like a private sector enterprise

- They typically have a range of non-financial objectives (eg service quality and value, sustainability, social responsibility), rather than the private sector's focus on the primary objective of profitability

- They are subject to government targets and formal regulation on a range of social responsibility and sustainability issues, reflecting the state's broad obligation to protect citizens' rights and preserve national resources.

Similarly, **voluntary sector** organisations (such as clubs and associations, charities, churches and pressure groups) may have a diverse range of stakeholders, including: their funders, their staff and volunteers/members, the beneficiaries of their services, and a number of target audiences of their marketing messages.

▸ **Assessment tip**

If you select a public or voluntary sector organisation as the subject of your assignment, you will need to be aware of these issues. You will also need to bear in mind that its relationships and marketing approaches may have different priorities and use different tools – often with fewer available resources – to those of private sector commercial businesses. We will highlight some of these differences in our The Real World examples and Activities.

1.1.2 Government as a stakeholder

At the national level, the government is a very important stakeholder.

- It has legal authority to regulate the activities of corporations (eg through company and competition law, employment law, consumer protection and so on)

- Its policies affect the economic environment in which organisations operate (eg through regional development, monetary and international trade policies, and infrastructure and skills development)

- It may be an important customer, as a very large buyer of goods and services

- It also (theoretically) represents the interests of the population as a whole.

National government has an interest in the activities of commercial organisations for a number of reasons. Organisations provide reports and returns (eg on labour trends and skilling) which contribute to government statistics and policy development. The spending patterns of large companies can have significant macro-economic effects (eg on inflation). A profitable private sector results in greater tax collection potential to support government spending. Government often also looks to private and not-for-profit organisations to share its social responsibilities: providing services, social benefits (such as employment), and funding and expertise for projects (such as the Virgin Group's use of its airline profits to fund research into alternative fuels).

Local government is also a stakeholder, through local policies on commercial development and employment, and the enforcement of local bye-laws (eg in regard to land use and development, outdoor advertisements, traffic flows, environmental protection and so on). It has an interest in local issues raised by organisational activity: for example, economic activity and employment, environmental damage and pollution, traffic congestion, and the use of local small suppliers.

International political bodies, such as the European Union, the World Health Organisation or the World Trade Organisation may also exercise influence. Much UK legislation (eg on competition, health and safety, employment rights and data protection) now comes from EU social policy and directives, for example.

1.1.3 Society as a stakeholder

Marketing activities can affect local communities and broader society on many levels. You might think immediately of examples such as the creation of jobs (or unemployment, due to redundancies or branch

closures); the provision of safe, healthy, accessible and reasonably priced goods and services (or not); business contributions to local events and charities; or environmental impacts such as traffic, pollution, damage to natural beauty or excessive energy/resource consumption.

However, consider the following more subtle examples of marketing impacts.

- Does the advertising of luxury goods create a greater sense of alienation by poorer members of society who will never be able to afford them?

- What about overseas societies and economies: do businesses have the right to 'dump' lower quality or obsolete goods on less-developed markets, or to increase profits by exploiting workers in low-wage countries (often with poor working conditions)?

THE REAL WORLD

In November 2010, Unilever launched a new corporate social responsibility programme.

Entitled the Sustainable Living Plan, it is a wide-ranging CSR programme from the Anglo-Dutch company, whose food, home and personal care brands include Lynx, Persil, Flora, Hellman's and Knorr.

By 2020, Unilever wants to help one billion people improve their health, to source all its agricultural raw materials from sustainable sources, and to halve the total environmental footprint of its products. At the same time, the company aims to double in size. The group's annual turnover for the last three years has been around €40bn, or £34bn.

Doubling the size of the business may be easier than achieving the CSR goals as the company is currently on the acquisition trail, with the home care arm of Sara Lee the latest addition.

For the 60 specific CSR goals set out in its Sustainable Living Plan, Unilever chief executive Paul Polman said: 'There might be targets that we miss. But if we do this we will be in a better place than we were before. We see no conflict between business growth and sustainable consumption. And we believe it is the right thing to do for the company, for our customers and for the planet.'

On its website, Unilever lists the key targets of the plan as:

- Improving health and well-being: By 2020 it will help more than a billion people take action to improve their health and well-being.

- Reducing environmental impact: By 2020 its goal is to halve the environmental footprint of the making and use of its products.

- Enhancing livelihoods: By 2020 it will enhance the livelihoods of hundreds of thousands of people.

You can read more at: http://www.unilever.com/sustainable-living/

Society as a whole, because of its diversity, may have low direct influence on the policies and activities of an organisation. However, society's interests are organised, focused and represented in various ways.

- **Government** policy, legislation and regulation (and the regulatory bodies that enforce them) are intended to protect the wider interests of citizens, economies and the environment.

- The concept of '**consumerism**', or the consumer rights movement, seeks to promote and protect the rights and interests of consumers (as a general group: not necessarily the customers or end-users of the organisation's products and services). It emphasises four basic rights: the right to safety (when using products and services); the right to be informed (through responsible product labelling and instructions, clear terms and conditions of service and accurate marketing claims); the right to choose (through the availability of choice/competition and restraint of coercive marketing techniques); and the right to be heard (through feedback, complaints and appeals).

- In their six markets model, Peck *et al* (1999) argue that there is a distinct '**influence market**', which has the potential to exert influence over the organisation on behalf of particular interests, and which therefore requires a marketing response. This market includes diverse constituencies such as pressure groups, the press and media, user and consumer groups and trade unions. Pressure groups are often the

The Chartered Institute of Marketing

interface between an organisation and society, since they have been formed specifically to pursue a higher degree of interest in issues and their social impacts: we will consider them specifically in sections 4 and 5 of this chapter.

- Members of **internal and connected stakeholder groups** are also members of society: damaging or alienating their interests would be counter-productive for an organisation which depends on, and competes for, labour, suppliers, customers and sustainable and synergistic business alliances.

ACTIVITY 2.1

How does your own work organisation, or one which you know well, impact (a) positively and (b) negatively on the local community (or communities) in which it operates?

1.2 External stakeholder analysis

The following is our overview analysis of the interests and impacts of some of the key general stakeholders in the external environment.

> ▶ **Assessment tip**
>
> As in Chapter 1, the tables given here are intended to be a useful starting point for your own work-based analysis of stakeholders, but please be aware that they are only a general framework: you will need to select the specific stakeholder groups that apply to the context of your chosen organisation.

Table 2.1   Factors to consider about external stakeholders

Stakeholder	Interests, needs and drivers	Influence/contribution
Government (national and local), government agencies and regulatory bodies	■ Corporate tax revenue ■ Healthy level of economic activity and balance of trade ■ Compliance with legislation ■ Reports and returns ■ Support for regional development and employment ■ Socially responsible, ethical and sustainable policies	■ Power to enforce requirements through legislation, regulation and sanctions ■ Control over taxation, grants and other financial constraints and incentives on business ■ Bargaining power as a large customer for goods/services ■ Power to send own marketing messages: mobilise public opinion (eg on green and social responsibility issues) ■ Direct control and funding of public sector organisations ■ Reliable, cost-effective guidance on obligations
News/information media	■ Access to information and news of relevance/interest to audiences (public right to know?) ■ Competitive advantage over other news/entertainment providers ■ Revenue from the sale of advertising space	■ Ability to expose abuses ■ Shape public/consumer awareness and opinion: may add positive or negative 'spin' to issues/crises ■ Control access to the public through publicity, editorial coverage ■ Provide media for promotional messages (eg ad space)

Stakeholder	Interests, needs and drivers	Influence/contribution
Pressure groups	▪ Promotion and increased awareness of a cause or issue (eg fair trade, environment) ▪ Protection of the rights or interests of the group (eg consumer protection, trade union) ▪ Access to information about company policies/practices ▪ Access to influencers and coalitions (to increase influence) ▪ Sponsorship or donation funding	▪ May shape public policy (eg through lobbying, input to advisory committees) ▪ Inform and mobilise public/consumer opinion for or against organisational practices ▪ Source of information about potential issues and impacts on the business: input to issues management ▪ Potential to collaborate to enhance green/ethical credentials of a brand ▪ Negative power to mobilise or conduct protests, boycotts
Trade unions	▪ Protect and promote the interests of their members: support in collective bargaining, employee relations and labour disputes ▪ Gain bargaining power to improve collective agreements on pay and conditions ▪ Greater participation in decision making in issues affecting members ▪ Recognition of trade union representatives and activities ▪ Attract members (for power and revenue)	▪ Collective bargaining power (representing large numbers of employees) ▪ Power to expose abuses and infringements of rights ▪ Political power: influence on government policy ▪ Expertise/training in areas beneficial to the firm (eg access to learning/training) ▪ Negative power to restrict or withdraw labour (eg through official go-slow or strike action)
The community and society at large	▪ Access to products/services ▪ Safe products ▪ Affordable prices for essential goods/services ▪ Access to employment ▪ Legal, ethical, fair and socially responsible business and employment practices ▪ Positive (or minimal negative) impact on the environment	▪ Pool for actual and potential customers, suppliers and employees: power to give or withhold support if interests damaged ▪ Power to organise/mobilise to influence government policy and consumer opinion ▪ Potential for mutual benefit through co-operation eg in infrastructure development, environmental clean-up, recruitment etc.

The Chartered Institute of Marketing

Eastborough is a large region of the UK with a rugged, beautiful coastline where rare birds have recently settled on undisturbed cliffs. Since mining ceased 150 years ago, its main industries have been agriculture and fishing. However, today, many communities in Eastborough suffer high unemployment. Government initiatives for regeneration through tourism have met with little success as the area has poor road networks, unsightly derelict buildings and dirty beaches.

Digwell Explorations, a listed company, has a reputation for maximising shareholder returns and has discovered substantial tin reserves in Eastborough. With new technology, mining could be profitable, provide jobs and boost the economy. A number of interest and pressure groups have, however, been vocal in opposing the scheme.

Digwell Explorations, after much lobbying, has just received government permission to undertake mining. It could face difficulties in proceeding because of the likely activity of a group called the Eastborough Protection Alliance. This group includes wildlife protection representatives, villagers worried about the potential increase in traffic congestion and noise, environmentalists and anti-capitalism groups.

You are a marketing assistant for Digwell Explorations. Write a short informal report for your Marketing Manager in which you:

(a)   Use Mendelow's mapping framework to analyse how the interest and power of stakeholder groups in Digwell Explorations' plans can be understood, and

(b)   Identify how Digwell might respond to each group.

---

2 Marketing ethics and CSR

2.1 Marketing ethics

> **▶ Key term**
>
> **Marketing ethics** are 'the moral principles and values that guide behaviour within the field of marketing, and cover issues such as product safety, truthfulness in marketing communications, honesty in relationships with customers and distributors, pricing issues and the impact of marketing decisions on the environment and society.' (Jobber, 2007, p191)

Ethics are a set of moral principles or values about what constitutes 'right' and 'wrong' behaviour. They are shaped by social (and sometimes religious) assumptions and beliefs, and – more deliberately – by public and professional bodies, in the form of agreed principles and guidelines (ethical codes or codes of practice) which are designed to protect society's best interests.

At the macro level, marketing itself has been subject to criticism from consumer, environmental and anti-globalisation groups for its harmful impacts: generating manufacturing activity and waste products which impact on the environment; encouraging over-consumption of scarce resources; encouraging consumption of harmful products (such as alcohol, tobacco and junk foods); invasion of privacy (eg through direct marketing and customer data collection); erosion of national cultures through globalisation; exploitation of workers and consumers in less-developed markets; and so on.

At the corporate level, ethical issues face a marketing organisation as it formulates policies about how it interacts with its various stakeholders. Some of these matters are covered by legislative requirements (eg in regard to product safety, truth in advertising or basic rights of employees). Others are subject to rules laid down by industry regulators, such as Ofcom for the communications industry, the Competition Commission (regulating merger and acquisition activity) and the Advertising Standards Authority (regulating media advertising).

An organisation may have a 'compliance-based' approach to ethics which strives merely to uphold these minimal requirements. Alternatively, it may pursue a more proactive 'integrity-based' approach, which pursues high ethical standards – whether or not they are illegal. (It is not currently illegal in the UK, for example, to promote extreme dieting among teenage girls, or to put genetically modified ingredients in food products – but both have been argued to be unethical, and leading brands have altered their policies accordingly.)

2.2 Corporate social responsibility (CSR)

Caroll & Buchholtz (2000, cited in Jobber, 2007) argue that there are four main 'layers' of corporate social responsibility:

2.2.1 Economic responsibilities

The firm must produce goods and services wanted by the market, profitably – otherwise it cannot survive, and will not be able to fulfil any other obligations to stakeholders. Economic responsibilities include: operating efficiently and effectively, aiming for consistent levels of profitability, and competing effectively in the market.

2.2.2 Legal responsibilities

Economic goals must be pursued within the framework of the laws of the society within which the firm operates. It is sometimes said that 'the law is a floor': it does not define best practice, but does set out the minimum principles and standards that are considered acceptable. The news is full of examples of how business practices can fail to comply with contract, employment, consumer protection, health and safety, and competition law and so on. Law and regulation may affect marketing practices, the organisation's business practices (trading, employment, environmental protection, financial management and so on) and its products and services (eg in regard to quality, safety, packaging or customer protection).

2.2.3 Ethical responsibilities

Ethical responsibilities comprise the expectations of society, over and above basic economic and legal requirements: honesty in business relationships, for example; not exploiting small suppliers and retailers; or not marketing manipulatively to children. This is a more discretionary area, because there are fewer direct sanctions against unethical behaviour. Ethical principles may be enforced via Codes of Ethics or Codes of Practice in an industry, profession or individual firm – but they are often also subject to stakeholder pressure (demands, protests, boycotts and so on).

2.2.4 Philanthropic responsibilities

Above and beyond even ethical dealings, society increasingly expects that marketing organisations be 'good corporate citizens': that is, that they proactively and positively contribute to the society in which they operate. Examples of philanthropy include corporations building community amenities, sponsoring local causes and events, donating money to charity, supporting local schools, promoting or campaigning on issues of concern, or offering grants and prizes for research/innovation of benefit to society. (A recent example of such corporate philanthropy is Marks & Spencer's relationship with Oxfam who help encourage Marks & Spencer's customers to recycle clothing while Marks & Spencer raises money to support the work of Oxfam).

Some key areas for CSR policies include matters such as:

- **Environmental responsibility**: control of pollution, waste and carbon emissions; promotion of recycling; repair of land degradation; protecting species; reducing resource use and so on

- **Ethical trading**: eg non-exploitative dealings with suppliers and intermediaries, avoidance of bribery/corruption in winning or awarding contracts, fair pricing of essential goods and services

- **Human rights**: eg the improvement of working conditions, protection of privacy, ethical investment (avoiding funding exploitative regimes and corporations)

- **Equal opportunities** (non-discrimination in employment and access to products and services) and diversity (structuring the workforce and supply chain to reflect the diversity of the population as a whole)

- **Sustainability**: operating in ways that do not compromise the wellbeing of future generations. This may include both environmental sustainability (eg controlling the use of non-renewable resources,

encouraging recycling) and economic/social sustainability (eg supporting small and local business, creating employment, or promoting health).

ACTIVITY 2.3

How does your work or other selected organisation fulfil its economic, legal, ethical and philanthropic responsibilities? Give at least two specific examples of responsibilities recognised by the organisation in each area, and at least one specific example of measures taken to meet those responsibilities.

How (and how well) are these responsibilities communicated to staff of the organisation, and to other stakeholders? What kinds of mission, ethical or CSR statements does the organisation make? Where, and for what audience(s)?

What is the general attitude of the organisation's culture to these responsibilities? Are they taken seriously – or are 'corners cut' on some issues? What measures might be taken to get them taken more seriously, more consistently?

2.3 Why should marketing organisations pursue CSR objectives?

2.3.1 Is there an argument *against* CSR?

Economist Milton Friedman took the view that 'the social responsibility of business is profit maximisation': that is, to give shareholders a return on their investment. He argued that spending funds on objectives *not* related to shareholder expectations is simply irresponsible: regard for shareholder wealth is a healthy discipline for management, providing accountability for decisions. The public interest is, in any case, already served by profit maximisation, because the State levies taxes on corporate profits.

Friedman went on to say that 'there is one and only one social responsibility of business – to use its resources and engage in activities designed to increase its profits so long as it stays within the rules of the game, which is to say, engages in open and free competition without deception or fraud.' (Friedman, 1970)

So does CSR service the interest of the firm? It can be argued that pursuing CSR policies is expensive – and that this represents an opportunity cost: the funds could have been spent on more directly value-adding (and profitable) priorities. It can also be argued that CSR has become so fashionable that it no longer has any credibility with consumers: they see it as a public relations exercise without real substance – and this robs it of any public relations value it may have had.

2.3.2 The business case for CSR

The consensus, however, is that CSR has many potential benefits for the marketing organisation.

- **Law, regulation and Codes of Practice** impose certain social responsibilities on organisations, and there are financial and operational penalties for failure to comply (eg 'polluter pays' taxes and compensation claims). Meanwhile, voluntary ethical and philanthropic measures may head off stricter legal and regulatory requirements.

- Increasing **consumer awareness** of social responsibility issues creates market demand for CSR – and risks for irresponsible firms. Failure to meet ethical expectations can cause reputational damage, negative media exposure, consumer boycotts and so on. The risk of reputational damage extends to 'responsibility by association' in supply chains: organisations are increasingly being held responsible for poor labour conditions or environmental damage by their suppliers, for example. Positive CSR can be regarded as a form of reputational and financial risk management.

- Positive CSR may **enhance corporate reputation and brand image**. A commonly cited example is The Body Shop, which has positioned itself strongly as an ethical and responsible brand.

- CSR creates **opportunities to add value** to products and services, or to develop new ones. Examples include recyclable packaging, environmental impact consultancy, and products specifically targeted at 'green' and health-conscious consumers (from low-energy light bulbs to low-GI foods).

- CSR can **offset or reduce costs** eg by increasing energy efficiency, creating markets for recycled products, or (as in the case of The Body Shop) reducing the need for expenditure on advertising.

- CSR maintains the **sustainability** of business dealings. Above-minimum standards for the treatment of employees, suppliers and other business partners may be necessary for the business to attract, retain and motivate them to provide quality service and commitment – particularly in competition with other firms. Ethical and responsible business activity helps to create a climate in which mutually-beneficial long-term trading relationships can be preserved.

2.3.3 Pressures for CSR

In addition to legislation and regulation on CSR issues, Jobber (2007) identifies three main social pressures on business to become ethical and responsible in their dealings with stakeholders.

- **Consumerism**: organised action by the consumer movement (consumer associations and pressure groups whose objective is to protect the rights of consumers) against business practices that are not considered to be in their interests. Consumer groups both campaign for change (eg restrictions on tobacco and alcohol advertising, or food ingredient labelling) and offer information (eg product reviews and comparisons) to guide consumer choice.

- **Environmentalism**: the organised movement of groups and organisations to protect and improve the physical environment. Environmental pressure groups (such as Greenpeace and Friends of the Earth) have influenced companies to adopt environmentally friendly practices (such as recycling and energy saving) and produce 'green' products (such as lead-free petrol and recycled paper).

- **Ethical consumption**: individual consumers taking ethical factors into account when making purchase decisions. Consumers are increasingly prepared to boycott products and companies with poor ethical profiles, and to support products which are identified as fair trade, organic, green or cruelty-free.

3 The role of marketing in CSR

3.1 Marketing responses to CSR issues

As you may have gathered, not all CSR issues are exclusively marketing issues! The human resources function will have the primary role in the treatment of employees; the procurement function, in management of the supply base; and the engineering and production function, in resource utilisation, recycling, pollution control and so on. However, marketing policy and practice can be influential in many ways – not least by managing stakeholders' expectations and perceptions.

The following may be a helpful overview, drawn from Jobber (2007).

Table 2.2   Responses to key issues

Dimension	Key issues	Marketing response
Physical environment	Combating global warming	Sustainable marketing
	Pollution control	
	Conservation of energy and other scarce resources	
	Use of environmentally friendly ingredients and components	
	Recycling and non-wasteful packaging	
Social (community involvement)	Support for the local community	Societal marketing
	Support for the wider community	Cause-related marketing

The Chartered Institute of Marketing

Dimension	Key issues	Marketing response
Consumer	Product safety (including the avoidance of harmful long-term effects) Avoidance of price fixing Honesty in communications Respecting privacy	Societal marketing
Supply chain	Fair trading Standard setting for suppliers (eg human rights, labour standards and environmental responsibility)	Fair trade marketing
Employee relations	Fair pay Equal opportunities Training and motivation Employee involvement, consultation and information provision	Internal marketing

ACTIVITY 2.4

Using the template, for each dimension of CSR, list key issues for your organisation. These may include some of those identified by Jobber and/or others. (Leave the third column blank for the moment.)

Dimension	Key issues	Marketing response
Physical environment		
Social (community involvement)		
Consumer		
Supply chain		
Employee relations		

Let's look briefly at some of those marketing responses

3.2 Societal marketing

Marketing aims to satisfy consumers' and society's immediate consumption needs: societal marketing seeks to protect and promote their wider, more long-term interests. Activities and marketing messages that are not in people's best interests (such as price fixing, invasion of privacy or promotion of harmful products) are avoided, and sustainable, healthy, ethical activities are pursued.

The most commonly cited example is rising concern about obesity, partly attributed to 'junk food': many food producers and fast food outlets (such as McDonald's, which came under intense consumer and media pressure) have launched not just healthy-eating options but added-value health promotion campaigns (healthy-eating advice, sponsorship of community sports programmes and so on).

3.2.1 Cause-related marketing

This may take the form of companies sponsoring charity, community or arts events; raising funds (through staff, customer and supply networks) on behalf of charities; providing resources (eg computers) for schools; or offering funding for initiatives tackling social or environmental problems. Many large corporations now have major cause-related marketing programmes.

Cause-related marketing has the potential to create mutual gains and positive synergy when the business and the charity/cause have **similar target audiences** and/or **similar messages**: for example, luxury car manufacturers sponsoring the arts, healthy food brands promoting community sports, or publishers donating textbooks to schools. Of course, brands may also use affiliations with causes to counteract *opposite* messages: for example, Virgin Airlines (which might be accused of having a fairly high carbon footprint and energy use) partnering with environmental groups to fund alternative fuel and carbon capture research.

ACTIVITY 2.5

- What cause-related marketing is carried out by your organisation?

- What matches are there between the target audiences and/or messages of the charity/cause and the organisation/brand that might create synergy?

- How might the association with the cause/charity attract customers and/or counteract negative marketing messages or PR?

- If your organisation does not currently carry out cause-related marketing, try and suggest two causes/charities that it might consider building an association with. Justify your choice.

3.3 Fair trade marketing

'Unfair' trading arises when large buyers exert their bargaining power to force down the prices of small suppliers to levels that bring severe economic hardship to producers, exacerbating poor wages and working conditions for their workers, and bringing no economic

 The Chartered Institute of Marketing

benefit to their communities. In the UK, there have been recent calls for formal regulation of the relationship between large supermarket chains and their suppliers, for example, because of the allegedly unfair 'squeezing' of prices. More commonly, however, fair trade issues arise in developing economies: the media has recently highlighted the plight of coffee and tea growers, and textile and garment trade workers.

Consumers are increasingly willing to support small and developing-country suppliers by buying genuine fair trade brands, often paying premium prices – which enable organisational buyers to provide higher prices, support and development programmes to their suppliers. In the UK, sales of fair trade products in 2010 reached £1.17 billion, an increase of 40% on 2009.

THE REAL WORLD

In 2007, **Marks & Spencer** launched a new CSR programme called **'Plan A'** (so called because 'There is no Plan B'), built on five CSR 'pillars':

- Climate change
- Waste
- Natural resources
- Fair partnership
- Health & wellbeing

In a report on progress in 2010, the company reported the following:

'In the last three years, thanks to Plan A, we've made a number of ground-breaking innovations that have changed the way we do business:

- We've motivated one million M&S customers to raise over £2.2m for Oxfam and saved 4 million items of unwanted clothes from going to landfill.

- We've improved energy efficiency by over 10% in our stores.

- We've reduced packaging on our foods by 16%, without compromising freshness, quality or shelf life – and cut costs in the process.

- We've improved fuel efficiency by over 20% and introduced our instantly recognizable 'tear drop' aerodynamic lorry trailers.

- We've made clothes hanger recycling 'mainstream' – with 120 million re-used or recycled each year.

- We've reduced the number of food carrier bags we give out by 400 million each year.

- We've purchased GreenPalm Certificates to cover all of the palm oil used in our M&S products. By doing this we are rewarding palm oil producers for working in a sustainable and responsible way.'

The full report is downloadable from http://corporate.marksandspencer.com/investors/reports_publications/2010

M&S is involving stakeholders, including employees, suppliers and customers (asking them to sign 'pledges' of commitment to each of the five pillars). Its website gives case studies for the various pillars, and updates on progress: http://plana.marksandspencer.com

---

3.4 Sustainable or 'Green' marketing

Consumer choice is increasingly exercised according to environmentally-related criteria (a trend reflected in the term 'green consumption'). High profile environmental issues at the moment – many of which are highlighted in the syllabus for Unit 2: *Assessing the Marketing Environment* – include:

- Global warming (embracing the issues of climate change, carbon emissions and the 'carbon footprint' of business activities)

- Environmental decline and degradation (eg soil erosion and deforestation), and loss of biodiversity through species extinction

- Over-consumption and waste of non-renewable natural resources, and the need to develop alternative energy sources

- The effects of pollution on air, waterways and ecosystems

- The disposal of waste products (especially those which contain harmful substances eg chemical and electrical waste)

- Pressure to increase industrial and household recycling.

Marketing organisations need both to manage the risk associated with poor environmental practices (or crises, such as an oil spill) and to capitalise on opportunities presented by green consumption: many brands are now marketed on their green, organic, energy-saving or recycling credentials.

Green marketing programmes may embrace measures such as:

- Conducting market research into demand for green products, potential green market niches and key environmental concerns of consumers

- Driving product modification and development: reducing packaging waste, increasing recyclability, developing 'green' products or product lines (eg electric, hybrid fuel/electric and recyclable cars)

- Developing positive relationships with environmental research and pressure groups

- Using marketing communications to emphasise the green credentials of the organisation or brand

- Using issues and crisis management to control negative public relations effects of environmental problems

THE REAL WORLD

Some creative marketing communication on environmental issues in the last few years include:

- Genesis Energy (New Zealand). In response to soaring energy costs, Genesis launched a direct marketing campaign emphasising to customers that the company was there to help them save money on energy bills. They sent out a leaflet of energy-saving tips printed in fluorescent ink (so they could be read with the lights off!)

- Oroverde (Tropical Rainforest foundation) sent out a package to potential donors reminding them of the threat to tropical rainforests from land clearing by burning. The package included a 'paint by numbers' picture of the rainforest – but only one colour ink: black.

3.4.1 Green relationships

Gummesson (2002) argues that marketing organisations can establish relationships with customers (and other stakeholders) specifically through environmental issues: green issues are not just costs or threats, but opportunities for relationship, value and revenue enhancement.

'The green relationship concerns the company's way of handling environment and health issues in its offerings and the relationships that are created with specific individuals and communities of individuals.' (*ibid*, p122). This may include:

- Collaborative relationships with **suppliers and distribution channels** to solve environmental problems and explore opportunities presented by increasing green interest (eg working with suppliers to develop recyclable products; with logistics providers to minimise pollution and fuel use; with retail outlets to promote green brands).

- Investment in constructive **network relationships** with authorities, the environmental movement and the media, to share information and best practice – and to manage any issues that might damage public relations.

The Chartered
Institute of Marketing

- Use of relationship marketing to establish relationships with environment- and health-conscious **customer segments** – and marketing communications to bring other customers into these segments.

'Building coalitions with all stakeholders keeps the company abreast of environmental regulations, issues, debates, technology and attitudes.' (*ibid*, p123).

3.5 Internal marketing

Most issues in the ethical treatment of employees are the responsibility of individual managers and the human resources function. Ethical employment practices are highly relevant to marketing, however, as a poor reputation in this area (eg allegations of discrimination, exploitation, poor working conditions, invasion of privacy or unethical redundancies) can alienate ethically-aware customers – and potential future recruits to the organisation!

Marketing may participate directly in employee relations, through **internal marketing**: programmes for developing, motivating, informing and involving employees in such a way as to enhance their ability to provide customer service, satisfaction and value. 'Customer-facing' staff (whether at the point of sale or via telephone or email) are at the interface between the marketing organisation and the customer, so effective internal marketing is crucial to successful external marketing.

We will examine internal marketing in detail in Chapter 9.

ACTIVITY 2.6

Complete the third column of the analysis started in Activity 2.4, by identifying specific marketing responses your organisation has used to manage each of the key issues you defined.

Highlight any areas in which the organisation does *not* appear to be addressing the issue, and consider what responses it might adopt.

3.6 Issues and crisis management

Issues management and crisis management fall broadly within public relations activity, and are particularly relevant to the handling of CSR and ethical issues.

3.6.1 Issues management

▶ **Key term**

Issues management is a proactive process of monitoring potential controversies or public relations problems in relation to the business, and initiating communication programmes to manage public perceptions about them. Hainsworth & Meng (1988) define it as: 'A management activity intended to bring some control to the impact caused by the discontinuity of the environment'.

Issues management endeavours not just to identify and fight fires as they arise, but to:

- Proactively initiate dialogue with the public and pressure/interest groups
- Express general responsibility and openness
- Educate stakeholders in the organisation's position and efforts on the issue
- Establish networks of goodwill and support.

According to Hainsworth & Meng (1988), there is an **issues life cycle**. Issues grow (in terms of the public's awareness the level of concern about them), towards a peak – and then typically fall away as the public's attention shifts, or as the issue is seen to be addressed.

- Organisations that **lag** in their management of the issue, failing to address them adequately as they reach their peak, suffer the maximum negative impact to their reputation and credibility: their failure to address the issue may create a crisis which prolongs the peak of the issue, keeping it 'live' in people's minds.

- Organisations that **lead** – giving attention to the issue early in its growth phase – gain positive benefits of being seen to be insightful, 'on the ball', responsible and proactive, and effectively speed up the fading of the issue as far as they are concerned.

THE REAL WORLD

Insurance giant **Swiss Re** has developed a systematic approach to proactive issues management, intended to:

- Meet the increasing demands of more critical stakeholders
- Manage emerging gaps between corporate action and stakeholder expectations
- Implement a global 'one voice' approach to communication on key topics.

It starts by defining the '**sensitivities**' of its key stakeholder groups. For clients, these are identified as capital strength, expertise, and payment of claims; for investors, profitability, capital management and transparency; for regulators, capital adequacy and transparency; and for the general public, reliability, corporate governance and restructuring.

The company has defined criteria for selecting and prioritising '**Top Topics**' which need to be monitored and managed. These are defined by: potentially significant impact on corporate value; need for interaction with external stakeholders; and need for action in terms of formulating and communicating a corporate position.

Swiss Re then utilises a five-stage process for **Top Topic issues management**:

- Topic identification: monitoring industry trends, product threats, regulatory issues and internal processes

- Topic analysis: by in-house experts

- Options development: should the organisation react, adapt or pro-actively shape the issue?

- Action: contingency planning and external and internal communication, co-ordinated by a Topic Manager (the top in-house expert on the topic)

- Process evaluation: effectiveness of communication, evolution of the topic.

3.6.2 Crisis communication

Crisis communication is the issuing of 'emergency' communications to minimise or counter the negative PR effects of crises (damaging events or revelations). A crisis in the field of CSR might include: the recall of a product due to safety defects; an ecological disaster such as the running aground of an oil tanker; the enforced withdrawal of an advertising campaign deemed offensive by the Advertising Standards Authority; or revelations of unethical behaviour by the organisation or its suppliers.

Effective crisis communication requires very careful handling: recognising and responding to the likely level of concern; telling the organisation's side of the story without appearing to excuse or 'cover up'; demonstrating care and concern about the impact of the event on the target audience; and demonstrating action to solve the problem. As ever, positive stakeholder relationships will be helpful in mobilising support (eg from an independent, credible 'champion' who can vouch for the organisation and its steps to resolve the problem).

THE REAL WORLD

In early 2010, reports emerged around the world about problems with the braking systems on several Toyota car models. The company's reaction to this problem was widely criticised when it took some time to acknowledge the problem and even longer to start a recall of affected vehicles in order to rectify the problem.

'Toyota has come under sustained fire from crisis experts for its global response to the brand crisis that has seen millions of cars recalled worldwide.

The Chartered Institute of Marketing

The company's crisis communications team has been criticised by a leading Japanese PR executive over its 'easygoing attitude'. Another PR agency head in Asia said that Toyota's slow and poorly co-ordinated response could spell the 'beginning of the end for old-style Japanese PR'.

Toyota has been criticised for a slow response that has placed the company on the back foot throughout the unfolding crisis. Global CEO Akio Toyoda has attracted particular attention for his low profile. Toyoda emerged last week to express contrition, two weeks after the crisis broke.

"There has been silence for some time on this" said Edelman international director of crisis and issues management, Mike Seymour. The Japanese are greatly inclined to want to wait until they have got all the facts. I'm surprised they aren't taking a global view of their communications.

Senior Toyota executives have released explanatory videos in the US and the UK. Last week, industry observers told PR Week that while its UK video struck the right tone, the response may be too late.

"It has never seemed that Toyota has ever managed to get ahead of the issue in terms of its communications – it has been incredibly reactive" said Bite global CEO Clive Armitage. The upshot of this is that trust in the Toyota brand is being massively eroded and it will take a huge effort to rebuild this trust over the coming years.'

(PR Week, 2010)

4 Pressure groups

> ▶ Key term
>
> A **pressure group** is a group of people who have got together to promote a particular cause or issue (a causal pressure group) or to promote the interests of a particular constituency (a sectional pressure group).

4.1 Types and interests of pressure groups

Individual stakeholders may be unable to exercise influence over an organisation, whether as consumers, employees or members of the public at large, in relation to a particular issue or infringement of their rights. In these circumstances, they may seek to enhance their power by joining or supporting a pressure group. There are many thousands of groups, ranging from major umbrella groups to small local and/or single-issue groups.

4.1.1 Causal pressure groups

Causal groups (also called promotional groups) are formed to promote a cause or issue: to raise awareness, mobilise public opinion and lobby for changes in government policy or regulation. Examples include:

- Political and human rights groups, such as the CND (Campaign for Nuclear Disarmament) and Amnesty International

- Environmental groups, such as Greenpeace, Friends of the Earth, the Worldwide Fund for Nature, RSPCA and Countryside Alliance (which promotes a range of rural agendas, such as support for local food production and rural sports such as hunting and fishing – against opposition from conflicting groups such as the Hunt Saboteurs Association!)

- Social welfare groups, such as Fairtrade and the NSPCC (National Society for the Prevention of Cruelty to Children).

4.1.2 Sectional pressure groups

Sectional groups (also called defensive or interest groups) are formed to defend the interests of particular groups in society, including:

- **Workers** in particular industries, occupations or professions.

  - Many workers are represented by the **trade unions** such as the National Union of Teachers, the public service union Unison, or the GMB under an umbrella group: the Trade Unions Congress (TUC). Trade unions mainly protect their members' rights and interests at work: better pay, benefits and conditions; fair treatment (eg in relation to dismissal from a job); access to information and consultation on matters affecting workers; access to training and development; and the right to pursue individual and collective disputes with the employer.

  - Professionals are represented by **professional associations**, such as the British Medical Association or the Law Society – and, of course, the Chartered Institute of Marketing! Professional associations usually focus on setting the educational, technical and ethical standards of members, but they also promote the standing and interests of the profession and create opportunity through member networking.

- **Business firms**. Groups of employers are represented by **employers' associations** and trade associations, under umbrella groups:

  - the Confederation of British Industry (CBI), which promotes the economic interests of commercial organisations, and has considerable power as a consultant on government policy.

  - The British Chambers of Commerce (BCC) is the national body for a powerful and influential Network of Accredited Chambers of Commerce across the UK. The BCC is a non-political, non-profit-making organisation, owned and directed by its members, democratically accountable to individual businesses of all sizes and sectors throughout the UK.

  - Smaller trade associations may band together for purely sectional interests (eg the Booksellers' Association opposing sales tax (VAT) on books).

- **Consumers**: represented by the Consumer Association and specific user groups. Such groups campaign for the interests of consumers on issues such as product pricing, safety and quality, food labelling, restriction of unsolicited marketing (especially spam e-mail marketing) and so on.

The diversity of interests and causes means that there is inevitably conflict and competition between pressure groups: a marketing organisation may find that its plans are supported by one pressure group and opposed by another.

THE REAL WORLD

In early 2011 Unilever, the maker of PG Tips and Lipton tea, agreed to stop testing its tea on animals after the intervention of an animal protection pressure group, People for the Ethical Treatment of Animals (PETA).

The Independent newspaper reported that PETA had planned a web and poster campaign to highlight the fact that the company was using animals to test health claims for tea. The campaign was to urge a boycott of the company's products under the slogan 'Crueltea'

Unilever said: 'We have an ongoing dialogue with consumers and NGOs (including PETA), and that dialogue suggested to us that we consider whether our position on animal testing was consistent with the leadership role we have taken in other areas such as environmental sustainability and ethical sourcing of tea... We have done a very limited amount of testing of tea ingredients on animals when no other alternative method was available. This will stop now.'

(The Independent, 2011)

The Chartered Institute of Marketing

List the specific causal and sectional pressure groups which are relevant to the sector and activity of your work organisation, or other selected organisation. Highlight those with which it has (or has had) direct dealings, relationships or problems.

Select one causal and one sectional pressure group from your list which has (or may have) an impact on, or involvement with, your organisation, and research:

- Its membership, size and budget
- Its aims and objectives
- The nature of its potential impact (positive or negative) on your organisation
- The nature of your organisation's relationship with the group (if any).

Format your findings appropriately for use in an appendix to a stakeholder audit report.

4.2 Pressure group influence

4.2.1 Sources of pressure group influence

Pressure group influence is based on the idea of banding together to form a coalition. Collective power both enlarges and leverages influence: it creates a larger presence or 'voice'; potentially attracts or co-opts influential members; and generates increasing networks, ideas and resources – which can be used for further promotion and growth in membership.

Methods used by pressure groups to wield influence include:

- Attempting to **influence government policy** (eg by employing lobbyists, making politicians directors of the group, providing members for government committees and consultative bodies, or donating funds to political parties)

- **Raising awareness and influencing public opinion** (and therefore exerting indirect influence on government or organisational policy) by:

  - Advertising. For example, the RSPCA advertised (initially unsuccessfully) for a dog registration scheme in the UK. This was more than just an appeal for donations: the campaign was specifically designed to change government policy.

  - Public relations and publicity: generating media coverage, publicity stunts, demonstrations and marches, petitions and 'direct action' (eg volunteers confronting loggers or whaling fleets, boycotting brands with poor environmental or ethical records and so on).

- **Using their legitimate power to influence organisational decisions**. Recognised trade unions, for example, have formal power to negotiate on behalf of their members, and to use the threat of legitimate industrial action (eg official strike action) to reinforce their position. They have legal rights to be consulted on matters of significant interest or concern to their members (such as future plans, changes to working conditions, health and safety risks and any threat of redundancies).

- **Offering information and advice**, to influence the decision-making and policy formation of an organisation. This may take the form of:

  - Raising awareness of an issue, and highlighting its potential impact on the business and its stakeholders

  - Providing research, statistics or other supporting information (eg signed petitions demonstrating public concern) to shape the organisation's thinking

  - Providing policy guidelines and benchmarks for best practice in relation to the issue

- Using case studies, conferences or business networking to demonstrate the practice of (and benefits to) organisations who are leading the way on the issue

- Offering incentives and rewards for the organisation to change its policy and practice on the issue (eg endorsement of its products, publicised awards, or co-promotions to sell the brand to the pressure group's membership and supporters).

■ Offering the **opportunity to gain CSR, ethical or environmental credentials** through association with the group or through showing support for the issue. Many organisations actively pursue relationships with pressure groups in order to enhance their brand image and reputation.

THE REAL WORLD

The Medinge Group, an international think-tank on branding and business, annually releases a Top Brands with a Conscience list. The international collective of brand practitioners meets in August in Sweden to develop the list, evaluating brands on criteria including expressed values of humanity, ethics and sustainability; evidence of consideration of the human implications of the brand; whether the brand takes risks in line with its beliefs; and positive transformations being made to improve the brand's humanity, responsibility or sustainability.

In announcing the winners of the 2010 awards, Stanley Moss, CEO of the Medinge Group said, 'This year's awards indicate that principles of compassionate branding are being applied globally, by businesses large and small, across categories from finance to retail to energy, in established and emerging economies, in new markets. Today, brands with conscience can work to build bridges of understanding between nations and societies.'

Ian Ryder, a founding Director of the Medinge Group, commented, 'Winning a BWAC award is more than public recognition. It is a clear statement of your organisation's values, one of the most powerful competitive differentiators in existence!'

You can get the 2011 update (a great source of short case studies on ethics, CSR and sustainability) at: http://www.medinge.org.

(Medinge Group, 2011)

4.2.2 Impacts of pressure group influence

Pressure group influence may impact on organisations in various ways.

It may bring about a change in **corporate strategy**. For example, producers may decide to introduce fair trade brands, or retailers to stock them. Corporate social responsibility, ethical and environmental objectives may be incorporated in the strategies of the organisation. Marketing strategies may respond to pressures for fair pricing or responsible advertising. Product lines may be developed, discontinued or adapted in response to the concerns of the market.

There may be pressure and/or positive opportunities to **develop new products** and services, or to improve existing ones, in line with public concerns. Examples include recyclable products, energy-saving household appliances, healthy and weight-reducing food products, chemical-free cleaning services and so on.

There may be a need for changes in **business processes**: the way products are developed, produced and marketed. For example, animal protection groups have created widespread pressure to find alternatives to animal testing in the development of cosmetics and pharmaceuticals. Production and logistics processes may be altered to incorporate recycling, manage waste, reduce emissions and energy usage, and create safer conditions for workers. Supplier management may incorporate monitoring to ensure that low-cost country suppliers treat their workers fairly. Ethical codes may be developed for all business dealings.

If there is a conflict of interest between the organisation and a pressure group, and the organisation is unable or unwilling to respond to its influence attempts, the pressure group may have the power to cause **negative impacts** for the organisation. It may generate negative publicity (using its contacts in the media and other influencing networks) which may affect customer support for the brand. It may also organise and mobilise public opposition (eg organise protests, boycotts or petitions), or lobby for government intervention and

The Chartered Institute of Marketing

regulation. All this could in turn damage the support or confidence of the organisation's investors and the financial markets, resulting in a lower share price.

ACTIVITY 2.8

It is important to realise that the organisation may regard pressure group influence *not* just as a potential nuisance, source of poor press and public relations, or constraint on decision making! Explain three ways in which pressure groups could represent a **positive resource** for the organisation.

An organisation may choose proactively to **ally or associate itself** with pressure groups which *reflect* its own corporate values, or those of its customers, in order to:

- **Support the aims of group which further its own purposes**. For example, a bus or train company may ally with anti-pollution groups: their interests coincide, in that getting more people to use public transport reduces traffic emissions – and promoting reduced traffic emissions encourages more people to use public transport!

- **Form an association in people's minds**, so that supporters of the pressure group or cause will be disposed to support the brand (affinity or cause-related marketing). This may be practically reinforced by promotions in which, for example, a percentage of profits from sales of a product are donated to a charity: a positive incentive for supporters of the charity to purchase the product.

- **Demonstrate its ethical and social responsibility credentials**, by promoting the fact that it is contributing to good causes (or causes supported by its customer base). Supermarkets, banks and other organisations that rely on a local customer base often have charitable fundraising and donation as part of their community involvement programmes, for example.

5 Marketing's role in managing pressure groups

Following from our discussion in section 3, you should be able to see that marketing has a specific role in the management of pressure groups, and the mitigation or exploitation of their impacts on the organisation.

- **Planned marketing communications** to encourage interaction and dialogue with relevant pressure groups. For key pressure groups, this may involve establishing direct contacts, with a view to discussing issues and potential for co-operation or sponsorship. There may be opportunities for contact at issues-based or industry conferences. More generally, the communications mix will include advertising, corporate reports and brochures, and public and media relations activity: stating the organisation's position on issues, demonstrating its commitment to social responsibility and ethics, and (where appropriate) highlighting its willingness to partner with pressure groups. These messages will be directed both at members of pressure groups and at the wider audiences who might be influenced by them.

- **Developing relationship strategies**, such as sponsorship deals, co-branding or co-promotions, or cause-related sales promotions (eg motivating extra purchases by offering to donate a percentage of the sales price to a cause or charity).

- **Developing marketing approaches** such as societal, cause-related, fair trade, green and internal marketing (discussed earlier), to pre-empt, address – and if possible exploit opportunities arising from – pressure group activity.

- **Developing specific product and service messages** derived from interactions with pressure groups, in order to maximise their benefit for sales, brand positioning and corporate reputation.

  - Marketing campaigns will be used to inform customers (and other interested publics) of value-adding changes to products and services resulting from listening to or consulting with pressure groups: eg greater product durability; greater environment-friendliness; fair trading principles; locally-sourced ingredients; health benefits; improved customer care package; and so on.

- In addition, the organisation's willingness to listen to, or partner with, the pressure group may be incorporated in these messages, to add third-party endorsement.

- Packaging may have to be re-designed to show endorsements, or to implement sales promotions – or indeed to make the packaging itself more compliant with pressure group demands (eg recyclable materials, product descriptions, safety instructions).

- **Issues and crisis management**: proactive approaches to managing the effects of unplanned and uncontrollable messages such as news stories, reviews, opinion articles or blogs which could put the organisation in a bad – or positive – light. Influential media should be monitored and emerging issues proactively handled by internal and external communication – as discussed in section 3.

The Chartered Institute of Marketing

- External stakeholder groups: government, society, consumerism and the influence market

- External stakeholder interests, needs, drivers and influence and contribution

- Definitions of marketing ethics and CSR: economic, legal, ethical and philanthropic responsibilities of the firm

- Marketing responses: societal marketing, cause-related marketing, fair trade marketing, sustainable (or green) marketing, internal marketing, issues and crisis management

- Green relationships (Gummesson): relationships based on environmental and health issues

- The business case for CSR: enlightened self interest

- Pressures for CSR: legislation and regulation, consumerism, environmentalism and ethical consumption

- Causal pressure groups: promoting a cause or issue (eg political, human rights, environment or welfare)

- Sectional pressure groups: defending the interests of particular groups (eg workers, professions, businesses or consumers)

- Sources of pressure group influence: lobbying, public opinion, legitimate power, information and consultancy, collaboration

- Impacts of pressure group influence: changes in strategy, new product development, process adaptation, negative impacts, opportunities

- Planned marketing communications to enhance engagement and dialogue

- Development of collaboration and association

- Product/service messages arising from changes and interactions

- Crisis and issues management

FURTHER READING

Green issues

Gummesson, E. (2002) *Total Relationship Marketing.* 2nd edition. Oxford, Elsevier Butterworth-Heinemann. Chapter 3: Section on *Relationship 15: The green relationship*

CSR and marketing ethics

Jobber, D. (2007) *Principles & Practice of Marketing.* 5th edition. Maidenhead, McGraw-Hill Education Chapter 6 and Case Studies on Microsoft and Fair Trade coffee.

Influence Market Domain

Peck, H. *et al* (1999) *Relationship Marketing: Strategy & Implementation.* Oxford, Elsevier Butterworth-Heinemann.
Chapter 4 and case studies, especially The Body Shop

Brooks, J. (2010) Analysis: Unilever shakes up strategy in CSR goals. *Packaging News*. http://www.packagingnews.co.uk/environment/analysis-unilever-shakes-up-strategy-in-csr-goals/ [Accessed 27 June 2012].

Carroll, A. B. and Buchholtz, AK (2000) *Business and Society: Ethics and Stakeholder Management*. Cincinnati, South-Western College.

Foley, S. (2011), PG Tips maker agrees to halt animal tests on its tea, *The Independent*, http://www.independent.co.uk/life-style/food-and-drink/news/pg-tips-maker-agrees-to-halt-animal-tests-on-its-tea-2202615.html. [Accessed 24 June 2012]

Friedman, M. (1970) The Social Responsibility of Business is to Increase its Profits. *The New York Times Magazine*. September 13, 1970.

Gummesson, E. (2002) *Total Relationship Marketing*. 2nd edition. Oxford, Elsevier Butterworth-Heinemann.

Hainsworth, B. and Meng, M. (1988) How corporations define issues management in *Public Relations Review*, Vol 14(4), pp18-30.

Jobber, D. (2007) *Principles and Practice of Marketing*. 5th edition. Maidenhead, Berks, McGraw Hill Education.

Kotler, P. *et al* (ed) (2002) *Social Marketing: Improving the Quality of Life*. 2nd edition. Thousand Oks, CA, Sage Publications.

Medinge Group (2011) http://medinge.org/brands-with-a-conscience/news-releases/. [Accessed 24 June 2012]

Peck, H. L. *et al* (1999) *Relationship Marketing: Strategy and Implementation*. Oxford, Elsevier Butterworth-Heinemann.

Sudhaman, A. (2010), Car giant Toyota slammed for 'easygoing' attitude to recall crisis. PR Week. http://www.prweek.com/uk/news/982303/Car-giant-Toyota-slammed-easygoing-attitude-recall-crisis/) [Accessed 24 June 2012]

QUICK QUIZ

1   Why is the government an important stakeholder?

2   What are the four basic consumer rights?

3   What are the interests/needs/drivers and influence/contribution of the news/information media?

4   Explain the concept of marketing ethics.

5   List the four 'layers' of CSR for an organisation.

6   Explain the benefits of pursuing CSR for an organisation.

7   What are (a) cause related marketing and (b) fair trade marketing?

8   List five current issues of concern in the area of environmental sustainability.

9   Distinguish between causal and sectional pressure groups, with examples.

10   List five sources of pressure group influence.

The Chartered
Institute of Marketing

Activity 2.1

Your own knowledge and research. Use our examples – or consider the statements made by the organisation on its 'corporate social responsibility' or 'corporate citizenship' reports or web pages.

Activity 2.2

REPORT

Stakeholder analysis for The Eastborough Mining Project
From: Your Name
To: The Marketing Manager
Date: Today

1   Background

Digwell has recently obtained government permission to undertake mining in the Eastborough area. However, difficulties are anticipated due to the opposition of the Eastborough Protection Alliance: an umbrella group for local pressure groups. This may pose a need for stakeholder management, and the analysis contained in this report is intended to help prioritise and plan such a strategy.

2   Stakeholder map

The key stakeholder and pressure groups identified in the scenario might be placed in a power/interest matrix as follows.

Level of interest

	Low	High
Low	Quadrant A Anti-capitalist groups	Quadrant B Local residents
High	Quadrant C Digwell shareholders & directors	Quadrant D Environmental groups? Government

Power/influence (row label, left side between Low and High)

3   Analysis of map and management strategies

(i)   **Anti-capitalist groups** are likely to have relatively low power (with relatively low numbers and credibility in relation to more directly affected stakeholders) – and relatively low interest (given the local scale of the mining operation, compared to, say, G8 summits). The recommended strategy for quadrant A is to expend minimal effort. However, Digwell can prevent these groups graduating to quadrant C with marketing messages clearly separating the concerns of legitimate stakeholders from those of the anti-capitalists.

(ii) **Local residents** have a high legitimate interest in Digwell's plans, both positive, in terms of employment and development, and negative, in terms of loss of amenity. They have relatively low power: although they have influence (as voters) on local government, their position is weakened by internal conflicts of interest and by their relatively small numbers. However, because of their high interest, there is a risk that they will co-opt more influential stakeholders (such as the media and interest/pressure groups). The recommended strategy for this quadrant is consultation and information: Digwell should show its willingness to take local residents' concerns into account by open consultation, and promote the economic and social benefits of the project – co-opting this group as supporters rather than resisters.

(iii) The various **environmental groups** have a high interest in the project, as it concerns the area of their specific remit and concern, and may even be seen as a 'test case' for other mining protests. Some individual groups may fall into the low-power category, but others may have considerable public credibility, media influence and lobbying power: grouped together, they may exert pressure for government to impose restrictions, or for public protest to disrupt Digwell's activities and ability to secure local labour and services. The recommended strategy for quadrant D 'key players' is to ensure that strategies are acceptable to them. Digwell should prepare an environmental audit and impact statements, and make plans to protect rare species, regenerate land, minimise pollution and so on.

(iv) **Government** has a high official interest, as the approver of mining grants: it also has an interest as beneficiary in the economic/social benefits to the area – and in the concerns of voters which pose a political risk. It has high power to revoke permissions and to monitor and enforce environmental and local government regulations. As a key player, government should be the target of ongoing stakeholder management, through proactive issues and crisis management and promotion of benefits (perhaps reinforced by extra community investment and political support).

(v) **Digwell's shareholders and directors** have a high degree of power over Digwell's strategy, as the strategic decision makers – and those to whom they are accountable. However, they may have relatively low interest in the specifics of this project: their interests are more generally in the performance of the company. The recommended strategy for Quadrant C is 'keep satisfied'. As long as Digwell upholds its reputation for maximising shareholder returns, is able to demonstrate compliance (and consideration for any CSR values its shareholders particularly care about), it should be able to avoid arousing more specific interest in opposition to its plans.

Activity 2.3

Your own research, using our examples as a guide. Note the different areas in which law may affect the marketer and the organisation:

- Marketing: advertising claims, no spam (opt-in for e-mail and fax marketing), advertising standards (truthful, non-offensive), consumer rights, data protection and privacy

- Products/services: quality and safety standards; particular issues for the sector (eg financial services regulation, transport safety); recyclable materials and packaging

- Business practices: environmental responsibility (eg pollution control); employment (health and safety, wages, equal opportunities, consultation with unions); competitive tendering for contracts in the interests of fairness and transparency (in the public sector); use of funds (in the charitable sector).

CSR-focused cultures can be reinforced by methods such as: CSR and ethics statements communicated to employees (and supply chain partners); values expressed and modelled consistently by top management and other key influencers in the firm (team leaders, 'heroes'); CSR/ethics objectives and performance measures set for functions and departments; CSR/ethics criteria used in staff selection, appraisal, rewards/bonuses and promotion; and CSR/ethics built into training and development programmes.

Activity 2.4

Your own knowledge and research. This may put some detail into your answer to activity 2.3. The specific issues faced by your organisation will depend on its industry sector, its current policies, and any pressure groups which make 'issues' out of them!

The Chartered
Institute of Marketing

Activity 2.5

Your own knowledge and research. Use our examples as a guide, and refine your list as you read further through the section. Keep in mind that this may all be useful preparatory work for your assignment!

Activity 2.6

Your own knowledge and research. Again, you can use some of the ideas covered in this section – but it would be good learning to review actual organisational practices, scan the website – or even ask a colleague, manager or mentor: 'What are we doing to respond to these issues for our firm?'

Activity 2.7

Your own research. As an example of the first part of the exercise, and an appropriate format (drawn from Peck *et al*, 1999, p140):

Greenpeace

Size and membership

- Founded in 1971, the total number of 'supporters' is now 279,000. 5,000 of these are 'Frontline supporters' who pay £10 per month in return for video updates on campaign activity, a magazine and invitations to regular campaign meetings.

- Total income in 1995 was £6,627,000. 80% of this was from subscriptions.

- Direct expenditure on campaigns and local group support was £3.5 million.

- Membership base is rising steadily, the charity has benefited from the recent high-profile battle with Shell Petroleum.

Aims

- 'Greenpeace has always been ready to campaign against things which we believe are morally or ethically unacceptable' (Annual Report 1995).

- Greenpeace is in the business of elimination of problems, not their management.

- It aims for long-term change. Recent projects have included: campaigning for new manufacturing technologies by commissioning the design of a Greenpeace fridge and car; championing energy saving schemes; protecting fishing stock; attempting to stop whaling vessels; and campaigning against genetic modification in the food industry.

Activity 2.8

Pressure groups may be a positive resource as:

- A useful **barometer** of government and consumer concerns. If a pressure group represents the views of a powerful constituency, it may be possible for the organisation to use its resources for stakeholder research and feedback-gathering.

- A source of **helpful advice and consultancy** in the group's area of concern and expertise. If the organisation recognises and seeks to remedy an area of concern in its policy or practices (eg to reduce its environmental impacts or improve its labour relations record), there may be potential for genuine collaborative problem solving.

- A potential source of **promotional and reputational advantage**. If the organisation is able to work with a pressure group to solve problems, it may receive its approval and endorsement: using the pressure group's profile and influence to its advantage. An example includes food products receiving the Heart Foundation 'Tick of approval', or cosmetic products being certified as involving no animal testing. Such endorsements are more persuasive than mere advertising claims to the same effect, since they are perceived as coming from a concerned and expert source.

1   Government has authority to legislate and regulate. Its policies shape the business environment and economy. It may be a large customer for goods and services. It represents the interests of society as a whole.

2   Four basic consumer rights are: the right to safety; the right to be informed; the right to choose; and the right to be heard.

3   See table in section 1.2 for a full answer.

4   Marketing ethics are the moral principles and values that guide behaviour within the field of marketing: eg product safety, truthful advertising, honesty in relationships, fair pricing and reduced impact of marketing on the environment.

5   The four layers of CSR are economic, legal, ethical and philanthropic (or good corporate citizenship).

6   Potential benefits of CSR include: no penalties for failure to comply with legislation/regulation; avoidance of risk of reputational damage and lost custom; enhanced corporate reputation and brand; opportunities to add value to products and services, or develop new ones; offset or reduced costs; and enhanced ability to compete for quality employees, suppliers and business allies.

7   Cause related marketing is activities in which a business forms a partnership or association with a charity or cause, in order to promote a product, brand or issues, for mutual benefit. Fair trade marketing is the development, promotion and selling of brands which treat suppliers and producers equitably, and the positioning of organisations on the basis of a fair trade ethos.

8   See section 3.4 for a selection of environmental issues.

9   Causal pressure groups promote a cause or issue (eg Greenpeace, Amnesty International, Friends of the Earth or the NSPCC). Sectional pressure groups promote and defend the interest of particular groups (eg trade unions, professional associations, employers associations or the Consumer Association).

10 Pressure groups may exert influence by: influencing government policy, raising awareness and influencing public opinion, using their legitimate power to influence organisational decisions, offering advice/consultancy to influence decision making, or offering opportunities to gain CSR credentials by association with or support for the group.

CHAPTER 3

Organisational relationships

Introduction

This chapter introduces the concept of organisational relationships, as a foundation for going on to consider the discipline of Relationship Marketing in Chapter 4.

We start by considering what the term 'relationship' means for an organisation: is it really possible (or desirable) for a consumer or other stakeholder to form a relationship with a commercial organisation?

In section 2, we examine some of the basic relationship configurations or types: from the basic one-to-one relationship of a customer and marketer/supplier; to the wider supply or value chain, in which each party contributes to the flow of value towards the customer; to the concept of the supply or value network, which acknowledges the more complex web of relationships surrounding organisational activity.

In section 3, we explore two influential models of the relationships between a given organisation (the core firm) and its environments or markets. The six markets model categorises the various aspects or 'domains' of the stakeholder environment, while Gummesson's 30R model distinguishes four types of relationships.

In section 4, we explore the differences between transactions (one-off exchanges or interactions) and relationships; the benefits and limitations of each for the marketing organisation; and the trade-offs that may need to be made between short-term and long-term marketing activities.

In section 5, we introduce the concept of relationship management (RM). We revisit stakeholder analysis (covered in Chapter 1) to consider how an organisation might audit and prioritise its relationships, and how it might develop a portfolio of different relationship strategies suitable to a range of stakeholder groups.

Topic list

What is a relationship? ①

Types of organisational relationships ②

The core firm and its relationships ③

From transactions to relationships ④

Relationship management ⑤

1.6	Evaluate the different options to developing a Relationship Management (RM) approach within a market oriented organisation:
	■ Transactional
	■ Long term mutually beneficial relationship with a defined customer:
	– group
	– partnerships
	– strategic alliances
	– e-relationships
	– networks
	– customisation
	– internal customer relationships
2.1	Explain the position and importance of key stakeholders in the market oriented organisation and establish relationship priorities for the organisation:
	■ Stakeholder maps/matrices
	■ For stakeholders with little power/interest in project/programme – minimal effort
	■ For stakeholders with interest but little power – keep informed and nurture
	■ For stakeholders with little interest but high power – maintain relationships
	■ Key players – high level of interaction in developing and maintaining relationships
	■ Classic market relationships
	■ Special market relationships ie, high income/high profile partners
	■ Green/mega/nano relationships (Gummesson 2003)

1 What is a relationship?

If you shop regularly at the same supermarket, does this mean you have a 'relationship' with that supermarket? If you regularly buy a particular brand, does this form a 'relationship' with the brand or the organisation that created it? And what if you have given your details as part of a sales promotion, and the marketer starts e-mailing you regularly with special offers: is this a 'relationship'? How can a person have a meaningful relationship with an organisation?

1.1 In what sense do organisations have 'relationships'?

Most writers on relationship marketing acknowledge that organisational relationships cannot be the same as interpersonal relationships. Most commercial dealings, particularly in consumer markets, are 'one-sided and emotionless', and marketers need to be careful about assuming that they have relationships with their customers – when all they really have are a series of impersonal exchanges. Repeat purchases don't necessarily imply loyalty! (Egan, 2004).

However, organisational relationships do have some of the same features as interpersonal relationships, and that enables us to use the concept to describe certain types of exchanges or interactions between organisations and their stakeholders.

- **Relationships imply longevity**

    Ford *et al* (2003, p38) use the term 'relationship' to describe 'the pattern of interactions and the mutual conditioning of behaviours over time, between a company and a customer, a supplier or another organisation.'

- **Relationships imply some kind of meaningful ties between the parties**

  Relationship ties, which bind two parties together, may take various forms.

  - **Recurring contacts**, interactions and communications between individuals. Personal contact development is often used in business-to-business marketing and business networking, for example.

  - **Linking of activities**: transactions, co-ordination of plans, collaboration (working together) or knowledge-sharing.

  - **Investment of resources**, such as time or finance, in the relationship. Close relationships often result from investment in adaptations made especially for the other party (a customised marketing mix, say, or the integration of supplier/buyer information systems) because they create mutual dependency.

  In network theory, these are called 'actor bonds', 'activity links' and 'resource ties' (Håkansson and Snehota, 1995), respectively.

- **Relationships imply some kind of commitment from both parties**

  Commitment to a relationship may be reflected in:

  - **Recognised importance or 'special status'**: that is, it isn't just casual or occasional contact. This has to be perceived and acknowledged by both parties – otherwise attempted intimacy from one will just be seen as inappropriate and intrusive by the other. (Egan, *op cit*)

  - The development of **mutuality**: that is, it is not a one-sided relationship. There are benefits to both parties and perhaps a degree of inter-dependency.

  - The development of **trust and transparency**: the willingness to share information.

  - The **frequency, regularity and intensity of interactions** and communication between the parties.

  - Efforts made to overcome **distance** (such as cultural differences) and **barriers** (such as conflicting interests).

ACTIVITY 3.1

Select any one stakeholder in your organisation, or another organisation of your choice, and identify whether the organisation has a relationship with it, using the factors listed above as a checklist. Explain how each factor applies or does not apply.

2 Types of organisational relationships

Relationships require at least two parties who are in contact with each other. If we focus on only two parties (for example, a supplier and its customer), the relationship will be a **'one-to-one'** or **'dyad'** (two-party) relationship.

However, basic supplier-customer exchanges usually happen within the wider context of a supply process: a producer of raw materials supplies a processing plant or producer of components, which supplies a manufacturing organisation, which supplies a distributor or retail outlet, which supplies the consumer. This configuration is often called a **chain** or **channel**.

However, even this picture is simplified. The fact is that each organisation in the supply chain has multiple other relationships with customers, suppliers, industry partners and so on. Many writers (eg Cox & Lamming, 1997; Christopher, 2005) have therefore argued that a more appropriate metaphor is a **network** or **web**.

We will look briefly at each of these types of relationship in turn.

2.1 One-to-one (dyadic) relationships

The relationship between a supplier and a customer is the classic two-sided relationship (dyad) of marketing (Gummesson, 2002). Marketing and supply management often focus on this dyad: focusing on how the firm could secure and exploit the contribution of its immediate upstream suppliers – and what it could offer to its immediate downstream customers: Figure 3.1.

Figure 3.1   Classic dyadic (one-to-one) relationships

(Gummesson, 2002)

Despite the trend towards looking at networks, the management of a firm's **immediate upstream and downstream relationships** is still crucial, as reflected in approaches such as customer relationship management (CRM) and supplier relationship management (SRM). In marketing, in particular, each supplier 'zooms in on the customer relationship' (*ibid*, p40) through approaches such as customer research, customer relationship management, personal selling, direct marketing, and customer loyalty/retention programmes.

Note that 'one-to-one' relationships may or may not imply interactions between individual people. The marketing organisation may be represented by a salesperson, customer service team member, negotiator or some another individual 'touch point' with an individual customer. The term **'one-to-one' marketing** has been coined for techniques which use (or simulate) direct person-to-person interactions with customers: personalised communications, for example, or offers tailored to the individual customer's past buying patterns and preferences. (If you have ever registered with an online store such as Amazon.co.uk, you will be aware of the extent to which a total offering can be personalised to you as an individual.)

In other words, one-to-one marketing means establishing relationships *not* just with 'customers' (mass marketing), nor even with 'this group of customers' (target marketing) but with 'this particular customer'. It has been made possible in recent years by developments in Information and Communication Technology (ICT), as we will see in Chapter 10.

Christopher *et al* (2002, p27) argue that: 'A prime objective of relationship marketing is to create superior customer value at the one-to-one level. The premise is that while it is impossible to have a relationship with a market or even a segment, it may be possible to establish a relationship with an individual customer or consumer'.

2.2 Chains and channels

> ▶ **Key term**
>
> The **supply chain** is 'that network of organisations that are involved, through upstream and downstream linkages, in the different processes and activities that produce value in the form of products and services in the hands of the ultimate customer.' (Christopher, 2005)

The supply chain is the classic example of chain or channel relationships in marketing: Figure 3.2

The Chartered
Institute of Marketing

Figure 3.2   A simple supply chain

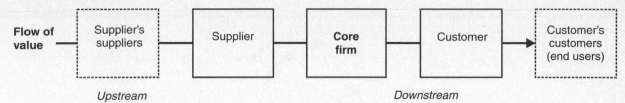

Of course, this is a simplified picture, because material and information flows in both directions up and down the supply chain: customers send specifications and orders upstream to suppliers; suppliers send goods and services downstream; and customers send payments upstream, for example. (Increasingly, they may also send goods back up the supply chain for recycling and re-use, a process called '**reverse logistics**' – which effectively turns the supply chain into a loop.)

The chain concept highlights several useful aspects of marketing relationships.

- It emphasises '**serial co-operation**': each player needs to add value through its contribution to the sequence or process.

- It emphasises the **linkages and interfaces** between members, and co-operation between them, because each link in the chain is essential to the completeness and strength of the whole. Weak links and breakages (ie poor supply chain relationships) may disrupt the flow of supply and value to the ultimate customer.

Supply chains are also sometimes referred to as **channels**, emphasising that they provide a structure for flows of materials, goods, information and so on. This metaphor also helpfully raises 'push' and 'pull' issues: whether flows are driven by supply-side (push) or demand-side (pull) factors. Push marketing strategies, for example, are aimed at getting goods into the front end of the pipeline by selling to distributors and retailers, while pull marketing strategies are aimed at stimulating consumer demand and drawing goods out of the pipeline at the other end.

It is worth noting that there are **internal supply chains**, as well as inter-business or external ones. The internal value chain describes the processes which integrate all the business functions and units responsible for the flow of materials and information into and through the organisation. This is why we can talk about **internal marketing** – as we do in Chapter 8.

ACTIVITY 3.2

Find out who are the key players in your organisation's supply chain, and map them using a simple chain diagram like Figure 3.2. (You may have more than one key supplier or customer at each point in the chain.)

2.3 Networks

The concept of the supply chain is helpfully sequential and linear – but doesn't really do justice to the complexity of the real picture! Any given firm in a supply chain in fact has its own relationships and connections with multiple other players: multiple suppliers and customers, industry contacts, partners/collaborators and advisers – any or all of whom may themselves be connected with each other: Figure 3.3.

Figure 3.3   Network relationships

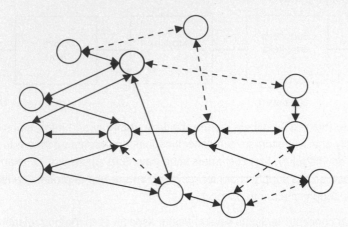

The network metaphor is arguably a more realistic model for mapping and analysing business relationships.

- It raises the possibility of a **wider range of connections and collaborations** (eg knowledge sharing, alliances and co-promotions) which may offer mutual advantages – and help to add value for the end customer.

- It also recognises the potential of what has been called the **'extended enterprise'**: extending the capability of a firm by tapping into the resources and competences of other network contributors (for example, by outsourcing activities like call centres to partners better equipped to undertake them). Some of this extended enterprise, these days, may well be 'virtual': that is, connected purely by Information & Communication Technology links, such as the internet. (You might never know, when you speak to the customer services department of a 'local' bank or telecom provider, that you are actually speaking to someone in India or South Africa.)

Christopher *et al* (2002, p126) argue that:

'The real competitive struggle is not between individual companies, but between their supply chains or networks. This view is sometimes challenged on the grounds that supply chains cannot truly compete since, because they frequently share common suppliers, for example, they are not unique configurations. But this view misses the point. What makes a supply chain or network unique is the way the relationships and interfaces in the chain or network are managed. In this sense, a major source of differentiation comes from the quality of relationships that one business enjoys, compared to its competitors.'

We will recommend readings on supplier relationships and external partnerships later, in Chapter 5, when we look at specific relationships.

3 The core firm and its relationships

A number of influential models highlight the nature of a marketing organisation as a hub of relationships – and the positioning of marketing at the interface between the organisation and the other parties to those relationships. We will look at the two models specified in the CIM syllabus and tutor guidance, although you may come across others in your wider reading.

3.1 The six markets model

The six markets model offers a helpful overview of the key categories of relationships for any given firm (sometimes called the 'core' or 'focal' firm, because we are looking at relationships from its point of view). It presents six role-related market domains or 'markets', each involving relationships with a number of parties –

organisations or individuals – who can potentially contribute, directly or indirectly, to an organisation's marketplace effectiveness (Peck *et al*, 1999, p5).

The model has developed since its formulation in 1991, to take account of changing views and priorities in marketing, but the most commonly used version of the framework is as follows: Figure 3.4. Note that the focal firm is not the centre of the relationship 'hub', although the model recognises that internal marketing supports relationships with all the other parties. Rather, the customer is placed at the centre, 'to focus on the purpose of relationship marketing: the creation of customer value, satisfaction and loyalty, leading to improved profitability in the long term' (Peck, et al 1999).

Figure 3.4   The Six Markets Model

Table 3.1   The six markets

Domain	Comments
Customer markets	The concept of relationship marketing (as we will see in Chapter 4) is based on the belief that firms must invest in building relationships with customers, in order to enhance profitability through customer retention and loyalty. The importance of customer relationships has long been recognised in professional and financial services, business-to-business marketing, and the market for regularly replaced consumer durables (such as cars). It is now 'catching on' in FMCG (fast-moving consumer goods) markets.
	▪ For consumer goods or services, the customer market domain represents end customers, users and consumers.
	▪ For business-to-business marketing, it also embraces channel intermediaries, including agents, retailers and distributors who are effectively 'customers' of the organisation, but operate between them and the end users.
	(In a later version of the model, these were included as two separate domains.)

Domain	Comments
Referral markets	Referrals, recommendations and endorsements by existing customers are an important source of new business: either directing potential new customers to the supplier (eg business-to-business sales 'leads' and professional referrals) or guiding consumer choice (eg through word-of-mouth recommendations or endorsements by trusted third parties).
	Potential sources of referrals must be cultivated and motivated. 'Given that satisfied customers will happily endorse the products or services of the supplier if prompted, relationships with existing customers are an unrecognised or underutilised facility for many organisations'. (Peck *et al*, *op cit*, p7) Companies can create formal or informal cross-referral agreements between themselves and suppliers of complementary products (eg a weight loss consultancy and a local gym). Such referrals may also add value for customers, as part of a total service.
	(This disappears as a separate market in later versions of the model, which argues that referrals are really *benefits* arising from successfully managed relationships with Customer and Influencer markets.)
Internal markets	The internal market comprises all employees, and other functions, divisions and strategic business units (SBUs) of the firm.
	The concept of 'internal marketing', as we have already noted, argues that employees and units throughout an organisation can contribute to the effectiveness of marketing to customers: most notably, through value-adding customer service and communications. It has been shown that employee satisfaction and retention (the aims of internal marketing) correlate directly with customer satisfaction and retention (the aims of customer relationship marketing) in service businesses (Schlesinger & Heskett, 1991).
Recruitment markets	The recruitment market comprises:
	■ The external labour pool and, more specifically, those with the attributes and competencies needed by the firm: that is, quality potential employees.
	■ Third parties, such as colleges, universities, recruitment agencies and other employers, who can give the firm access to those quality potential employees.
	Relationships with these markets must be cultivated in order for the firm to be able to compete with other employers to attract the best people, particularly in times, regions and disciplines in which there are acute skill shortages.
	(This disappears as a separate market in later versions of the model, as it can really be included within Influencers.)
Influence markets	■ As we will see in Chapter 6, customers' buying decisions are often made with input from a group of key influencers, referred to as a 'decision-making unit' (DMU).
	■ A range of external third parties also exercise influence over consumers – and over the marketing organisation itself. These influencers include governments and government agencies, the press/media, investors and pressure groups.
	As we saw in Chapter 2, relationships with these markets can be exploited to generate positive PR (and/or minimise negative PR); influence public opinion in the organisation's favour; gain access to markets (eg through cause-related marketing); and enhance or replace other marketing activities (as in The Body Shop's exploitation of referral, media and pressure group relationships, in place of advertising).
	'While relationships with these parties may not directly add value to a product or service, they can directly influence the likelihood of purchase or prevent an offer from ever reaching the market' (Peck et al, 1999).
Supplier & alliance markets	The supplier market refers to the relationships that the firm must cultivate with its supply chain or network, in order to enable reliable, flexible, value-adding, cost-effective flows of supplies into and through the firm to the end customer. The concept of supply chain management recognises the need for long-term, collaborative relationship development with a small number of suppliers, particularly for strategic or critical items – rather than hard-bargaining, adversarial, one-off transactions (which may still be used for routine items, where price is the main criterion).
	The alliance market recognises a wide range of opportunities to add value through collaborative relationships between the core firm and partners (other than its immediate suppliers) in joint promotions, strategic alliances, joint ventures, knowledge-sharing networks, 'virtual' collaborations, and so on.
	(In later versions of the model, these were included as two separate domains.)

The Chartered Institute of Marketing

Regroup your list of stakeholders in your own organisation (prepared in Chapter 1) under the appropriate six markets headings. For each group, pick out the key relationship aims mentioned in our table.

THE REAL WORLD

Coutts Bank: It's not just about clients

Coutts considers at the way it services five distinct markets, in addition to its traditional client market, to make sure it maintains consistent, high quality relationships with them.

- **Internal markets**: Coutts communicates with all staff – client account managers, product managers and support staff – about its relationship management priorities. The aim is to ensure there is no weak link in the chain that makes up the Coutts service offering.

- **Referral markets**: Lawyers, consultants and financial advisers are a significant source of new business for the bank: they meet prospective clients every day and advise them on how best to invest their wealth. Coutts contacts these sources regularly and delivers regular, tailored information to them so that the bank is in their minds when they are advising their clients.

- **Supplier markets**: Although the bank is a service provider, it needs to ensure that its tangible offerings – brochures, events, premises or staff lapel badges – match its service quality image. It works closely with a few suppliers who, over time, get to know its ways and standards.

- **Recruitment markets**: In banking, new client account managers can often bring a portfolio of business with them, so Coutts works hard to sustain its quality image among its peers, and to be an organisation that people want to work for, in order to attract the best recruits.

- **Influence markets**: One of Coutts' key influence markets is the governments and financial authorities in the countries in which it operates. They may actively seek the bank's views on legislative changes and new product opportunities that might attract investment to their countries.

(Adapted from Christopher *et al*, p81, 2002)

3.2 Gummesson's 30R model

Evert Gummesson (2002) defines relationship marketing as 'marketing *seen as relationships, networks and interaction*'. The key question for relationship marketers is: 'If we view marketing through relationship eye-glasses, what do we see and how can we use what we see?'

After on-going research into marketing practices with 'relationship eye-glasses' on, Gummesson formulated a framework of thirty relationships (what he described as the 30Rs) which may be part of a company's marketing and business planning. They are grouped into market relationships and non-market relationships.

In the descriptions below, we list each of Gummesson's R numbers so that you can trace them in his original book if you decide to do so.

3.2.1 Market relationships

Market relationships are the externally-oriented relationships between the suppliers, customers, competitors and intermediaries who operate in a market, which have traditionally been the focus of marketing.

- **Classic market relationships** are the focus of traditional mainstream marketing management: the supplier-customer dyad (R1); the triad or three-way relationship of supplier-customer-competitor (R2); and the distribution network (R3).

- **Special market relationships** (R4-R17) focus in on certain aspects of the classic relationships, such as:

  - The **interfaces** between two parties: eg multiple contact points between suppliers and customers (especially in business-to-business marketing); and interfacing through full-time marketers (who directly create customer relationships) and other business functions (which indirectly influence them).

  - The various means through which parties **interact**: eg the service encounter (the interaction between a customer and front-line personnel), customer membership of loyalty programmes, and electronic relationships (interaction via IT networks).

  - The **status and condition** of relationships: eg distant and close relationships, and relationships to dissatisfied customers.

  - The **basis** of relationships: eg relationship with objects (such as an iPod) and symbols (such as brands and corporate identity); law (contracts and compliance); non-commercial objectives (in the public/voluntary-sectors and families); and green relationships (based on environmental and health issues).

3.2.2 Non-market relationships

Non-market relationships are relationships outside the market, but which indirectly influence the efficiency of the market relationships.

- **Mega relationships** (R18-R23) are those which exist 'above' the immediate marketplace, in the economy or society in general. These include:

  - **Personal and social networks**, friendships and ethnic bonds, which often determine business networks (and can be exploited eg for word-of-mouth marketing and recruitment)

  - **Non-market networks** (relationships with governments, legislators and influential individuals) and mega-marketing (eg lobbying and public relations activity) to support marketing on an operational level

  - **Mass media relationships**, which can be supportive or damaging to marketing

  - **Alliances** (relationships and collaboration between companies) and knowledge relationships (since knowledge acquisition is a key reason for forming alliances)

The Chartered Institute of Marketing

- **Mega-alliances** (alliances beyond single companies, industries or nations: for example, the EU or North America Free Trade Agreement) which shape the macro environment of marketing

- **Nano-relationships** (R24-R30) exist 'below' the market relationships. They involve internal (*intra*-organisational) relationships, which may support or undermine the firm's external (*inter*-organisational) relationships and marketing. Examples of nano-relationships include:

  - Relationships between **internal customers and internal suppliers** in an organisation: how different tiers, functions and business units interact with one another as members of an internal supply chain

  - Concepts (eg total quality management) and organisational structures (eg matrix, product or account management) which can be used to **build bridges between different functions**, supporting integration and customer focus

  - Internal marketing: relationships with the 'employee market' which support external customer relationship marketing

  - Relationships between the **marketing function and external providers** of marketing services (advertising agencies, market research institutes, logistics providers, outsourced call centres and so on)

4 From transactions to relationships

4.1 Transactions

Transactions are single exchanges between an organisation and a customer or other stakeholder: a single market exchange in the form of a purchase (goods exchanged for money), or an exchange of information or influence (such as an offer and a response, in marketing).

The focus of **transactional marketing (TM)** is to look to each transaction or encounter as an opportunity to maximise short-term gains for the marketing organisation, without necessarily considering future contacts, or the effect of *this* transaction on the potential for future contacts. The fact that a customer has bought a product, even several times, does not mean that she is more likely to do so again. She may repeatedly use the same supplier because of the cost or inconvenience of switching to another supplier, without feeling any particular commitment or loyalty to that supplier, and without desiring to enter into any kind of relationship with it.

The focus is therefore on **winning customers** (either creating new customers or attracting dissatisfied customers away from competitors) to achieve **sales volume** and increased **market share**. This is achieved through market research and targeting, an emphasis on customer satisfaction through product features and product quality, and the use of mass media advertising, promotion and short-term sales incentives to stimulate purchase. There is little emphasis on customer service or customer contacts, over and above what is necessary to process each transaction.

4.1.1 Benefits of transaction focus

At its best, and in appropriate markets, this is a realistic and efficient approach to marketing, which the CIM defines as 'identifying, anticipating and satisfying customer requirements profitably'.

- If customers are buying FMCG goods (such as groceries) or commodities (such as metals), say, all they really want to know is that the products are available when you need them, and that they offer standard features and adequate quality at a competitive price. This audience can be reached cost-effectively through mass marketing. A transactional approach may therefore offer adequate customer satisfaction, profitably.

- 'A consumer may only buy a home on a single or a few occasions in a lifetime and rarely has surgery on the appendix more than once' (Gummesson, 2002) – so customer loyalty is not always relevant or worth marketing investment.

- Customers are increasingly empowered to 'shop around' (eg by using the internet for global price comparison and bargain hunting): it may be unrealistic to expect to win their loyalty.

- Similarly, with suppliers, it may not matter if you alienate a supplier by your adversarial negotiating approach and hard bargaining on price – as long as there are plenty of equally good suppliers competing for your next purchase: you are maximising value for your organisation, without undue risk.

- A transactional approach may be useful for meeting short-term objectives such as: raising revenue and maintaining cash flow; countering competitor initiatives; winning new customers; and enlarging market share (with the potential to create barriers to the entry of new competitors).

A short-term focus on transactions has some key limitations, however.

4.1.2 Limitations of transaction focus

At its worst, transactional marketing can be seen as a manipulative or exploitative approach (Egan, 2004). Customers may be fooled or forced into short-term purchases which will disappoint them – since it is not a priority to *keep* customers (or to keep them happy).

ACTIVITY 3.5

Before you read on, from everything we have already said about the importance and nature of relationships, see if you can come up with some potential disadvantages of taking a short-term transactional or 'one-shot deal' approach to customers.

More generally, it has been recognised that:

- Transaction marketing is inadequate to cope with today's business environment. A focus on customer acquisition and volume growth works where populations and markets are growing, and competition is relatively stable – but in many markets, those conditions no longer exist. In the face of global competition and overcapacity (or market saturation), the focus has to switch:

    - From volume growth to **profit growth**, based on building and leveraging longer-lasting relationships with more profitable customers

    - From short-term customer satisfaction based on product quality (easily emulated by competitors) to **long-term customer satisfaction** through a wider and more sustained value and service proposition.

- It is more **expensive** to continually win new customers (especially if you later lose them 'out the back door') than it is to keep existing customers happy, thereby encouraging them to make repeat and extended purchases (eg Christopher *et al*, 2002). Customer retention is potentially more profitable than customer acquisition, since in many markets, customers' spending *increases* over time while the cost of selling to them *decreases* (Reichheld, 2001).

The Chartered
Institute of Marketing

- Focus on the short-term profitability of a customer or supplier is a poor guide to **long-term profit potential**: firms should consider the income, cost savings and other economic benefits which might be derived through a long-term association. Banks, for example, have traditionally offered incentives for young people to open accounts: while representing a cost in terms of short-term transactions, this may pave the way for a long-term relationship which becomes increasingly profitable over a lifetime (as the account-holders enter the market for housing loans and other products, and increase the value of their investments).

- A focus on single transactions fails to **leverage the potential** inherent in the customer base, and other relationships, to add value for the organisation and for the customer. For example, it fails to gather on-going customer feedback which could be used to refine marketing strategy; or to seek the collaboration of key suppliers in improving products or reducing costs; or to share knowledge and best practice with other companies to improve the performance of the industry as a whole.

These arguments, and others, have brought about 'a shift in the nature of marketplace transactions from discrete to relational exchanges, from exchanges between parties with no past history and no future to interactions between parties with a history and plans for future interaction' (Weitz & Jap, 2000, cited in Egan, *op cit*, p25). We will look at them further when we consider a detailed justification for relationship marketing in Chapter 4.

4.2 Relationships

Relationships, as we saw at the beginning of this chapter, are more than just one-shot deals. They imply longer duration, repeated contacts and two-way (rather than just one-way) communication, a degree of co-operation or collaboration, mutual investment for mutual benefits, and the development of mutual commitment and loyalty ('plans for future interaction'). A sales transaction is not seen as the end of a process, but the start of a potential on-going relationship with the customer.

Marketing relationships are thus built on:

- The creation and delivery of **superior customer value** on a **sustained basis** (Christopher *et al*, 2002). Note that:

  - The concept of **customer value** now implies more than product features and benefits: it encompasses a wide range of satisfactions that may be derived from dealing with the supplier and purchasing, owning and using the product over its lifetime

  - The focus has shifted from customer acquisition to **customer retention**: from 'getting' customers to 'keeping' them. Marketing effort is directed towards encouraging repeat (and/or further) purchases, the development of loyalty (and therefore fewer 'defections' to competing brands), and greater customer profitability (increasing revenue while decreasing selling costs).

- Creating **multiple contacts** with customers, with opportunities for **two-way dialogue and engagement**: eg giving customers opportunities to give feedback, join user communities, generate content on websites, earn rewards through loyalty programmes and so on.

- **Personalising and customising contacts**, where possible, to simulate one-to-one relationships: eg personally addressed communications, allowing web page personalisation, giving customer service staff access to customer ID and account details through computer-telephony integration, or tailoring offers to customers' past buying preferences.

- **Co-operative relationships** with a range of external and internal stakeholders, in order to build value-creating networks which support the delivery of customer value – while bringing benefits to all their members.

The following examples (drawn from Gummesson, 2002, pp6-7) illustrate the importance of relationships in a variety of marketing situations.

- Within a few years, **Amazon.com** became one of the world's largest bookstores. Founder Jeff Bezos used the opportunities inherent in the capabilities of the internet to reach out globally, create an apparently **individual relationship with each customer**, effectively interact with customers and encourage customer interaction with each other. As a customer you can not only order books (and other products) but read reviews, lists and web logs by writers and other customers, and contribute your own. You can share personal profiles and 'wish lists' within your own social networks. Amazon is also a learning network which registers which type of products you order and offers you further recommendations and special offers that fit your profile.

- Instead of letting a large number of **suppliers** fight for contracts at lowest price, companies increasingly choose to develop intimate relationships with a limited number of suppliers. Information technology (IT) can facilitate the creation of close customer-supplier networks. An extreme example is **Procter & Gamble**, the world's largest producer of packaged goods, which has joined forces with **Wal-Mart**, the world's largest retailer. They have set up an online information system which co-ordinates the product and delivery of the goods with the sales in the stores.

- Resources are increasingly being built through **networks of co-operating companies**. In the early 1990s, **IBM** had formed alliances with several of its major customers, competitors and suppliers. Some of the most important were Toshiba (joint factory in Japan for colour screens), Mitsubishi (selling IBM mainframes in Japan under its own name), Intel and Siemens (joint development of microchips), Apple (joint development of operating systems and technology for the integration of multi-media), Lotus (IBM acting as agent for Lotus software), and Sears (joint ownership of home shopping software).

4.2.1 Levels of relationship

Relationships can be viewed on a continuum from very *low* levels of frequency, intensity, mutuality and commitment to very *high* levels of each. A transaction is, arguably, a relationship – but at a very low level. There are several different levels of customer-supplier relationship, classified according to the purpose and frequency of interaction from the supplier side. (Note that these classifications could also be used to analyse relationships with other stakeholder groups as well.)

Table 3.2   Relationship levels

Basic (transactional)	The organisation sells the product/service without initiating or inviting any further contact with the customer
Reactive	The customer is invited to contact the organisation if there are any problems with the product/service.
Accountable	The organisation follows up the sale, contacting the customer to ask if there have been any problems, and inviting feedback for future product/service improvements.
Proactive	The organisation contacts the customer on a regular basis, for a range of purposes (additional offerings, incentives, updates, loyalty rewards, feedback opportunities).
Partnership	Organisation and customer exchange information and work together over a long-term relationship, with the specific aim of enhancing customer value. This is most appropriate for high-value 'key account' customers and B2B (Business-to-Business) markets where firms have few high-profit customers.

Broadly speaking, the greater the number of customers and the smaller the profit per unit sold (as in FMCG markets), the greater the likelihood that relationship marketing will be basic. At the other end of the continuum, where a firm has few customers of high value/profitability, a partnership approach may be both necessary and worthwhile. This is the norm in industrial and service markets, where a complex total offering is tailored to the

customer's needs – and mutual investment in this process makes it more likely that the relationship will be on-going.

Many marketing organisations, however, have begun to move from basic or reactive to proactive relationships – even in consumer markets. Car dealerships, for example, no longer just sell cars, but subsequently offer to service them and keep in touch with buyers (with service reminders or invitations to test drive new models). Some even offer valued customers special benefits such as Owners' Clubs for particular models, deals on insurance (in collaboration with motoring insurance providers), opportunities to undertake special advanced driving courses or drive on racing circuits and so on.

4.3 Transactions v relationships?

From our discussion so far, you may have gathered that marketing on the basis of transactions is somewhat different to marketing on the basis of relationships! The differences can be directly compared as follows (Egan, 2004, p26; Peck *et al*, 1999, p44).

Table 3.3   Transactions versus relationships

Transaction focus	Relationship focus
Focus on obtaining new customers: single sales and sales volume	Focus on retaining existing (profitable) customers: repeat purchases and loyalty
Short timescale	Longer-term timescale
Customer satisfaction through product features	Customer satisfaction through (sustained) value delivery
Quality as the concern of production	Quality as the concern of all staff
Primary concern with product quality	Concern with relationship quality (including supportive network relationships)
Little emphasis on customer service	High emphasis on customer service
Limited, discontinuous customer contact	High, continuous customer contact
Limited commitment to meeting customer expectations	High commitment to meeting customer expectations

It would be a mistake to think, however, that a firm can or should simply switch from a transactional to a relationship focus.

ACTIVITY 3.6

Which of the above approaches most closely resembles your organisation?

4.3.1 Balancing customer acquisition and retention

There is certainly a danger in placing too much focus on customer acquisition, if customers are lost (and the investment in acquiring them is wasted) because too little effort is given to retaining them. However, the organisation *has* to acquire customers before it has any customers to retain (Grönroos, 1995). Like a leaky bucket, the customer base has to be continually filled up – as well as having the holes plugged to prevent them trickling away!

'To succeed, a company must both have a flow of new customers and restrict customer exit. The aim is to keep or, where company objectives call for it, increase the number of customers available to the company. To achieve profitability the dual strategies of acquisition and retention must work in tandem' (Egan, *op cit*, p58).

Customer acquisition and retention will require different strategies – and appropriate proportions of the marketing budget (Egan, 2004). A company in a start-up situation, in a growing market or in a fledgling industry will need to focus its resources in winning new customers; a well-established company in a mature market will need to focus on retaining existing customers and developing supply chain partners (in order to differentiate its offering through whole-supply-chain value).

4.4 Approaches to developing relationships

Long-term, mutually-beneficial relationships with a defined customer or other stakeholder may be developed using a number of approaches – the following are just some of these approaches; you may come across others as you explore this subject further.

Table 3.4   Relationship approaches

Relationship approach	Comments
Partnerships	Close, collaborative, mutually beneficial long-term relationships, usually with other members of the business system or supply chain: eg suppliers or service providers, distributors, retailers and (in B2B markets) customers. Partnership relations focus on aligning the objectives of both parties, and allowing both to share in the value gains created by the collaboration (Reichheld, 2001). The relationship between a client and a long-term advertising agency, business consultancy or major supplier will often be classed as partnerships, for example. Some organisations also see their relationship with their employees as a partnership: working together to the same ends, and to mutual benefit. (We look at supply chain partnerships in Chapter 5.)
Strategic alliances	Formally structured relationships, in which two companies legally contract to cooperate in limited, specified ways (eg collaborative promotions or product cross-selling) to achieve specific commercial objectives that are of benefit to both parties. One example is the various promotional alliances between credit card companies and airlines, to offer joint loyalty incentives. (We look at external alliances in Chapter 5.)
Joint ventures	Formal arrangements whereby two independent companies establish a new company which they jointly own and manage. Their other businesses remain separate from this new, shared venture. (Where more than two companies enter the arrangement, it is called a 'consortium'.) Joint ventures are often used to overcome barriers to entry into international markets: Western companies operating in eastern Europe, India and China, for example, have often been required to form joint ventures with local partners. One provides technical and managerial expertise and investment, while the other supplies access to labour and local markets.
Networks	Looser, dynamic, more informal affiliations of autonomous and broadly equal organisations, which exchange information and pursue ongoing (typically long-term) relationships for mutual benefit. Rather than direct contractual or financial obligations, the relationships are held together by collaboration, communication, trust and mutual advantage.
Virtual organisations	A special form of network, where companies (or units of a single company) collaborate, co-ordinate their activities and share data using information communications technology (ICT) as their main – or only – point of contact. Relationships may also be formed in virtual communities (customer-to-customer or C2C networks), such as online clubs, Facebook or LinkedIn, for example, which support user networking and content sharing.
E-relationships	Relationships, networks and interaction based on information and communication technology (ICT): email, websites, e-commerce, e-procurement, e-learning, e-publishing, internet banking, virtual teamworking, virtual communities and so on. (We look specifically at the way technology impacts on relationships in Chapter 10.)

Relationship approach	Comments
Customisation	Relationship ties developed through the adaptation of processes, products, services and messages to the specific requirements of an individual customer or other party: a form of 'one-to-one' marketing. Customisation may be a way of adding unique value through a relationship: Dell Computers, for example, allows individual customers to configure their own hardware and software requirements. It may also represent integration and mutual dependency (eg a supplier developing equipment or systems specifically for a major customer), which ties the parties together.
Internal customer relationships	Relationships between functions, units and levels in an organisation. Organisations comprise internal supply chains, communication networks and markets. Each link in the value chain towards the end consumer can be seen as the 'customer' of the one before it: service must be delivered, and value added, particularly in cross-functional relationships, in order to co-ordinate the activities of the firm towards customer value. (We look at internal relationships in Chapter 9.)

THE REAL WORLD

McDonald's: Championing supplier partnerships

McDonald's restaurants won a Responsible Supply Chain Award in 2011 from Business in the Community, a business-led UK charity focused on promoting responsible business practice.

The company won the award because of its development of what it calls its 3E framework: an initiative to drive ethical, environmental and economic outcomes with its suppliers. It now favours long-term rather than short-term contracts with suppliers, the majority of whom having been supplying McDonalds for over ten years. This has particularly helped British and Irish farmers, 17,500 of whom were supported through the initiative.

Read more about the award at http://www.bitc.org.uk/resources/case_studies/mcdonalds_suppliers.html

---

5 Relationship management

5.1 What is relationship management?

▶ **Key term**

Relationship management is the process of analysing, planning and controlling organisational relationships, with the particular goal of leveraging more important relationships to the organisation's benefit.

Some writers have argued that attempting to apply a rational planning and control framework to relationships is forcing a managerial perspective on something that cannot really be 'managed'. However, 'management planning and decision making are necessary to co-ordinate the direction and resource allocation of any organisation, and important factors in creating the organisational climate in which relationships can flourish' (Egan, 2005, p228).

Relationship management encompasses a range of activities (and related information systems) designed to:

- **Gather and analyse information on stakeholders**, in order to attempt to predict and manage their behaviour.

- **Segment and prioritise stakeholders**, based on their relative profitability or potential impact on the organisation (eg most profitable customer segments, key account customers, strategically important suppliers and other 'key players' on the power/interest matrix). This may involve sales or spend analysis or stakeholder profile analysis, for example.

- **Develop plans for each key relationship**, with objectives, strategies (eg partnership or alliance building, or tailoring the marketing mix to stakeholder needs) and tactics (eg selecting communication channels, tools and messages).

- **Co-ordinate information-sharing, communication and contacts** with stakeholders to ensure coherence, consistency and service quality in day-to-day relationship handling. This is often supported by centralised database systems, such as Customer Relationship Management (CRM) and Supplier Relationship Management (SRM) systems. These systems allow a range of users (in sales, field sales, marketing, order processing, accounts, customer service and so on) to access real-time information on all dealings and contacts with a customer or supplier.

- **Monitoring and evaluating the effectiveness** of relationship handling, in terms of attainment of desired outcomes, development of the relationship, stakeholder satisfaction and return on investment for the organisation. This may include marketing/campaign analysis, stakeholder contact history analysis, stakeholder satisfaction measurement and/or profitability analysis, for example.

We will follow up on these processes in later chapters.

5.2 Stakeholder relationship auditing

'Regular assessment of a stakeholder relationship is a prerequisite for conscious, purposeful intervention in it. Assessment is particularly valuable when any major change in the relationship is being considered, such as developing or adapting an offering or investing in operational capability for the relationship' (Ford *et al*, 2003, p75).

5.2.1 Basic relationship audit

A simple checklist of topics for relationship assessment, based on the requirements of CIM's specimen assignment and tutor guidance, might be as follows.

- Who the main stakeholders in the organisation are

- The needs/interests/concerns of each stakeholder

- The power/influence and potential impact on the organisation (positive or negative) of each stakeholder

- Current organisational strategies or thinking in relation to each stakeholder group

- The type of relationship established with each stakeholder group

- The length and degree of development of the relationship

- The importance/value of the relationship to the organisation

- The personnel involved in managing the relationship (ie contact or 'touch' points with the stakeholder) and what their roles are

- The level and type of contacts, interactions and 'ties' with the stakeholder

- The current methods used to communicate with the stakeholder

- Any problems or issues (perhaps reflected in particular incidents) arising from the handling of stakeholders, or a particular stakeholder.

ACTIVITY 3.7

Use the above checklist to audit your organisation's relationship with any ONE of its key stakeholders.

5.2.2 Relationship SWOT analysis

Another simple approach to assessing a relationship is to analyse its Strengths and Weaknesses, and the Opportunities and Threats which might arise from them.

- **Strengths** are things the relationship (or a party within it) is good at: things that are going well and enhance the relationship

- **Weaknesses** are things that the relationships (or parties within it) are less good at: things that are not going well or that limit the relationship

- **Opportunities** are ways in which the organisation could enhance and exploit the relationship for greater benefit, or external factors which make this possible

- **Threats** are factors which may damage the relationship, increase its costs or erode its benefits.

These elements can be plotted in a matrix: Table 3.5.

Table 3.5 Example SWOT matrix for a B2B customer relationship

Strengths	Weaknesses
Long history of dealings	Little co-ordination of contacts
Good personal contacts with buyers	Little collaboration to develop offering
Information-sharing via extranet	No proactive plans to deepen relationship
High satisfaction with products/service	Little learning from occasional problems
Opportunities	**Threats**
Scope for deepening relationship	Contacts may conflict or be neglected
Potential benefits from collaboration	Build up of problems over time
ICT developments support linkages	Strong competing suppliers

SWOT is used to identify areas where responses are required to improve the relationship.

- Plan to build on strengths and/or minimise weaknesses – in order to be able to capitalise on the identified opportunities (or create new ones) and to cope better with the identified threats

- Plan to convert threats into opportunities – by developing strengths and contingency plans to counter them, and by being prepared to learn from them.

ACTIVITY 3.8

Carry out a SWOT analysis on your organisation's relationship with any ONE of its internal or external stakeholders. (Use a different relationship to the one you assessed in Activity 3.7, so that you are not covering the same territory.)

Brainstorm some ways in which you might minimise the effect of the relationship's weaknesses, and/or use its strengths, to exploit opportunities.

5.3 Prioritising relationships

5.3.1 When is a relational approach needed or appropriate?

It is worth stating, again, that not all stakeholder relationships will be equally worth attention and investment. Organisations need to prioritise their stakeholders, in order to decide those for which relationship development strategies (or relationship marketing) will be most appropriate and beneficial. These may be:

- Stakeholders who are most potentially **beneficial or profitable** to the organisation, or offer a high return on relationship investment

- Stakeholders who present a **potential risk** to the organisation, its brand or reputation, which must be managed

- Relationships which offer **realistic potential** for adding value, on-going development and deepening.

Expecting to develop close relationships may be **unrealistic** (and the attempt counter-productive) if:

- There is little likelihood of repeated purchases or contacts: one off transactions or interactions are all that is required

- One or both parties want to avoid being locked in to a relationship – for example, if it could mean losing out on opportunities for better prices or options elsewhere

- Transaction processes are formalised or automated, so that there is little opportunity to develop a more emotional/social relationships. (This may be desirable to maintain objectivity and fairness: it is, for example, legally required in public sector purchasing.)

- The market is characterised by opportunistic transactions to get the best short-term deal available, which would be hampered by relationship loyalty.

In any of these scenarios, a stakeholder may resent or resist attempts to force a relationship, to gather information or to initiate frequent contact.

5.3.2 Stakeholder maps and matrices

At this point, the syllabus refers again to the need to assess relationship priorities for the organisation using stakeholder maps and matrices.

- We have already looked at the key examples – Mendelow's **power/interest matrix** and **Egan's stakeholders in change** – in section 7 of Chapter 1: if this doesn't ring a bell, please go back and revise that material!

- We will look at a more specialised matrix for prioritising relationships with **suppliers** in Chapter 5.

5.4 A portfolio of relationship types

In practice, a combination or 'portfolio' of transactional and relational approaches will be required, to suit the needs and potential of different stakeholder groups and marketing strategies. Some relationships will be long-established and others more recent; some will be highly profitable and important, and others less so; some will be high-involvement, and others low-maintenance.

'Together, the choices about individual relationships and the interconnections between them are a problem of **relationship portfolio management**. Underlying the portfolio concept is the idea that the different [stakeholder] relationships of the company represent expensively acquired, valuable assets. The problem is how to balance the investment of time, money and resources in each relationship asset and maximise the return across the portfolio. This rate of return cannot be expressed in narrow financial terms and a company may seek many different types of contribution from its relationships, such as technological, operational or commercial learning or network access.' (Ford *et al*, 2003, p83)

In other words, it is quite appropriate to have different types of relationship strategy for different stakeholders.

The Chartered
Institute of Marketing

- Definition of relationship

- Key components of relationships: longevity, ties and commitment

- One-to-one relationships (eg the customer-supplier dyad), channels (eg the supply chain) and networks (webs of multiple relationships)

- The six markets model (Peck *et al*): referral, customer, supplier/alliance, influence, recruitment and internal market domains

- Classic and special market relationships; mega ('above' market level) and nano ('below' market level) relationships (Gummesson)

- Transactions (short-term 'one-shot deal' exchanges): benefits and limitations

- Relationships: based on customer value, multiple contacts, two-way dialogue, personalisation and/or customisations.

- Transaction focus vs relationship focus

- Levels of relationship interaction: basic, reactive, accountable, proactive, partnership

- Longer-term relationship options: partnerships, strategic alliances, joint ventures, virtual and e-relationships, networks, customisation, internal customers

- Definition of relationship management and activities

- Relationship auditing: assessment checklists and SWOT analysis

- Prioritising relationships: conditions when relational approaches are needed, appropriate and realistic; maps and matrices for analysis

FURTHER READING

One-to-one, chain and network relationships

Gummesson, E (2002) *Total Relationship Marketing.* 2nd edition. Oxford, Elsevier Butterworth-Heinemann
Relationship 1: *The Classic Dyad* and Relationship 3: *The Classic Network*

Six markets model

Peck, H *et al* (1999) *Relationship Marketing: Strategy & Implementation.* Oxford, Elsevier Butterworth-Heinemann
Chapter 1: *Relationship Marketing: the six markets framework.*

30Rs framework

Egan, G (2004) *Relationship Marketing.* 2nd edition. Harlow, Pearson Education
Introduction to Part II: *The Core Firm and its Relationship*

Gummesson, E (2002) *Total Relationship Marketing.* 2nd edition. Oxford, Elsevier Butterworth-Heinemann
Chapter 1: section: *The 30Rs – introductory specification of thirty relationships*

Peck, H *et al* (1999) *Relationship Marketing: Strategy & Implementation.* Oxford, Elsevier Butterworth-Heinemann
Chapter 1: Figure 1.6

REFERENCES

Anon (2011) McDonald's: Championing Supplier Partnerships, in Business in the Community, http://www.bitc.org.uk/resources/case_studies/mcdonalds_suppliers.html [Accessed 24 June 2012].

Christopher, M. (2005) *Logistics & Supply Chain Management.* 3rd edition. London, FT Pitman.

Christopher, M. *et al* (2002) *Relationship Marketing: Creating Stakeholder Value*. Oxford, Elsevier Butterworth-Heinemann.

Cox, A. and Lamming, R. (1997) Managing Supply in the Firm of the Future in *European Journal of Purchasing & Supply Management*. Vol 3, No 2.

Egan. J. (2004) *Relationship Marketing: Exploring Relational Strategies in Marketing.* 2nd edition. Harlow, Essex, Pearson Education.

Ford, D. *et al* (2003) *Managing Business Relationships*. 2nd edition. Chichester John Wiley & Sons.

Grönroos, C. (1995) Relationships marketing: the strategy continuum in *Journal of Marketing Science*, Vol 3 No 4.

Gummesson, E. (2002) *Total Relationship Marketing* (2002) Oxford, Elsevier Butterworth-Heinemann.

Håkansson, H. and Snehota, I. (1995) *Developing Relationships in Business Marketing*. London, Routledge.

Peck, H.L. *et al* (1999) *Relationship Marketing: Strategy and Implementation*. Oxford, Elsevier Butterworth-Heinemann.

Reichheld, F. (2001) *The Loyalty Effect*. Harvard Business School Press.

Schlesinger, L.A. and Heskett, JL (1991). Breaking the cycle of failure in services. *Sloan Management Review, Spring*, pp17-28.

Weitz, B. A. and Jap, S. D. (2000) Relationship marketing and distribution channels, in Sheth, JN & Parvatiyar, A (eds) *Handbook of Relationship Marketing*. Thousand Oaks. CA: Sage.

QUICK QUIZ

1   What are actor bonds, activity links and resource ties?

2   What is 'one-to-one marketing'?

3   Explain why the network concept may be more useful than the supply chain concept.

4   List the six market domains in the six markets model.

5   What are 'special market relationships'?

6   Give two examples each of mega and nano relationships.

7   What are the limitations of a short-term transaction focus?

8   Contrast a transaction focus and a relationship focus.

9   What are (a) strategic alliances, (b) e-relationships and (c) customisation?

10   List the key activities of relationship management.

The Chartered Institute of Marketing

Activity 3.1

Your own research.

Activity 3.2

Your own research. Supply chain mapping is useful for analysing key relationships in the chain.

Activity 3.3

This will depend on your own research (see our Assessment tip).

Activity 3.4

Your own research.

Activity 3.5

The answer is outlined in the text that follows the activity.

Activity 3.6

This will be specific to your own organisation. Make sure that you keep this activity (and the next two) because you may find it helps you directly in preparation for your assessment work.

Activity 3.7

This will be specific to your own organisation. Note that this is likely to be useful preparation for an assignment.

Activity 3.8

Your own application of the frameworks given in the text. Note that this is likely to be useful preparation for an assignment.

QUICK QUIZ ANSWERS

1   Actor bonds are recurring contacts and relationships between individuals; activity links are transactions, co-ordinated plans and collaboration; and resource ties are the investment of resources in, or adaptations made specially for, a relationship.

2   One-to-one marketing is a term for techniques which use or simulate direct person-to-person interaction with a single customer or client.

3   The network concept portrays the complexity of business relationships more realistically. It raises the possibility of a wider range of connections and collaborations, and recognises the potential of the 'extended enterprise' to bring resources and competencies to the firm.

4   Customer (including consumers and intermediaries); internal; referral; influence; recruitment; and supplier/alliance.

5   Special market relationships are market relationships (externally-oriented relationships between players operating in a market) seen with a focus on certain aspects of relationship, such as interfaces, means of interaction, the status/condition of the relationship or the basis of the relationship.

6   See section 3.2.2 for a full list to choose from.

7   A transaction focus is limited in its ability to cope with highly competitive non-growth markets. It ignores the greater profitability of customer retention (compared to customer acquisition); the long-term profit potential over a customer lifetime; and the potential of relationships to add value.

8   See the table in section 4.3 for a detailed comparison.

9   Strategic alliances are contractual relationships for co-operation in limited, specified ways to achieve specific commercial objectives of benefit to both parties. E-relationships are relationships, networks and interaction based on information and communication technology (ICT). Customisation is the adaptation of processes, products, services and messages to the specific requirements of an individual customer or partner.

10   The key activities of relationship management are: gathering and analysing information on stakeholders; segmenting and prioritising stakeholders; developing plans for key relationships; co-ordinating contacts; and monitoring and evaluating relationship effectiveness.

CHAPTER 4

Relationship marketing

Introduction

This chapter introduces the concept of Relationship Marketing, a marketing approach which has developed in response to the move from transaction focus to relationship focus, which we discussed in Chapter 3. This concept underlies the whole syllabus, and is consequently explored in detail throughout the rest of this text.

In section 1, we explain the concept and approach of relationship marketing, building on our discussion of relationships in Chapter 3. In section 2, we go on to look at various influential models of relationship development, on a continuum from basic transactions to long-term partnerships, and the role of relationship marketing in developing **customer loyalty and retention**.

In section 3, we look at the values underlying the concept of relationship marketing: ideas such as trust, commitment, co-operation, value creation and mutuality – and their importance to customers. And in section 4, we survey some of the techniques used in relationship marketing at a tactical level.

In section 5, we *evaluate* relationship marketing, exploring its importance and benefits for a marketing organisation – and some of its limitations.

Finally, in section 6, we extend the relationship marketing concept beyond the customer to the broader stakeholder audience.

The topic of customer retention is central to relationship marketing. We discuss the role of relationship marketing in developing customer loyalty in this chapter. However, we examine specific methods and programmes for customer retention and loyalty in Chapter 5, alongside other relational strategies directed at creating value for (and through) a range of stakeholders.

Topic list

What is relationship marketing?

Models of relationship development

Key values of relationship marketing

Relationship marketing at the tactical level

Why pursue relationship marketing?

Beyond the customer 6

2.2	Explain the concept of relationship marketing and its approach in developing customer retention, encouraging customer loyalty, stakeholder interest and engagement both internally and externally:
	■ Relationship lifecycle model
	■ RM ladder of loyalty

1 What is relationship marketing?

1.1 Definition of relationship marketing

▶ **Key term**

Relationship marketing has been variously defined as:

- 'The process whereby both parties – the buyer and provider – establish an effective, efficient, enjoyable, enthusiastic and ethical relationship: one that is personally, professionally and profitably rewarding to both parties' (Porter, 1993, p14)

- 'A disciplinary framework for creating, developing and sustaining exchanges of value, between the parties involved, whereby exchange relationships evolve to provide continuous and stable links in the supply chain' (Ballantyne, 1994, p3)

- 'The process of creating, maintaining and enhancing strong, value-laden relationships with customers and other stakeholders' (Kotler *et al*, 1999, p11)

- 'Marketing based on interaction within networks of relationships' (Gummesson, 2002, p3)

- 'All marketing activities directed towards establishing, developing and maintaining successful relational exchanges' (Morgan & Hunt, 1994, p22)

- 'To identify and establish, maintain and enhance, and when necessary terminate relationships with customers (and other parties) so that the objectives regarding economic and other variables of all parties are met. This is achieved through a mutual exchange and fulfilment of promises.' (Grönroos, 2000, p242)

As you can see, definitions of Relationship Marketing vary in scope and emphasis. Some focus on buyer-supplier relationships and others on wider stakeholder networks. Some focus on the management of relationships, while others focus on their 'win-win' nature – and this in turn is variously thought of in economic or wider social terms.

▶ **Assessment tip**

It is worth noting that the initials RM are variously used in the literature – and in guidance from CIM – to denote both '**relationship management**' (the process of analysing, planning and managing relationships, with the particular goal of focusing marketing effort on more profitable customers) and '**relationship marketing**' (the wider process defined above). If you see either phrase, or the initials RM, in an assignment, it is worth making sure, from the context, that you understand exactly which discipline is intended. If this is not clear, you will need to state your assumptions, define your terms and justify whichever interpretation of the term you choose to adopt.

It may be helpful to think in terms of the definition provided by Gummesson (*op cit*, p3): 'Relationship *management* is the values and strategies of relationship *marketing*... turned into practical application.' [italics ours]

1.2 Principles and characteristics of relationship marketing

There are different schools of thought on the exact scope and nature of relationship marketing, and the term tends to be used to express a wide range of 'relationship-type' strategies. However, surveys of the literature (Christopher *et al*, 2002; Egan, 2004) highlight a number of distinctive features of Relationship Marketing as a broad philosophy and strategic approach.

- A shift from marketing activities which emphasise customer acquisition to those which emphasise **customer retention (in addition to acquisition)**, with an intentional balance between the two – based on the economics of customer retention (discussed in section 4).

- The development of **on-going (and, if possible, constantly deepening and improving) relationships**, as opposed to one-off transactions. A key principle is to extend the duration, or lifetime, of a customer's purchasing relationship with the firm, and therefore to maximise their 'lifetime value': that is, the future flow of net profit arising from the relationship.

- Recognition of the potential for customer/supplier **co-operation, collaboration or partnership**. Traditional marketing could be seen as adversarial, with firms battling not only competitors, but customer bargaining power: if the customer won (say, on price or quality standards), the supplier lost – and *vice versa*. Relationship marketing is co-operative: by working together, customer and supplier can create, share and exchange more value, to mutual benefit (Gummesson, 2002; Grönroos, 1996).

- This idea has been borrowed from industrial and service markets, where firms often have fewer, higher-value customers, demanding a more complex total value offering (product/service customisation, on-going service or consultancy, user training, collaboration on quality management, flexibility and so on) which requires long-term mutual investment and commitment.

- The aim of **long-term customer profitability**, or maximum lifetime value. Not all customers are equally profitable: the firm must use relationship *management* techniques to identify and prioritise potentially profitable customers – and avoid over-investing in unprofitable customers. Marketers may need to communicate in different (perhaps even contradictory) ways with customers and potential customers, depending on their status and worth to the firm.

- Emphasis on providing **sustained and complex value** to the customer, over and above the short-term satisfaction of product features and quality. This includes the recognition that:

    - High levels of service quality are required at every touch point with the customer

    - Quality, customer service and marketing are interdependent processes, and need to be more closely integrated

    - The marketing mix concept (4Ps) does not adequately describe all the elements which must be addressed to build and sustain relationships with key stakeholders: the additional 3Ps of the service mix (particularly people and processes) are crucial

    - Customers are the ultimate definers of the value they wish to receive.

- A move from functionally-based marketing to **cross-functionally-based marketing**: customer value and quality are the responsibility of all employees, not just those who work in the marketing department. Internal marketing is recognised as critical in achieving external marketing success. (One co-founder of Hewlett-Packard is said to have remarked that 'marketing is too important to be left to the marketing department'!)

- The importance of **relationship values** such as trust, co-operation, commitment and mutuality (discussed in section 3). To have an on-going relationship, both parties need to trust each other and keep the promises they make: marketing moves from one-off potentially manipulative exchanges towards cooperative relationships built on mutual value exchange.

- The development of **supportive network relationships** with other internal and external stakeholders, rather than a focus on the customer-supplier dyad. Relationship marketing principles are extended to a range of diverse market domains (as in the Six Markets Model, discussed in Chapter 3), not just customer markets. Relationship marketing may even be defined by this full range of relationships, networks and interactions (as in Gummesson's 30R model).

2 Models of relationship development

2.1 The relationship life cycle

We saw, in Chapter 3, that relationships develop and mature over time. The stages of this development can be represented as a relationship 'life cycle' – as it were, from the 'birth' of the relationship to its 'death'. Each stage presents its own challenges and opportunities for the participants. (You may be familiar with a similar concept in terms of the product life cycle or PLC model.) At its most basic, the life cycle model highlights the need for marketers to manage:

- **Relationship 'birth'**: selecting suitable relationship partners; attracting them into relationship; negotiating each party's terms and expectations from the relationship; and setting up systems for interactions, joint activities and communication.

- **Relationship growth**: progressively upgrading the relationship by increasing co-operation, closeness, inter-dependency and (hopefully) the benefits to both parties. This involves managing the risks of closer involvement; improving communication and integration; managing issues and conflicts; and continually checking that expectations, objectives and synergies are being fulfilled to both parties' satisfaction.

- **Relationship decline**: progressively downgrading the relationship, or disengaging from it. Most relationships run their course: they become stale, cease to be profitable, come up against limitations, or run into problems. The needs and circumstances of either or both parties may change. As a relationship declines, roles will have to be re-defined and resources diverted. Internal and external stakeholders will have to be informed and supported through the change.

- **Relationship termination**: ending a relationship. This can be done constructively, with a view to: keeping the door open to future relationship or further business; learning lessons for future relationship management; and avoiding unnecessary conflict and reputational damage from the termination (eg law suits for breach of contract by suppliers, or negative PR due to poor handling of staff redundancies or termination of sponsorships).

There are various models of the stages of the relationship life cycle, most of which were formulated to describe **business-to-business relationships** (whether buyer-supplier or external partnerships), because these are more usually based on formal long-term commitments and interdependencies. We will focus on the models covered by your Key Texts.

2.1.1 A five-stage model

Dwyer *et al* (1987) set out a five-stage model of the life cycle of buyer-seller relationships, although it could be applied to any long-term stakeholder relationship.

- **Awareness**: parties become aware of each other as potentially profitable exchange partners, and position or portray themselves in such a way as to attract each other into partnership

- **Exploration**: research and trial is conducted to establish the terms of the relationship, and size up obligations, benefits and costs. This includes sub-phases such as attraction, communication and bargaining, the negotiation of the balance of power in the relationship, the development of norms for working together (eg contract terms) and the development of relationship values and expectations (eg trust and commitment)

- **Expansion**: there is continual increase in benefits obtained by exchange partners, and they become increasingly interdependent

- **Commitment**: trust and mutual benefit have developed to the point where it is understood (or explicitly stated) that both parties intend to continue the relationship, and are committed to its success

- **Dissolution:** if the relationship has run its course, one or both parties may seek to disengage.

This can be depicted as follows:

Figure 4.1 The relationship life cycle

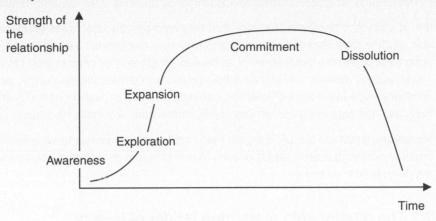

ACTIVITY 4.1

At what stage of this life cycle model do you think Relationship Management begins?

2.1.2 A four-stage model: the development of trust

Tsokas & Saren (2000, described in Egan, *op cit*, p196) set out a life cycle model with four stages, and suggest that each stage:

- Involves different relationship activities
- Requires different kinds of knowledge and information
- Develops different kinds of trust between the partners.

Table 4.1 Tsokas & Saren relationship life cycle stages

Stage	Activities and knowledge requirements	Basis of trust between the parties
Introduction	Exploration and information-seeking to develop a mutual understanding of: ■ Each others' capabilities and concerns ■ Potential for strategic, operational and cultural 'fit'	Rational evaluation, calculation
Experimentation	Action-based learning about each other: undertaking joint tasks to test the relationship and enhance appreciation of each others' capabilities. ■ Pilot projects and joint activities ■ Information sharing ■ Testing promises	A working knowledge of the partnership
Identification	Closer and higher-level collaboration begins to dissolve boundaries between the partners, making new shared tasks possible. Organisation and relational skills, and openness in sharing information, are required to take the process forward.	Identification: a mutual sharing of purpose and values
Continuous renewal – or dissolution	If the relationship has run its course, it can be terminated at this point. But if the partners can find new purpose and reinvent the relationship, there may be renewal, based on: ■ Creativity ■ New horizons/possibilities ■ Potential for further integration	Integration: trust is integral (built in) at this stage.

2.1.3 Evaluation of life cycle models

Life cycle models usefully highlight Relationship Marketing's role in continually deepening and enhancing customer (and other stakeholder) relationships, by fostering trust, commitment and co-operation.

It is important to be aware, however, that they represent an ideal linear progression. In practice, relationships ebb and flow: the degree of closeness and trust may rise and fall as each party's needs change, as opportunities present themselves, or as barriers temporarily or permanently get in the way. Many relationships – even in B2B markets – never reach the commitment or identification stage: participants may be content to collaborate at a lower level of intensity, avoiding the risks of over-dependency and over-commitment (which may 'trap' the organisation in an unsuitable partnership, and make dissolution costly and traumatic).

Meanwhile, Egan (*op cit*, p66) argues that: 'doubt must remain as to whether this level of solidarity could possibly exist in consumer goods or even many consumer service markets, where many exchange relationships are discrete [transactional].'

2.2 The relationship marketing ladder of loyalty

The ladder of loyalty (Kotler, 1997; Peck *et al*, 1999) is designed to illustrate how relationship marketing seeks to increase the loyalty of customer groups (including buyers, intermediaries and consumers), in order to reap the benefits of their retention, support and engagement: Figure 4.2. It can be applied in many relational settings: for example, charities and pressure groups use it to gauge the loyalty of donors, volunteers and members.

Figure 4.2   Ladder of loyalty

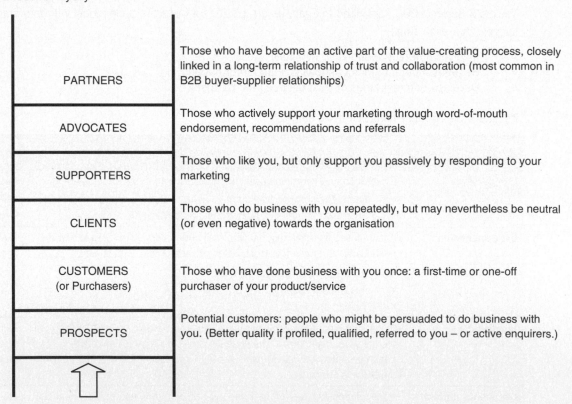

PARTNERS — Those who have become an active part of the value-creating process, closely linked in a long-term relationship of trust and collaboration (most common in B2B buyer-supplier relationships)

ADVOCATES — Those who actively support your marketing through word-of-mouth endorsement, recommendations and referrals

SUPPORTERS — Those who like you, but only support you passively by responding to your marketing

CLIENTS — Those who do business with you repeatedly, but may nevertheless be neutral (or even negative) towards the organisation

CUSTOMERS (or Purchasers) — Those who have done business with you once: a first-time or one-off purchaser of your product/service

PROSPECTS — Potential customers: people who might be persuaded to do business with you. (Better quality if profiled, qualified, referred to you – or active enquirers.)

Finding **prospects** and converting them into **customers** (ie securing purchase) is the preoccupation of traditional or transactional marketing. Relationship marketing emphasises the conversion of new or one-off customers into repeat customers – followed by progressive conversion to each higher rung of the ladder, which represents a strengthening of the relationship over time.

The Chartered Institute of Marketing

Getting customers to **advocate** level is a particularly helpful source of leverage, as recommendations and referrals by existing customers are an easy and cost-effective way of both getting new prospects and converting them into customers and clients.

Few consumer relationships go beyond the advocate level to **partnership** (which is mainly a feature of B2B buyer-supplier relationships). However, some ladder models include an intermediate stage called '**membership**', which implies genuine affiliation of some sort. This has long been a feature of voluntary sector relationships: membership of political parties and charities, for example, requires commitment and cost/effort, and offers corresponding opportunities for active involvement in fund-raising and policy development. In the consumer sector, some organisations have introduced tactics to create or simulate membership-type relationships.

'Travel organisations are perhaps the furthest advanced and many (particularly airlines) have developed clubs where members are seen to enjoy privileges that ordinary consumers do not enjoy. Some organisations, for example British Airways, have taken this a step further by openly differentiating between levels of membership dependent on the customer's commitment (determined by expenditure) to the airline. Executive Club Members (who can be blue, silver or gold card holders) receive different levels of privileges dependent on their status.' (Egan, *op cit*, p68)

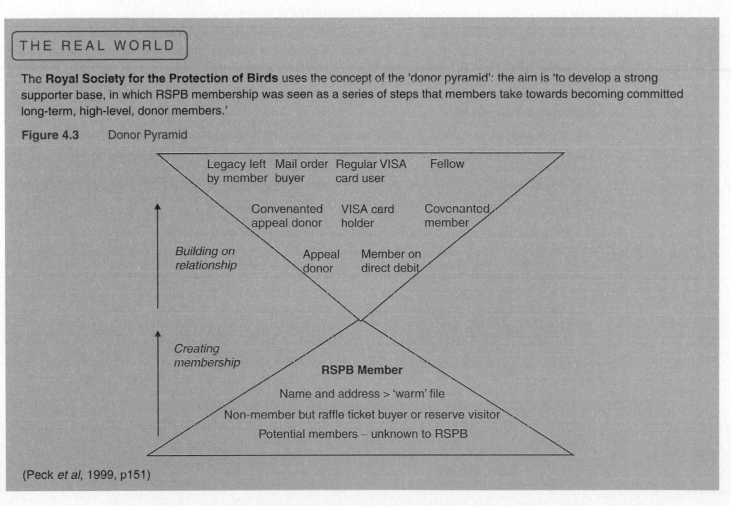

The **Royal Society for the Protection of Birds** uses the concept of the 'donor pyramid': the aim is 'to develop a strong supporter base, in which RSPB membership was seen as a series of steps that members take towards becoming committed long-term, high-level, donor members.'

Figure 4.3   Donor Pyramid

Legacy left   Mail order   Regular VISA   Fellow
by member   buyer   card user

Convenanted   VISA card   Covenanted
appeal donor   holder   member

Building on   Appeal   Member on
relationship   donor   direct debit

Creating
membership

RSPB Member

Name and address > 'warm' file

Non-member but raffle ticket buyer or reserve visitor

Potential members – unknown to RSPB

(Peck *et al*, 1999, p151)

Important note: it is not necessarily desirable to progress a relationship with *every* customer or customer segment. Some may not justify the investment required to turn them into supporters, advocates or members: it may be too expensive to change marketing activities and increase marketing expenditure to build the relationship, compared to the benefits obtained from doing so.

How does your work organisation, or another organisation that you know well, go about:

- Finding prospects?
- Converting prospects to customers?
- Converting customers to clients?
- Creating advocates?

If it has a defined relationship 'scale' or 'ladder' of involvement, status or membership – like the RSPB's 'donor pyramid' – draw this and add explanatory notes where necessary.

3 Key values of relationship marketing

The syllabus notes that 'relationship marketing is based on trust, commitment and co-operation'. We have already seen how these factors represent a deepening of relationship, in the life cycle and ladder of loyalty models discussed earlier. Here, we will briefly explore the importance of some of the key relationship qualities or values pursued by RM, which are sometimes called 'relationship drivers'.

3.1 Service encounter

On-going customer-supplier relationship (and, by definition, customer retention) depends on a supplier's ability consistently to fulfil customer expectations and to create a positive experience of doing business, at every encounter and touch point with the organisation.

Service encounters may be called **episodes**: *'specific interactions between customers and... employees that are especially satisfying or unsatisfying'* (Bitner *et al*, cited in Egan, *op cit*, p111). Some episodes are merely routine. Others are 'critical': that is, the continuation of a relationship depends on them, either positively (because they are particularly satisfying) or negatively (because they are particularly dissatisfying).

A single disappointing service encounter – and/or a firm's subsequent poor response to handling the problem – may be sufficient to reduce loyalty and make the customer more amenable to switching brands in response to competitor offers. Customers may tolerate **negative critical incidents** for the time being, but they are taken into account in the long-term evaluation of the supplier's performance. In the worst case scenario, a single disappointment (and related loss of trust) may be sufficient to induce the customer to take her business elsewhere – and to further damage relationship marketing by spreading negative word-of-mouth about the supplier.

On the positive side of this equation, **positive critical incidents** (unusually satisfying service encounters) are an important source of added value for customers, a part of the package of benefits that helps to attract and retain them, and potentially a key differentiating factor between the supplier and its competitors.

First Direct is a telephone and online bank in the UK – a subsidiary of the international bank HSBC.

One customer told a story of how, on a business trip to London, she had lost her purse containing cash and several credit cards.

Sensibly, she immediately phoned the various banks to cancel her cards and found that in general they handled it well, taking her details in a courteous and efficient manner and cancelling her cards as requested.

The final call was to First Direct, where the operator asked her how she was feeling and sympathised with her over the incident before the card cancellation process got underway – a nice touch.

At the end of the process the First Direct operator asked how the customer was going to get on without money or cards in the next couple of days. When the customer replied that she hadn't worked that out yet, the First Direct operator replied, 'Well, I can arrange for you to collect £200 from the nearest HSBC bank?' and went on to identify where the nearest branch to the customer's hotel was, adding, 'If you tell me what you'll be wearing, I'll get them to look out for you and you can collect your money!'.

This is an example of a member of staff not only being well trained, but also being empowered to "go the extra mile" for the customer by using their own initiative in the situation.

First Direct regularly wins the UK's 'most recommended' bank in surveys.

(Hanselman, 2011)

We will discuss the service elements of the marketing mix in detail in Chapter 6, but note that the concept of the critical episode or service encounter is also important in relationship marketing to the **broader stakeholder audience**.

- Suppliers, intermediaries and potential network allies may choose not to develop a relationship with an organisation if they have a poor experience of dealing with it – especially if the potential value from the relationship is relatively small or unprofitable for them.

- Critical incidents also apply to relationships with internal stakeholders. If their rights are violated, or their expectations within the 'psychological contract' of employment disappointed, employees may become less committed to their work (damaging productivity, quality and flexibility) and less loyal (increasing the risk of employee turnover, especially where other employers are competing for scarce skills). In some cases, they may withdraw from the relationship altogether, through industrial dispute or resignation.

3.2 Trust

Trust is central to the success of relationship marketing strategies (Morgan and Hunt, 1994, p22), as it reduces the perception of risk and supports mutual investment in relationship.

Without trust, the investment of time, money and commitment in a relationship – on either side – would simply be too risky: there would be no reason to believe that the benefits, promised in exchange, would accrue. The parties are also less likely to share information, and this limits the depth of the relationship. If customers distrust a supplier, they are unlikely to make large purchases, disclose personal information, recommend the supplier to others, or try new, potentially risky products or services (eg buying financial services, or buying over the internet).

On the positive side, trust can:

- Generate willingness to engage in co-operative behaviour

- Reduce relationship-damaging suspicion and conflict

- Allow the use of flexible, value-adding organisational forms (such as outsourcing, network and virtual relationships, and *ad hoc* work groups) which do not allow for direct control and supervision of participants

- Decrease transaction and relationship costs (eg less need for checking)
- Facilitate fast, constructive response to crises
- Encourage openness to new, potentially risky, products/services because they are offered by a trusted provider or endorsed/certified by a trusted third party.

ACTIVITY 4.3

What factors do you think are required to establish trust in a relationship between an organisation and its customers (or other stakeholders)?

Note that, again, this is highly relevant to both customer and wider stakeholder relationships. Think how important mutual trust would be in an organisation's relationship with its suppliers (especially if they also supply its competitors, say, or if the goods and services they supply are critical to the business) and industry networks (eg if sensitive information is shared with partners). Think about how important it is for wider stakeholders to trust the organisation's advertising and PR messages (especially in a crisis).

3.2.1 Transparency

Transparency is the **willingness to share information.** It depends on trust, because information can be *misused*: used to the advantage of the one party at the other's expense (eg exploiting information on a supplier's costs or problems to strengthen one's bargaining position in price negotiation); released to unauthorised third parties (eg giving customer data to commercial mailing lists, or leaking unfavourable company reports to the press); or even given to a firm's competitors (eg divulging information about a firm's new product or marketing plans).

Transparency supports a relationship by fostering a mutual understanding of both parties' needs, concerns and potential contributions. It is essential for higher-level collaboration, both to demonstrate trust and commitment, and to provide the flows of information necessary for the parties to share and coordinate activities in any meaningful way. Buyers and suppliers in partnership, for example, may need to exchange information about their strategies and plans, cost structures, capabilities and problems (in order to plan collaborative solutions and improvements) and product specifications (including confidential patents and designs).

If information is withheld, particularly in 'bad news' areas, trust may be damaged – and damaging rumours may be allowed to circulate and escalate. Consider the effect on shareholder relationships if the directors appear to lack transparency in their reports to annual general meetings, for example; or on employee relationships, if information is not disclosed about rumoured redundancies; on customer relationships, if information is withheld about the reasons for a product recall; or on wider stakeholder relationships if there appears to be a 'cover up' of an environmental or ethical critical incident.

This news item appeared in the Daily Telegraph on January 27th 2012:

'Lloyds Bank pulls out of charity credit card market

State-owned Lloyds Banking Group is pulling out of the charity credit cards market, because it says that offering cards that donate to good causes is "no longer cost-effective". The company has been offering these cards for over 23 years, but has written to customers informing them that their charity cards will be replaced by standard credit that do not offer a charity donation.

The charities hit by the withdrawal include Cancer Research UK, which has received over £15m from the credit cards, as well as the NSPCC and the Scottish SPCA. Lloyds said it had offered to help each charity find a new issuer "should that be the route they wish to pursue in the future".

Charity credit cards, which are still offered by other providers such as MBNA and the Cooperative Bank, work by donating a small percentage of the amount spent on them to charity. Typically the charity also receives a larger amount the first time that the card is used.

A spokesman for Lloyds said that the cards were held by fewer than one per cent of its customers. 'Following a recent review, which noted the limited demand for charity cards in recent years, we have decided that we will no longer offer a charity credit card. We remain committed to charitable giving and will work to support Cancer Research UK, NSPCC and the Scottish SPCA in any way we can in the future.'

Draft some questions you would want to ask the bank about their decision, highlighting the relationship marketing issues raised by this extract.

3.3 Commitment

> **▶ Key term**
>
> **Commitment** may be defined as the intention or desire of one or both parties to continue in a relationship, and to invest in activities to maintain it.

Committed parties are more likely to be loyal to the relationship, and therefore more reliable. They are also likely to seek proactively to contribute more to the relationship than is strictly required by contract terms or basic expectations.

High levels of relationship commitment are associated with:

- Trust: which reduces the risk of commitment
- Time: since commitment is a late stage of relationship development
- Perceptions of the potential benefits or rewards of the relationship: which make commitment worthwhile
- Investment in the relationship, in terms of time, effort, resources and identification (psychological attachment): which increases the financial and emotional costs of terminating the relationship
- Limited opportunity or desire to seek alternative relationships
- Limited opportunity or desire to seek short-term gains at the relationship's expense (eg opportunistic behaviour which takes advantage of the other party).

Meaningful commitment is likely to be fairly low in many **consumer markets**, such as the FMCG sector – despite marketers' heavy investment in so-called loyalty schemes! High levels of competition and low switching costs encourage opportunistic or 'promiscuous' buying behaviour – although it may be argued that some consumer brands evoke strong loyalty and commitment from users, against all competition: Apple's iPad might be one example.

However, commitment is highly desirable for mitigating risk and adding value in long-term **buyer-supplier** relationships and in **voluntary-sector** relationships (eg high donation/involvement members of charities, churches and political parties).

The concept of commitment may also be useful in relation to attempts by the marketing organisation to gain the interest, engagement, support and co-operation of **wider stakeholders**. In this case, commitment is most likely to be fostered by shared values and aims (eg in the case of affinity and cause-related marketing) and relationship benefits (eg in the case of sponsorships and alliances).

3.4 Co-operation and collaboration

One of the key principles of relationship management, as we saw earlier, is that relationships can be co-operative rather than adversarial or competitive: buyers and suppliers, and even industry competitors, can work together to add value, to mutual benefit. It is widely acknowledged that in order to compete successfully in the global marketplace, firms cannot 'go it alone'.

- They depend on the contribution of their total **supply chains** to enable them to deliver value to the customer better and more profitably than competitors, through: better quality materials or access to scarce materials; reliable and flexible delivery; cost savings on materials and logistics; streamlined processes enabling late customisation of products (eg Dell Computers, the specifications for which are put together by the individual buyer, from a menu of components); and the quality of service given by intermediaries to the end consumer.

- They may also depend on a range of **network alliances** to provide access to: markets (eg through joint ventures with overseas partners); technology and intellectual property (eg through licensing); resources and competences (eg through strategic alliances or outsourcing); wider distribution, brand profile or reputational credibility (eg through co-branding, joint promotion, sponsorship, endorsements and affiliations). Such partnerships are often based on shared interests and objectives (eg associations between commercial organisations and pressure groups to promote causes or raise funds, while enhancing the ethical or environmental credentials of the business).

We look at the development of collaboration in these two key relationships in more detail in Chapter 5.

Collaboration is increasingly also embracing **customers and consumers**, who were previously regarded as passive recipients of marketing activity and offerings. For example:

- **Customer self-service.** Customers are being empowered to 'self-serve' products, services and marketing information. Examples include: self pick-up and home assembly furniture (eg from Ikea); online information and customer support via database searches and FAQs; self-administered purchase-and-payment transactions via e-commerce; online travel and entertainment bookings; and so on.

- **User-generated product and marketing content**. Examples include: magazine readers being allowed to nominate feature content; TV viewers contributing news and current affairs content, via online and SMS services; web-based blogs and wikis (eg Wikipedia) written by users; 'viral' marketing via word-of-mouth, content-sharing (eg on YouTube) and so on.

ACTIVITY 4.5

What techniques, if any, does your organisation use to involve customers in the process of value creation and delivery? How does it actively involve them in marketing communications: whether customer-to-business (C2B), customer-to-customer (C2C), or even customer-to-government (C2G)?

3.5 Mutuality

The concept of **exchange or mutuality** means that both parties gain some benefit from the relationship. This is key to the development of trust and commitment, and to continued investment in the relationship: organisations expect to reap enhanced value (ultimately, in the form of profits) in return for the enhanced value they offer customers – and *vice versa*.

The Chartered
Institute of Marketing

We will discuss the nature of the value exchange in detail in Chapter 5. For now, however, note that mutuality is central to any sustainable stakeholder relationship: if both parties don't get something out of it, the relationship will be exploitative – and probably short lived.

4 Relationship marketing at the tactical level

At the tactical marketing level, relationship marketing is reflected in a number of practical techniques.

4.1 Database marketing

▶ **Key terms**

Database marketing is an interactive approach which builds a database of all communications and interactions with customers (and other stakeholders) and then uses individually addressable marketing media and channels to further contact with them (for promotional messages, help and support, and relationship-building contacts). Customer data held in computerised databases can be interrogated and manipulated in various ways, through the process of data mining.

Data mining is the process of sorting through data to identify patterns and relationships between different items. Data mining software using statistical algorithms to discover correlations and patterns is frequently used on large databases. In essence, it is the process of turning raw data into useful information.

Database marketing techniques may be used for a range of relationship marketing projects (Allen *et al*, 2001) including:

- Identifying the most profitable customers, using RFM analysis (Recency of the latest purchase, Frequency of purchases and Monetary value of all purchases).

- Developing new customers (eg by collecting data on prospects, leads and referrals).

- Tailoring messages and offerings, based on customers' purchase profiles. (Actual customer buying preferences and patterns are a much more reliable guide to their future behaviour than market research, which gathers their 'stated' preferences.)

- Personalising customer service, by providing service staff with relevant customer details

- Eliminating conflicting or confusing communications: presenting a coherent image over time to individual customers – however, differentiate the message to different customer groups. (For example, don't keep sending 'dear first-time customer' messages to long-standing customers!)

4.2 Customer Relationship Management (CRM)

▶ **Key term**

Customer Relationship Management (CRM) is an umbrella term describing the methodologies and ICT systems that help an enterprise to manage its customer information and customer relationships in an organised and profitable way.

CRM is a more comprehensive approach to the use of database technology, designed to:

- Enable marketers to predict and manage customer behaviour, by allowing them to learn and analyse what customers value (eg about products, services, customer service and web experiences)

- Segment customers based on their relative profitability or lifetime value to the organisation

- Enhance customer satisfaction and retention by facilitating seamless, coherent and consistent customer service across the full range of communication channels and multiple points of contact between the customer and the organisation.

A CRM system involves a comprehensive database that can be accessed from any of the points of contact with the customer, including website contacts, field sales teams, call centres and order processing functions. Information can be accessed and updated from any point, so that participants in customer-facing processes – sales, customer service, marketing, maintenance, accounts and so on – can co-ordinate their efforts and give consistent, coherent messages to the customer. Information can also be analysed (through a process called 'data-mining') to determine profitability, purchasing trends, web browsing patterns and so on.

We will look at other Information and Communication Technology (ICT) contributions to customer relationships in Chapter 10.

4.3 Customer loyalty programmes

Customer loyalty or reward programmes are specifically designed to incentivise and reward loyal behaviour such as repeat purchases, escalating purchases and recommendations and referrals. They include schemes such as Air Miles, various retail discount/rebate/bonus/dividend cards and voucher schemes.

Loyalty programmes, among other tools of customer retention, will be discussed separately in Chapter 5.

THE REAL WORLD

Tesco Clubcard (UK)

'Clubcard is one of the ways in which we can be responsive to local customer needs. In addition to rewarding customers for their loyalty, Clubcard provides us with insight from millions of customer transactions. From this we can develop tailored ranges, promotions and marketing by country or region – in fact right down to the individual customer via their Clubcard mailing. The knowledge and expertise of operating Clubcard was developed in the UK but has now been rolled out to a further 11 countries across the Group, with more members in Asia and Europe than at home in the UK.'

(Tesco, 2011)

4.4 Relationship marketing communications

Relationship marketing communications place a high emphasis on frequency, quality and personalisation of contact with customers (and other stakeholders).

- **Multiple on-going customer contacts**, using multiple touch points within the marketing organisation: eg sales or direct marketing, customer research and feedback-seeking, customer service, after-sales service/maintenance, the web site, loyalty programmes, newsletters, product updates, maintenance reminders, invitations to launches and other events, notification of special offers and so on.

  Designated account managers or customer contacts may be used to focus initial contact on an individual touch point, to create personal familiarity and add value by having a single 'gatekeeper' to direct customer queries to other parts of the organisation.

- **Two-way dialogue** with customers: not just marketing messages (business-to-customer or B2C) but **customer-to-business (C2B)** communication, through mechanisms such as feedback and suggestion seeking, the creation of customer communities, customer-generated web and advertising content, and so on.

  This may be augmented by encouraging **customer-to-customer (C2C)** communication via discussion boards, user groups, customer networking events and so on. C2C happens anyway, so it makes sense for the organisation to monitor the exchanges (to gather information on customers' perceptions and interests); create a sense of belonging or affiliation (adding a social benefit to the total product/service offering); and offer social/entertainment value which draws people repeatedly to the website and other mechanisms (where they can be targeted with promotional messages).

- **Personalised and customised contacts**: making customers feel recognised and valued, and that their individual needs are being catered for. Examples include: customer 'recognition' by customer service staff (enabled by computer-telephony integration); the use of customer data to send birthday cards or service reminders (such as you might get from a dentist or car dealership); the personalisation of mailings, e-mail and web pages; and the customisation of offers on the basis of customers' previous purchases.

THE REAL WORLD

Amazon.com is a retail organisation specialising in books (and an increasingly diversified range of other products). It has developed a world-leading relationship marketing strategy which utilises to the full the technological opportunities provided by online marketing and database management. Some of the relationship-building devices it uses include:

- Complete personalisation of the site for registered users

- The option to receive targeted e-mail recommendations, reminders and offers

- A virtual community of users through interactivity, notice boards, personal reviews and recommendations, blogs and customer home pages

- Customer choice as to communication/contact/privacy preferences

- Transparency about the sources and uses of personalised information

- Added-value site services such as free e cards, gift certificates and out-of-print book searches

- Convenient and secure online purchase transactions, follow-up and order tracking

- A very friendly, personal, up-beat tone.

The best way to get a flavour of how this works is to get online! Check out http://www.amazon.com or http://www.amazon.co.uk.

4.5 Referrals management

As the ladder of loyalty indicates, customer referrals, endorsements and 'spreading the word' (word-of-mouth promotion) are an important marketing resource. The organisation should develop formal processes to capture and follow up referrals from existing customers – rather than just letting them happen. Sales and customer service staff can be briefed to ask for referrals, for example, and incentives may be offered to customers to 'introduce a friend': a low-cost reward might be entry in a prize draw, say.

5 Why pursue relationship marketing?

5.1 Customer loyalty and retention

Relationship marketing intentionally aims to **retain customers** (keep them purchasing repeatedly over time) and foster **customer loyalty** (create a favourable attitude or bias which drives repeat purchase).

People trade repeatedly in some goods or services over a lifetime (eg purchasing cars or banking and insurance services) – and it makes sense for the marketing organisation to secure as large a share of the value of that lifetime expenditure as possible (where this can be done profitably). 'The lifetime value concept suggests that a company should avoid taking a short-term view of the profit (or indeed loss) of any individual but rather should consider the income derived from that company's lifetime association with the customer.' (Egan, 2005, p69)

5.1.1 The economics of customer retention

Research by Frederick Reichheld, a management consultant at Bain & Co, found a high correlation between customer retention and company profitability: retained customers are more profitable than new customers for several reasons (Reichheld, 1996). There are some cautionary notes to this view (Egan, op cit), which we have also included – but don't miss the force of Reichheld's findings.

Table 4.2   Benefits of customer retention

Profitability of retained customers	Cautionary note
Retaining customers **costs less** than winning new ones.	This is true for firms with high acquisition costs: eg from using personal selling, supplying equipment to customers, or gathering extensive customer data (as for finance services marketing). It is less true for FMCG retailing, where there are low per-head acquisition costs.
Retained customers are amenable to **cross-selling** (selling other products of the firm) and **up-selling** (selling higher-value products of the firm), so their spending increases over time.	This is true in industries with low customer turnover, but less so in markets where customers shop around, or for firms with a limited portfolio of products/services to sell (eg British Telecom or British Gas).
Retained customers **cost less to serve**, as they place frequent, consistent orders (allowing better inventory planning and capacity forecasting, say).	This may be true in stable retail settings, but not in the FMCG sector. Increased competition and more demanding customers tend to *increase* retention costs.
Retained customers may become less sensitive to price over time, and may be willing to pay **price premiums** for products which they know and trust.	Customers are increasingly promotion-literate, and supported (eg by the internet) in making price comparisons: they expect to be rewarded, not penalised, for loyalty.
Retained customers are a cost-effective source of word-of-mouth **referrals and recommendations** to potential new customers	Referrals may not be a major source of revenue growth, due to other factors (eg competition or market decline).

Reichheld (2001) argues that the profit potential of a customer relationship increases the longer the relationship continues, because of revenue growth over time, cost savings over time, the addition of referral income and the potential for price premiums.

ACTIVITY 4.6

Thinking in terms of making a simple product sale, why do you think it would cost more to sell to a new customer than to an existing one?

How readily would you change: (a) the model of car you drive? (b) the bank or building society with which you have an account?

5.2 Competitive advantage

Creating bonds which tie a customer to a firm or brand, and create a psychological investment in it, may minimise the **risk of switching**: customers changing brands or service providers in response to competition. This can be seen in the relative stability of buyer-supplier relationships in industrial markets, for example. The creation of relationships may therefore represent a source of competitive advantage (if it can be achieved) in consumer markets, where weak preferences can easily be overcome by competitor promotions, and switching is relatively hassle-free and low-cost.

Relationship management also supports competition by creating a **point of differentiation** of the organisation's offering from that of competitors: customer service and relationship building are distinctive, value-adding competences, which may not be easy for competitors to emulate.

The competitive strength of a brand in the marketplace is also supported by close relationships with:

- **Suppliers**: eg through collaborative product development and quality management, the ability to customise, or the ability to maintain access to materials in times of shortage or disruption

- **Intermediaries**: eg through more extensive (perhaps even exclusive) market coverage, preferential point-of-sale displays and promotions, or access to competitor and sales information (through point of sale systems)

- **Employees**: eg through empowering and motivating them to deliver competitive levels of service to customers. Top service companies like Federal Express, IBM and Singapore Airlines make training a central element of their company brand-building plans (Jobber, *op cit*, p343).

5.3 Risk management

The development of stakeholder relationships supports risk management, which is a high priority for firms in highly complex and fast-changing business environments.

In terms of customer relationships, for example, long-term customers provide relatively predictable revenue and turnover. Loyal customers reduce the impact of risk events: they may support a supplier when market and economic conditions are bad, or when supply is temporarily disrupted (eg through supply shortages, or supply chain or production breakdown) or following a public relations crisis (eg a product recall due to quality or safety concerns).

ACTIVITY 4.7

How might business risk be reduced by establishing relationships with (a) suppliers and (b) shareholders?

In addition, as we saw in Chapter 2, poor, unethical or exploitative relationships may themselves be a source of financial, compliance and reputational risk for the firm. They may fall foul of legislation (eg on customer privacy or consumer rights, unfair selection of suppliers, or unfair dismissal of employees). They may attract the opposition of pressure groups, with negative publicity and potential for direct action (eg consumer boycotts). Or, given increasing consumer concern about corporate social responsibility, they may cause the firm's reputation to suffer in the marketplace, hindering its ability to recruit and retain customers, staff, suppliers and network partners. Constructive relationship management helps to minimise these risks.

5.4 Support for marketing activity

Relationship marketing aims to build rapport and interactive dialogue with customers, which potentially enables:

- Cost-effective marketing communication channels to be established (with greater openness to further contact, related products/services and incentives)

- Information on customer needs and wants to be more effectively gathered

- Issues and crisis management, and public relations generally, to be enhanced

- Positive word-of-mouth promotion and referrals to be exploited as a powerful and cost-effective sales support and public relations tool

- Customer networks and communities to become self-generating and self-sustaining sources of interest, commitment and engagement – and information for marketers.

In the **wider influence/stakeholder market**, relationship marketing is designed to create interest, engagement and, if possible, co-operation from government bodies, financial markets, the media, pressure groups and wider society. This similarly supports marketing activity in opening channels for communication and public relations aimed at these audiences. The relationships themselves may, as we saw in Chapter 2, be a source of positive support and promotion (or at least help to minimise resistance). They may also help to mitigate the effects of negative PR, by creating a willingness to trust the organisation's issues management and crisis communications.

5.5 Value creation

As we will discuss in more detail in Chapter 5, relationship management adds value for the organisation, for example by:

- Creating added value for the customer – which in turn adds value for the firm through customer retention and loyalty

- Focusing on leveraging the long-term potential of the organisation's most profitable customers and other beneficial stakeholder relationships

- Mobilising the capabilities and resources of internal and external supply chain partners to support the organisation's value-adding activities

- Giving the organisation access to knowledge and learning through networking, information-sharing and feedback, especially as trust develops over time

ACTIVITY 4.8

Summarise the benefits of strong customer relationships (a) to the organisation and (b) to the customer.

Present your findings in a table, such as you might include in the appendix of a report.

5.6 Some problems with relationship marketing

It is worth noting again that:

- While fashionable, relationship marketing is not a universal panacea or 'magic wand' for all marketing problems

- Not all customers will be *worth* the cost and effort of progressing them up the loyalty ladder

- Not all customers in all markets will *want* multiple, multi-source communications from organisations, or welcome requests for two-way dialogue and involvement – even from firms from whom they have purchased products or services in the past!

Permission marketing is an important concept, based on the belief that people should be given the choice of whether to receive further marketing communications or not – and that customers are likely to respond more positively to contacts that they have requested (or given permission for) than to unsolicited approaches. This was a major issue for 'junk mail' promotions, and is equally important in regard to internet/email marketing: spam (unsolicited online direct mailings) is a major source of consumer resistance to e-marketing.

Many countries have **legislated** against unsolicited and intrusive marketing, and the sharing of personal data given to one organisation with other organisations. For some years, organisations have clearly stated their privacy policies and offered 'opt out' clauses ('if you do not wish to receive other offers, tick this box'). Many countries are now legislating for 'opt in' clauses ('If you wish to receive other offers, tick this box'.)

The UK **Privacy & Electronic Communications Regulations 2003,** for example, updated legislation covering unsolicited email, phone calls, faxes and the internet. It covers matters such as: explaining to customers the

purpose of cookies (programs which personalise customer contacts with a website) and describing how to block them; obtaining permission for e-mail/SMS/text advertising to individuals; telephone marketing subject to 'opt out' ('Do not call') requests; and fax marketing to individuals by 'opt in' (request) only.

6 Beyond the customer

We have already noted how the key principles and drivers of relationship marketing can be applied not only to customers but to the broader stakeholder audience.

- The aim of securing repeat purchases may not be relevant – but the aims of enhancing levels of **interest, trust, co-operation, identification, loyalty and commitment** (and in some circumstances, partnership) are. Think about the contribution to the firm of:

    - Loyal and committed employees: fewer labour turnover costs (such as recruiting and training new employees) and more motivated performance (over and above compliance with rules and targets).

    - Loyal shareholders: keeping their finance in the business (especially in periods of high risk or low returns).

    - Collaborative long-term suppliers: preferential treatment in the face of supply shortages or urgent orders; willingness to work together on quality or design improvements; willingness to do their best for your business (especially if they also supply competitors); protection of sensitive information and intellectual property (eg product designs).

- There may not be a 'service encounter', as such – but there will be **'critical episodes'** in dealings with wider stakeholders, which must be managed to maintain trust, commitment and/or co-operation.

- The collaborative **creation and exchange of value** is central to developing and deepening all stakeholder relationships: adversarial (win-lose) and exploitative relationships do not foster trust or commitment. Both sides must see some contribution to their own objectives, if they are to be motivated to maintain and invest in the relationship. This applies even to secondary stakeholders: the organisation must offer them something (promotion of the cause/aims of a pressure group, say, or social benefits for a local community) in return for their support for – or non-resistance to – its plans.

- Regular, coherent, consistent, targeted **contacts and messages** are as necessary in wider internal and external stakeholder communication as they are in customer communications.

- Relationship marketing itself recognises the importance of the **web of internal and external stakeholder relationships** in supporting customer marketing.

- The activities of relationship marketing **benefit** a range of internal and external stakeholders, as well as customers.

    - Suppliers, intermediaries and network partners gain access to opportunities, information, resources and a share of value gains through improved, on-going relationships.

    - Internal stakeholders gain psycho-social benefits. A cross-functional focus on customer service, quality and relationships adds value, responsibility and significance to employees' jobs throughout the organisation, for example. Peters & Waterman (1982) found that these values were a key source of employee morale, job satisfaction and identification with a strong, positive organisation culture.

    - Pressure groups may gain the co-operation of the organisation in pursuing their aims (promoting them, raising funds for them, or simply complying with them in its own policies and practices).

    - Local communities and wider society gain through being kept informed about, and where possible involved in, decisions that effect them – and through whatever investment the organisation makes in maintaining stakeholder goodwill (eg community investment, sponsorships, research grants and so on).

- Definitions of relationship marketing

- Key principles and characteristics of relationship marketing

- Tactical level techniques of relationship marketing: database marketing, CRM, customer loyalty programmes, relational marketing communications and referrals marketing

- The relationship life cycle (RLC): staged models of relationship development

- The ladder of loyalty: a progression of increasing customer loyalty

- Service encounter

- Trust and transparency

- Commitment

- Co-operation and collaboration

- Mutuality

- Benefits of relationship marketing for the organisation: customer loyalty, competitive advantage, risk management, support for marketing, value creation

- The value of customer loyalty and retention: the economic arguments for retention over acquisition

- The aims of stakeholder marketing: interest, engagement, co-operation, sustainable relationships

- Application of RM to broader stakeholder audiences

FURTHER READING

Nature of partnerships

Reichheld, F. (2001) *The Loyalty Effect*. United States, Harvard Business School Press
Chapter 10.

Stakeholder analysis and plan stakeholder management

MindTools (http://www.mindtools.com) – interesting articles and free downloadable templates for both tasks.

General consolidation

Egan, G. (2004) *Relationship Marketing*. 2nd edition. Harlow, Pearson Education
Chapters 1-5.

Allen, C. *et al* (2001) *One to One Web Marketing*. 2ⁿᵈ edition. New York: Wiley & Sons.

Ballantyne, D. (1994) Marketing at the crossroads in *Asia-Australia Marketing Journal* Vol 2, no 1 pp1-7.

Bitner, M. J. *et al* (1990) The service encounter: diagnosing favourable and unfavourable incidents in *Journal of Marketing* No 54 pp71-84.

Christopher, M. *et al* (2002) *Relationship Marketing: Creating Stakeholder Value*. Oxford, Elsevier Butterworth-Heinemann.

Dwyer, F. R. *et al* (1987) Developing buyer-seller relationships in *Journal of Marketing* No 62, pp1-13.

Egan, J. (2004) *Relationship Marketing: Exploring Relational Strategies in Marketing*. 2ⁿᵈ edition. Harlow, Essex, Pearson Education.

Grönroos, C. (1996) Relationship marketing: strategic and tactical implications in *Management Decisions*, Vol 34, no 3, pp5-14.

Grönroos, C. (2000) *Service Management and Marketing*. Chichester, Wiley.

Gummesson, E. (2002) *Total Relationship Marketing* (2002) Oxford, Elsevier Butterworth-Heinemann.

Hanselman, A. (2011) A first class tale about customer delight. http://www.andyhanselman.com/2011/01/25/a-first-class-tale-about-customer-delight/ [Accessed on 18 June 2012]

Kotler, P. (1997) Method for the millennium in *Marketing Business*. February, pp26-27.

Kotler, P. *et al* (1999) *Marketing: An Introduction*. Sydney, Prentice Hall Australia.

Jobber, D. (2007) *Principles and Practice of Marketing*. 5ᵗʰ edition. Maidenhead, Berks, McGraw Hill Education.

Morgan, R. M. and Hunt, S. D. (1994) The commitment-trust theory of relationship marketing in *Journal of Marketing*, Vol 58(3), pp20-38.

Peck, H. L. *et al* (1999) *Relationship Marketing: Strategy and Implementation*. Oxford, Elsevier Butterworth-Heinemann.

Peters, T. J. and Waterman, R. H. (1982) *In Search of Excellence*. NY, Harper Collins.

Porter, C. (1993) quoted in *The Marketing Strategy Letter*, May 1993, p14.

Reichheld, F. (2001) *The Loyalty Effect*. Boston, Mass, Harvard Business School Press.

Tesco, (2011) http://ar2011.tescoplc.com/pdfs/tesco_annual_report_2011.pdf [Accessed 24 June 2012]

Tsokas, N. and Saren, M. (2000) Knowledge and relationship marketing: where, what and how?: *Second www.Conference on Relationship Marketing*, 15 Nov 1999 – 15 February 2000, paper 4.

1   List seven of the key characteristics of relationship marketing.

2   What are the five stages in Dwyer's relationship life cycle model?

3   Draw the relationship ladder of loyalty.

4   What are 'episodes' or 'critical incidents' and why are they important?

5   Explain why trust is important in stakeholder relationships.

6   Why is customer retention potentially more profitable than customer acquisition?

7   What is permission marketing and how is it relevant to RM?

8   Define database marketing and customer relationship management (CRM).

9   List three features of relational marketing communications.

10   How might stakeholders other than customers benefit from RM?

ACTIVITY DEBRIEFS

Activity 4.1

Relationship Management really begins at the end of the exploration stage (past the first transaction) – *if* the organisation chooses to go further and develop a long-term, closer relationship with the stakeholder.

Activity 4.2

Some examples might include the following.

- Finding prospects: conferences and trade exhibitions; 'introduce a friend' and referral schemes; sales promotions (eg competition entry)

- Converting prospects to customers: personal selling, direct marketing, advertising, sales promotions – to induce first purchase, sampling or trial

- Converting customer to client: repeat purchase incentives (eg through loyalty programmes), excellent quality/service

- Creating advocates: referral seeking (eg 'introduce a friend' incentives), customer-generated content and word-of-mouth (eg discussion boards, blogs, reviews and testimonials), delighting levels of service or personalisation, encouraging identification/involvement/membership (eg with 'clubs' and communities).

Activity 4.3

The establishment of trust in a relationship depends on factors such as: demonstrated (and/or a reputation for) honesty, integrity and fairness; demonstrated (and/or a reputation for) reliability and consistency of performance and brand qualities; and consistency in delivering on promises made or expectations raised (which is why managing – as well as fulfilling – expectations is so important). Trust is built up by experience: the more consistently positive experiences a stakeholder has with the firm, the greater the level of trust.

Activity 4.4

- How will this decision affect Lloyds' relationship with:

    - Its customers who already hold one of these cards?
    - The charities who benefited from the cards?

- How was the decision communicated to cardholders? Were they offered alternatives of value to them?

- How was the decision communicated to the charities concerned? Were alternative sources of income offered to the charities concerned?

Activity 4.5

Your own research, drawing on our examples if you need to.

Activity 4.6

Reaching new customers takes longer and costs more, because you don't have existing contact with them. New customers require more information: free samples, product brochures, sales staff time etc. At the end of the process, a percentage of the prospects reached will not be converted to customers. Existing customers can (ideally) be easily contacted (for example, through databased information): they already have the information and the trust and predisposition to purchase.

Cars are generally subject to 'pull' switching factors: competitors easily 'win' customers by more attractive features and deals. Banking is said to be more subject to 'push' factors: requiring suppliers to 'lose' customers by mistakes or poor customer relations (although this may be changing, with customers able to 'shop around' online).

Activity 4.7

Partnerships with suppliers reduce supply risks. They give the buyer more control over supply, motivate the supplier to greater dependability, and make it more likely that they will be flexible if risk events occur (eg supply disruption, shortages or urgent orders).

Shareholder loyalty minimises the risk that shareholders will withdraw their investment: stabilising the financial system and the company's share price; allowing long-range planning (as cash can be put back into the business); and lowering the cost of capital (as share finance is less costly than loans).

Activity 4.8

Jobber (*op cit*, p899-900) summarises the benefits.

1   See section 1.2 for a fairly comprehensive list to choose from.

2   Awareness, Exploration, Expansion, Commitment and Dissolution.

3   See Figure 4.2.

4   Episodes are specific interactions between customers and employees that are especially satisfying or unsatisfying: they are 'critical' if the continuation of a relationship depends on them. They are important because if they are particularly dissatisfying, the relationship may be damaged or broken off.

5   Trust is important in stakeholder relationships because it reduces the risk of entering into the relationship, sharing and exchanging information, and trying out potentially risky activities, methods or purchases for the first time.

6   See section 5.1.1 for a full list of points.

7   Permission marketing gives people the choice of whether of not they receive marketing communications and in what form: in other word, opt out and opt in clauses. It is important (a) because legislation may provide for it in some instances and (b) because not all customers in all markets want multiple, multi-source communications from organisations, and attempting relationship marketing without their consent will simply be counter-productive.

8   Database marketing uses stored data on all communications and interactions with customers, and individually addressable marketing media and channels, to further contact with customers in relationship-building ways. CRM is a more comprehensive approach to the use of database technology, designed to help the organisation to manage its customer information and relationships in an organised and profitable way.

9   Relational marketing communications feature: multiple on-going customer contacts from multiple touch points; two-way dialogue; and personalised and customised contacts.

10 See section 6 of the chapter for a brief survey.

The Chartered
Institute of Marketing

CHAPTER 5

Value-creating relationship strategies

Introduction

Following on from Chapters 3 and 4, this chapter examines ways in which a marketing organisation can develop and maintain closer relationships with various connected stakeholder groups.

We start by exploring the concept of value creation. This is only mentioned briefly in the syllabus, but it is an important underlying strand in relationship marketing, which may be the focus of an assignment. So in section 1, we round up points from across the syllabus to give you a framework for thinking about relationship marketing from the point of view of creating value for the customer *and* for the organisation.

In section 2, we focus on a key area of relationship marketing, by evaluating various approaches to fostering customer retention and loyalty. This builds on the discussion of the ladder of loyalty and the economic rationale for customer retention in Chapter 4. (Of course, there are many other aspects to customer relationships: these are covered throughout this text, as they are relevant to specific syllabus topics.)

In sections 3 to 6, we look specifically at shareholder, supplier, intermediary and network relationships. If, for example, the assignment asks you to select a stakeholder group for analysis, you may well choose a shareholder, supplier, intermediary or network partner. So we have gathered together an outline of some of the key relationship issues for each group here.

Topic list

Creating and adding value	①
Customer retention and loyalty	②
Shareholder relationships	③
Supplier relationships	④
Intermediary relationships	⑤
External collaborations	⑥

2.2	Explain the concept of relationship marketing and its approach in developing customer retention, encouraging customer loyalty, stakeholder interest and engagement both internally and externally: ▪ Relationship lifecycle model ▪ RM ladder of loyalty
2.3	Explain how relationship marketing is based on trust, commitment and cooperation and the importance of this concept not only to customers but the broader stakeholder audience: ▪ Service encounter ▪ Collaboration ▪ Transparency ▪ Creation of value
2.4	Explain how relationship marketing can contribute to both long-term and short-term customer retention: ▪ Improve customer experience and develop brand loyalty ▪ Superior service levels ▪ Develop stakeholders as advocates ▪ Profile strategies – sponsorship, use of celebrities versus advertising

1 Creating and adding value

1.1 What is value?

Michael Porter (1980) argued that competitive advantage comes from the value a company creates for its customers. Value is the 'worth' of the product or service: what it costs the organisation to produce and what the customer is willing to pay for it. In other words:

▪ A firm *creates* value – by performing its activities and satisfying customers better, differently or more efficiently than its competitors. (The term '**added value**' refers to a product or service being given greater value as a result of the processes that support it: customer service, product customisation and home delivery are some obvious examples.)

▪ Customers *purchase* value – basing purchasing decisions on the perceived value they will receive, relative to the perceived costs, over the lifetime of the purchase.

From an accountant's perspective, added value is measured by the amount customers are willing to pay for a product or service *above* the cost to the firm of carrying out all its value-creating activities: in other words, profitability. From this point of view, the organisation gains value *either* by inducing its customers to pay more *or* by reducing its costs.

From a marketing point of view, added value resides in augmenting the 'product': the total bundle of benefits that offer customers value. The **augmented product** (Kotler & Armstrong, 2003) may include a range of tangible and intangible elements which add value (and differentiate competing products): enhanced features and optional extras, warranties, delivery and credit facilities, after-sales service, installation, brand image and fashionability, customisation, the esteem/prestige value of ownership, value for money – and the total 'customer experience' of purchasing and using the product/service.

Value is effectively 'in the eye of the customer', and organisations must seek to understand exactly what aspects of their offering customers will place value on. Dell Computers, for example, promise to configure computer equipment to an individual customer's specifications and to have it delivered and up and running within days: the value here is mainly based on customisation and service – rather than, say, technology, image or price.

Customer loyalty is built on the creation and delivery of superior customer value (that is, greater than that offered by competitors) on a sustained basis.

Jobber (2007, p15) defines value using the following equation:

'Customer value *equals* perceived benefits *minus* perceived sacrifice'

Using a fast food outlet (such as McDonald's or Pizza Hut) as an example, identify some perceived benefits and perceived sacrifices of doing business with the organisation.

1.2 The value exchange

Relationship marketing can be seen as a process of value exchange between the organisation and each of its stakeholders or markets.

- The organisation provides value to the customer through the total '**value proposition**': that is, all the reasons why a customer should buy the company's product/service. As we have seen, this includes product plus service plus added financial and psycho-social benefits (such as peace of mind from dealing with a trusted supplier, or an enjoyable working relationship with a supplier contact).

- The customer provides value to the organisation through the economic benefits of acquisition and retention: new and repeat business, competitive advantage, profits, feedback information, support/advocacy and so on.

1.3 Relationship marketing: creating value for the customer

The shift from transactional marketing to relationship marketing, as we saw in Chapter 4, reflects a shift in focus (Egan, 2004, p130) from what you can do *to* customers (persuade, capture, exploit) to what you can do *for* customers (added benefits) and *with* customers (dialogue and co-operation) to ensure customer satisfaction. Relationship marketing may add to the flow of value to the customer by:

- Understanding that value, as perceived by the customer, includes not just product benefits but a **bundle of less tangible benefits**, relating to the quality of the customer's total experience of the product, service episodes and relationship with the supplier. Christopher *et al* (2002) argue that relationship marketing reflects the alignment of quality, customer service and marketing strategies, giving each a sharper focus and higher priority, to the benefit of the customer.

- Adding benefits that specifically come with **relationship** (Kotler *et al*, 1999), in order to foster customer retention and satisfaction over time.

  - Adding **financial benefits** to the relationship: eg airline frequent-flier programme; hotels giving room upgrades to regular guests; retail groups giving 'Fly-Buys' or regular customer discounts.

  - Adding **social benefits** to the relationship: eg personalising products and services to individual customers' needs and wants (eg recording purchase and payment preferences, sending birthday cards, referring to customers by name); offering involvement and affiliation (eg customer/user clubs, web communities, opportunities to create web content); or building positive personal working relationships (eg with industrial buyers).

  - Adding **structural ties**: eg a business marketer supplying customers with equipment or computer linkages to help manage orders and inventory; or an Internet Services Provider supplying a starter kit with software and router.

- Mobilising **wider value chains and networks** (employees, suppliers, distributors and alliance partners) to contribute a total package of benefits to the customer which the organisation may not be able to achieve – or even come up with – alone.

- Spreading customer focus and customer service values **across the marketing organisation** – not just the marketing function – so that customer experience of dealing with the firm is consistent, coherent, seamless (without inter-departmental barriers) and service-oriented, no matter which department they are talking to.

- An emphasis on **quality of customer service** (at all touch points, in all activities and throughout the life cycle of the customer-supplier relationship).

- The **tailoring of offers** to meet the precise needs and drivers of the customer: allowing customers to define the value they want from the organisation. This can be achieved through market analysis and **segmentation** on the basis of the value customers desire, enabling the design of targeted value propositions for each segment. However, it is also increasingly possible on an individual customer or **'one-to-one'** basis (eg in the case of Dell Computers), where customer and supplier work together to create a unique or customised value proposition, through dialogue and involvement.

- Using **database marketing** to progressively gather and utilise customer information to enhance customer service and to target offerings and messages to individual customers.

1.4 Relationship marketing: creating value for the organisation

The customer's value to the organisation is the *outcome* from the organisation providing and delivering superior value to the customer; deploying improved acquisition and retention strategies; and utilising effective channel management (Christopher *et al*, *op cit*, p39).

You may recognise the following points from our discussion of the advantages of pursuing relationship marketing in Chapter 4, but recapping them here is intended to be helpful if you are specifically 'dipping into' this section for an assignment on value creation.

1.4.1 Value flowing from the customer

Relationship marketing, with its focus on customer lifetime value, may enhance the flow of value back to the organisation in various ways.

- Recognising the need for **customer relationship management**: segmenting the market in such a way as to identify the most potentially profitable customer segments, and prioritising relationships with them. (Note that market segmentation delivers *customer* value, by enabling offers to be targeted to specific groups – and *organisational* value by focusing relationship investment on groups that will be most profitable.) **Profit and loss accounts** might be drawn up for each customer segment (and/or each large individual client, in a B2B market, say), as the basis for identifying those whose profitability and potential lifetime value justifies investment in deepening relationship ties.

- Seeking to understand and exploit the **economics of customer acquisition and retention**.

  - Seeking to acquire more, and specifically more attractive/profitable, customers, more cheaply: eg by targeting promotional campaigns, encouraging customer referrals and using more cost-effective communication channels (eg the internet).

  - Placing greater emphasis on customer retention, on the basis that keeping existing customers is (generally) more profitable than winning new ones. We discuss customer retention methods in detail later.

- Using the **ladder of loyalty** to leverage potentially value-adding relationships: progressing customers toward repeat purchase, support and – where possible – advocacy and partnership. These higher loyalty levels add value in the form of: recommendations and referrals; positive public relations and issues management; information, resource and other collaborative inputs; and so on.

- Identifying and exploiting opportunities for **cross-selling** (related products) and **up-selling** (higher value products) to existing customers, increasing revenue from them over time. Cross-selling and up-selling

The Chartered
Institute of Marketing

activities may include: widening the product range, linked offers, special offers, training staff to link products ('would you like fries with that?', 'would you like to supersize that?'), in-store design and promotion to link items, and loyalty programmes.

One framework which you might like to use to review the full range of potential value/profit opportunities for an organisation (Christopher *et al*, *op cit*, p63) is expressed by the acronym **ACURA**: Acquisition, Cross-selling, Up-selling, Retention and Advocacy: Figure 5.1

Figure 5.1   The ACURA model

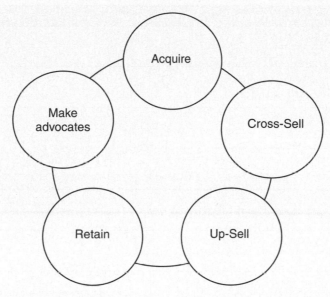

(Adapted from Christopher *et al, op cit*, p64)

You might appraise an organisation's opportunities for enhancing profitability through relationship marketing by asking:

■ Which of these activities is the organisation doing, or doing well, for each customer segment (or other stakeholder group)?

■ How profitable is each activity, and each strategy pursued within each activity, for each customer segment?

For your own work organisation, or another organisation you know well:

- List the activities carried out by the organisation to pursue each of the ACURA aims

- For each activity, assess its profitability (marking it with £ for profitable, ££ for very profitable and £££ for extremely profitable

Acquire	Cross-sell	Up-sell	Retain	Advocacy

1.4.2 Value flowing from other stakeholder relationships

Extending the principles of relationship marketing to other stakeholders may create value for the organisation by:

- **Supporting the organisation in providing customer value**: eg by streamlining customer service (employees); enabling swift delivery or customisation (suppliers, intermediaries); providing trusted endorsement of a product (influencers); or offering feel-good 'affiliations' or support for a cause (pressure groups).

- **Adding value to the organisation's activities**: eg by providing long-term capital (shareholders); enhancing productivity (employees); collaborating to achieve materials cost reductions, quality gains or new product development (suppliers); giving the organisation access to brand strength, competences, resources or new markets (intermediaries, external network alliances); providing physical infrastructure and skills (the community at large); and supporting – rather than resisting – the organisation's plans (any and all stakeholders!).

We will look further at these possibilities in sections 3-6.

2 Customer retention and loyalty

Customers give loyalty in exchange for their expectation that value will flow to them from a relationship with a supplier. Customers are more likely to become repeat customers, loyal customers and perhaps even active advocates or recommenders of the product or service if they:

- Consistently experience satisfaction – or better!
- Are acknowledged and rewarded for their loyalty, and
- Perceive that they have a relationship with the supplier.

In this section, we evaluate relationship marketing methods for contributing to short- and long-term customer retention, under four broad headings.

- Service quality
- Barriers to exit
- Loyalty programmes
- Brand engagement.

2.1 Service quality

As we saw in Chapter 4, a high, consistent and competitive level of customer service (seen as an on-going chain of satisfying service encounters or episodes) is a key to customer satisfaction and loyalty – and therefore to long-term relationships of mutual advantage – in many industries. It is also one of the main ways in which an organisation can add customer value.

There are many factors involved in the delivery of customer service – and they are not confined to what happens during the service encounter that the customer experiences. Here are some of the wider factors that affect the delivery of great customer service:

- The creation of a **corporate culture** which expresses and models customer-focused values and reinforces those values through its selection, appraisal and reward systems, and the messages it sends employees at every level

- The creation of **service-supporting internal relationships** and internal marketing: the recruitment of skilled customer-facing people; the supply of appropriate training; the empowerment of staff to take decisions that will satisfy and retain customers; and the reward and recognition of staff who deliver outstanding service

- **Gathering, analysing, communicating and acting on customer feedback**. Feedback and adjustment (addressing customer concerns and complaints) are crucial in minimising dissatisfaction and demonstrating commitment to customer value. Constructive handling of problems and complaints (sometimes called '**service recovery**') may lead to restored satisfaction – and even strengthened relationship, because of the supplier's demonstrated commitment

- Establishing a **partnership approach** to relationships with other stakeholders, such as suppliers and intermediaries (distributors, retail outlets, call centres), in order to support high levels of service at all links in the value-delivery chain

- Ensuring **promise fulfilment** (Jobber, 2007, p902): making realistic promises (to manage customer expectations); enabling staff and service systems to deliver on promises made; and keeping promises during service encounters

- Offering **support services** (eg warranties, servicing, user training and help lines) to facilitate customers in using the product safely and satisfyingly, and support them through changes and difficulties

- Reinforcing customer loyalty with **incentives and rewards**, to show that the organisation values its 'valued customers'

- Establishing **customer-friendly systems**. It is no good expecting staff to give great service to customers if the systems, procedures, technology and information flows do not support their efforts.

We will look at customer service in more detail in Chapter 6, as part of the extended marketing mix.

It is worth noting that while high levels of customer service are *essential* for customer retention, they may not be *sufficient*. No amount of service ultimately makes up for products that don't work, fall apart or otherwise disappoint, for example (Lele & Sheth, 1991). Moreover, high levels of service may get taken for granted over time, and cease to be an incentive to loyalty, in the face of competitor offers.

ACTIVITY 5.3

An organisation conducted a survey of their managers asking about key benefits of the customer care scheme implemented two years ago.

The results of this survey are shown below.

Benefit	% of managers citing benefit
Improved customer retention	67
Enhanced reputation of the organisation	59
Competitive advantage in the marketplace	52
Attraction of new customers	42
Increased profitability	27
Improved staff morale and loyalty	26
Cost efficiency	10

You have been asked to present this information in a report to your Board of Directors, to help justify the implementation of a new customer care programme.

Bearing in mind your aims, and the directors' needs in this situation (as customers of your internal marketing message), format this information in a way that will show the cited survey results to best effect.

▶ **Assessment tip**

You may choose (or be asked) to use simple graphic formats in your assignment, to display summary data (as in Activity 5.3) or to illustrate an argument (for example, if you are discussing the ladder of loyalty). Unless asked for, however, diagrams and graphs should only be used if they are *relevant* and *applicable* to the situation being described (and if you can draw them neatly and label them accurately!)

2.2 Barriers to exit

Customer exit is the term used to describe a situation where a customer decides to end the relationship and switch to another brand or provider. In competitive markets, there may be many (or a few strong) alternative sources of a product/service, and this may make it comparatively easy for the customer to switch – unless the organisation can increase the costs of switching, or erect '**barriers to exit**'.

'**Switching costs** are effectively barriers to exit from the company, from the perspective of the consumer' (Egan, *op cit*, p70).

Some of these barriers are generated by the customer themselves, as the result of genuine satisfaction and added value created by the supplier. This is arguably the most constructive and ethical approach to building exit barriers, since it involves willing participation and an exchange of value. Examples of such barriers are:

- **Emotional costs**: emotional investment in relationship with an organisation, brand or particular personnel (eg an account or contract manager)

- **Social costs**: loss of social networks and affiliations created by dealing with the supplier (eg membership in a user club)

The Chartered Institute of Marketing

Some barriers are a natural consequence of the **relationship**. The marketer can exploit this by drawing customers' attention to the costs of going elsewhere: emphasising the value of trust, familiarity and so on. Examples of such barriers are:

- **Search costs**: time and energy spent looking for another supplier

- **Learning costs**: time and energy spent developing dealings with a new supplier, or learning to use a new product/brand

- **Risk**: potential costs or difficulties of using an unknown supplier or brand

- **Inertia**: the psychological difficulty of breaking long-term habits or patterns. Some barriers are deliberately applied by the supplier to '**lock customers in**' with the threats of penalties. This is less effective from an RM point of view, as the implied threat may alienate customers (especially if the product and service elements are less than satisfactory) – making it more likely that they will defect as soon as they can.

- **Financial costs**: formal financial penalties for exiting the relationship (as when switching gym membership, telecom providers or mortgage providers) or loss of rewards built up over time (eg no-claims insurance bonuses, customer loyalty points or employee share option schemes)

- **Legal barriers**: for example, a fixed-term contract with a supplier (with no early opt-out clause).

Some barriers are deliberately applied by the supplier to **encourage retention** via incentives and opportunities to build up rewards (eg in loyalty programmes). This can be effective (as we will see below), if the rewards represent genuine value.

2.3 Loyalty programmes

The purpose of loyalty programmes, for an organisation or brand, is to establish a higher level of customer retention in profitable segments, by providing increased satisfaction and value to certain customers (Egan, 2004, p44).

Some schemes focus on securing **multiple on-going purchases**, usually with the incentive of earning points for each purchase, which can be redeemed for rewards or discounts. Reward cards memorise the redeemable points, and generate information on the holder's purchasing behaviour for the provider. Such cards lend themselves to co-branding and other forms of alliance: consortia of retail, financial services and other providers have been formed to pool resources and share information in joint loyalty schemes (eg the Nectar Loyalty Card Scheme).

Some schemes are based on receiving **added value benefits** once you reach a higher category of status/value (eg frequent flyer clubs, or 'patrons' of arts organisations).

Others use affinity marketing, by linking purchases with donations to a charity or other cause (eg building up points towards donation of books or computers to local schools). **Affinity cards**, which link a business with a charity or cause, have become a popular way for consumers to identify with a cause and donate to charity from their spending. Such schemes have been exploited for fundraising by the RSPCA, Save the Children and some commercial football clubs. (But see Activity 4.4 in Chapter 4 about one bank withdrawing such affinity cards).

Most loyalty programmes have some kind of 'club' aspect to them, and offer a variety of **member benefits**. The Waterstones Card, for example, offers points which build towards cash discounts on further purchases; email newsletters (with book reviews, offers and competitions); a free copy of the quarterly magazine; and invitations to exclusive shopping events. (If you're curious, go to http://www.waterstones.com and click on the Waterstones Card link.)

The intention of a loyalty scheme for the organisation is that:

- A brand preference or habit will develop from repeat purchase and familiarity, which creates psychological barriers to switching

- A sense of belonging to a community or club (even if 'virtual') will reinforce the relationship

- The brand will be differentiated from similar competing brands and/or defended against the effect of competitors' loyalty programmes

- The incentives and their accessories (VIP cards and so on) add economic and social benefits, which will be valued and desired by customers – creating further barriers to switching (if similar benefits are not available elsewhere)

- Customer data gathered from the scheme (details provided by the customer or point-of-sale data) can be used to fine-tune the marketing mix – which in turn may create a genuine bias or commitment to the brand. This data reflects actual customer behaviour and preferences, and is therefore 'much more valuable for customised product offerings than is any of the aggregate data about the 'average' customer or market segment typically used in traditional marketing practices.' (Varey, 2002).

- Additional revenue can be raised through repeat purchases, cross-selling and up-selling, on the back of customer loyalty. Incentives can also be added for short-term sales promotions (eg 'double points' on selected purchases).

2.3.1 Limitations of loyalty programmes

The **profitability** of loyalty programmes has been questioned (Egan, 2004; Jobber, 2007).

- The costs of the schemes can be high, if you include technology, software, staff training, administration, communications, cards and rewards.

- Over time, the rewards may get taken for granted as part of the organisation's offering. They may even become the norm for a sector – particularly since the providers of loyalty scheme technology are promoting their products heavily to marketers (Varey, 2002, p241): schemes may not provide competitive differentiation for long.

- The costs may therefore become another unavoidable cost of doing business – without necessarily creating a corresponding impact on sales.

- Meanwhile, in order to keep customers motivated, the organisation may get caught in a costly spiral of offering higher and higher rewards.

ACTIVITY 5.4

In your experience, are loyalty programmes genuine attempts to build lasting relationships with customers? Can you think of ways in which they may *not* create genuine loyalty and relationships?

Egan (2004, p45) argues that all this is, in the end, counterproductive: 'Over time, customers who receive, in effect, only bribes are likely to become promiscuous and seek the highest bribe available, as that is the only satisfaction they receive from the exchange'.

So should a firm implement, or continue, a loyalty scheme? It should certainly regularly assess whether it is gaining any of the **benefits** listed above, set against the **costs** of pursuing them. It should also assess whether focusing on one group of customers (eg frequent flyers) risks losing, through neglect, others who are potentially equally profitable. However, in markets where key competitors are operating loyalty schemes, it may simply be seen as too risky not to have one, or to discontinue one.

The Chartered Institute of Marketing

Assess the following loyalty programmes. What is the basis of each scheme? Does it provide meaningful incentives to repeat purchase – and in what way (if at all) might this be an expression of genuine loyalty? How vulnerable might this 'loyalty' be to competing offers? How costly do you think the scheme would be to manage? How have the organisations exploited wider stakeholder relationships in support of the scheme?

- **Tesco**: http://www.tesco.com. Click on the Tesco ClubCard link. (Note also the 'community' and 'environment' links: what messages are these giving to wider stakeholders, and how might this be tied in to customer loyalty?) Alternatively, Tesco is written up as a case study in Peck, Payne & Christopher *Relationship Marketing* (1999) at the end of Chapter 2.

- **Virgin Atlantic**: http://www.virginatlantic.com. Click on the Flying Club link.

- **Hertz Rent-a-Car**: http://www.hertz.com. Click on the Hertz Gold Plus Rewards link.

- **Nectar Loyalty Points Card**: http://www.nectar.com. Alternatively, this is written up as a case study ('Nectar: Loyalty brings sweet rewards') in your key text: Jobber *Principles & Practice of Marketing* (5th edition, 2007: Pearson Education), at the end of Chapter 15 on Direct Marketing – and think through the questions at the end.

2.4 Brand engagement

> **▶ Key term**
>
> A **brand** is defined as any words, symbols, design or style in any combination that distinguishes a company's offering from competing offerings in the perceptions of the target audience. In other words, brands have an **identity**, which may begin with a product name, such as 'Kleenex' or 'Coca Cola', but extends to a range of features which assist in reinforcing recognition and attachment: product and packaging design, slogans, people (like Richard Branson as a visible part of the Virgin brand) and values (like the Body Shop's ethical and environmental commitments).

In addition to forming relationships through engagement with the supplier organisation (through interactions, dialogue and developing contacts) or through rewards and incentives, marketers can attempt to foster a bias, preference or commitment towards a **brand**.

Branding has various uses in promotion, and particularly in fostering customer loyalty.

- It aids product **differentiation**, helping customers readily to identify the product or service, and reinforcing their bias or preference for it over competing offerings.

- It aids **recognition** of, and **identification** with, the brand, which helps to create brand loyalty.

- It supports **market segmentation and targeting** of the value proposition, since different brands of similar products may be developed to meet the specific needs of categories of users. (Think of all the different cereal brands – Cornflakes, Special K, All Bran, Sultana Bran – produced by Kelloggs, for example.)

- It supports **brand extension or stretching**. Other products can be introduced into the brand range to 'piggy back' on the articles already known to the customer (but ill-will as well as goodwill for one product in a branded range will be transferred to all other products in the range).

More specific branding tactics which can be used to support customer loyalty – or wider stakeholder engagement – include the following.

Table 5.1   Branding tactics

Tactic	Explanation
Brand positioning	Brand positioning is the process of associating a brand with certain values or characteristics in the perceptions of consumers: for example, value for money, quality, convenience, trendiness or ethics. If this can be targeted to the values that are important to customers (and wider stakeholders), they are more likely to form an emotional connection or engagement with the brand. Examples include The Body Shop's positioning as an ethical brand; Marks & Spencer for quality and value; Rolls Royce for premium quality and luxury; or Dyson for technological innovation.
Brand profile	The presence, visibility, credibility and congeniality of a brand may reinforce customers' loyalty by confirming the reasons why they prefer the brand – and affirming them for preferring it. Brand profile strategies may, for example, include the use of: ■ Sponsorships, which associate the brand with community involvement (eg sponsorship of local events, arts or sport) or worthwhile causes (eg sponsorship of a charity, fundraiser or awareness campaign) or other high-profile brand (eg sponsorship of a major sporting team or event) ■ Celebrity spokespersons and endorsements (eg various music artists' associations with the Apple iPod, or celebrity advertisements for Pepsi).
Affinity marketing	Brands can be linked to other brands, organisations or causes, in order to extend goodwill and loyalty from them to the brand. ■ Product-based co-branding links two or more existing brands to form a single offering: for example, Siemens Porsche Design products, or various computer brands partnered with Intel microchips ■ Communication-based co-branding links two or more brands in promotional campaigns: for example, Whirlpool washing machines endorsing Ariel washing powder, or (a few years ago) McDonald's restaurants having exclusive rights to promote new Disney films and merchandise ■ Brands can be linked to charities or pressure groups, to win the engagement of their supporters, eg through the use of affinity cards, cause-related sponsorships and fund-raising.
Brand communities	Communities, or virtual communities, can be built up around brands, in order to create opportunities for relational interaction and social bonds, which offer customers the psycho-social benefits of belonging and participating (which in turn become barriers to switching). Examples include: ■ User groups or 'clubs', where owners get together for social events and/or brand related events (eg private viewings, new model previews, anniversary-of-ownership celebrations) ■ Involvement in online user groups and clubs, through discussion boards, e-mail newsletters, chat rooms and so on ■ Brand loyalty programmes which foster a sense of membership and status ■ Membership of the organisation itself, in the case of a charity, political party, pressure group or football club, say. This may involve various types and levels of involvement.
Customer/ stakeholder advocacy	Influential stakeholders can be developed as advocates for the brand, either informally (by progressing them up the ladder of loyalty, so that they become active supporters) or formally, by for example: ■ Using customer testimonials in advertising ■ Enlisting customers in 'Introduce a Friend' or referral schemes ■ Securing brand endorsement by, or co-branding with, influential pressure groups (eg food brands marked with the Heart Foundation 'Tick')

The Chartered Institute of Marketing

Explore the websites of some of the following organisations. What methods do they use to develop relational interactions with (and between) their customers or other stakeholders? What benefits are offered by these interactions for the customer or stakeholder? What benefits do you think accrue for the organisation?

- Your favourite football club. (If you don't have one, you might like to look at **Manchester United**: http://www.manutd.com)
- **Amazon.com** (http://www.amazon.co.uk)
- **Nike Plus** (http:// nikeplus.nike.com).

3 Shareholder relationships

As we saw in Chapter 1, shareholders are important stakeholders in a firm, as they collectively own it, and individually contribute finance (in the form of share capital) to fund its activities.

The firm's relationships with its shareholders are subject to a discipline called **corporate governance**: the system by which organisations are directed and controlled. Corporate governance issues came to prominence in the 1970s and 1980s, with high profile corporate scandals and collapses. In particular, concerns about the transparency and truthfulness of financial reporting – and resulting risks for shareholders – were raised by many investors. Shareholder confidence was being eroded, and steps were taken in the UK during the 1990s to protect their interests and the stability of the financial system. The **Stock Exchange Combined Code** (1998) seeks to:

- Ensure that the board of directors does not have unchecked power, and that it has a balance of executive and non-executive directors (adding independent judgement on decisions)

- Ensure that directors present balanced and understandable assessments of the company's financial position and prospects in the annual accounts and other reports to shareholders (and other stakeholders)

- Improve accountability and transparency on key issues (including the remuneration of directors)

- Strengthen internal controls and auditing, to avoid fraud and/or mismanagement of funds and financial reporting

- Improve communication with shareholders. Companies should be prepared to communicate directly with institutional shareholders, and to use the Annual General Meeting (AGM) to communicate with private investors.

From a tactical marketing point of view, however, the most important issues in **shareholder marketing** may be:

- The potential to **maintain proactive communication** with shareholders, other than in formal financial reports (eg through an 'investors' page on the company website) so that they remain positive about the organisation's management and prospects, and may therefore be sufficiently loyal to hold onto their shares (ie leave their capital in the firm).

- The need for **issues management** in order to avoid alienating shareholders (eg through allegations of fraud, mismanagement or reputational damage through ethical/environmental problems) and/or to avoid making them nervous about the security of their investment (eg through rumours of losses or senior management defections).

- Emphasising **'good news' messages** eg about the support and enthusiasm shown by shareholders at the AGM, the growth or maintenance of dividend payments to shareholders, or added-value 'partner' benefits given to shareholders (eg discounts on products/services, invitations to special events).

- Demonstrating **effective and profitable marketing activity**, so that shareholders have confidence in the future profitability of the enterprise (and their own prospects for dividends and share value growth).

4 Supplier relationships

4.1 Value-adding potential of supplier relationships

High-quality, motivated and committed suppliers have the potential to contribute significantly to the business in several ways.

- **New product development and innovation**: contributing ideas and refinements based on their expertise in the materials/components involved; and confirming that materials and components will be available at the right price for the product to be profitable. (The term 'early supplier involvement' is used for this early-stage collaboration on product development.)

- **Product/packaging quality**: ensuring the quality of the materials/components used by the firm; collaborating with the firm's procurement and operations functions to improve quality management processes; training the firm's staff in the properties of the materials; or sharing information and planning for continuous improvement programmes.

- **Availability/delivery:** offering swift, flexible delivery of materials/components, so that the manufacturer can keep less inventory (and benefit from lower inventory costs) while still being able to fulfil orders (this is known as 'Just in Time' supply).

- **Customisation:** pre-assembling product modules, so that the final manufacturer can swiftly configure and deliver customised products to consumer specification (eg Dell computers).

- **Value for money:** keeping materials, supply and stock-holding costs low, or collaborating with the organisation in cost-reduction programmes.

- **Marketing activity**: providing marketing services such as market research, merchandising, marketing consultancy, copywriting and design, printing, website design and management, media buying etc.

4.2 Adversarial and collaborative supplier relationships

4.2.1 Adversarial relationships

Relationships with suppliers have traditionally been adversarial (or competitive). The buyer and supplier **compete to maximise benefits** for their own organisation, at the expense of the other party: this often focuses on hard bargaining on price. Buyers use multiple suppliers to stimulate competition, and contracts are typically short, to allow opportunistic switching to cheaper suppliers when available. There is minimal sharing of information, because there is little or no trust – and little consideration of the potential for co-operation. Contract terms, product specifications and service level agreements are rigidly enforced, as a substitute for supplier loyalty and commitment.

The intended **benefits** of such a relationship strategy for the buying organisation are primarily price reduction (for greater profitability), compliance (where this is all that is required) and supply security (because if one supplier fails, you can switch to another).

The **drawbacks** of such a strategy, however, are that each party fails to get the full benefit of the other party's expertise. There are inefficiencies in identifying, evaluating, negotiating with, motivating and managing different suppliers each time. Suppliers are unlikely to be motivated by small, short-term contracts: effort will have to go into performance management – and there is little potential for collaborative improvements.

4.2.2 Collaborative supplier partnerships

In a collaborative approach, the buyer seeks to develop longer-term relationships with a smaller number of preferred suppliers. The strategic view is that both organisations can benefit from seeking ways of adding value in the supply chain, to the ultimate benefit of the end consumer. Relationship management is based on trust, mutual obligation and benefit (rather than compliance with contract terms), and information sharing. The supplier participates with the buyer in looking for improvements and innovations: they jointly set targets for improvements in cost and quality, and meet regularly to discuss progress towards achieving these targets. Information is shared more or less freely (in areas of shared activity) in both directions, in order to support joint problem solving and development.

Collaboration can be seen on a spectrum. At the tactical end, suppliers may be invited to participate in new product development projects, quality drives or cost-reduction programmes, say. At the high-trust, high-integration end of the spectrum are:

- **Outsourcing relationships**: a supplier carries out part of the firm's activities (eg production, data processing or telesales) on its behalf, under contract

- **Strategic alliances**: contractual collaboration in particular areas (eg co-branding or joint entry into a new international market)

- **Partnership relationships**: buyers and suppliers agree to collaborate closely over the long term, sharing information and ideas for development.

The **benefits of collaborative supplier relationships** can be summarised as follows (Profex, 2007).

Table 5.2   Mutual benefits of collaborative supplier relationships

Benefits to the supplier	Benefits to the buyer
There will be established points of contact, enabling the development of trust	Purchasing attention is focused on developing deeper relationships with fewer suppliers
Better information about the buyer and its needs enables the supplier to manage the buyer's expectations and offer better service	Better information, supplier commitment and collaborative improvement-seeking should result in better service and quality gains
Better information (and/or systems integration) allows forward planning	A smaller supplier base and systems integration lead to process efficiencies and reduced sourcing costs
Joint improvement, development and value gains will be shared by the supplier	The buyer may get preferential treatment (eg in the case of supply shortages or emergency orders) arising from goodwill
The supplier is likely to get more business, as preferred supplier	The buyer should be able to develop a high degree of trust and confidence in the supplier

Collaborative strategies are currently fashionable, but it is important to note that a collaborative approach is not necessarily the 'best' approach to supply chain relations in all circumstances. Co-operative or partnership relations take time and effort to develop, and may not be worth the investment for the purchase of routine items – especially since the buyer will also be missing out on opportunities to drive price down by adversarial bargaining.

There are also drawbacks, risks and obstacles in getting close or 'cosy' with suppliers, or in getting 'locked in' to long-term supply contracts. There is the risk of being locked into a relationship with the 'wrong' partners (incompatible – or unethical, which brings additional reputational risk from being associated with them). There is risk in exchanging information, possibly losing control over confidential data and intellectual property. Over-dependence on a small group of suppliers may make the buyer vulnerable to supply risk if they fail or suffer disruption. Long-term supply partners may get complacent and cease to give excellent service or prices. And high switching costs may be a constraint if better alternative suppliers emerge in the market.

Appraise your own organisation's relationships with its suppliers. Are they adversarial, collaborative – or somewhere between?

What suppliers are used by the marketing function – and what type of relationships does it have with them?

What are the features and tools of collaborative supplier relationships, as practised in your organisation?

4.3 Prioritising supplier relationships

As with wider stakeholders (using Mendelow's power/interest matrix) and customers (using Customer Relationship Management), it is important to know *which* suppliers are worth investing in closer relationships with – and which are not.

An influential tool for prioritising supplier relationships is Kraljic's (1983) **procurement positioning matrix**: Figure 5.2.

Figure 5.2   The Kraljic matrix

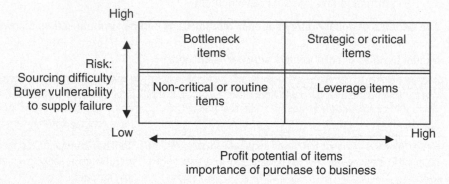

- For **routine items** (such as common office stationery items) a non-relational contract supply approach will provide routine efficiency, which is all that is really required

- For **bottleneck items** (such as specialised components, which could cause production delays if supply was disrupted), the buyer's priority will be ensuring continuity and reliability of supply – which may suggest entering into longer-term contractual relationships with suppliers

- For **leverage items** (such as local produce bought by a major supermarket) the buyer's priority will be to secure best prices and terms, and this might suit a transactional or even adversarial (hard bargaining) approach

- For **strategic items** (such as key sub-assemblies for a car maker, or an advertising agency for an organisation) there is mutual dependency and investment – and therefore a need to develop long-term, mutually satisfying partnership relationships.

4.4 Approaches to supplier marketing

At a tactical level, relationship marketing to suppliers may involve activities such as:

- **Reverse marketing**: instead of suppliers marketing to buying organisations, the buying organisation takes the initiative in seeking out quality suppliers and persuading them to meet its supply requirements

- **Supplier relationship management (SRM)**: the equivalent to CRM. The focus is on segmenting suppliers for importance and appropriate relationship, selecting the right vendors and integrating communications (and, where possible, systems)

The Chartered
Institute of Marketing

- **Internal co-ordination**: establishing clear procedures and contact points for the buyer-supplier interface and ensuring that supplier inputs (deliveries, information) flow efficiently to the right people in the internal supply chain

- **Supplier communication**: ensuring that suppliers have all the information they need (clear specifications, orders, schedules, quality standards and so on) to tender for contracts and, once contracts have been won, to meet the organisation's needs. In partnership relations, information systems may be linked, or suppliers may have access to a corporate extranet, for real-time information sharing

- **Supplier involvement**: consulting suppliers on areas in which they may add value (eg new product development) and other plans in which they are stakeholders (eg cutting down the supply base, changing transport providers or computerising the purchasing system)

- **Supplier performance management**: agreeing performance targets and incentives; monitoring supplier performance; providing feedback for learning and improvement; and rewarding excellence (eg with supplier awards or 'approved supplier' status)

- **Supplier development**: supporting or assisting suppliers to be able to meet the buyer's requirements better (eg by training, investment in equipment or systems integration, information exchange and so on).

THE REAL WORLD

Tesco develops supplier relationships

Supermarket giant Tesco launched an 'academy for suppliers' in Poland during 2011 to improve supplier relationships in the country.

The academy builds on the seven regional meetings for current and future local suppliers that have already been held in the country. The company offers its suppliers advice on working with the company by sharing knowledge on customer trends, and providing training on product safety and quality and reducing carbon emissions. Last year almost 300 suppliers took part in these workshops.

Tesco takes its supplier relationships seriously and regularly surveys its suppliers. In March 2010, the company surveyed 3,887 suppliers – 54% of its international supply base – seeking their views on the relationship. The results are published on the company's website which shows that in 2010, 83% of its UK suppliers responded positively to the statement 'I am treated with respect'.

(Tesco, 2011)

4.5 Stages of relationship development in industrial markets

It is worth being aware that a slightly different relationship life cycle model may be used to analyse the stages of relationship development between industrial suppliers and buyers (Ford, 1980, cited in Jobber, 2007 p 173).

Table 5.3   Supplier relationship life cycle

Pre-relationship stage	Evaluation of a potential supplier: risks of change and 'distance' (unfamiliarity, incompatibility etc).
Early stage	Contact and negotiation of trial deliveries (or development of a specification for a capital purchase): testing each other out.
Development stage	Purchases built up (or contract for capital purchase signed): increasing familiarity, trust, info sharing, problem solving.
Long-term stage	Several major contracts have been performed: high trust and proven commitment lead to mutual dependence. Investment in adaptation, integration and greater partnership.
Final stage	Established patterns of trading (in stable markets over long time periods).

5 Intermediary relationships

5.1 Intermediaries

Firms may distribute products or services direct to consumers, or they may choose from a wide range of intermediaries: wholesalers, dealers, agents, franchisees, retailers or multiple stores. Some of the options, and the distribution channels they create, are illustrated in Figure 5.3.

Figure 5.3   Channel intermediaries

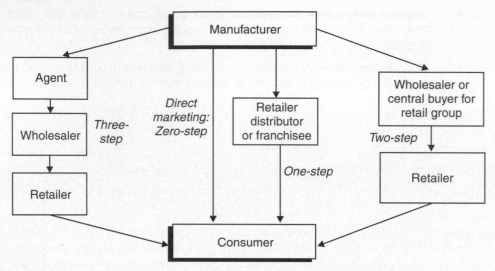

- **Wholesalers** stock a range of products from (potentially competing) manufacturers, to sell on to other organisations such as retailers. They command discounts for buying in bulk, then break bulk (enabling retailers to buy smaller quantities) at a marked-up price, to make a profit.

- **Distributors and dealers** contract to buy a manufacturer's goods and sell them to customers. Their function is similar to that of wholesalers, but they usually offer a narrower product range, sometimes (as in the case of most car dealerships) the products of a single manufacturer. In addition to selling, distributors may also promote the products and add value by providing after-sales service.

- **Agents** differ from distributors, in that they do not purchase and resell the goods at a profit, but sell goods on behalf of the manufacturer and earn a commission on the sale (eg insurance brokers).

- **Franchisees** are independent small businesses which, in exchange for an initial fee and (usually) a share of sales revenue, are allowed to trade under the name of a parent organisation. Examples include Kodak Express photo labs and Kall Kwik print shops.

- **Retailers** are outlets which stock a range of products and sell on to consumers, marking up prices to earn a profit.

5.2 Relationships with channel intermediaries

The six markets model (Peck *et al*, 2004) explained in section 3.1 of Chapter 3 includes intermediaries as a sub-set of customers, since the marketing organisation is selling goods/services to them. All the principles of relationship marketing discussed in Chapter 4 therefore apply as much to channel customers as to consumers.

However, channel intermediaries are *businesses*, and this highlights some particular issues.

- **Value exchange is likely to be more explicit,** because the intermediary has its own commercial objectives for doing business with the supplier. Intermediaries do not stock products or run promotions as a 'favour' to the supplier!

    - The **terms** of the relationship will need to be negotiated and contracted.

- Intermediaries will need to be **selected, prioritised and managed** for long-term profitability; added value (eg provision of sales and customer information from electronic point of sale or EPOS systems); contribution to customer value (eg convenient access to the product, customer service); and compatibility with marketing strategy (eg matching the brand's positioning, targeting the right customer segments).

- The **benefits** of the product or collaboration will have to be promoted to the distributor, through trade advertising, promotion and personal selling.

ACTIVITY 5.8

What benefits might a manufacturer offer a retailer, dealer or franchisee in order to persuade them to stock the product or brand? (Think beyond obvious financial incentives such as discounted prices.)

- Intermediaries may have equally committed relationships with the firm's direct **competitors** (eg a supermarket promoting both Pepsi and Coke). Marketers will need to differentiate their products and promotions, be discreet in sharing confidential information – and be aware of opportunities to gain useful competitor intelligence (eg a new product or promotion plans).

- Intermediaries are in the **front line of contact with consumers**. Marketers need to gather information from them as to consumer buying patterns and preferences, and respect their advice as to what products/promotions will work (or not).

- **Major retailers** (eg supermarkets) have considerable buying power in their markets, and good working relationships must be preserved with them. This may come at the expense of profit (eg giving large supplier discounts or paying for point-of-sale display and promotions). It may also involve some loss of control over promotion (eg in-store display, price promotions) or distribution (eg granting a major distributor exclusive rights to sell the product).

- There may be significant mutual benefits from **promotional collaboration**. If the supplier promotes the product to consumers through PR, advertising and consumer incentives, the intermediary will benefit. If the intermediary promotes the product to consumers – eg through in-store display and promotions – the supplier will benefit.

6 External collaborations

Relationships with suppliers, intermediaries and customers are often referred to as **vertical relationships** (or 'partnerships'), because they involve parties at different levels in the hierarchy of supply. **Horizontal relationships** involve collaboration between organisations at the same position on the supply chain: direct competitors and other organisations serving the same markets or addressing the same target audiences. This can be shown as follows.

Figure 5.4   Vertical partnerships and horizontal collaborations

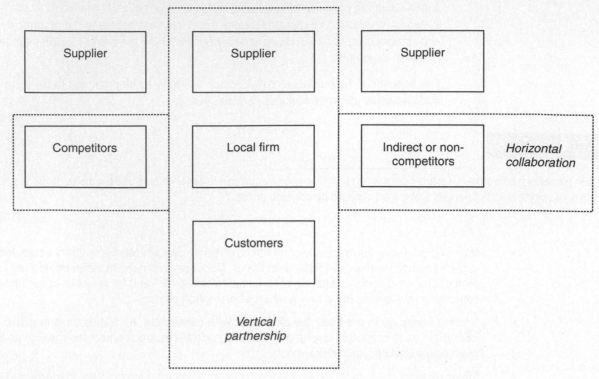

(Adapted from Egan, *op cit*, p173)

Although **networks between consumers** are a growing trend (eg through consumer networking websites, support groups and self-help sites, auction websites like eBay and content-sharing sites like YouTube, Flickr and SlideShare), collaborative networks are mainly in the **business-to-business (B2B)** sector.

6.1 Different types of collaboration

Industry collaboration involves alliances with competitors in the same market sector. It may be used to:

- **Develop infrastructure** (eg distribution channels, servicing or support facilities, employee skills)

- **Share and promote best practice** (eg through industry benchmarking, cross-organisational visits and training, or joint codes of practice)

- **Stimulate industry growth**. This potentially creates value gains for all parties – although they will still compete over who gets the biggest share of those gains! Examples include the Star Alliance network within the airline industry.

Star Alliance is the most-used example of network collaboration. It is a network of airlines, allowing customers to conduct flight searches, bookings and ticketing across the full range of participating airlines: one-stop shopping for flights. Customers can purchase regional 'air passes', valid for all participating airlines.

Participating airlines also share:

- Loyalty programmes (frequent flyer programmes, status-level rewards)

- Airport lounge facilities

- Connection centres at key airport hubs: monitoring in-bound and out-bound flights and arranging with airport staff to minimise any connection problems (eg by arranging direct bus transfers between terminals)

- Terminal locations ('Move under one roof') to minimise transfer times

- A website with tools for flight search, fare calculators, visa and health requirements search, baggage track-and-trace and currency conversion.

The benefits of the network to customers are so great (in terms of convenience and lower airfares) that it has been granted specific immunity from anti-trust (anti-competition) regimes. Meanwhile, at a time when the market for global travel is reportedly declining, the airlines gain access to a wider customer pool and share administration costs – while avoiding legal restrictions on mergers and acquisitions.

For more details, see: http://www.staralliance.com. Star Alliance is also used as a case study in Egan (2004, p201).

External collaboration involves organisations from different industries or market sectors contributing different competencies and resources to the relationship. The purpose may be:

- To **improve the total package offering** to consumers (eg the collaboration between an airline, car rental company and hotel/travel group)

- To **create competitive advantage** through sharing brand strengths and affiliations (eg co-branding, co-promotions and sponsorships)

- To **gain access to distinctive, competitive or value-adding expertise**, technology, resources, distribution channels or markets

- To **share resources and competences** to develop new markets (eg retailers collaborating with website, credit card and logistics providers to develop online shopping and delivery services)

- To **outsource activities** that are not 'core' to the business, and that could be carried out more competitively and cost-effectively by another organisation (with resulting savings for the outsourcer, in terms of staff downsizing, sale of assets, greater managerial focus and so on).

'Increasingly, the value-creating process is no longer confined to a single firm but instead is rooted in a confederation of firms each of which contributes specialist skills and capabilities. The value chain, in effect, now spans several organisations that work as partners in creating and bringing products to market.' (Peck *et al*, 2004, p174).

6.2 Requirements for successful alliances

Quinn (1992) argues that successful alliances are built on a number of foundations.

- **Openly stated, jointly developed goals and plans**: making expectations and desired outcomes clear, and avoiding subsequent disappointment and conflict.

- **Avoiding territorial conflict**: agreeing (for the period of the alliance) not to compete directly with the ally in niche areas which are strategically important to it.

- **Setting up specialist teams** to project manage shared processes. These teams must be championed by senior management and empowered to take decisions.

- **Clear communication links**, with defined contact points at top management, project management and operational levels.

- **Analysis and management of cultural issues**. Cultural conflicts may occur between allies from different national cultures (eg due to differences in language and norms of business behaviour) or from different industry or leadership cultures (eg entrepreneurial or creative companies frustrated by the rigidity and slowness of bureaucratic, safety-seeking allies).

- **Deliberate learning processes**: transferring knowledge and expertise from one party to those in the other party who can best use and apply them. This may also involve project teams getting together periodically to review the relationship and its results, and identify lessons that need to be learned.

THE REAL WORLD

Apple iPod and Nike

Apple have developed a unique partnership with sportswear giant Nike, on the basis that many walkers and runners like to listen to music using their iPods. The partnership includes various aspects including:

- A jointly-engineered and co-branded Nike+iPod Sport Kit. Nike+ shoes have a built-in pocket under the insole for a Nike+iPod sensor, which enables the shoe to 'talk' to an iPod nano, tracking the runner's workout in real time (time, distance, calories) and giving voice feedback (progress reports and congratulations on personal bests).

- Nike Sport Music content, available from Apple's iTunes music store, including playlists put together by top athletes, and special workout mixes (including personal coaching and motivational tips spoken over the music).

- Nike+ clothing designed to hold the iPod Nano during the run.

- The facility to synchronise workout data from the i-Pod to a computer, either via iTunes or nikeplus.com.

Check out the attractive co-branding proposition: http://www.apple.com/ipod/nike or http://nikeplus.nike.com – which also allows users to log their workout data and compete in virtual races against other users worldwide.

At http://www.apple.com/itunes, you might also browse the **Partner with iTunes** menu, which sets out opportunities for:

- Music labels and content providers to promote their music or videos via iTunes

- 'Affiliates' to provide links to iTunes on their websites, for a commission (on revenue resulting from a click-through from the link)

- Sales and marketing organisations to use weblinks to iTunes songs, TV shows or podcasts, to enhance the multi-media content of their promotional messages.

6.3 Potential downsides of alliances

It is worth noting that, like close supplier partnerships, there may be drawbacks to getting 'locked in' to collaborations with culturally or operationally incompatible allies, or being too closely associated with organisations whose ethical, quality or environmental standards may cause reputational damage.

Performance can actually suffer, rather than gain, from the alliance. For example, if one or both parties gets complacent, or if the process requires costly layers of relationship management, or if one party does not pull its weight in the partnership and has to be subsidised by the other.

There is also the risk of losing control over confidential data and intellectual property (eg designs and patents). And in some legal regimes (eg the USA and European Union), close collaboration may be open to interpretation as illegal collusion, if its effect is to fix prices or stifle competition.

What industry or external collaborations is your organisation currently involved in?

What benefits and costs/disadvantages does it experience from its involvement?

If it is *not* currently involved in alliances, brainstorm some ideas about other organisations which share audiences or values with your organisation, and what areas might be explored for collaboration.

'The advice provided by a marriage counsellor is surprisingly well suited for the advice needed for a company entering an alliance: choose your partner carefully, invest in a win-win relationship, stay attractive to your partner, develop a sound economy, and search for a division of labour that works for all parties. Good vibrations are needed, even if it is not passionate love. Still we know that decisions on cohabitation are taken under uncertainty with no guarantee whatsoever of the outcome.' (Gummesson, 2002, p161)

- The nature of value

- Value for the customer

- Value for the organisation: flowing from customers; flowing from other stakeholder relationships

- Service levels

- Barriers to exit

- Loyalty programmes

- Brand engagement

- Shareholder relationships: corporate governance and shareholder communications

- Supplier relationships: adversarial or collaborative; the Kraljic matrix; relationship management

- Intermediary relationships: types of intermediaries; relationship management

- External collaborations: industry and external collaboration; requirements for successful alliance; downsides of alliances.

FURTHER READING

General

Christopher, M. *et al* (2002) *Relationship Marketing: Creating stakeholder value.* Oxford, Elsevier Butterworth-Heinemann
Chapters 1: *Creating value for the customer* and 2: *Creating value for the organisation*.

Reichheld, F. (2001) *The Loyalty Effect.* United States, Harvard Business School Press.
See Chapter 9: *Transforming the Value Proposition* and case studies

Customer relationships

Egan, G. (2004) *Relationship Marketing.* 2nd edition. Harlow, Pearson Education.
Chapter 6: *Customer Partnerships*.

Ford, D. *et al* (2003) *Managing Business Relationships.* 2nd edition. Chichester, John Wiley.
Chapter 4: *Relationship with Customers*.

Peck, H. *et al* (1999) *Relationship Marketing: Strategy & Implementation.* Oxford, Elsevier Butterworth-Heinemann.
Chapter 2: *The Customer Market Domain*

Supplier relationships

Egan, G. (2004) *Relationship Marketing.* 2nd edition. Harlow, Pearson Education
Chapter 8: *Supplier Partnerships*.

Jobber, D. (2007) *Principles & Practice of Marketing.* 5th edition. Maidenhead, McGraw-Hill Education
Chapter 5: *Understanding Organisational Buying Behaviour* (the sections *Developments in Purchasing Practice*, *Relationship Management* and *How to Build Relationships*).

Ford, D. *et al* (2003) *Managing Business Relationships.* 2nd edition. Chichester, John Wiley
Chapter 5: *Relationships with suppliers*.

Peck, H. *et al* (1999) *Relationship Marketing: Strategy & Implementation.* Oxford, Elsevier Butterworth-Heinemann.
Chapter 3: *The supplier and alliance market domain*

Intermediary relationships

Christopher, M. *et al* (2002) *Relationship Marketing: Creating stakeholder value.* Oxford, Elsevier Butterworth-Heinemann
Chapter 4

Ford, D. *et al* (2003) *Managing Business Relationships*. 2nd edition. Chichester, John Wiley
Chapter 6

Peck, H. *et al* (1999) *Relationship Marketing: Strategy & Implementation.* Oxford, Elsevier Butterworth-Heinemann.
Chapter 2

External partnerships

Egan, G. (2004) *Relationship Marketing.* 2nd edition. Harlow, Pearson Education.
Chapter 9

Christopher, M. *et al* (2002) *Relationship Marketing: Creating stakeholder value.* Oxford, Elsevier Butterworth-Heinemann.
Chapter 4

Gummesson, E. (2002) *Total Relationship Marketing.* 2nd edition. Oxford, Elsevier Butterworth-Heinemann.
Chapter 4

REFERENCES

Christopher, M. *et al* (2002) *Relationship Marketing: Creating Stakeholder Value*. Oxford, Elsevier Butterworth-Heinemann.

Egan, J. (2004) *Relationship Marketing: Exploring Relational Strategies in Marketing.* 2nd edition. Harlow, Essex, Pearson Education.

Gummesson, E. (2002) *Total Relationship Marketing* (2002) Oxford, Elsevier Butterworth-Heinemann,.

Jobber, D. (2007) *Principles & Practice of Marketing.* 5th edition. Maidenhead, Berks. McGraw Hill Education.

Kotler, P. and Armstrong, G. (2003) *Principles of Marketing.* 10th edition. New Jersey, Prentice Hall, New Jersey.

Kotler, P. *et al* (1999) *Marketing: An Introduction*. Sydney, Prentice Hall Australia.

Kraljic, P (1983) Purchasing must become supply management, *Harvard Business Review*, Sept edition.

Lele, M. M. and Sheth, J. N. (1991) *The Customer is Key: Gaining an unbeatable advantage through customer satisfaction* New York, John Wiley.

Peck, H. L. *et al* (2004) *Relationship Marketing: Strategy and Implementation*. Oxford, Elsevier Butterworth-Heinemann.

Porter, M. E. (1980) *Competitive Strategy.* New York, Free Press.

Profex Publishing (2007) *Strategic Supply Chain Management.* 2nd edition. Maidenhead, Berks, Profex.

Quinn, J. B. (1992) *Intelligent Enterprise,* New York, Free Press.

Tesco (2011) Tesco plc interim results 2010/11.
http://www.tescoplc.com/files/pdf/results/2010/interim/interims_2010-11.pdf [Accessed on 18 June 2012]

The Emirates Group (2011) Skywards continues its winning streak – eight awards and counting. [Accessed 10 June 2012]

Varey, R. J. (2002) *Marketing Communications: Principles & Practice*. Abingdon, Oxon, Routledge.

QUICK QUIZ

1   What is 'added value'?

2   What does ACURA stand for?

3   List five dimensions of service delivery.

4   Identify eight sources of switching costs.

5   What are the aims of a loyalty programme from the point of view of the organisation?

6   Distinguish between product-based and communication-based co-branding, with an example of each.

7   What is corporate governance?

8   What are the benefits for the buyer of collaborative relationships with suppliers?

9   What value can intermediaries offer the organisation?

10   Distinguish between industry collaboration and external collaboration.

ACTIVITY DEBRIEFS

Activity 5.1

Perceived benefits: taste of the food, known/consistent product (low risk purchase), speed of service, cleanliness of the outlet, low price, sociable setting, good facilities (eg parking, toilets), drive-through, family friendly.

Perceived sacrifice: distance to the outlet, negative image of fast food, price/cost, pressure from children to eat there, negative publicity re packaging waste, down-market image

Note that the outlets will do what they can to promote the benefits and reduce the sacrifices (eg by offering healthy food options, reducing packaging, offering meal deals and so on).

Activity 5.2

Your own research.

Activity 5.3

You want to present the benefits of customer care: their statistical prevalence is really secondary. The directors do not need excessively detailed information in a visual presentation. We suggest the following (a simple horizontal bar chart).

The Chartered
Institute of Marketing

Figure 5.5   A simple bar chart

BENEFITS OF CUSTOMER CARE	% of managers who have experienced the benefit
Improved customer retention	67
Enhanced organisation reputation	59
Competitive advantage in the marketplace	52
Attraction of new customers	42
Increased profitability	27
Improved staff morale and loyalty	26
Cost efficiency	10

Activity 5.4

It is worth noting that commentators see many loyalty programmes as:

- More or less heavily disguised sales promotions: creating short-term customer retention (repeat transactions) – but not loyalty (emotional commitment to the organisation or brand)

- Merely tactical moves designed to defend a brand's market position in the face of competitors' offers or loyalty schemes: creating short-term disincentives to switch

- Mere reinforcing mechanisms – since they often reward customers who are already loyal, rather than creating loyalty.

Activity 5.5

Your own research and evaluation. You might like to consider sharing these.

Activity 5.6

Activities with a group of fellow students, presenting your findings to each other and discussing your evaluations.

Activity 5.7

Your own research. Note that your findings may be useful preparation for an assignment task.

Activity 5.8

Benefits offered may include: potential profits through sales; sales force awards and incentives (eg commissions); promotional support (eg advertised stockist lists, point-of-sale display materials); product-related support (eg sales staff training, warranties, exchange/repair services); trade sales promotions; status through association with the brand; or 'membership' benefits (eg of a dealership network or franchise).

Activity 5.9

Your own research and suggestions. Again, these may be useful for an assignment task, so it would be worth writing your answers down, rather than just running through them in your head!

1   Added value is the extra value given to a product or service as a result of the processes that support it, such as customer service.

2   ACURA stands for relationship marketing strategies: Acquire, Cross-sell, Up-sell, Retain and Advocacy.

3   See section 2.1 for a full list of dimensions.

4   Switching costs include: search costs, learning costs, emotional costs, social costs, financial costs, risk, inertia and legal barriers.

5   The aims of a loyalty programme are: creating brand preference or habit through repeat purchase; reinforcing relationship through belonging; differentiating the brand; adding economic and social benefits to create barriers to switching; gathering customer data; and raising additional revenue.

6   Product-based co-branding links two or more existing brands to form a single offering eg IBM/Intel computers. Communication-based co-branding links two or more brands in promotional campaigns eg Whirlpool endorsing Ariel washing powder.

7   Corporate governance is the system by which organisations are directed and controlled, with particular reference to the relationship between directors and shareholders.

8   See the table in section 4.2.2 for a full list of benefits.

9   Intermediaries can offer profitability, added value (eg information sharing), contribution to customer value (eg providing customer service), co-promotion and compatibility with marketing strategy (eg quality/price positioning or market targeting).

10   Industry collaboration involves alliances with competitors in the same market sector. External collaboration involves organisations from different industries or market sectors contributing different competences used and resources to the relationship.

CHAPTER 6

The stakeholder marketing mix

Introduction

This chapter recaps the concept of the marketing mix, which you should have covered in your studies for Unit 1: *Marketing Essentials.* Rather than focusing on the marketing mix to customers, however, we explore how a co-ordinated marketing mix can be used to meet the needs of an organisation's broader stakeholder audience.

From the indicative content given in the syllabus, it appears that the intended focus is the **wider or secondary stakeholder environment**: building corporate social responsibility elements into the marketing mix. However, the guidance notes state that you also need to differentiate marketing mix requirements for a **range of target audiences**: although it is difficult to think in marketing mix terms for all stakeholders, we suggest how this might be approached.

In section 1, we recap the elements of the marketing mix (the four Ps) and how each can be used to add value for secondary stakeholders. (The 'promotion' element will be picked up again, in more detail, in Chapter 8 on marketing communications.)

In section 2, we focus on the service mix (the three Ps), the role of people, process and physicals in adding value for secondary stakeholders and supporting relationship marketing approaches. (The importance of the 'people' element will be picked up again, in more detail, in Chapter 9 on internal stakeholders.)

In section 3, we briefly note that relationship marketing has added an extra two Ps to the extended mix: political power and public opinion.

In section 4, we emphasise the need to tailor the mix for different stakeholder groups or target audiences, some of which have different or conflicting needs and interests. We also examine how the elements of the mix can be interpreted in relation to non-customer groups, in order to think in terms of a distinct marketing mix for each stakeholder audience.

Finally, in section 5, we highlight the importance of co-ordinating the marketing mix and marketing resources, in order to present a consistent and coherent value proposition.

Topic list

The stakeholder marketing mix (4Ps) (1)

The service mix (3Ps) (2)

The influence mix (the 8th and 9th Ps) (3)

Tailoring the mix to stakeholder needs (4)

Co-ordinating the mix (5)

1.5	Specify the role of marketing in managing these pressure groups effectively:
	■ Planned marketing communications eg, PR and advertising, brochures, encouraging interaction and dialogue
	■ Product messages – design, technical features, production process durability and distribution
	■ Service messages derived from interactions with pressure groups
	■ Proactive management of unplanned messages such as news stories, Blogs – Hainsworth and Meng issue lifecycle model.
3.1	Explain how a coordinated marketing mix can be used to meet the needs of an organisation's broader stakeholder audience:
	■ Product development eg, ethical clothing ranges, smoothies for children
	■ Renewable resources
	■ Price-value versus supply
	■ Place – direct distribution, e-distribution
	■ Promotion – bluetooth, compliance with regulation eg football clubs sponsored by alcohol companies removing sponsorship on children's replica kits, not advertising foods high in fat, sugar and salt (HFSS), products in children's programmes
	■ People – recruitment, working conditions, equal opportunities
	■ Process – recycling, alternative power sources, fair trade
	■ Physical environment (décor, corporate image, livery, etc)
3.3	Explain the dependencies of people, place and process in supporting relationship marketing approaches:
	■ Employee satisfaction versus customer satisfaction
	■ Reichheld Service Profit Cycle
	■ Customer and stakeholder management
	■ Product development
	■ Place

1 The stakeholder marketing mix (4Ps)

1.1 Quick recap: the marketing mix

▶ **Key term**

The **marketing mix** or **Four Ps** is a set of controllable marketing tools or elements which a firm can intentionally manipulate and co-ordinate to produce a desired response from its target market(s). These elements are: product (or service); price; place (provision or distribution); and promotion (or marketing communications).

'The marketing mix consists of everything that the firm can do to influence the demand for its product. An effective marketing program blends all of the marketing mix elements into a **co-ordinated program** designed to achieve the company's **marketing objectives** by delivering **value to consumers**. The marketing mix constitutes the company's operational tool kit, used to establish strong positioning within target markets.'

(Kotler *et al*, 1999, pp36-37)

The marketing mix (four Ps) can be summarised as follows.

Table 6.1   The 4Ps

Element	Explanation	Example tools
Product	The bundle of benefits that makes up the offering to the target market, in the form of goods and/or services	Product range/variety; quality; design; features; brand identity; packaging; services; warranties
Price	The amount of money customers have to pay to obtain the product (eg price, fees, fares, rent, tuition)	List price; discounts; payment periods and credit terms; different pricing for different market segments
Place (provision)	Activities that make the product available to target customers (ie not just *where* they access the product)	Distribution channels (direct or intermediary); coverage (local, national, global); outlet locations; transport and logistics
Promotion (marketing communication)	Activities that communicate the merits of the product and persuade target customers to buy it	Advertising, personal selling, sales promotions, public relations, direct marketing, web marketing

1.2 The marketing mix and the wider stakeholder audience

As we saw in Chapter 2, today's marketing environment increasingly requires organisations to take responsibility for the social and environmental impacts of their actions, and marketing mix decisions are increasingly influenced by:

- The agendas set by government policy, public opinion and pressure groups, and their ability to mobilise consumers for or against an organisation or brand

- Corporate objectives, values and policies to do with business ethics, corporate social responsibility and environmental sustainability

- The need to respond to the potential marketing threats (and opportunities) presented by consumers' awareness of ethical and environmental issues, and their influence on buying decisions

- The desire to be good corporate citizens, minimising negative impacts and pursuing positive impacts of marketing and business activity on society as a whole.

Stakeholder marketing is based on the idea that marketers need to **understand** the needs, concerns and expectations of different stakeholder groups, and **adapt the marketing mix** accordingly – in order both to create and deliver **value** for stakeholders *and*, in return, to build **trust**, **loyalty and commitment** from them.

How can marketers respond to these wider stakeholder drivers through the marketing mix? Let's look at each element in turn.

1.3 Product

Products are bundles or packages of benefits, although we tend to think of them as 'things' with 'features'. The benefits offered by a product may include:

- A **physical aspect**, which relates to the components, materials and specifications (colour, size etc) of the product: for example, a size 12 pullover made of 100% pure wool

- A **functional aspect**, which relates to how a product performs and the purpose for which it is bought: the wool pullover may give warmth and comfort, say

- A **symbolic aspect**, which represents the qualities the product suggests to, or confers upon, the buyer: the '100% pure wool' label may represent quality, status or ecology (as a natural rather than synthetic product), say.

Each of these elements could be reviewed from the point of view of the **needs, concerns and expectations of stakeholders,** and adjusted during new product development and/or product improvement (with the added

marketing benefits of 'refreshing' a product that may have reached the mature or declining stages of its life cycle).

1.3.1 Product decisions for stakeholder marketing

In response to wider stakeholder needs and concerns, the physical components or materials in products (and services) could be made:

- **Safer**

  Examples: Reducing the use of harmful chemicals (such as lead paint), or child choking hazards from small parts; developing child- and tamper-proof packaging for potentially dangerous goods; adding safety warnings and detailed product labelling (eg about food containing nuts which might cause allergic reactions).

- **More environmentally friendly**

  Examples: Recyclable or biodegradable products or packaging; product return and recycling services and instructions (eg for electrical and electronic goods); less packaging and disposable extras (eg plastic bags given by supermarkets as part of their service); products and services that consume less energy, and cause less pollution and carbon emissions (eg hybrid or electric cars).

- **More ethical**

  Examples: Environmentally sustainable materials sourced with fair treatment and payment of suppliers (as in 'ethical clothing' ranges or fair trade coffee brands); produced by workers in safe, hygienic working conditions for fair wages; and addressing – rather than contributing to – social problems (eg healthier food options, reduced alcohol beverages and low-tar cigarettes; sizing clothing products to reflect real body shapes and avoid promoting over-dieting).

- **More socially sustainable**

  Examples: Building a longer useful life into products (rather than built-in obsolescence) for less over-consumption and disposability; using components/materials from local, diverse, small-business suppliers.

- **Compliant** with all relevant safety, quality and environmental standards and codes of practice issued by government, regulatory bodies, industry associations and pressure groups.

ACTIVITY 6.1

How could the functional and symbolic aspects of products likewise be used to respond to wider stakeholder needs and concerns?

Again, the purpose of such benefit-building is both to create and deliver value for stakeholders – and, in return, to elicit trust, loyalty and commitment from them.

1.3.2 Product development

A marketing organisation will constantly seek to **update its products/services** (eg by new features or packaging), so that products that have failed, or have reached the maturity or decline stages of the **product life cycle** can be 'refreshed' and re-launched as 'new and improved'. It will also seek to **develop new product ideas**, so that it constantly has new products with growth/profit potential 'coming up' within its product portfolio, as other products become obsolete, or saturate their markets, and cease to generate profits.

The **new product development process** is typically represented by a seven-stage process:

1 Idea generation
2 Idea screening
3 Concept testing
4 Business analysis
5 Product development
6 Test marketing
7 Commercialisation.

ACTIVITY 6.2

You will have studied the stages of new product development process more fully in your *Marketing Essentials* studies. In the context of stakeholder marketing, what role could the following stakeholders play in the various stages of the process?

- Customers
- Suppliers
- Employees
- Distributors

In addition, however, product development and updating may be seen as an opportunity to:

- Meet new, or newly recognised, customer and **stakeholder needs**: eg increasing consumer demand for dietary food products, healthy snacks and educational toys for children, 'green' products such as recycled paper, and ethically-produced clothing.

- Respond **to pressure group concerns** and address problems with existing products, which might impact on stakeholders: eg replacing hazardous materials, or developing low-emission and low-fuel-consumption car engines.

- Develop commercial **solutions to social or environmental problems**: eg developing alternative energy products such as bio-fuels or electric/hybrid cars.

- **Consult or collaborate with external stakeholders** on new products, product improvement and/or branding, in such a way as to build mutually beneficial relationships – and perhaps gather stakeholder endorsements: eg sunglasses and sun-protection products developed in consultation with the Cancer Council and endorsed or co-branded by them.

THE REAL WORLD

'Innovation' features highly in the marketing press, and in companies' self-image, in regard to new product development.

Engineering company **Dyson UK** (innovators in vacuum cleaners and washing machines) pride themselves on innovation, R & D and quality. Their website (http://www.dyson.co.uk) features advice for inventors, information on the product testing/development process and so on.

Consider how each of these examples seeks to deliver value to wider stakeholders – and how they might establish beneficial stakeholder relationships.

1.3.3 Corporate responsibility issues concerning products

Jobber (2007, p367ff) highlights three major ethical issues in regard to product.

- **Product safety**. New risks are emerging all the time as new technologies are applied to products in an attempt to win competitive advantage. One example is the genetic modification of food products – without, as pressure groups have argued, detailed study of its long-term effects. (This is an area in which pressure group concerns and resulting public outcry have changed corporate policy: Monsanto halting further development, for example, and supermarket chains removing GM foods from their shelves.) Safety and health-promoting features are likely to be a major product element in the marketing mix – from passenger-side air bags in cars, to sharp-edge-folding tin openers, to low-tar cigarettes and low-sugar cereals.

- **Deceptive packaging**. Packaging may mislead consumers if:

  - It gives the impression that the contents are larger or more generously packed than is actually the case (eg large, partially filled cans or boxes)

  - Labels are misleading: omitting country of origin; using the term 'Lite' which implies low-calorie but may only mean 'lightly flavoured'; implying that flavourings are natural when they may be synthetic; and so on. Loose language and meaningless terms should be avoided, so as not to create false expectations and impressions.

- **Branding and its effect on developing economies**. Some advocates argue that branding concentrates power and wealth in the hands of a few corporations, weakening the ability of equivalent products to compete, and forcing them to compete on price. This has a negative impact on small local producers and especially on developing countries, where low wages are exploited by brand manufacturers. As we have seen, large brands such as Nestlé, Nike and Gap are now being held accountable by consumer groups for more ethical and sustainable sourcing policies.

In addition, there may be stakeholder responsibility issues in the management of the **product portfolio**. For example:

- There may be an impact on stakeholders if a company decides to **discontinue** a product or service on which a group has come to rely, or to which it has become accustomed. Think of the difficulties faced by older people as over-the-counter banking services are phased out in favour of ATMs and Internet banking, say. There may be a trade-off between profitability (in the interests of shareholders) and responsibility (subsidising an unprofitable product in the interests of wider stakeholders).

- It may be considered unethical if consumers who choose one product are effectively **'forced' to buy others in the product line**, because they are compatible with it and competitor offerings are not. One high-profile example concerns computer software, such as Microsoft Windows, and its compulsory bundling with Microsoft application software. As a result of EU pressure, Microsoft launched their Browser Choice update to allow all users of Microsoft Windows the option of choosing which internet browser they use rather than forcing them to use Internet Explorer which was previously built-in to the Windows operating system.

1.4 Price

> **Key term**
>
> **Price** can be defined as a measure of the value exchanged by the buyer for the value offered by the seller.

The ultimate objective of pricing is to produce the level of sales required to fulfil the organisation's **marketing and financial objectives**, on behalf of its shareholders, by: covering costs and maximising profits; maintaining or increasing market share (through price competition); getting a new product adopted and accepted quickly (through low introductory or 'market penetration' pricing); or increasing short-term sales volume (eg through discounted pricing).

However, there may be a trade-off between the interests of the shareholders and directors of the company (essentially, pricing for profitability), and the **interests of wider stakeholders**, including:

- **Customers and consumers**, who would (all other things being equal) prefer to keep prices low, or at least within a range that represents good value for the quality and benefits received.

- **Suppliers** (whose own prices and profits may be 'squeezed' to allow the organisation to set competitive prices and still make a profit) and intermediaries (whose profit margins and cash flow may be affected by high manufacturer pricing).

The Chartered Institute of Marketing

- **Wider stakeholder groups**.

  - High prices may put desirable (or even essential) products or services out of reach of ordinary consumers.

  - Very low prices or price wars may cause a lowering of product/service quality. They may also stimulate over-consumption, resulting credit card debt and environmental damage from subsequent disposal of waste goods.

  - The squeezing of supplier and intermediary profit margins, or the raising of prices to business customers, may put enterprises out of business, creating negative economic and social effects such as unemployment.

  - Government and regulatory bodies protect consumer interests in regard to price: the pricing of essential goods and services may be regulated (as in the case of gas and electricity) or subsidised (as in the case of certain medicines). Meanwhile, anti-competition law outlaws collusion on pricing between competitors, or 'price-fixing', as this prevents consumers benefiting from price competition.

  - Pressure groups (consumer groups, trade unions, fair trade organisations) are often sensitive to the fairness and impact of pricing: eg if high prices are not reflected in prices paid to suppliers or employees; or if prices do not represent value for money.

Another corporate responsibility issue in pricing may be the way pricing decisions are **communicated** to stakeholders. Prices must be easy to understand and calculate, and without hidden costs 'in the small print'. Changes to prices which may have a significant impact on stakeholders should, where possible, be notified in advance and carefully explained.

Price can also be used in the development of **sustainable stakeholder relationships**, through: incentive pricing for repeat purchases; price-based rewards for loyal customers; the donation of a price percentage to a charity, cause or research valued by stakeholders; or generous price negotiation to support a supplier or intermediary (enhancing sustainability and loyalty).

ACTIVITY 6.3

The following is a **brand positioning map** plotting consumer respondents' views on different family cars, asked whether they perceived them to be value-for-money or premium, environmentally friendly ('green') or not environmentally friendly.

Figure 6.1   Brand positioning map for family car brand

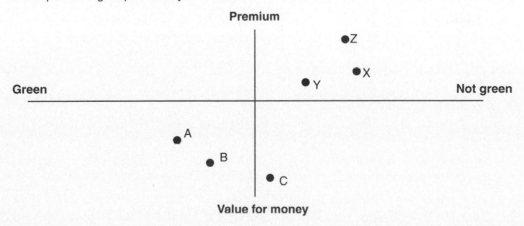

How would you report on the performance of Car X in this brand positioning exercise, if you were its marketing co-ordinator?

1.4.1 Approaches to pricing

Pricing decisions are affected by a range of factors, both internal and external to the organisation, in the competitive environment. These factors can be briefly summarised as follows.

Table 6.2   Factors affecting pricing

Internal factors	External factors
■ **Marketing objectives**: profit maximisation; market share leadership; brand targeting and positioning.	■ **Competition**: the extent of competition in the market; whether there is price or non-price competition; competitor pricing and promotions; likely response to price changes.
■ **Marketing mix strategy**: factoring in the cost/price implications of quality, distribution, brand differentiation.	■ **Demand**: the sensitivity of customer demand to changes in price (do they buy measurably more if prices go down, or less if they go up?)
■ **Costs**: at least setting the lowest viable price at which the company can afford to make and sell the product	■ **Customer perceptions** of price and what it means for quality and value.
■ **Price-setting methods**: negotiated by sales reps, set by management, arrived at by customer auction (eg on eBay).	■ **Suppliers and intermediaries**: impacting on costs; reacting to price decisions to protect their own margins.
■ **Product portfolio strategies**: launch/new-product incentive pricing; 'loss leaders' (low-priced products which draw customers in to the brand); high-profit products which subsidise less profitable ones; or other variations.	■ **Environmental factors**: economic factors influencing affordability; government price watchdogs; social responsibility dictating affordability; changing social perceptions of 'value'; technology lowering production costs.

You should be familiar with basic price-setting strategies from your studies in *Marketing Essentials.* You might like to remember the key factors in pricing strategy as the four Cs: **C**osts (ie pricing to cover costs), **C**ustomer (ie pricing to stimulate demand), **C**ompetition (ie pricing to gain or maintain competitive advantage) and **C**ompany (ie pricing to achieve corporate objectives and policies).

The Chartered Institute of Marketing

The UK supermarket chain Iceland has had to work hard to broaden its marketing away from purely price-led promotions to emphasise its product range and service levels.

As its website states: "Iceland is one of Britain's fastest-growing and most innovative retailers, recognised as one of the best companies to work for in the UK.

Read about our amazing history of success (with one dark patch), what makes us such a great place to work, the man who started it all in 1970 and the good causes we support."

An excerpt:

'In 2005, sales were running at minus 10% on the previous year, having declined every year since 2001. Over the same four years overheads had escalated on a massive scale, with head office employee numbers growing from 800 to 1,400 and a further £16 million being spent on the services of external consultants. The product range had expanded chaotically and prices were well out of line with the market. Morale was at an all-time low and the company was in such a precarious financial state that suppliers could not even obtain credit insurance.

A new management team, installed in 2005, worked hard to turn the company around.

2009 began with the announcement that Iceland had agreed to buy 51 stores from the receivers of Woolworths, massively accelerating the current year's planned store opening programme. Iceland planned to open 70 new stores in 2009 throughout the UK, from Fraserburgh in the north of Scotland to Exmouth in Devon, creating some 3,500 new jobs. The company also planned to open a further 20-30 new stores in 2010. This is Iceland's fastest rate of expansion since it bought Bejam 20 years ago.

In March 2009 Iceland was recognised in the annual Sunday Times '100 Best Companies to Work For' survey as one of the 20 best big companies to work for in the UK.

In a statement released to coincide with the company's 2010-11 results, Iceland Chief Executive Malcolm Walker said, "We continue to thrive in a highly competitive market place by offering customers the best everyday value in frozen foods and for their daily purchases of grocery and chilled foods, underlined by our round-sum pricing policy. Iceland is the main driver of innovation in the UK frozen food market, launching more than 200 new products during the last 12 months.'

(Iceland, 2012)

This case illustrates the fact that a low-price policy does not have to preclude product innovation.

1.4.2 Stakeholder issues in pricing

Jobber (*op cit*, p485) identifies a number of ethical issues in pricing, some of which have been mentioned in our summary earlier.

- **Price fixing**: agreement between producers *not* to compete on price. This restricts or distorts competition – which in turn robs consumers of the benefits of competition (choice, lower prices, better quality). Such collusion is banned in many legislative regimes, including the EU, under competition law.

- **Predatory pricing**: price cuts designed to force competitors out of the market. The short-term loss of profit is balanced by the prospect of higher profits later.

- **Deceptive pricing**: misleading price comparisons or incentives. Examples include retail stores setting artificially high prices shortly before sales, so that the sale price looks like more of a bargain. (This practice is restricted by UK law, which sets a minimum period over which the 'regular' price must be charged, before it can be used as a comparison or reference price in a sale.)

- **Penetration pricing**: charging low prices to gain more customers. This is a legitimate marketing practice, but is ethically questionable where the product is arguably against the best interest of consumers (eg low prices charged for fast food, making it attractive to young people, to the potential detriment of their health).

- **Price discrimination**: offering different prices for the same product to different groups of buyers. This is again a legitimate marketing practice, used to smooth fluctuations in demand (eg 'off-peak' low fares on public transport) and potentially beneficial for some stakeholders (eg 'concession' fares for pensioners, children and students). However, it may be used to exploit some markets or create unfair competitive advantage.

- **Discounting and dumping**: exporting obsolete, excess or poor quality products, which cannot be sold in the domestic market, to overseas countries at very low prices. This may even apply to products ruled unsafe by the regulatory regime in the domestic country, but tolerated by less stringent regimes overseas.

- **Profit taking**: buying materials from developing or rural economies at very low prices, which barely give suppliers a livelihood, and selling in western markets at high prices. Profitability is a legitimate responsibility of marketing firms, but fair trade organisations, as we have seen, argue that gains should be equitably shared with poor producers in the interests of sustainability.

1.5 Place

> ▶ **Key term**
>
> **Place** is concerned with the selection of distribution channels to deliver goods to target customers, and with the storage and physical distribution of goods (logistics).

Place decisions are mainly focused on the interests of:

- **Target customer groups**: where and how they can best access the product or service.

- **The marketing organisation and its shareholders**: how the product/service can be delivered to customers most effectively, efficiently, competitively and cost-effectively; how information on consumer behaviour can flow back to the organisation to improve planning.

- **Channel intermediaries and service providers**: how their resources and expertise can best be secured, utilised, supported and rewarded.

However, place decisions may also be targeted to the needs and concerns of wider stakeholder groups in various ways.

ACTIVITY 6.4

Before you read on, see if you can think of some of the ways in which place or distribution decisions may be adapted for greater corporate social responsibility, or the interests of wider stakeholder groups.

- Reducing the environmental and social impacts of **transport and logistics**: eg efficient route planning to avoid unnecessary fuel use and pollution; transport planning to minimise traffic congestion at pick-up/delivery hubs; training and incentives for drivers to drive safely.

- Ensuring **compliance** with legislation and regulation in areas such as the transport, storage and handling of hazardous goods; the health and safety of warehouse workers; the monitoring of drivers' working hours.

- Distributing through **small local retail outlets**, which maintain the ambience and prosperity of local communities – rather than out-of-town mega-malls and retail chains.

- Ensuring that **franchisees** are adequately supported, to reduce the rate of small business failure and its local socio-economic impacts.

- Ensuring, as far as possible, that intermediaries **offer reliable supply and good levels of service** to consumers: offering sales and inventory management support, or staff training in demonstration or servicing of the product, if necessary. This will impact on the supplier's relationships not just with the intermediary, but also with customers, since point-of-sale, delivery and after-sales service are part of the total offering of value to the customer. Responsibility for such matters should be clearly apportioned by negotiation between suppliers and intermediaries, and performance monitored.

The Chartered Institute of Marketing

- Supporting **'reverse logistics'**: that is, the return of products from the consumer back to the manufacturer, for replacement or refund (eg in the case of a product recall due to safety concerns), repair or maintenance, or, at the end of the product's useful life, safe disposal or recycling. This requires relationship management with intermediaries who may have to mediate returns, exchanges or refunds. However, it is primarily seen as a benefit to consumers and to wider society, mainly in terms of environmental responsibility (encouraging recycling and safe waste disposal).

- Allowing wider – and perhaps more equitable – **access to products and services**, through extending the distribution network to cover more areas or centres. This may further social policies of supporting remote communities and less-developed regions, and perhaps also enhance the national interest by establishing cultural and trading links with other nations (through international distribution).

- Giving wider access to products through **direct distribution** (supplying direct to customers, without intermediaries) and/or **e-distribution** (supplying products and services over the internet: for example, downloadable books or music, or banking and e-learning services). This enables remote or un-serviced communities to access goods and services without having to find a retail outlet, and is of particular social benefit for some important services (eg banking, education, legal/medical advice). It may also support less mobile segments of the community, such as the elderly and disabled, in accessing goods and services through home or online delivery.

1.5.1 Stakeholder issues in direct and e-distribution

Direct distribution and e-distribution are growing trends, and represent significant cost savings for the organisation. They may be used as part of a relationship marketing strategy, as a way of establishing **direct contact with consumers** which can be developed into a relationship over time. Customers may, for example, have to register on a website in order to make a purchase, and may thereby be exposed to a range of membership benefits (as in the example of Amazon.com, say). Direct and e-distribution strategies may form key parts of brand identity, as with iTunes (digital entertainment downloads) or First Direct (HSBC's telephone banking subsidiary).

It is worth noting, however, that direct and e-distribution strategies may create issues in relationships with other stakeholders, for which **trade-offs** may have to be made. For example, they put the marketing organisation in the position of competing against its channel intermediaries for sales. This may damage relationships unless it can be carefully justified and mutual benefits negotiated (eg by including stockist lists on the website). Such strategies may also damage communities eg in the case of local bank branch closures (in favour of internet banking), or impact on businesses (eg CD and video stores going out of business due to competition from downloadable formats).

It is worth noting, too, that while many products can be ordered on the internet, they cannot all be *delivered* electronically. **Fulfilment or physical distribution** of high-volume, global orders may cause problems for customer relationships. A US survey by the Boston Consulting Group found a variety of problems, which internet marketers will need to overcome.

	% respondents citing the problem
- Hard to contact customer service	20%
- Product took much longer than expected to arrive	15%
- Returned the product	10%
- Tried to contact customer service and failed	8%
- Ordered product that never arrived	4%
- Wrong product arrived and couldn't return it	3%

So much for sustained, value-adding, relationship-building service encounters!

1.5.2 Channel decisions

A number of considerations will determine the choice of distribution strategy.

- The **number of intermediate stages** to be used. As we saw in Chapter 5, there could be zero (direct distribution), one, two or three levels of intermediaries.

- The level of **support given to intermediaries**. It may be necessary to provide after-sales and repair services, or to agree to immediate exchange of faulty products returned by a retailer's customers, or to make weekly or monthly stock-checking and replenishment visits to intermediaries. The manufacturer may also need to consider offering advertising and sales promotion support, to encourage consumers to buy from retailers.

- The extent to which the manufacturer wishes to **control and integrate marketing activity** up to the point of sale to the consumer. Layers of intermediaries may distance the manufacturer from the consumer, in terms of controlling how products are handled, displayed, explained, promoted and serviced.

- **Customer preferences** in regard to where and how they buy, and the kind of shopping experience they want.

- **Product characteristics**. Speed of delivery is a key factor in place decisions. For example, perishable goods such as fresh fruit or newspapers must be distributed very quickly or they become worthless. Complex or technical goods need to be accompanied by expert sales and after-sales service, and the manufacturer may need to ensure this by for example training intermediaries, or using a franchise model to give greater control.

- **Distributor characteristics**: the location, customer base, performance, promotion and pricing policies of different types of distributor and specific distribution outlets.

1.6 Promotion (marketing communications)

Although the word 'promotion' is widely used, it implies that the seller is doing all the talking – as we have seen, this is an old-fashioned, transactional view of marketing. For a marketing-oriented business, there needs to be a two-way dialogue, where the buyer's input and responses are as important as the seller's awareness- and preference-creating messages. Hence the growth of the term 'marketing communications' – except that it doesn't start with a P!

It could be argued that all the other Ps are also elements of the marketing communications mix: product and packaging have quality, design and brand values that 'communicate' a great deal to the customer; price communicates the implied quality and desirability of the product and the choice of distribution outlet likewise reflects brand values and the extent of the organisation's customer focus.

We will look at the elements of the promotional (or marketing communications) mix in detail in Chapter 8. Here, we will simply explore some of the ways in which the mix as a whole can be used to meet the needs of the broader stakeholder audience. First, however, it may be worth recapping just how extensive a 'mix' of available tools we're talking about: Figure 6.2.

Figure 6.2 The marketing communications mix

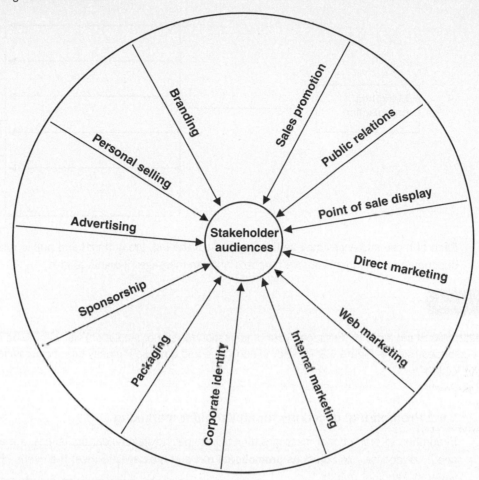

1.6.1 Stakeholders as target audiences

All stakeholder groups are potentially target audiences for the organisation's marketing messages (and sources of relevant information in return). The ability to identify and analyse stakeholder groups (as discussed in Chapter 1) should allow the marketer to determine:

- Appropriate **channels of** communication to target relevant groups, to gain efficient access for the message. (Who are the contact points, information gatherers, advisers and influencers who could be 'gone through' to get to the target group?)

- Appropriate **media of communication** to suit their needs and characteristics, to attract them to the message. (Do they read newspapers or magazines, and if so which ones? Do they watch television, and if so, what and when? Might they be amenable to – and worth investment in – personal selling or discussion?)

- Appropriate **modes of communication** to express the message in a way that reflects their interests, motives and objectives, adds value and establishes and maintains constructive, on-going relationships. (What offers will be made? What impressions will be made? What influence will be used: negotiation or bargaining, persuasion, an appeal to fear/concern, an appeal to self-interest?)

Kotler (1992, cited in Egan, 2004) suggests that, in addition to suppliers, intermediaries, employees and consumers, there are six major audiences in the wider environment: Figure 6.3.

Figure 6.3   Target audiences in the wider stakeholder environment.

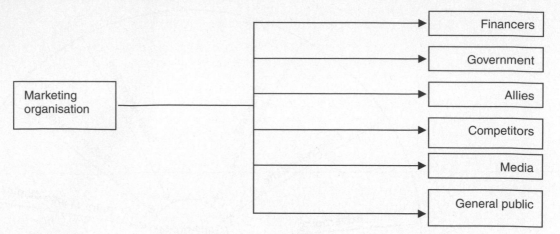

Each of these audiences may be the target of advertising, promotional and public relations campaigns, depending on the organisation's purposes and the messages it wants to give.

ACTIVITY 6.5

Give some examples of the kinds of messages your organisation (or any organisation) will want to be sending to each of the stakeholder audiences listed in Figure 6.3, in order to add value and develop mutually beneficial relationships with them.

1.6.2 Promotional decisions for stakeholder marketing

In addition to promotional messages directed at specific stakeholder audiences, a marketing organisation may need – or choose – to **adjust its promotional mix** and messages to meet the needs of, or add value for, the wider stakeholder market.

One important aspect of this is **compliance** with legal and/or voluntary industry regulations in regard to advertising and promotion.

- There are **restrictions on the advertising of harmful products** (such as tobacco and alcohol), particularly in contexts where children may be the prime audience. So, for example, football clubs sponsored by alcohol companies are removing branding from children's replica kits and cigarette manufacturers have to add severe health warnings to all packaging and advertisements.

- **Standards of truth and ethics in advertising** are monitored by the Advertising Standards Authority, Independent Television Authority and similar bodies. All claims must be fair and accurate, or not misleading, and messages must not be discriminatory or offensive. Recruitment advertising is also covered separately by equal opportunities legislation, outlawing discrimination in wording or implication on the basis of sex, sexual orientation, race or ethnicity, religious belief or age.

- The **privacy of consumers** is protected by privacy and data protection legislation:

  - Requiring 'opt in', or allowing 'opt out', in regard to unsolicited marketing messages (eg junk mail, telesales and e-mail and fax marketing).

  - Restricting the use of personal details obtained from promotions, contacts and websites, and sharing these with other parties (eg selling e-mail lists).

Corporate social responsibility in promotion may take other, voluntary, forms, depending on the ethical issues raised by particular products/services or campaigns. For example:

- Many companies are now refraining from advertising 'junk food' or foods high in fat, sugar and salt (HFSS) during children's TV programming.

- Fashion brands and retailers are refraining from using very young and very skinny models in advertising, with the deliberate aim of encouraging realistic body image among women, and particularly reducing potential causes of hyper-dieting and eating disorders among teenage girls.

- Car advertising is focusing on attributes such as passenger safety, fuel economy and reduced emissions – rather than speed (which may promote illegal and irresponsible driving).

Promotional activities are also, of course, used directly for **philanthropic**, **social and environmental ends**. Pressure groups, religious groups, charities and self-help groups, trade unions and professional associations all use marketing communications to promote wider stakeholder interests. In addition, business organisations may co-promote issues or causes, in order to enhance their CSR credentials.

THE REAL WORLD

In June 2011, McDonald's launched a UK TV campaign to highlight the company's environmental initiatives as well as its approach to staff development and community involvement.

McDonald's UK vice-president of marketing Alistair Macrow said: 'Over the last three years our advertising focus has been primarily around the ingredients that go into our food and where those ingredients come from. Whilst our brand advertising will continue to satisfy this interest, we feel now is the right time to start celebrating some of the good work we do in other areas of our business. I believe that even our most dedicated followers will learn something new about McDonald's from the advertisement.'

Watch the advertisement here: http://www.youtube.com/watch?v=dxVCVEFrjSM, then consider the range of McDonald's stakeholders that this was aimed at:

- Customers
- Employees
- Suppliers
- The wider community
- Any others you can think of?

ACTIVITY 6.6

Identify the external stakeholder audiences of your own organisation, or one you know well (perhaps as an external stakeholder yourself). How regularly, and in what circumstances, does the organisation communicate with each group? What means of communication are used? How does this shape the relationship between the organisation and each stakeholder?

This needn't be a detailed analysis (although such an analysis would be useful groundwork for an assignment). You may like to discuss the answers with a group of fellow students or employees.

---

2 The service mix (3Ps)

> **Key term**
>
> A **service** may be defined as: 'Any activity or benefit that one party can offer to another that is essentially intangible and does not result in the ownership of anything. Its production may or may not be tied to a physical product.' (Kotler *et al*, 1999a)

Egan (2004, p131) notes that in marketing, the term 'service' is used in two main ways.

- To describe businesses where the greater part of the company's central offering is intangible or non-physical: **'service industries'**. Examples include entertainment, transport, banking, insurance, consultancy, cleaning and hairdressing: the core of the offering is *doing* something for the customer, rather than transferring ownership of a physical product.

- To describe the features of any offering or exchange which extend beyond the core product or service, adding value (and perhaps, over time, relational benefits) as a result of the contacts between the buyer and the seller: in other words, '**customer service**'.

The discussion that follows mainly focuses on the distinctive nature of services (as opposed to physical products), and therefore applies to marketing in service industries (or '**service marketing**'). However, the issues are also relevant to the provision of customer service.

The major contributors to national output are the public and private service sectors. The extension of the service sector and the application of market principles across what were previously publicly-owned utilities has made a large number of service providers much more marketing conscious.

The service sector extends across the **public sector** in the legal, medical, educational, military, employment, credit, communications, transport, leisure and information fields. The private sector includes areas such as arts, leisure, charities, religious organisations and educational institutions, as well as business and professional services involved in travel, finance, insurance, management and consultancy, the law, construction, commerce and entertainment.

▶ **Assessment tip**

You may well select a service organisation, rather than a manufacturing organisation, as the subject of your assignment. If so, all that we have said about products (which includes services), price, place and promotion will still be relevant – but pay particular attention to the *differences* between products and services discussed here.

2.1 Characteristics of services

Services are different from physical products or goods in five main ways: intangibility; inseparability; heterogeneity; perishability and non-ownership. Let's look briefly at each in turn.

2.1.1 Intangibility

Intangibility refers to the lack of substance involved in service delivery. Unlike goods, there are no material or physical aspects to a service: no taste, feel or object that can be handled or owned. This creates difficulties for marketers and customers: it is difficult to describe the offering and to make comparisons between rival offerings. 'The customer may have no prior experience of a service in which he or she is interested, nor any conception of how it would satisfy the requirements of the purchase context for which it was intended.' (Morden, 1993)

Marketers and consumers need to try to overcome this problem, in order to reduce the stress and risk of the purchase decision. This can be done by:

- Increasing the level of tangibility: adding tokens or evidences to give the service a tangible aspect (eg a programme for a concert, or a ticket for transport)
- Focusing attention on the benefits of the offering: for example through images or testimonials of past customers' experience and satisfaction
- Differentiating and reputation-building: enhancing customer value by offering excellence in the delivery of the service, or relationship benefits over time

2.1.2 Inseparability

Products can be produced in one location and delivered in another – services can't. The production, delivery and consumption of services are simultaneous. Think of having dental treatment or taking a bus ride: neither exists until they are being experienced or consumed by the patient/passenger. 'With services, marketing becomes a means of facilitating complex producer-consumer interactions, rather than being merely an exchange medium' (Egan, 2004, p132).

In addition, the customer's impression of a service is inseparable from the person who provides it. Consequently, increasing importance is attached to the need to instil values of quality, reliability and customer focus in service staff – as we will see in Chapter 9.

2.1.3 Heterogeneity

Heterogeneity means lack of 'sameness' or consistency: in other words, variability. Many services face the problem of maintaining consistency in the standard of output. The quality of the service may vary widely depending on who it is that delivers the service, and when and where it takes place. Booking a holiday using standard procedures may be quite different on a quiet winter's afternoon than on a hectic spring weekend, and may also vary according to the individual facing you across the travel agency desk. In addition, variability may be caused by the individuality of customers' needs and wants (in the case of hairdressing or consultancy, say). It is difficult to monitor and control 'production' of services to ensure consistent standards.

Variability highlights the need for marketers to develop and maintain processes for:

- Consistent quality control, with clear and objective quality measures
- Consistent customer service and customer care, standardising as far as possible
- Effective staff selection, training and motivation in customer care
- Identifying and prioritising potential critical touch points or 'moments of truth', which could be a source of critical episodes (both positive and negative)
- Monitoring service levels and customer perceptions of service delivery

2.1.4 Perishability

Services cannot be stored. Seats on a bus, a hotel room or the services of a doctor exist only for 'windows' of time: they cannot be kept aside for later use, nor produced in advance and stockpiled to allow for peaks in demand!

This presents specific marketing challenges. Meeting customer needs depends on staff being available as and when they are needed – which must be balanced against the need for a firm to minimise unnecessary staff levels (and wages costs). Anticipating and responding to levels of demand is, therefore, a key planning priority, in order to balance the needs of internal and external stakeholders. Policies must seek to smooth out fluctuations in the supply/demand relationship, or allow for contingencies, for example by:

- Using price variations to encourage off-peak demand (eg on travel services)
- Using promotions to stimulate off-peak demand (eg free mobile calls between certain hours)
- Using flexible staffing methods to cover fluctuations in demand (eg part-time and temporary working, or outsourcing customer service to call centres)

2.1.5 Non-ownership

Services do not result in the transfer of property. The purchase of a service only gives the customer access to, or the right to use, a facility – not ownership. This may lessen the perceived customer value of a service – particularly if the benefit does not accrue until some time in the future (like a pension, or a voucher for future use). There are two basic approaches to addressing this problem.

- Promote the advantages of non-ownership. This can be done by for example emphasising the benefits of low up-front costs, flexibility.
- Make available a symbol or presentation of ownership such as a certificate, voucher, merchandise item or receipt. This can come to embody the benefits owed or enjoyed.

A national charity wants to send out a mail shot to attract donations. Describe what you would suggest that recipients should find in the envelope in order to persuade people to donate, and begin to create a relationship with the donor. (Note: the charity faces the same problems as a typical service provider. The key is to overcome the lack of a physical product and ownership.)

2.2 The extended marketing mix

Marketers of services have long argued that the four Ps are insufficient to describe the elements in providing and marketing a service. A service does not primarily involve a physical product: if you buy a ticket to go on a train journey, for example, you own nothing at the end of the exchange. Your experience of a service depends on the people who deliver it, the processes or systems by which it is delivered, and any physical aspects that can be used to add something tangible to the service (such as your train ticket). Most physical products have these elements of service in them, too, whether in the selling of the product, or in customer support or maintenance after you've bought it.

The marketing mix has therefore been extended to include the three Ps of the service marketing mix (People, Processes and Physicals) and the seven Ps together are known as the **extended marketing mix**.

The service mix elements can be summarised as follows.

Table 6.3   The extended marketing mix

Element	Explanation	Example tools
People	The employees and intermediaries who create and deliver service.	Staff selection, training, motivation, empowerment and performance management: internal marketing.
Process	The activities, information flows and supporting procedures and systems which create and deliver service.	Policies and procedures; administrative, information and transaction processing systems; customer management; quality management; product development.
Physicals	Tangible evidences of purchase, and physical factors in the purchase environment, which influence the service experience of customers.	Point of sale environment; staff uniforms; tickets, vouchers and merchandise; discount/loyalty cards.

Let's look at how each element can be applied to the wider stakeholder audience, and to the development of sustainable stakeholder relationships.

2.3 People

The people employed by an organisation are an important ingredient in the marketing mix and the organisation's relationships with the wider environment.

People play a crucial role in **delivering stakeholder value**, whether in service marketing or in customer service and stakeholder relationship management. The higher the level of contact involved in the delivery of a product or service, the greater the potential for added value and relationship development.

In some cases, the **physical presence** of people actually performing the task is a vital aspect of customer satisfaction. Think of counter staff in a bank, or table waiting staff in a restaurant – or builders leaving your house tidier than they found it! The people involved are performing or 'producing' the service; selling the service; co-operating with the customer to promote the service, gathering information and responding to customer needs; and creating interpersonal relationships which may evolve into loyalty to the firm.

Arguably, however, **all members of the organisation are involved in 'marketing'**: all personnel should have the skills, motivation and attitudes to do their jobs to a professional standard and with a customer value focus, and should be rewarded and valued accordingly. As we will see in Chapter 9, this requires policies for employee selection, training and development, motivation, empowerment and communication.

2.3.1 The Service Profit Cycle

It is often argued that '**employee satisfaction** and **customer satisfaction**' may not always be compatible: customers may have expectations or make demands which are impossible, difficult or unpleasant for employees to satisfy – and employees may have to behave as if 'the customer is always right' when they know this is not the case!

However, marketing literature has suggested that, rather than a trade-off, there is a positive correlation between customer satisfaction and employee satisfaction.

- Peters & Waterman (1982) argued that customer- and quality-focused values are a powerful source of **job satisfaction** for employees, giving their jobs meaning and significance beyond the mere performance of tasks. Such strong values also enable the organisation to direct and control employees' activities without resorting to close supervision and detailed rules, and this style of control is regarded as **empowering** rather than restricting by employees.

- Other writers on service marketing (Grönroos, 2000; Heskett *et al,* 1997) have suggested that employee satisfaction and customer satisfaction are linked in a **service profit cycle or chain**: Figure 6.4.

Figure 6.4   The Service Profit Cycle (adapted from Egan, *op cit*, p145)

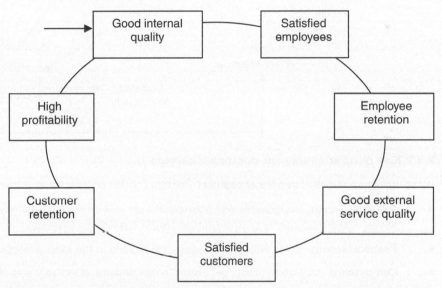

Reichheld (2001) developed a **loyalty-based cycle**, based on the firm's relationships with three core stakeholders: employees, customers and investors. This model shows the linkages between loyalty, value and profits: Figure 6.5.

- Superior service and value creates loyal customers
- Revenues and market share grow as the best customers are prioritised, building repeat sales and referrals
- Sustainable growth enables the firm to attract and retain the best employees
- Consistent delivery of superior value to customers increases employees' loyalty by giving them pride and satisfaction in their work
- Long-term employees get to know long-term customers, enabling further service and value enhancement, which in turn further enhances customer and employee loyalty

- Loyal long-term employees generate superior productivity. This surplus can be used to fund superior rewards, tools and training – which further reinforce employee productivity, reward growth and loyalty

- Increased productivity and the efficiency of dealing with loyal customers generates cost advantages over competitors – and higher profits

- High profits make it easier for the firm to attract and retain high-quality investors

- Loyal investors stabilise the system, funding investments that increase the company's value creation potential.

Figure 6.5   Reichheld's loyalty-based cycle of growth (simplified!)

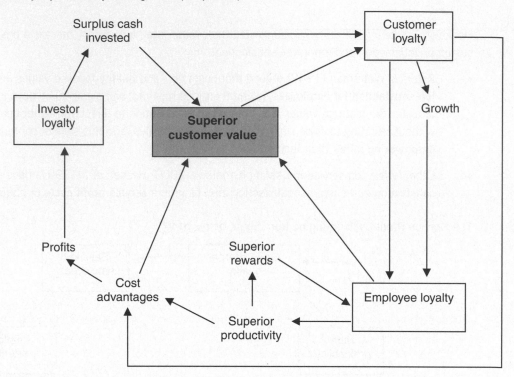

2.3.2 Key people values for customer service

What makes an effective **service encounter**? Overton (2002) suggests that it involves the following key values.

- **Reliability**: being dependable and consistent – not only to ensure repeat business, but as a matter of ethics, if the customer is buying a future benefit (eg financial services)

- **Responsiveness**: being willing and ready, and flexible in the face of needs

- **Competence**: skill and knowledge, ability to use systems effectively and efficiently

- **Accessibility**: minimising queuing/waiting times, offering speedy service, approachability of service personnel

- **Courtesy**: being polite, considerate, respectful and friendly (without excessive informality, in some cultures)

- **Communication**: communicating clearly, using language the customer/stakeholder will understand, listening effectively

- **Credibility**: projecting an image of honesty, believability and trustworthiness

- **Security**: minimising risk and doubt for the customer/stakeholder; ensuring physical safety, protecting rights, ensuring confidentiality where appropriate

- **Understanding**: appreciating the customer/stakeholder's needs and concerns

- **Tangibles**: the service area, accessories and evidences of service are consistent with the service provided

- **Focus**: an attitude that puts the customer first.

High-level people skills are especially required to handle **complaints** from customers or other stakeholders. Effective complaint-handling requires acknowledgement and management of the stakeholder's feelings about the problem – as well as dealing with the problem itself swiftly, fairly and helpfully. The aim is to minimise the potential for lasting dissatisfaction; restore satisfaction and (if possible) reinforce loyalty; and uphold the credibility – and profitability – of the organisation.

2.3.3 People in wider stakeholder marketing

In the context of **wider stakeholder needs** (beyond *customer* service), the people element of the extended marketing mix may include corporate decisions about how people should be treated, in order to build their trust, loyalty and commitment – and in order to maximise their potential contribution to the objectives of the enterprise.

- **Internal marketing** is the process whereby employees are equipped and empowered for their contribution to marketing, stakeholder relationships and customer service. It embraces recruitment, motivation and reward, training and development, communication and empowerment – as we will see in Chapter 9.

- **Employee relations** is how the organisation conducts the relationship with its employees. It includes issues such as: fair pay and benefits; safe and healthy (and if possible, congenial) working conditions; equal opportunity (non-discrimination) and diversity (welcoming of differences, representation of minority groups); employee consultation and involvement (both formal, through trade unions, and informal); flexible working arrangements (to help employees with work-life balance and family responsibilities); fair disciplinary and grievance-handling frameworks (clear rules and fair handling of disputes); employment security (eg protection from unfair dismissal or redundancy without notice); and the attitudes, values and style of management in regard to workers.

- **Ethics and corporate social responsibility** impose constraints and principles on how people in general (employees, suppliers, external stakeholders) are treated by the organisation. This includes principles such as equal opportunity and diversity; equal access to goods, services and business opportunities; fair treatment and non-exploitation; ethical dealings; and minimisation of negative impacts on people's rights and interests.

2.4 Processes

> **Key term**
>
> **Processes** are the way in which tasks are carried out: Peck *et al* (1999, p408) defines them as 'the way we do things: linked sets of activities that enable market demand to be satisfied'. Core business processes include new product development, order fulfilment, supplier management and customer management – all of which, ultimately, deliver customer value.

Owners of BMW cars in the UK can now take advantage of what BMW calls its 'Fast Lane Service.' This is promoted as a four-step process:

 1

Contact our Service Department.
Our team will immediately check whether the work can be completed as a Fast Lane Service, how long it is expected to take and how much it will cost.

 2

Bring in your BMW.
You arrive prior to the appointment and your BMW is checked in immediately so work can begin without delay.

 3

Enjoy our hospitality.
Relax, finish some work, enjoy the wide range of facilities and your short stay can be productive.

 4

Drive away.
With all work completed within the agreed time, your BMW is ready for the road.

(BMW, 2012)

During Step 3, customers can use the customer lounge which is equipped with TV, wi-fi access and tea and coffee among other facilities.

What aspects of the three service Ps do you think BMW had to consider when introducing this service?

Process issues for stakeholder marketing include the following.

- The formation of **policies and codes of conduct** in regard to ethical dealings and corporate social responsibility (a key issues for many stakeholders)

- Procedures for **efficiency and standardisation** of all service provision, transactions and communications; the reduction of queuing/waiting times for services or contacts; capacity management (to match supply to demand in a timely and cost-effective way – overcoming the perishability factor in service provision)

- Efficient and ethical **information-gathering, processing and communication** mechanisms for customer service and stakeholder relationships. If possible, these mechanisms should be integrated to handle all stakeholder contacts, communications and transactions: for example, in Customer Relationship Management or Supplier Relationship Management systems (discussed in Chapter 4).

- Equitable and convenient **accessibility** of facilities, premises, personnel and services to all stakeholders. This may embrace CSR and diversity issues such as disabled access to premises, the use of different languages in communications (or Braille for the sight-impaired, or displays for the hearing-impaired),

 The Chartered Institute of Marketing

adjustment of premises and duties for disabled employees, and so on. However, it also includes distribution issues: processes for getting goods and services to remote or isolated areas or customers, say.

Such provisions are particularly important in service marketing, because of the characteristic of heterogeneity or variability: the organisation needs to **standardise service provision** as far as possible, preserving minimum standards and reducing customer/stakeholder risk (or perception of risk).

2.4.1 Processes for wider stakeholder marketing

In addition, the **wider stakeholder marketing mix** may be underpinned, as we have already seen, by processes for:

- Stakeholder-sensitive, responsible and ethical **product development** (or adaptation)
- **Stakeholder management**: prioritising, needs analysis, contact planning, relationship monitoring
- Ethical **supplier management** and **fair trading**
- **Green supply and manufacture**: establishing processes for recycling and reverse logistics; using or developing alternative energy sources.

2.5 Physicals

Physical elements are designed to overcome the intangibility and lack of ownership of services, and to:

- Convey the nature of the service
- Transmit messages and information
- Imply aesthetic qualities, CSR, ethical values or other aspects of corporate image
- Reassure customers about the professionalism or security of the service
- Differentiate the service and its provider from competitors.

Physical elements include tangible evidence of purchase (such as a receipt or voucher, or a bank statement), accessories (such as merchandise or concert programmes), factors in the environment of purchase (eg showroom décor, furnishing and ambience), and brand identity (eg staff livery or uniforms, brand logos).

What physicals could be provided by:

(a)   A provider of adventure sport activities?
(b)   A provider of tourist information services?
(c)   A provider of travel services?
(d)   A TV rental provider?

The following are examples of items of physical evidence that can be used in the marketing mix.

Table 6.4   Physical evidence examples

Service environment	Facilities	Evidence of purchase
Décor	Vans/vehicles	Labels and other printed information
Layout	Equipment/tools	Tickets, vouchers and purchase confirmations
Staff uniform/livery		Packaging design

Service environment	Facilities	Evidence of purchase
Noise, music, smells and general ambience		Logos and other visible evidence of brand identity
Website design (for online service provision)		On-going contacts: reports, statements, reminders

The layout, décor and 'branding' of a bank or travel agency, for example, are likely to be an important part of the customer's **experience** of receiving services which are otherwise 'virtual'. Likewise, the appearance, user-friendliness and branding of a company's website gives a visible, interactive face to a virtual entity.

A service can be **presented** in tangible (and promotional) physical form: consider how travel tickets are presented in branded envelopes (or more sophisticated document wallets), with vouchers for added services, information leaflets and other added-value elements – despite the fact that all the customer has purchased is the promise of a future benefit.

Note that physical evidences can also be used as a **relationship marketing tool**: promoting brand awareness and recognition, creating opportunities for marketing messages and after-sales contacts and so on.

ACTIVITY 6.10

Check out the websites of the following organisations and appraise their service marketing mix. How do their people, processes and physicals support relationship marketing? (Think about service quality; website browsing appeal and any incentives to revisit the site; loyalty programmes; branding; signs of user recognition, personalisation and status; downloadable physical elements).

- Barclays Bank: http://www.barclays.co.uk

- British Airways: http://www.britishairways.com

- Sainsbury's online: http://www.sainsburys.co.uk (Don't neglect the Corporate Responsibility, On-line Community, Recruitment and Nectar links: all good stakeholder marketing!)

- Free rice: http://www.freerice.com (This is an interesting one: what stakeholders does it address – and benefit? Warning: the site can also become addictive!)

3 The influence mix (the 8th and 9th Ps)

Egan (*op cit*, p15) mentions two additional Ps for the extended marketing mix, which are particularly relevant to relationships with external stakeholders.

- **Political power**: using various types of power (discussed in Chapter 1) to influence stakeholders; mobilising coalitions of stakeholders; or lobbying representative bodies (such as government or trade unions) on behalf of the interests of the organisation

- **Public opinion**: mobilising the awareness, interest and engagement of the general public (directly or through intermediaries such as pressure groups or the media) to support the interests or objectives of the organisation.

Peck *et al* (1999) include these factors in the influence market of the organisation. Note that they work both ways. The organisation can use them to **influence stakeholders**: using power to control employee or supplier behaviour, or mobilising public support for a policy (perhaps against pressure group opposition), say. However, they can also be mobilised **by stakeholders** to promote their own interests in relation to the organisation: applying pressure to change organisational policy and practice (as we saw in Chapter 2).

4 Tailoring the mix to stakeholder needs

4.1 Difficulties of applying the mix to stakeholder groups

In relationship marketing theory, as we saw in Chapter 4, the marketing mix is regarded as inadequate to tell the whole story of management decisions in relation to customers. It is argued (Egan, 2004; Grönroos, 1996; Gummesson, 2002; and others) that the four Ps model is core-firm-oriented rather than customer-oriented (what we do 'to' customers, rather than 'for' or 'with' them); that it fails to address key features of service and B2B marketing; and that it focuses on manipulating 'tools' at the expense of relationships.

'There has been a shift in thinking from exchange to relationship, or sequences of exchanges within a relationship. The focus is on the value-creating process rather than merely on outcome. Promises are made and given – and fulfilled – mutually. Thus, many facets of the required decision making for the management of the relationship **fall outside of the marketing mix framework**.' (Varey, 2002).

The vocabulary of the marketing mix can be simplistic when trying to describe the **complex value proposition** sought by relationship marketing. In Chapter 5, we noted that, in the process of creating customer value, the 'product' is not just a simple product: it involves the customer's total experience of purchasing it, using it and relating to its supplier. Likewise, 'price' is not just sale price, but a complex of costs or sacrifices the customer is willing to make to obtain the promised benefits.

The use of marketing mix terms is perhaps even more complicated when talking about **non-customer stakeholder groups**. What 'product' is offered to shareholders or suppliers, for example? What do 'price' or 'place' mean in the context of employees or trade unions? If we are to think about the marketing mix for such stakeholder audiences, we need to broaden our definitions.

4.2 A broader definition of mix elements

Van Waterschoot and Van den Bulte (1992) have described the four Ps of the marketing mix as four **generic marketing activities** that bring about exchanges with stakeholders.

- Configuration of some **offering** that will be valued by the other party [Product]
- Determination of the **value** (compensation or sacrifice) desired from the other party in exchange for the offering [Price]
- Facilitation of the exchange by making the offering **accessible** to the other party [Place or provision]
- **Communication** of the offering to bring it to the attention of the other party and to influence feelings and preferences about it [Promotion].

In these terms, it may be easier to see how the mix could be analysed and applied to non-customer marketing exchanges.

Check out the websites of the following organisations, and appraise how each has responded to pressures for Corporate Social Responsibility (or their own values in this area) by adapting their marketing mixes. Work through each of the 7Ps in turn, and explain how (if at all) each has been adapted for CSR objectives.

- Federal Express (FedEx): http://www.fedex.com

- John Lewis Partnership: http://www.johnlewis.com

- Toyota: http://www.toyota-global.com (in particular, look at Toyota's "Approaches to Stakeholders" at http://www.toyota-global.com/sustainability/stakeholders/

- Any other organisation of your choice.

You might also like to note any brand or corporate **alliances** promoted by these organisations, and any messages specifically targeted at **non-customer stakeholder groups**.

4.3 A more relational marketing mix?

Kotler *et al* (1999b) argued that the marketing mix represented the firm's view of marketing and argued that in a marketing-oriented organisation, the 4Ps should be viewed from the *customer's* perspective, as 4 Cs. These have since been augmented to include the service mix (Ace, 2001), as follows.

Table 6.5   Customer-focused marketing mix

Producer/provider-focused activity	Customer/consumer-focused activity
Product Plan product/service mix	**Choice** Consider how customers make choices: differentiate and inform to support the purchase decision
Price Consider all elements of the price mix	**Cost** Consider how customers perceive value for money
Place Manage distribution channels	**Convenience** Consider what customers find convenient: they may not like the channels (eg the internet) that are most 'efficient'
Promotion Persuade customers that the product meets their needs	**Communication** Enter into dialogue with customers: inform and support their decision making: they are increasingly aware that promotion is being used to persuade or manipulate
People Select, train and manage staff in service delivery	**Care** Communicate and implement customer care values to all staff
Processes Organise, plan and control systems and operations	**Corporate competence** Understand customer expectations and convey commitment to deliver: customers don't need to know *how* things are done (much less how difficult they are to do...)
Physical evidence Manage all physical factors (premises, logos etc)	**Consistency** Ensure that customer contacts and experiences are alike, to establish recognition, positive associations and loyalty

You should be able to see that the 7Cs are much more relationship-focused, and could be applied to a wider range of stakeholder groups, for whom concepts such as 'product', 'price' and 'place' may not be directly applicable.

4.4 Differentiating stakeholders' marketing mix requirements

CIM's tutor guidance states that 'students will be expected to differentiate between the marketing mix requirements for each stakeholder group or target audience and to tailor the mix for different groups.' How might you go about this?

Most importantly, you need to identify and appreciate the different **needs, expectations, interests and drivers** of different stakeholder groups. The purpose of tailoring the marketing mix is to satisfy as many of these as possible, as effectively and profitably as possible. Our surveys of stakeholder groups in Chapters 1 and 2 should give you a good basis for more detailed analysis of particular stakeholders. A 'one size fits all' approach will not work, given the multiple, differing – and sometimes conflicting – needs and expectations of different stakeholders.

For each key stakeholder group, work through the 7Ps or 7Cs, to identify how each element of the mix might be used to **add value** for the group, and to **build relationship** with it. There may need to be a distinct marketing mix plan for:

- Different customer groups or market segments. The concept of market segmentation and targeting should be familiar from your studies in *Marketing Essentials*. Basically, it involves 'the subdividing of a market into distinct sub-groups of customers, where any sub-group can conceivably be selected as a target to be met with a distinct marketing mix' (Cannon, 1980). Customers may be segmented on the basis of geographical area, demographics (age, gender, socio-economic group or family life cycle stage, say), psychographics (lifestyle, opinions and interests), buyer behaviour (eg user status or usage rate), the kinds of value and benefits they look for in the product – or the value they represent to the organisation (eg 'key account' or high-profitability customers).

- Different external stakeholder segments. Similarly to customer segmentation, pressure and interest groups and wider community stakeholders can be segmented according to the nature of their interest in the organisation. The marketing mix can then be targeted to the cause or interests being promoted or protected: emphasising 'green' values to environmental groups, say, and ethical supply policies to fair trade groups.

- Different stakeholder groups. As we saw in Chapter 1, employees, shareholders, suppliers and intermediaries (among other stakeholder groups) each have their own needs, interests and drivers. You might define the 4Ps using the generic factors identified by Van Waterschoot and Van den Bult (see section 4.2), and put together an offering best-suited to the needs of each relationship.

- Different stakeholder audiences. The need to tailor marketing communications and messages for different audiences is perhaps the most obvious – and easiest – way of tailoring the marketing mix to different stakeholders. Product, price and place may not be easy to apply or adapt to multiple, specific and potentially conflicting needs – but the way they are communicated can always be targeted to the expectations, needs and concerns of different audiences. We will explore this in detail in Chapter 8.

We will also look at some formats for preparing marketing mix plans in Chapter 7.

Which elements of the marketing mix do you think would be the main priority and focus of interest for:

- Shareholders?
- Employees?
- Suppliers?
- Pressure groups?
- The news media?

5 Co-ordinating the mix

5.1 What is 'mix co-ordination'?

We have referred throughout this chapter to a 'co-ordinated marketing mix', but perhaps this requires some further explanation.

- Mix decisions are not taken in isolation: they must be **aligned** with the overall corporate objectives of the organisation (for example, profitability and social responsibility), and its marketing objectives (brand positioning, market share, customer retention, price leadership).

- The elements of the marketing mix **work together** to create a total value proposition for the customer (and other stakeholders). Each element contributes to the total proposition and the impression it creates in the mind of the customer or stakeholder. Mix decisions need to ensure **coherence** and **consistency** in the messages they convey: creating positive synergy (2 + 2 = 5) rather than undermining or conflicting with each other.

- For example, if an organisation wants to position a product as a luxury or high-quality 'premium' brand, it should price the product accordingly (on the grounds that consumers assume they 'get what they pay for'). It should also ensure a matching quality image in its intermediaries or dealerships, and should select promotional media and messages on the same lines (advertising in up-market media, no 'get one free' sales promotions).

- The overall **stakeholder marketing mix** also needs to be coherent and consistent. It will be no good marketing products to customers on the basis of corporate social responsibility and ethics – if opposite messages are sent by the firm's treatment of its suppliers, intermediaries or employees, say. The charity Oxfam, for example, had its credibility undermined when it was discovered that suppliers of its 'Make Poverty History' wristbands were themselves guilty of exploiting workers with minimal pay and poor working conditions.

- Mix decisions must be taken with the needs of a **range of market/stakeholder segments** in mind. The product mix or product portfolio, for example, can be adapted to cover a range of stakeholder and customer needs: think of Nestlé's range of coffee brands, for example, which covers luxury, economy, fair-trade and health-conscious (de-caffeinated) brands. The distribution mix can similarly cover the needs of different regions, urban and rural lifestyles, isolated or less mobile consumers (eg internet buying and/or home delivery).

- Mix decisions may need to acknowledge **trade-offs** between the needs and interests of different stakeholder groups, prioritising some over others – or ensuring that each group at least gets a 'partial win' through some elements of the mix. We drew attention to some of the conflicting interests in Chapter 1: shareholder interests (profitability) versus customer interests (quality and value), for example. So price and product elements may have to be juggled to create a short-term compromise – or shareholder marketing may emphasise the long-term benefits of putting customers first (for a long-term win-win solution).

- The **resources** available for marketing – human, financial and physical – need to be prioritised and co-ordinated in order to deliver an effective marketing mix. We will look at budgeting in Chapter 11, in relation to the marketing communications mix, but you should be aware of the principle that resources are limited – and sometimes scarce. They need to be allocated where they will have most effect on profitability and long-term sustainable relationships: marketers sometimes use the term 'leverage' to express the idea that a small amount of resource has a disproportionately large impact. So, for example, there will need to be a balance between expenditure on customer acquisition and customer retention; between product development and enhancement, service quality and promotion.

▶ **Assessment tip**

This is a useful reality check for any proposals you may make in your assignment.

- Is your proposal for any one element of the marketing mix **coherent and consistent** with other elements? Does it create harmony and synergy – rather than conflicting or undermining messages, with potential for stakeholder confusion?

- Does your proposal for any one element of the marketing mix **use – and ideally**, **leverage – available resources**? Does it use no more than its 'fair share' of the resources that need to be allocated across the marketing mix – or will it leave other elements neglected?

- Will your proposal for a marketing mix for one stakeholder be **broadly acceptable to other stakeholders** – or will it cause stakeholder conflict in other areas?

5.2 An overview of integrated marketing planning

The following (Fill, 2002) is a model showing how all the different elements need to be brought together in a co-ordinated or integrated way: Figure 6.6.

Figure 6.6   Integrated marketing

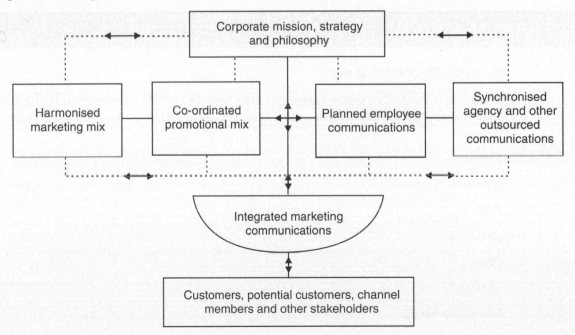

- Definition/recap of the 7Ps: Product, Price, Place (distribution), Promotion (marketing communications), People, Process, Physicals

- Potential of each element to add value for wider stakeholders

- Potential of each element to develop sustainable relationships

- Characteristics of services and their influence on the extended marketing mix (3Ps)

- Elements in delivering service value: people, processes, physicals

- The Service Profit Cycle (Reichheld): the interrelationship between employee satisfaction and loyalty, service quality, customer satisfaction and loyalty, and corporate profitability

- What it means to tailor the marketing mix to different stakeholder audiences

- A generic view of product (offer), price (cost/sacrifice), place (making the offer accessible) and promotion (communicating the offer) for marketing to non-customer stakeholders

- Customer/stakeholder focused alternatives to the 7Ps: the 7Cs (Choice, Cost, Convenience, Communication, Care, Competence and Consistency)

- The need for coherence and consistency of mix messages

- Inter-dependency of mix elements

- Trade-offs required by multiple and conflicting interests

- Co-ordination of resources across the mix.

FURTHER READING

Elements of the marketing mix

Jobber, D. (2007) *Principles & Practice of Marketing*. 5th edition. Maidenhead, McGraw-Hill Education. When reading the relevant chapters, think how the content applies to the wider stakeholder audience, not just customers.

Product

Chapter 9, 10 and 11

Price

Chapter 12

Place

Chapter 17

Service marketing

Chapter 22
Pay particular attention to the sections applying the service mix to retail and not-for-profit organisations, if these are your areas of interest.

General

Egan, G. (2004) *Relationship Marketing*. 2nd edition. Harlow, Pearson Education.

The Chartered
Institute of Marketing

Reichheld, F. (1996) *The Loyalty Effect: The hidden force behind growth, profits, and lasting value* Harvard Business School Press.

REFERENCES

Ace, C. (2001) *Successful Marketing Communications*. Oxford, Butterworth-Heinemann.

BMW (2012) http://www.bmw.co.uk/bmwuk/owner/servicing_programmes/fast_Lane/0,,1312___,00.html?cnr=3 [Accessed 24 June]

Cannon, T. (1980) *Basic Marketing: Principles & Practice*. Thomson Learning.

Egan, J. (2004) *Relationship Marketing: Exploring Relational Strategies in Marketing.* 2nd edition. Harlow, Essex, Pearson Education.

Fill, C. (2002) *Marketing Communications: Contexts, Strategies & Applications*. 3rd edition. Prentice Hall.

Grönroos, C. (1996) Relationship marketing: strategic and tactical implications in *Management Decisions* Vol 34, No 3, pp5-14.

Grönroos, C. (2000) *Service Management and Marketing*. Chichester, Wiley.

Gummesson, E. (2002) *Total Relationship Marketing*, Oxford, Elsevier Butterworth-Heinemann.

Heskett, J. *et al* (1997) *The Service Profit Chain*. New York, Free Press.

Iceland (2012) http://www.iceland.co.uk [Accessed on 24 June 2012]

Jobber, D. (2007) *Principles and Practice of Marketing.* 5th edition. Maidenhead, Berks, McGraw Hill Education.

Kotler, P. (1992) Total Marketing in *Business Week Advance, Executive Brief* No 2.

Kotler, P. *et al* (1999a) *Marketing: an introduction*. Sydney, Prentice Hall.

Kotler, P. *et al* (1999b) *Principles of Marketing.* 2nd edition. New York, Prentice Hall.

Morden, A.T. (1993) *Elements of Marketing*. Continuum International.

Overton, T. (2002) Customer Service, *Business Basics*. Sydney, Australia.

Peck, H.L. *et al* (1999) *Relationship Marketing: Strategy and Implementation*. Oxford, Elsevier, Butterworth-Heinemann.

Peters, T.J. and Waterman, R. (1982) *In Search of Excellence*. New York, Harper & Row.

Reichheld, F. (2001) *The Loyalty Effect*. Boston, Mass: Harvard Business School Press.

Van Waterschoot, W. and Van den Bulte, C. (1992) The 4P classification of the marketing mix revisited, in *Journal of Marketing*. No. 56, October, pp83-93.

Varey, R.J. (2002) *Marketing Communications: Principles & Practice*. Abingdon, Oxon, Routledge.

1   List the seven Ps of the extended marketing mix.

2   List the seven Cs devised as the customer-focused version of the seven Ps.

3   Give three examples of how (a) product and (b) price can be made more corporately responsible.

4   Give three examples of how distribution decisions can be targeted to the needs of wider stakeholders.

5   Identify six potential audiences or publics – other than customers – for marketing messages.

6   Give three examples of ethical issues in promotion.

7   List the five distinctive characteristics of services.

8   Explain the service profit cycle.

9   For what different groups might different marketing mixes be required?

10   Identify six senses in which the marketing mix needs to be co-ordinated.

ACTIVITY DEBRIEFS

Activity 6.1

The **functional aspects** of products and services could be 'ethically enhanced' eg by providing responsible safety and usage instructions (especially for potentially dangerous equipment or tools) in multiple languages (to give equal access to different stakeholder groups); providing advice and trouble-shooting services (eg help lines for the best use of washing powders and washing machine settings); or providing training or tutorials (eg bundled with computer software packages).

The **symbolic aspects** will be closely related to the way the product is promoted. However, as we saw in Chapter 2, brand characteristics can be used deliberately to appeal to wider stakeholder drivers: for example, the ethical values of The Body Shop, Fair Trade coffee brands, healthy/nutritious/weight-loss food brands and so on.

Activity 6.2

Customers could be involved at the concept testing stage (for example, being involved in focus groups to research the concept). They would clearly also be involved in the test marketing stage.

Employees would, of course, be involved at all stages – but think which employee groups would be involved at each stage – R&D, finance, production departments for example.

Suppliers could be consulted at the concept development stage to ensure that components for the proposed new product were available; costs of materials from suppliers would also be a fundamental part of the business analysis stage.

Distributors would need to be involved before any test marketing or commercialisation was carried out; however, they may also be a source of new ideas as they are a step closer to the end-user.

The Chartered
Institute of Marketing

Activity 6.3

You may or may not be pleased that your brand was perceived among the most expensive – depending on whether it was intended to be positioned as a luxury or premium model. If it was intended to be a value-for-money family car, the fact that it was perceived as expensive would be a problem – particularly since there are other models (eg A, B and C) which are perceived to be both less expensive and 'greener'. You would probably worry, in the current climate, that X is perceived to be not particularly environmentally friendly: people seeking green cars are presumably buying A, B or C. You would also be a bit concerned that people see little to choose between your model X and competing models Y and Z: it may come down to price deals or sales force persuasion at the dealership. You might be pleased to see that there is a great opportunity for a 'green' car in the premium price bracket: there is no competition at the moment, and if people are buying models X, Y and Z for their premium quality – how much more will they buy a model that represents quality/luxury *and* 'it's good for the planet too'?

Activity 6.4

The answer is provided in the text following the activity. This activity was intended to get you into the habit of thinking through the wider stakeholder implications of every marketing activity and decision you come across.

Activity 6.5

Financers: financial stability and performance of the organisation; confidence in future profitability; well managed and forward looking; good/safe investment; existing investor satisfaction (eg with dividends, returns); endorsements and awards by financial press.

Government: compliance with all law and regulation; proactive stance on CSR; willingness to support or challenge policies depending on their impact on the industry and organisation; political power (eg coalition of business interests).

Allies: 'safe' partner (eg reputationally sound, good risk management, trustworthy re confidential information); positive synergy (eg shared audience, messages); potential benefits of collaboration; willingness to partner and invest in partnership; expectations of mutual benefit; appreciation of value added by partners.

Competitors: willingness to compete aggressively; willingness to compete fairly and ethically; willingness to collaborate in interests of the industry and best-practice sharing.

Media: identity as trusted source of information; information resources available; newsworthiness of activities (appeal to media's own audience); 'human' interest of activities (eg community involvement); desire for collaboration/consultation on publicity.

General public: corporate social responsibility and ethics; community involvement; environment-friendly; support for local businesses; fair trading; good employer; etc.

Activity 6.6

Your own research and thoughts/discussions.

Activity 6.7

You may well have received such a mailshot yourself. One received by the author from the National Society for the Prevention for Cruelty to Children (NSPCC) contained five items in an envelope printed with a black and white photo of a sad and neglected little girl. The five items were:

- A letter printed on paper with a recycled feel, with more photos of neglected children. The letter told the story of the child shown on the envelope ('Ellie'), and in emotive language, asks for 'just £15' – and describes what good could be done with the money.

- A donation form. You can tick a box saying '£15' or fill in your own amount. You can give your credit card details. You can also opt *not* to receive further mailings. On the reverse, Ellie's story and NSPCC action is described again in a sort of brief 'photo-story'.

- An envelope addressed to the Director of the NSPCC at a freepost address (but suggesting that if you use a stamp it will save the charity postage).

- A 'Thank you' card with a picture of Ellie smiling on the front, and a thank you message in a 'hand-written' typeface.

- A car sticker saying 'Support the NSPCC'.

Activity 6.8

The most important factors in efficient complaint-handling, according to the general public (in a MORI survey for the UK Citizen's Charter Unit) were:

- The speed of response
- Being kept informed
- Feeling that the problem was fairly investigated
- Clearly communicated complaints procedures
- Friendliness and helpfulness of the staff handling the complaint
- Having a named contact person to deal with
- Receiving written apologies and/or explanations.

Activity 6.9

The following are just some simple suggestions.

(a)   A photo or video of the activity is a common one, or perhaps merchandise such as a T-shirt or baseball cap.

(b)   A map or brochure, guide book or souvenir.

(c)   An itinerary, tickets, accommodation vouchers, perhaps a document wallet.

(d)   A rental schedule, reminder card or customer card.

Activity 6.10

Your own research and evaluation.

Activity 6.11

Share with fellow students, if possible, so that you can get different opinions and insights.

Activity 6.12

Shareholders: Performance of the whole marketing mix, expressed as financial results. The 'product' for them is the quality of the investment vehicle: it needs to represent value for the 'price' of their investment.

Employees: The People element of the mix, as this embodies the way the organisation treats them. Processes will also be important, as this is what they have to work with: a source of frustration or satisfaction. Physicals will be important as the environment in which they work. Of the rest of the marketing mix, Product and Promotion will probably be the elements they will identify with most strongly.

Suppliers: Price (in the sense of the price the organisation is willing to pay for supplies/services) will be a priority for most suppliers in taking on a contract. Product and place will be the next priority (in the sense of materials specifications, service level agreements and delivery instructions). Processes and People will be important in co-ordinating supply activity and managing supply relationships.

The Chartered Institute of Marketing

Pressure groups: Priorities will depend on the nature of the group. A trade union, for example, will focus on People issues. Causal groups may focus on Product (safety, 'green' packaging etc) and Processes (eg recycling, fair trading). The Advertising Standards Agency will focus on Promotion. Government agencies may focus on Price (eg fair pricing of public services, avoidance of price fixing). And so on.

News media: Media will depend on Promotion for press releases and corporate information. They may, however, be interested in any element of the mix that provides newsworthy content.

QUICK QUIZ ANSWERS

1   7Ps: Product, Price, Place/provision, Promotion, People, Process, Physicals

2   7Cs: Choice, Cost, Convenience, Communication, Care, Corporate competence, Consistency

3   (a)   See section 1.3.1, 1.3.2 and 1.3.3 for a full range of examples.
    (b)   See section 1.4 for a full range of examples.

4   See section 1.5 for a full range of examples.

5   Six possible audiences (according to Kotler) are: financers, government, allies, competitors, media and the general public.

6   Ethical issues in promotion include: restrictions on the advertising of harmful products; standards of truth in advertising; consumer privacy and data protection; and promotion for philanthropic, social and environmental ends.

7   The distinctive characteristics of services are identified as: inseparability, intangibility, homogeneity (variability), perishability and non-ownership.

8   The service profit cycle argues that good internal quality and relationships lead to employee satisfaction; which leads to employee loyalty and retention (reduced labour turnover); which leads to better external service quality; which leads to customer satisfaction; which leads to customer loyalty and retention; which improves profitability (for reasons discussed in Chapter 4); and profits can be invested back into internal quality – renewing the cycle.

9   Different marketing mixes may be required for different customer groups or market segments; different stakeholder segments (eg different pressure groups); different stakeholder groups; and different stakeholder audiences.

10 The marketing mix needs to be co-ordinated in the sense of: alignment with corporate and marketing objectives; elements working together for coherence, consistency and synergy; consistency across stakeholder groups; appeal across a range of market/stakeholder segments; recognising trade-offs between stakeholder groups; and effective allocation of limited resources.

CHAPTER 7

Planning and evaluating the stakeholder mix

Introduction

This chapter introduces a number of concepts which will be useful in planning and controlling a co-ordinated marketing mix.

In section 1, we explain some of the key influences on the behaviour and opinions of stakeholder decision-making units. Understanding these influences can help the marketer to design and co-ordinate a marketing mix that is responsive to stakeholders' needs and drivers – and, where possible, adds value to them.

In sections 2 and 3, we focus more specifically on customers, and outline some of the key factors in consumer (personal) and organisational (industrial) buying behaviour. This material will also be useful underpinning knowledge for planning a promotional (marketing communications) mix, covered later in this text.

In section 4, we give you some basic tools that should enable you to apply everything you have learned so far, by formulating a simple marketing plan for a stakeholder or group of stakeholders. (In an assignment you may be asked to recommend improvements to the marketing mix of your chosen organisation. Presenting your recommendations as part of a simple marketing plan will enable you to justify the recommendations by demonstrating to examiners that you have fully understood the context within which your recommendations apply.)

Finally, in section 5, we recap some of your learning from Unit 1: *Marketing Essentials*, by explaining the methods available for monitoring and measuring the success of a co-ordinated marketing mix aimed at multiple stakeholders.

Topic list

Understanding stakeholder needs and drivers	(1)
Personal buying behaviour	(2)
Organisational buying behaviour	(3)
Formulating stakeholder marketing plans	(4)
Measuring and evaluating the mix	(5)

3.2	Analyse the behaviour and opinions of the decision making units in order to design and co-ordinate a marketing mix that is responsive to stakeholders' needs and adds value to them:
	■ Involvement theory
	■ Perceived risk – cost/value
	■ Attitudes
	■ Group influence and opinion leadership
	■ Organisational buying behaviour – stakeholder
	■ Personal buying behaviour and influence
3.4	Explain the methods available for measuring the success of a coordinated marketing mix aimed at multiple stakeholders:
	■ Inquiry tests
	■ Recall tests
	■ Recognition tests
	■ Sales
	■ Tracking studies
	■ Financial analysis
	■ Media evaluation
	■ Stakeholder satisfaction surveys

1 Understanding stakeholder needs and drivers

1.1 Stakeholder decision making

We have already seen, in Chapter 6, that the marketing mix needs to be tailored to the needs, expectations and drivers of key stakeholders, in order to:

■ Respond to their concerns or perceived threats to their interests

■ Create value which is significant to them, drawing them into a value exchange

■ Secure their support, or minimise their resistance, to the organisation's plans

■ Build interest, engagement, trust, loyalty and commitment – in other words, deepening relationship and involvement, to mutual benefit.

So what are those needs, expectations and drivers?

We saw, in Chapters 1 and 2, that different stakeholder groups have different specific needs, interests and priorities. We might call these **content** factors: they refer to *what* stakeholders want from the organisation, or what is important to them, that motivates them to respond to the organisation in a given way.

In addition, however, there are what we might call **process** factors: *how* stakeholders go about deciding what they want and what is important to them. These are the kinds of factors mentioned at this point in the syllabus, and we will explore them here.

First of all, as we will see when we discuss buyer behaviour (in sections 2 and 3 below), it is important to note that stakeholder decisions, like purchase decisions, often involve more than one person. There will be a number of people who have an influence or interest in the decision: stakeholders in the decision, if you like. The term **Decision-Making Unit** (DMU) is given to a group of people who participate in or influence a decision.

One of the first factors to be considered in planning a marketing mix targeted to a stakeholder group is therefore: who are the key **influencers** and **participants** responsible for **making decisions** and **leading opinions** within this stakeholder group? Who is the immediate target audience for the marketing mix and messages?

This information will enable you to **reach** and **target** the people who are most **influential** (potentially able to bring the rest of the stakeholder group with them) and most **amenable** to the idea of relationship or value exchange with the organisation – with the least expenditure of effort and cost. In other words, it helps you to **leverage** your marketing activity to greatest effect.

Having identified the decision-making unit, what factors and processes will they be using to make decisions about how to respond to your organisation and its plans? We will look at four main factors identified in the syllabus:

- Motivation and involvement
- Perceived risk
- Perceptions and attitudes
- Group influence and opinion leadership.

1.2 Motivation and involvement

1.2.1 Motivation

> **Key term**
>
> **Motivation** may be defined as an inner state that energises, activates or moves; that directs or channels behaviour towards goals.

There are various complex theories of what motivation is and how it works. 'Need' theories are perhaps most immediately helpful: they propose that human beings have certain needs and will choose to behave in ways that satisfy those needs. Motivation can be thought of as the **recognition of a need**, followed by **action to satisfy it**.

People may have a range of needs at any given time. Abraham Maslow (1954), in his influential 'hierarchy of needs' theory, classified and arranged basic human needs in order of importance or urgency as follows.

- **Physiological needs**: for food, water, sleep
- **Safety/security needs**: for shelter, safety, security, reduced risk
- **Social needs**: for belonging, relationships, identification with others
- **Esteem needs**: for self-esteem, status, recognition, the regard of others
- **Self-actualisation needs**: for growth, fulfilment, realisation of one's potential.

Once each level of need is satisfied, people will focus on satisfying the next level of need. A value proposition or marketing mix may motivate a stakeholder group to enter into a relationship or exchange with the organisation, if it offers a benefit or outcome which appears to satisfy the stakeholder's highest-priority needs at the time.

'We prioritise the effort we make towards satisfying our needs, generally giving more time and effort to those needs that have **higher costs and benefits** and that are more **important, interesting and relevant** to us.' (Varey, 2002, p50). This is the justification for tailoring the marketing mix to the needs and concerns of stakeholders: making the value proposition more important, interesting and relevant to them, in order to motivate them to act in the way the organisation wants.

1.2.2 Involvement

The more an issue, offer or decision touches our core motivations, the greater our involvement with it. Involvement reflects the importance and relevance of the benefits and costs we expect to result from a given decision or action. It may be defined as the degree of **perceived relevance and importance** of a brand choice or other decision. Egan (2004, p98) uses the alternative term **'salience'** to describe the level of importance or prominence that an exchange or relationship may have for a stakeholder. Whichever term is used, the importance and relevance of an issue or situation will impact on decision makers' behaviour.

'We judge things in terms of importance and relevance to us in a given situation or context. Involvement is a judgement relating to a feeling of risk of negative outcome, social sanction and ego. For example, will buying

that jacket be a mistake (poor value for money, say), will it make me look out of place in my social group, and does it seem right for my own sense of my image (self-image)? Involvement is an important concept for marketing... because it relates to the likelihood that a person [or stakeholder group] will pay attention to a [marketing] activity.' (Varey, op cit, p50).

- **Low-involvement decisions** (such as the purchase of a grocery item, or a fact-finding meeting between a stakeholder group and a marketing organisation) bear little risk and low cost. Comparatively little information-gathering, analysis or evaluation will be required to make the decision: simple choice tactics are used to reduce time and effort, rather than attempting to maximise outcomes. (In other words, parties don't 'sweat the small stuff'!) All that is required is awareness and sufficient interest to 'give it a try': if the experience is satisfactory, this may lead to repeat purchase or further contacts.

- **High-involvement decisions** (such as the purchase of a house or car, or entering into a strategic alliance with another organisation) mean high cost, high risk, long-term commitment and complex and uncertain factors – in return for significant, long-term potential benefits. A high degree of information-gathering, analysis and evaluation will be required: cost/benefit analysis, weighing up of alternative options, research into the other party, negotiation of terms and so on.

Ford *et al* (2003, p72) note that business relationships can also be low-involvement or high-involvement, in a different sense: the greater the actor bonds, activity links and resource ties between two parties (see Chapter 3 if these terms don't ring a bell), the more closely they are involved in a relationship. However, it is worth noting that entering into a high-involvement *relationship* is also a high-involvement *decision*! It offers high long-term benefits, but requires considerable investment of resources and time, and a significant element of risk.

ACTIVITY 7.1

What can you see as the implications of a high-involvement decision situation for marketers? How might marketing activity be tailored to support the customer, or other stakeholder, in making the decision?

1.3 Perceived risk

Process theories of motivation suggest that people are motivated to act in a given way, depending on a calculation of whether it is **worthwhile** for them to do so. The same is true of any decision. Decision makers calculate:

(a)   The **benefits or value** that are expected to accrue from the decision, how *likely* they are to accrue and how *important* they are to the decision maker

weighed against

(b)   The **costs, sacrifices or downsides** that may have to be endured to secure the benefits.

We saw in Chapter 5 that this calculation is important in the way stakeholders perceive **value**: potential benefits weighed against cost/sacrifices in obtaining them. It is also a measure of **perceived risk**: what is the likelihood that a decision will lead to a net gain or loss for the stakeholder?

Risk may be defined as the **perceived probability of loss**. Note the word 'perceived': risk is highly subjective, depending on the perceptions of the decision maker. Some stakeholders may be more 'risk-averse' than others: that is, they may have a low tolerance for risk and uncertainty, and be less willing to take risks that others may perceived as moderate.

Much relationship marketing literature suggests that the greater the perceived risk of a purchase or action, the greater the likelihood that stakeholders will seek to engage in relationship-type behaviour.

'One reason why so-called high-risk purchases [or other types of transactions] may benefit from Relationship Marketing strategies is that a relationship, over time, is likely (but not certain) to **lower the**

perceived risk as the consumer [or other stakeholder] learns more about the terms and security of the arrangement and, more generally, gets to know the supplier. Relationship marketing may also be well suited in cases where the unforeseen future is continuously defined and redefined by those involved in the relationship... The existence of risk, therefore, creates an opportunity for trust that would not be needed if actions could be taken with certainty and no risk.' (Egan, 2004, p99).

In situations characterised by high risk, stakeholders may enter into contact with the organisation seeking specific reassurance, a measure of control and/or the possibility of adjustment over time: such situations may require the development of trust and frequent communication, associated with relationship marketing. In low-risk situations, there is little motivation for the stakeholder to seek a trust-based relationship – and little need for the organisation to devote time and resources to anything more than basic reassurances (eg as to product safety or intention to comply with agreed terms).

A tailored and co-ordinated stakeholder marketing mix should, however:

- Make it possible for stakeholders to **carry out cost/benefit (or cost/value) analysis** eg by clearly conveying information about the value proposition and 'price' or costs involved in the exchange. The higher the perceived risk (importance and likelihood of loss), the more information – and the more reassuring messages – may have to be given.

- Ensure that the **benefit/value outweighs the cost**. Benefits should be not just emphasised in marketing messages, but genuinely built into the value proposition. Measures should be incorporated to reduce risk where possible (eg warranties on purchases, pre-planned dispute-resolution mechanisms, trial projects, opportunities for review and so on).

1.4 Perceptions and attitudes

1.4.1 Perception

Perception may be defined as the process by which people select, organise and interpret data into meaningful and coherent pictures. Individuals don't relate to the world 'as it really is' – but to the 'picture' they have of it. **External stimuli** from the environment (what we see, hear, taste, smell and touch) are one type of input to the perceptual process: there are also **internal inputs** in the form of our motives, interests, expectations (based on past experience) and beliefs. We filter out data that is irrelevant or unpleasant, and focus on data that matches our needs, interests and expectations: to an extent, we really do 'see what we want to see' and 'hear what we expect to hear'.

This is important for marketers to realise, because decision factors such as risk, trust, value and salience (relevance, importance) are largely subjective: they depend on the perceptions of the stakeholder – which may be quite different to those of the marketer. In trying to tailor the marketing mix to the needs of stakeholders, marketers need to recognise that they first have to 'get inside the heads' of stakeholders and see the value proposition from *their* point of view.

1.4.2 Attitudes

> ▶ **Key term**
>
> **Attitudes** are an enduring mixture of evaluations, feelings and tendencies which pre-dispose an individual or group to respond in a certain way to a given object or idea.

Varey (2002) defines attitude as 'a learned tendency to respond to something in a consistently positive or negative manner... Attitude is an evaluation: what we feel about a concept (brand, category, person, ideology and so on)' p54.

Attitudes lead us to behave in a fairly consistent way towards people, situations and ideas. They are a kind of 'short-cut' in decision making, because we do not interpret and evaluate things each time we encounter them; we already have a 'standpoint' (positive or negative) towards them.

Consumers may have formed attitudes towards organisations, products, brands and media. Brand messages may match or conflict with their attitudes towards consumption, the environment, globalisation, ethics and so on. Similarly, other stakeholder groups are likely to have strong attitudes towards issues in their area of interest, and perhaps towards the organisation (if it is perceived to be a positive or negative influence on those interests). It is therefore important for marketers to understand what attitudes may be supporting or undermining the value proposition, and to address them through the marketing mix.

Attitudes can be inferred from behaviour: for example, positive or negative **consumer** attitudes can be inferred from sales, and positive or negative **employee** attitudes from factors such as absenteeism, labour turnover, disputes and productivity.

Attitudes can also be **measured** using attitude surveys, which often use scaled questions such as: 'How would you rate the importance of x on a scale from 1 to 10?' or 'How would you rate x on the scale: poor, fair, good, very good, excellent?' More qualitative information about stakeholder attitudes may be gathered from talking to them, studying their statements about themselves (eg mission statements, reports, website), perhaps interviewing representative individuals, or seeking feedback.

Attitudes are stable and difficult to change, so the marketing mix should generally be tailored to **appeal to stakeholders' existing attitudes** if possible. It may be necessary to **change attitudes**, however: this is the objective of many pressure groups, but it also applies to government (eg changing public attitudes to smoking and alcohol) and commercial marketing (turning round poor employee relations, instilling quality focus in suppliers, or overcoming consumer resistance to innovative products or internet sales, say). Where necessary, attitudes can be shifted by:

- **Powerful contrary information**, especially from a **respected or influential source**. If stakeholders' attitudes don't 'fit' the evidence or the source, it is less mentally uncomfortable for them to change the *attitude* than it would be to deny the evidence or revise their opinion of the source. (Technically speaking, this mental discomfort is called 'cognitive dissonance'. We feel it when our beliefs, expectations, attitudes, actions or experiences don't fit well with each other. We then tend to change something in order to make a 'better fit' – and reduce the discomfort or tension.)

- **Changing behaviour**: for example, getting consumers to trial products they think they dislike, or to explain their benefits as part of a promotional competition – or asking resistant employees to act as coaches or champions of a plan. There is less cognitive dissonance in changing their attitudes to match their behaviour than there would be in admitting that their behaviour is inconsistent with their attitudes.

1.5 Group influence and opinion leadership

The immediate social environment in which decision makers operate has an important influence on behaviour, because of the basic human needs for belonging and esteem. The family, work groups and friendship groups are important influence on personal decision making, because they establish shared norms of thinking and behaviour – and apply powerful incentives (continued belonging and acceptance) to fall in with those norms. Pressure and interest groups may also influence decisions, through membership of, or advocacy by, the group.

Reference groups is the term given to groups 'with which an individual identifies so much that he or she takes on many of the values, attitudes or behaviours of group members' (Dibb & SimKin, 1996). These include:

- **Primary membership groups:** generally informal groups, to which individuals belong and within which they interact (family, friends, work groups, neighbours, and even virtual communities such as internet chat rooms, Facebook, Myspace, fan sites or eBay)

- **Secondary membership groups:** generally more formal, allowing less involvement and interaction (trade unions, professional bodies)

- **Aspirational groups**, to which an individual would like to belong. (This is an important factor in 'aspirational' buyer or relationship behaviour: people buying products or allying themselves with organisations to create an image of status, lifestyle or values leadership, above what they currently enjoy. It also accounts for many fashions, through which people seek to identify with celebrity or 'in' groups.)

The task of marketers is to **identify the reference groups** of a given target audience and:

- Offer **value propositions** (and associated images and messages) that help them to identify with the group

- Use **images and values** associated with, or approved by, the group to arouse interest and engagement

- Use **members of aspirational groups** (such as celebrities, successful business figures) to endorse products or services.

Part of the power of group influence is that people tend to evaluate whether others, particularly those whose opinion is important to them, would approve or disapprove of a given decision. (By acting in ways our influencers will agree with, we avoid the cognitive dissonance of admiring them but going against their opinions.)

Opinion leaders are 'people within a reference group who, because of special skills, knowledge, personality traits or other characteristics, exert influence on others' in regard to a particular product or decision area. (Kotler *et al*, *op cit*, p98). Some people are active in receiving data, interpreting it and communicating about their judgements with others – and these people are a good target for marketing messages, because they act as a hub for communication with others who look to them for leadership. In other words, they are a good source of entry and leverage for marketing messages.

Opinion leadership can also be created by the marketing organisation: for example, by using product testimonial advertising, or getting recommendations, referrals and endorsements from pressure groups and other respected authorities on a given issue.

ACTIVITY 7.2

If you are using this text, CIM – or the marketing profession – is probably one of your 'aspirational' groups. What other groups do you aspire to belong to or be like?

Who are the 'opinion leaders' in your network? How does this affect the kinds of products/services you buy – and the kind of marketing messages you respond to?

1.6 Understanding buyer behaviour

Dibb *et al* (*op cit*) suggest that the study of buying behaviour is particularly important for a number of reasons.

- The buyer's reaction to the organisation's marketing strategy has a major impact on the **survival and success** of the organisation.

- If organisations are truly to implement the marketing concept, they must examine the main influences on what, where, when and how customers buy. Only in this way will they be able to devise a **marketing mix** that satisfies customer needs.

- By gaining a better understanding of the factors influencing their customers and how customers will respond, organisations will be better able to plan effective **marketing communications and activities**.

The variables in buying behaviour are wide-ranging and complex. However, they can be broadly categorised as:

- **Stakeholders and participants** in the buying decision

- The **decision-making processes** by which information is used to solve problems, make choices and reach the decision to purchase

- Various **factors and characteristics** which influence buyers' perceptions, judgements, choices and decisions.

We will look at each of these, starting with **consumer** (or personal) buying behaviour, and then looking at **organisational** (industrial) buying behaviour.

---

2 Personal buying behaviour

> **▶ Key term**
>
> **Consumer buyer behaviour** refers to the buying behaviour of final consumers, those individuals and households who buy goods and services for personal consumption. (Kotler *et al*, 1999)

2.1 The consumer decision-making unit (DMU)

Purchase decisions, as we saw earlier, often involve more than one person. This is usually the case in organisations, where specialist purchasing or other decision-making teams ensure that a range of different factors and stakeholder interests are taken into account. However, even consumer purchase decisions (which brand of toothpaste will you buy? Should you get a DVD player?) may involve input from a number of stakeholders who have an influence or interest in the purchase. The **Decision-Making Unit** (DMU) is the group of people who participate in or influence the purchase decision at any stage in the buying process.

There are a number of different models of the DMU, but most identify the following roles.

Table 7.1   DMU roles

Gatekeeper	Accesses and controls the flow of information about the product or service to the others
Initiator	First draws attention to a particular product, or suggests the idea of buying it. May be influenced by a **trigger** – an identifiable event or item of information which highlights the need for the purchase
Influencer	Stimulates, informs or persuades at any stage of the buying process. Examples include children who urge their parents to buy, friends who recommend the product – or the 'expert' in a TV advertisement
Decider	Makes the decision that the product should be bought
Buyer	Implements the purchase decision by ordering or purchasing the product/service
Financer	Sets the budget and authorises or provides the funds for the purchase
User	Uses, consumes or benefits from the product or service

An individual may exercise one or more of these roles in a given purchase process: the decider/buyer/financier/user, for example, may be the same person. However, an example may help to clarify the various roles. A father browses the 'food' section of the newspaper (gatekeeper) and comments that there is a new brand of cereal on the market (initiator). The mother approves of its nutritional content and the younger child begs for the promotional toy that comes with it (influencers). The mother (in charge of grocery buying in this traditional household!) decides to try the cereal (decider), determines that it is within the weekly grocery budget (financer) and purchases the cereal at the supermarket (buyer). The children enjoy the cereal (users).

The people who make up a consumer DMU will vary according to the context in which the purchase decision is made and the stakeholders who will be affected by and involved in the decision. Consumers may be influenced by a number of different groups and networks: family, work groups, friends and other social and interest groups. Marketers may position products or services to appeal to these various stakeholders: appealing to family values; projecting status and professionalism (to fit in with the work group); depicting products being enjoyed by (or attracting) friends; or addressing pressure group values and concerns, say.

ACTIVITY 7.3

Produce a flow chart representing the stages in any major purchase you have recently been involved in at work or at home. Identify all those who were involved in the purchase, their DMU roles and how each step in the purchase decision was made. (In our answer, we chart a family's decision to purchase a holiday for their parents to celebrate a wedding anniversary.)

2.1.1 The DMU as a target audience

Although the buyer may appear to be the 'customer' at the point of sale, the entire decision-making unit can be identified as the target audience for the marketing mix.

The marketing organisation needs to understand the complexity of the DMU in each market and market segment in which it operates. It is clearly relevant to marketers whether, for example, the woman or man in a household is the primary buyer/decision maker; whether a young or older person is the user; and which gender or age group consumes which advertising media. This kind of information determines the product's positioning, media choices and target audience.

The communication mix should **leverage** stakeholder influence on the purchase decision: reaching and persuading the most influential role in a given purchase with the least expenditure of effort and cost. The decider may be an obvious target, but for price-sensitive decisions, for example, it may be important to target the financer; if deciders are difficult to reach, it may be important to target gatekeepers; and for shared or complex decisions, it may be more cost-effective to target influencers (co-opting them to share the work of promotion).

- Identify **gatekeepers** (who is mostly likely to be open to, or in charge of acquiring, product information?) and the most effective information **media** to reach them (where do they prefer to gather product information and in what format?)

- Identify **indicators/initiators** (who is most likely to notice and draw attention to product information?) and target them with messages that arouse **interest** (how is the product relevant to the needs, wants or interests of the DMU?)

- Identify **influencers** (whom will the decider consult or listen to?) and target them with persuasive information to arouse or reinforce **desire** (how does the product solve a problem or meet a need? How can it be endorsed or validated?)

- Identify **deciders** (who will have the final say?) and target them with information to arouse or reinforce **intention** (what are the decisive benefits of the product for meeting needs and wants? How can the perceived risks of the decision be lowered – and the benefits of acting quickly be conveyed?)

- Identify **buyers** (who actually makes the purchase?) and target them with messages which facilitate **action** (what does the buyer need to do next? How can it be made easy?)

- Identify **financers** (who pays or authorises payment?) and target them with information to help them to **justify** expenditure (what benefits can be weighed against the costs?) and to complete the transaction (how can payment be made easy?)

- Identify **users** (who uses, consumes or benefits?) and target them with practical information to enable them to **use** the product safely and satisfyingly (what are possible areas of ignorance or difficulty? What on-going support may be required?)

As we will see in section 4, the marketing organisation will also seek appropriate forms of **feedback** to fine-tune its marketing mix in satisfying the needs of the DMU. (Is product packaging effectively attracting the attention of initiators? Are promotional messages effectively persuading influencers and deciders? Is customer service effectively satisfying users?)

ACTIVITY 7.4

How might you target your communications in the ways suggested above if you were marketing a new model of family car?

THE REAL WORLD

There are many different models of the psychological process customers go through to reach a buying decision. The 'buyer readiness' model suggests that consumers progress through six stages:

- **Awareness**: the consumer knows the product exists
- **Knowledge**: the consumer knows something about the product
- **Liking**: the consumer has favourable feelings about the product
- **Preference**: the consumer favours the product over competing alternatives
- **Conviction**: the consumer believes that the product is the best one for his/her needs
- **Purchase**: the consumer decides to purchase the product.

When **Subaru** introduced its four-wheel-drive Forester model in Australasia, it began with an extensive public relations campaign. Motoring journalists were encouraged to write newspaper and magazine articles, to create name familiarity and knowledge of its design and purpose [*awareness*]. Later advertisements showed the car mud-splattered at the back, fresh from the action – but polished at the front ready for the city [*knowledge*].

Subaru's marketers used a combination of the promotion mix tools to create successively stronger positive feelings about the model [*liking, preference, conviction*]. Advertising extolled its advantages and uniqueness. Press releases, test drives and other public relations activities stressed the car's innovative features, versatility and performance. Dealer salespeople told buyers about options, durability, value for price and after sales service.

Special promotional prices, special showings (by personal invitation from dealers) and other incentives might be used to motivate convinced buyers to take the final step of *purchase.*

(Kotler *et al* 1999)

2.2 The decision-making process (DMP)

A number of complex or 'comprehensive' models have been developed in the attempt to describe or explain the dynamics of consumer behaviour. At its simplest level, however, decision making can be seen as a linear process with a number of steps. Not every decision will involve an orderly progression through all the steps, but such a model provides a useful framework for considering systematic decision-making activities by consumers – and how marketing can be used to influence them.

The decision-making process (DMP) for consumers may be illustrated as follows: Figure 7.1. (We have added the DMU roles to suggest how the process may be shared by different stakeholders.)

Figure 7.1   The consumer decision-making process

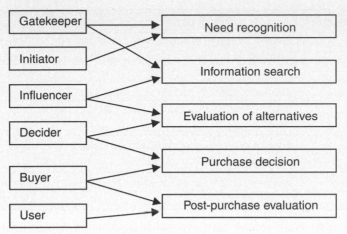

Before reading on, think about a recent purchase of a fairly major item that you have made. Did you go through the stages listed above? Explain what the need was, how you searched for information and so on.

2.2.1 Need recognition

The process begins when the consumer recognises a need or problem: the difference between a **desired state** and the **actual state** (s)he is experiencing. This sense of need can be triggered by **internal** stimuli – such as thirst or a desire for status – or **external** stimuli such as the smell of coffee brewing or a TV ad showing someone being admired and respected (for having chosen an up-market brand, say).

The marketer's task will be to identify (through consumer research):

- What kinds of **needs and problems** the target audience experiences (in order to develop a marketing mix that offers satisfaction or solutions)

- What stimuli **trigger the target audience's awareness** of the need or problem (in order to stimulate the sense of need, through marketing messages).

2.2.2 Information search

Once aroused, consumers may have accustomed ways of satisfying the need (products that have worked for them in the past) or the need may be so strong that they simply buy the nearest satisfying product at hand. If the need is not immediate, or the 'best' product not obvious, the consumer may:

- Develop **heightened attention**: become more receptive to information about the product category that might satisfy the need, from advertising, conversations or point of sale displays.

- Actively **search for information**. If additional information is relatively easy or satisfying to locate, and the consumer believes that it will materially improve the quality of the decision, this may be an extensive process. (Think about how you research a foreign holiday destination, say, or the purchase of a car.)

The marketer's task will be to determine which information sources will be most consulted and most influential: for example, by researching consumer information-seeking behaviour and asking where existing customers 'first heard about the product'. Kotler *et al* (1999) identify four major sources of product information:

Table 7.2   Sources of product information

Source	Description	Supporting marketing activity
Personal	Family, friends, neighbours, work colleagues, networks	Product samples/trials, customer satisfaction, creating 'virtual communities' of users, referrals management
Commercial	Advertising, selling, packaging, point of sale display, direct marketing, sales promotions, websites	By definition, all marketing activities
Public	Mass media, consumer rating and watchdog organisations	Positive public and media relations
Experiential	Handling, examining and using the product	Product demonstrations, samples and trial promotions

Consumers generally receive most information from commercial sources (initiated by the marketer) which inform them about the product. However, personal sources have been shown to be more effective – particularly in service markets – because they also endorse the product, pre-evaluating it for the potential buyer. Some of this effect can be harnessed by the use of expert, celebrity or distributor recommendations, but it is also a strong argument for relationship marketing: moving customers up the ladder of loyalty to become advocates for the product within their networks.

2.2.3 Evaluation of alternatives

There is no universal model of how consumers process information to arrive at the choice of a particular brand. It may involve the rational calculation and weighing up of benefits and costs; comparisons of competing brands; recommendation by friends, sales people or consumer guides; and so on. In other cases, it may involve purchase on impulse, instinct or emotion, with little or no logical evaluation. The task of the marketer is thus to find out *how* buyers evaluate brand alternatives, so that they can support the process appropriately.

Kotler suggests that, as the consumer is trying to satisfy some need with the buying process, (s)he will be looking for certain **benefits** from the product and/or the relationship with the supplier: each purchase will be seen as a 'bundle of attributes' which deliver value. The task of the marketer is thus to determine what attributes, benefits or value consumers want from a product (and/or relationship with the supplying organisation); the relative importance they attach to each benefit; and the extent to which they believe a given brand will deliver the most valued benefits. The marketing mix can then be targeted at **creating and promoting the most effective value proposition**.

ACTIVITY 7.6

What do you think are the key elements of value sought by the target audience in the following consumer markets?

- Domestic white goods (refrigerators, washing machines)
- Pharmaceuticals
- Education
- Snack foods
- Cars
- Financial services.

If convenient, you may like to discuss this question with fellow students, friends or family: an informal 'market research' exercise into consumer needs and perceptions.

The Chartered Institute of Marketing

2.2.4 Purchase decision

As a result of evaluation, the consumer forms the **intention to purchase** the brand which most readily promises to satisfy the need. The task of the marketer is primarily to ensure that the purchase decision is easy to put into effect, through availability, stockist information, prominent point of sale display, effective customer service and so on.

2.2.5 Post-purchase evaluation

Having purchased the product, the consumer will either be satisfied or dissatisfied/ disappointed with the value received, depending on how the experience matches up to his or her expectations. The task of the marketer will be:

■ To **manage consumer expectations**, by making accurate and realistic claims for the product or service

■ To **manage consumer experience** of the purchase, product and contact with the supplier, to ensure satisfaction – or, if possible, delight (experience *exceeding* expectation) through offering added value

■ To **manage the post-purchase relationship**. This may involve dealing with dissatisfied customers, to minimise damage: for example, by accepting the return of products that do not give full satisfaction; swift acknowledgement and adjustment of complaints; encouraging feedback and responding constructively. It may also involve proactive follow-up of satisfied customers, to further the relationship, as discussed in Chapter 4.

2.3 Key influences on consumer buying behaviour

The basic process of decision making described above will be influenced by a wide range of internal and external variables, which may be broadly classified as follows: Figure 7.2. Some of these factors were discussed earlier.

Figure 7.2   Influences on consumer behaviour

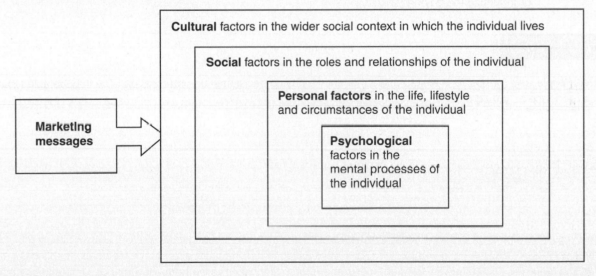

3 Organisational buying behaviour

▶ **Key term**

Organisational buying behaviour refers to the buying behaviour of organisations which buy goods and services to use in the production of other products and services that are sold, rented or supplied to others.

3.1 The organisational decision-making unit

The DMU of a buying organisation is often called its **buying centre**. This is not to be confused with a purchasing or procurement function or team: it is a set of buying roles exercised by different individuals and units that participate in the decision-making process. As Kotler *et al* (1999) note, 'the buying centre concept presents a major marketing challenge. The business marketer must learn who participates in the decision, each participant's relative influence and what evaluation criteria each decision participant uses.'

The buying centre will involve those formally involved in purchase decisions, such as department managers, purchasing managers and accountants. It may also involve less obvious, informal participants who may initiate or influence the buying process.

ACTIVITY 7.7

List five people who (or positions which) might influence a buying decision in an organisation. You may be able to use your own work experience as a guide.

THE REAL WORLD

Post-it Notes

'Surprisingly, Post-it Notes failed in concept, prototype and launch testing. In a last ditch effort, 3M sent the product to the secretaries/PAs of CEOs in large companies. They were asked to use the product and give feedback. In this case, the *connectors* were the secretaries/PAs and the consumer-brand connection came from allowing consumers to use the product. Now just count the number of Post-it Notes on your desk today!'

(Rob Smithson, 2005)

As in consumer marketing, it is helpful to consider the information needs of different roles (and individuals, if known, within a corporate buying centre).

- **Users** may be targeted with information on the technical characteristics, reliability, performance and service contracts pertaining to a product, since this will be relevant to their desired outcomes – and they may have influence in this area.

The Chartered Institute of Marketing

- **Influencers** may have technical expertise, or may be concerned with rational criteria such as cost/benefit analysis and competitor comparison. Influencers are a particularly useful contact where the purchase relies on technical knowledge: the sales person can become a respected technical adviser. Trade journals, professional bodies and consultants are also used as a source of influential information, so trade/public/media relations will be an important component of the promotional mix.

- **Deciders/buyers/financers** are likely to be powerful individuals or teams: the marketer may need to take into account a variety of personal, organisational and task objectives. Buying centres may be politically complex: there may, for example, be conflict between the interests of users, influencers/deciders and financers. Marketers may need to facilitate decision making in such situations, offering a cost/benefit analysis that will satisfy all parties.

- Even junior personnel may be **gatekeepers** for marketing information: a lesson to the marketer to use his or her relationship-building, public relations and persuasive skills at *every* contact with the customer.

3.2 The organisational buying process

A similar process to the consumer DMP will apply in organisational buying, but steps may be added to reflect the **formal requirements** of buying policies and criteria, and the greater **involvement** (risk and importance) of large-scale purchase contracts and supply relationships. A systematic business buying process can be shown as follows: Figure 7.3.

Figure 7.3   The organisational buying process

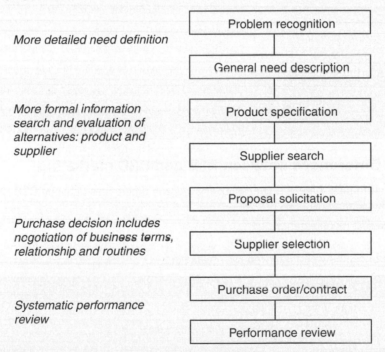

Whether the organisation will go through all these stages in a given case will depend on the nature of the **buying situation**.

- Some purchases will be a **straight re-buy** or the routine topping up of stocks without changing supplier or product specifications: for example, the re-ordering of stationery supplies. (This may be done on an automatic re-ordering system by the purchasing department, or even by the supplier, requiring only post-purchase review to ensure satisfaction.)

- Some purchases will be a **modified re-buy**: the organisation wants to change product specifications, prices, terms or suppliers (which should stimulate competitive offerings from existing and alternative suppliers). Any or all stages of the buying decision may be revisited.

- Some purchases will be a **new task** situation: the organisation is buying a product or service for the first time. In such circumstances, an extensive and systematic decision-making process may take place. This

is an opportunity to reach key members of the buying centre and to offer support and information in making the decision.

3.3 Influences on organisational buyers

Webster and Wind (1972) identify four main groups of influences on business buyers.

Table 7.3   Four groups of influences on business buyers

Environmental factors	▪ Health and prospects of the economy and market sector in which the business operates (affecting ability to invest) ▪ Scarcity of materials (affecting importance of secure supply) ▪ Cultural factors (eg business ethics and customs) ▪ Legal/political influences (eg obligation to seek tenders) ▪ Technological factors (eg use of e-procurement, e-auctions)
Organisational factors	▪ Objectives of the organisation (requiring cost efficiency, long-term supply continuity, risk management, quality) ▪ Policies, procedures and systems (buying policies, quality assurance, authorisation requirements) ▪ Structure (purchasing responsibilities, communication and decision-making channels, cross-functional procurement teams or projects)
Interpersonal factors	▪ Nature and distribution of influence within the buying centre (based on authority, status, expertise, control over resources. Who 'really' makes the decision?) ▪ Flow of information into and within the buying centre (who are the gatekeepers?) ▪ Interpersonal skills of buyers (negotiating, persuading, conflict resolution, networking)
Personal factors	▪ Personal needs, preferences and perceptions of the buyer (authority, expertise, values, professionalism, attitudes to risk and cost, and so on)

3.4 Differences between B2B and B2C marketing

To summarise, here is a chart showing a dozen differences between B2B (business-to-business) and B2C (business-to-consumer) marketing, drawn from Powers (1991). Note especially the different emphases in the marketing mix elements.

Table 7.4   Differences between B2B and B2C marketing

Area	B2B marketing	B2C marketing
Purchase motivation	Multiple buying influences and stakeholders Support company operations	Individual or family need
Emphasis of seller	Long-term economic needs	Immediate satisfaction
Customer needs	Each customer has different needs for complex total offering	Groups of customers (market segments) have similar needs
Nature of buyer	Group decisions	Purchase by individual or family unit
Time effects	Long-term relationships	Often, short-term relationships
Product details	Technically sophisticated	Lower technical content
Promotional decisions	Emphasis on personal selling	Emphasis on mass media advertising, sales promotion
Price decisions	Price negotiated Terms are also important	Prices are substantially fixed Discounts are also important

Area	B2B marketing	B2C marketing
Place decisions	Limited number of large buyers: short channels	Large number of small buyers: complex channels
Customer service	Critical to success	Arguably, less important in some markets
Legal factors	Contractual arrangements	Contracts only on major purchases
Environmental factors	Affect sales both directly and indirectly	Affect demand directly

4 Formulating stakeholder marketing plans

4.1 Marketing planning and control

Planning is the process of deciding what should be done. **Control** is the process of checking whether it has been done, and if not, doing something about it. The combined process of planning and control are known as a **control cycle**: Figure 7.4.

Figure 7.4   A basic control cycle

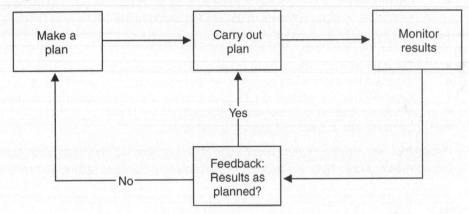

4.2 Objective setting

The first step in planning is to set objectives, so that you know what you are aiming to achieve. Effective objectives are often described using the acronym 'SMART'. We prefer to think of them as SMARTER, in the context of stakeholder marketing.

- **S** pecific
- **M** easurable (using clearly defined criteria)
- **A** ttainable (or realistic, given the resources available)
- **R** elevant (to the company's aims and strategies)
- **T** ime-bounded (with clear deadlines for completion)
- **E** valuated (to ensure that benefits outweigh costs)
- **R** esponsible (or Relational: taking stakeholder needs into account)

Examples of marketing objectives may include: 'Increase sales volume by 5% in the year 201X – 201Y', say, or 'Achieve and maintain for five years a 25% share of the domestic market for product x'. There may also be objectives for customer retention or conversion of first-time customers to repeat customers, and (less easily quantified) for stakeholder satisfaction.

Suggest some general objectives or 'Key Performance Indicators' (KPIs) for relationship marketing activity. (Don't worry about the detailed SMARTER elements: just suggest what you think RM should be aiming for, and how it might measure its success.)

4.3 Budgets

In practice, overall marketing budgets are often already set, or set based on last year's budget, or set as a percentage of projected turnover for the year. So if you are planning or proposing a marketing activity or marketing mix, you need to be aware that there will probably be resource constraints! There are often budgets for:

- **Regular or core marketing spend**, which maintains the marketing/selling cycle: catalogues, sales force support, agency retainers, public relations and so on

- Spend on individual products and services, for launch and maintenance marketing

- **Contingencies**. If you are lucky, there may be an amount to be used at the marketing department's discretion, to cover any new or unforeseen opportunities (or threats) that crop up during the year.

The main **budgetary control tasks** can be summarised as follows.

- Estimate all the costs involved in the proposed event/activity
- Compare the estimated total cost with anticipated returns, benefits and objectives
- Establish that the estimated total cost is within the department's expenditure budget
- Monitor actual expenditure against the budget
- Compare actual total cost against actual returns.

Budgeting is considered in more detail, in relation to marketing communication activity, in Chapter 11, but this brief overview should help you to put it in the context of objective setting and control.

> **Assessment tip**
>
> The financial aspects of marketing are not a major part of this syllabus, but you should nevertheless remember to take into account the **cost/budget implications** of any marketing plan you put forward in your assignment. Your proposals are supposed to be realistic in the context of your chosen organisation – and this means 'affordable', given the resources available. This is likely to be a major challenge for micro-enterprises, small-medium-enterprises (SMEs) and charities, for example, and you will be expected to appreciate the resource constraints to their marketing activity, if they are the kind of organisation you select for your assignment.

4.4 The marketing plan

You may be asked to prepare a basic marketing plan at a tactical level, as part of your assignment. There is no set format for such a plan, but you might use the following general outline.

Table 7.5   Example marketing plan

MARKETING PLAN	
1 **Executive summary**	A short summary of the major points of the plan to orient the reader, if the plan is a lengthy report
2 **Marketing objectives**	▪ What the marketing plan is intended to achieve (SMART objectives if possible) ▪ Marketing strategies within which the plan has been developed

The Chartered Institute of Marketing

MARKETING PLAN		
3	Stakeholder background	▪ Identification of the stakeholder group targeted by the plan ▪ Identification of the stakeholder's importance to the organisation (eg using the Mendelow matrix) ▪ Summary of key needs, concerns, expectations, interests and drivers of the stakeholder group
4	Marketing mix	Action plans for each of the elements of the (extended) marketing mix, to achieve stated objectives. ▪ Product action plan ▪ Pricing action plan ▪ Distribution action plan ▪ Promotion/communications action plan ▪ Service action plan
5	Timetable	Realistic timescales for implementation of plans
6	Monitoring and control	How progress and results will be monitored, reviewed and measured against objectives (see section 5 of the chapter)
7	Summary/conclusion	If required. There may also be an appendix (or appendices) with supporting documents and data which are too detailed to include in the body of the plan (for example, your detailed stakeholder audit).

> ▶ **Assessment tip**
>
> As one of the tasks in an Assignment Brief you may be asked, for example, to recommend how the marketing mix could be developed to be more responsive to the needs of certain stakeholders.
>
> This would not necessarily involve producing a complete marketing plan as described above. However, by including objectives for your proposals, identifying the target audience(s) you are trying to reach and showing that you have considered the resources necessary to implement your proposals you will demonstrate to the examiner that you understand the need to justify your proposals rather than simply presenting a list of suggestions.

4.5 The relationship marketing plan

A slightly different structure and approach may be used if you are asked to come up with a broad relationship marketing plan for the full range of organisational stakeholders. Again, the following is just one possible outline.

Table 7.6   Example relationship marketing plan

RELATIONSHIP MARKETING PLAN		
1	Marketing objectives	▪ Relationship marketing and/or other marketing objectives which the plan is designed to pursue
2	Stakeholder background	▪ Identification of key stakeholder groups targeted by the plan ▪ Identification of stakeholders' importance to the organisation (eg using the Mendelow matrix)
3	Customer relationship plan	▪ SMART objectives for customer marketing ▪ Summary of key needs, concerns, expectations, interests and drivers of customers ▪ Marketing mix plans to add customer value and build relationship
4	Supplier relationship plan	▪ SMART objectives for supplier marketing ▪ Summary of key needs, concerns, expectations, interests and drivers of suppliers ▪ Marketing mix plans to exchange value and build relationship

RELATIONSHIP MARKETING PLAN		
5	**Shareholder relationship plan**	▪ As above but specific to shareholders
6	**Internal marketing plan**	▪ As above but specific to internal stakeholders
7	**External stakeholder relationship plan**	▪ As above but specific to external stakeholders
8	**Timetable**	Realistic timescales for implementation of plans
9	**Monitoring and control**	How progress and results will be monitored, reviewed and measured against objectives
10	**Summary/ conclusion**	If required. There may also be an appendix (or appendices) with supporting documents and data.

ACTIVITY 7.9

You may already have gathered sufficient data, from previous activities, to begin experimenting with one or both of these marketing plan templates.

Start with the single stakeholder plan. Select any one stakeholder of your organisation, tackle each section of the outline plan – and see how far you get.

5 Measuring and evaluating the mix

You should already have learned about the measurement of marketing activities for Unit 1: *Marketing Essentials.* However, measuring the success of a co-ordinated marketing mix aimed at **multiple stakeholders** may require a slightly broader range of methods: you need to get feedback not just from customers, but the wider stakeholder audience as well.

5.1 Criteria for success

How do you know if the marketing mix, or a particular marketing activity, is a success? First, it should be evaluated according to whether it meets the specific **objectives** set for it: increased sales, increased stakeholder or customer awareness and recognition of the brand, customer retention (or cross-selling or up-selling), increased supplier reliability, less bad publicity (or increased generation of positive word-of-mouth) – or whatever the stated objectives of the plan are.

- If stakeholder marketing objectives are expressed in terms of sales or market share, performance measurement would focus on the **sales or market-share effects** of marketing activity.

- If stakeholder marketing objectives are expressed in terms of communication and relationship, performance measurement would focus on **communication effects** (eg increased awareness, recognition or response/enquiry rates as a result of marketing activity) or **relationship effects** (eg repeat purchases, up-selling or cross-selling in regard to customers; extent of integration and collaboration with suppliers, intermediaries or strategic allies; or changes in word-of-mouth, publicity and wider stakeholder attitudes/opinions).

- If stakeholder marketing objectives are expressed in terms of **specific stakeholder groups**, performance measurement would focus on factors relevant to those groups. For example, if trade marketing is important, the firm may monitor the stock/order levels of intermediaries, their awareness of the product, their attitudes to the organisation, their level of co-operation in display and promotion and so on.

In general terms, however, there are certain attributes of a viable and suitable marketing activity which can be measured and evaluated. Rather neatly, these can all be expressed as 'e' factors.

- **Effectiveness.** Does the activity fulfil the marketing function's objectives of adding value for its owners, customers and other stakeholders? Does it fulfil the specific marketing objectives set for it?

- **Efficiency.** Does the activity allow the marketing function to use its resources in such a way as to maximise benefit for cost, or return on investment?

- **Economy.** Does the activity fulfil the marketing function's financial objectives? Does it, for example, bring in the budgeted revenue or contribution, and/or fall within or below budgeted expenditure costs?

- **Elegance**. Does the activity look and feel 'right' for the company and the brand? Does it enhance the corporate image, dovetail with (or add value to) stakeholders' needs, or create positive synergy (2 + 2 = 5)?

- **Ethicality**. Does the activity fulfil the company's sense of corporate social responsibility and marketing ethics? Does it have low impact on the environment, encourage diversity, or promote socially responsible images/products, say?

- **Engagement.** Does the activity build and maintain long-term, mutually satisfying relationships with key stakeholders?

There are a number of different approaches and tools for measuring marketing effectiveness. We will discuss the measurement of **marketing communications or promotional activity** in Chapter 11, as it is highlighted by a separate learning outcome in the syllabus. Here, we will survey the various tools listed in the indicative content for this section of the syllabus.

5.2 Measuring the success of stakeholder communications

5.2.1 Response/inquiry measurement

One measure of the effectiveness of stakeholder communications is how many **responses** are received. This indicates that messages are getting to the target audience(s) *and* that they are effective in arousing awareness and interest.

Tools for measuring response rates include:

- **Response (sale, enquiry or request for more information) coupons** in direct mail and print advertising. The number of coupons received can be measured, and the data can further be broken down according to what media the coupons come from (if each medium is given an identifying code printed on the coupon) and what stakeholder group or segment the responses come from (if identifying data is collected on the coupon).

- **Response/enquiry telephone lines**, the number of which is communicated in advertising, corporate literature and other contacts with stakeholders. Again, the number of calls can be measured, with the additional advantage that call centre staff can ask questions about where callers saw the information and so on.

- **Website traffic monitoring**. 'Hits' on the corporate website, and the browsing patterns of users, can be automatically monitored, to show how many people were interested and in what areas of the site.

- **Inquiry tests**, which compare the number of inquiries generated by particular communications campaigns (and/or particular media), and the 'cost per inquiry' (ie cost of the campaign or media space divided by the number of inquiries generated).

5.2.2 Recall and recognition tests

Recall tests are designed to measure how much of the content of marketing messages members of the target audience remember. They can be used to measure the 'memorability' of advertising, press/publicity, sponsorships and branding campaigns – both before the campaigns run (pre-testing, using mock-ups) and afterwards (post-testing).

Survey or panel interviewees may be asked what advertisements and other communications they remember or have noticed. (This is called unprompted or unaided recall.) They may then be reminded of some details of the

campaign, such as the theme of a series of advertisements or press articles, and asked what else they remember, or which ads/articles in the series they remember (prompted recall).

Recognition tests are similarly used to test the *penetration* of advertising and other marketing messages: how much of the target audience have they reached? Survey or panel interviewees are asked to look through newspapers, magazines or journals they have already read, and to identify which marketing messages they remember.

| THE REAL WORLD |

'How are we doing?'

The following 'research facts and figures' were posted on the Virgin Group website (http://www.virgin.com)

- 100% brand awareness in the UK; 96% in Australia; 56% in USA
- No 1 brand to represent Britain in the future
- No 1 most respected brand amongst men
- 2nd most 'responsible' brand (after The Body Shop)
- Forbes' 4th best marketed brand in the world (after Dell, Sony and Harley Davidson)
- More trusted than the Bank of England.

How does the publication of these 'statistics' communicate with internal and external stakeholders?

5.3 Measuring relationships and their results

5.3.1 Internal diagnostics

The planning and control systems of the organisation should make information and reports available for measuring the success of marketing plans and relationships.

- **Moving standards** (such as monthly targets) allow the same performance measurement on an on-going control basis. Have sales – or on-time-in-full deliveries from suppliers, or the number of negative mentions in the press – slipped this month compared to last month?

- **Diagnostic standards** monitor how stakeholder markets are responding to marketing activity, to give continuous performance feedback (eg via electronic point of sale information or market/stakeholder research). Examples include:

    – Monitoring the volume and/or growth of sales, or market share (and any year-on-year changes)

    – Monitoring customer complaints and product returns – or repeat sales, recommendations and referrals

    – Monitoring supplier performance: eg on-time-in-full orders, response and delivery times, flexibility in response to urgent orders, number of improvement suggestions made

    – Monitoring shareholder loyalty: eg sales of shares, movements in share price.

5.3.2 Sales and market share

It is all very well knowing that a marketing campaign has increased brand awareness or recall by 20% and brand preference by 10% - but it is perhaps more important to know whether customers have converted their awareness and preference into *action*: that is, have **sales** increased?

Kotler *et al* (1999) note that the **sales effects** of marketing are often harder to measure than the **communication effects**, because sales are affected by many factors besides promotion – such as product features, price, sales team activities, dealer enthusiasm, supplier performance securing availability, and

publicity and word-of-mouth about the product. For this very reason, however, sales are a good indication of the effectiveness of the whole stakeholder marketing mix.

'One way to measure the **sales effect** of advertising [for example] is to compare past sales with past advertising expenditures. Another way is through experiments. For example, to test the effects of different advertising spending levels, Pizza Hut could vary the amount that it spends on advertising in different market areas, say major cities, and measure the differences in the resulting sales levels. It could spend the normal amount in one market area, half the normal amount in another area and twice the normal amount in a third area. If the three market areas are similar, and if all other marketing efforts in the area are the same, then differences in sales in the three cities could be related to advertising level. More complex experiments could be designed to include other variables, such as difference in the advertisements or media used.' p355.

Sales may be monitored using the organisation's own financial records, or via electronic point of sale (EPOS) data supplied by retailers, for example.

- **Sales analysis** compares actual sales revenue to forecast or target sales revenue. This may trigger further analysis to investigate the reasons for any shortfall. Were fewer products sold than anticipated – or more lower-priced products? Has a major client been lost? Is a particular region or intermediary under-performing?

- **Market share analysis** compares the company's performance to that of its competitors in the market.

5.3.3 Tracking studies

Tracking studies are a market research technique which analyses the responses of a particular group of consumers or stakeholders **over an extended period of time**. The effectiveness of stakeholder marketing can be measured by tracking studies which monitor variables (such as brand/product awareness and attitudinal change) before and after marketing activity, and as stakeholder relationships develop over time.

Tracking studies may be done by surveys, or by panel research. For instance, the Taylor Nelson Sofres Superpanel monitors changes in the grocery shopping behaviour of 8,500 UK households. The research company has placed portable bar code scanners in homes, and families undertake to use the device to record purchases made. The data is collated every week and gives diagnostic information: for instance, if the panel buy less of a particular brand, it is possible to identify what brand they have switched to instead.

With tracking studies, it is important to try to examine all possible reasons for any changes in stakeholder behaviour. As we saw earlier with sales, changes in behaviour, attitudes and relationships may – or may not – be directly attributable to marketing activity. Even so, marketing may need to *respond* to these changes.

5.3.4 Financial analysis

The technical details of financial analysis is beyond the scope of the syllabus. However, you should be aware at a basic level that financial analysis may be carried out at the corporate and/or functional level, to indicate whether marketing activity has been profitable, economical and cost-effective.

- Has marketing activity been carried out within relevant **expenditure budget** constraints?

- Has there been a measurable **economic contribution** attributable to the activity (ie increased profit) – and has this outweighed the costs of the activity?

- Have developments in stakeholder relationships **reduced costs**? For example, have the costs of supply been reduced through collaboration with suppliers or intermediaries? Have the costs of quality inspections been reduced by suppliers taking more responsibility for quality? Have the costs of poor public relations (eg in lost sales and reactive PR responses) been reduced by improved pressure group relations? Have the costs of disputes, absenteeism and labour turnover been reduced by improved employee relations?

- Have the costs and/or contribution attributable to marketing **gone up or down** in the past year? Is this a one off effect or a worrying (or beneficial) trend? How can it be corrected (or maintained)?

Cost analysis is used to establish the expense of an activity. **Profitability analysis** deducts costs from sales revenue to establish the activity's profit performance.

The term **return on relationship (ROR)** is used to describe the long-term net financial outcome caused by the establishment of an organisation's network of relationships (Gummesson, 2002).

It is worth noting that stakeholder marketing may also have **non-financial benefits** for the organisation, which might be difficult to quantify in financial terms: for example, supplier loyalty, intermediary commitment, pressure group support (or non-resistance) or improved reputation for corporate social responsibility. A comprehensive **cost-benefit** analysis of stakeholder marketing should take into account these qualitative measures of added value.

Skandia uses a wide variety of performance indicators. The following are of particular relevance to relationship marketing (Gummesson, 2002, p244):

- With the focus on customers: annual sales/customer numbers; customers lost, average duration of customer relationship, rate of repeat customers, average customer purchases per year, average contacts by customer per year, points of sale, customer visits to the company, days spent visiting customers, and satisfied customer index.

- With the focus on employees: motivation index, empowerment index, employee turnover, and average years of service with the company.

In contrast, Feargal Quinn (founder of **Superquinn** supermarkets) argues that leadership is not making all decisions based on numbers, but instead making qualitative evaluations. For example, Superquinn stores introduced playrooms for children so that the mothers would be free to shop. If the children enjoy the playroom, mothers were likely to stay longer, buy more and return. But it is not possible to measure the profitability of this investment in hard, short-term figures.

5.4 Measuring stakeholder satisfaction

As we have just noted, some of the objectives and measures of stakeholder marketing effectiveness will be qualitative in their nature: that is, they cannot be reduced to statistical or financial measures. Customer satisfaction and loyalty may partly be measured using sales and repeat sales. One might also infer the satisfaction of other stakeholders from their behaviour and economic results for the marketing organisation: suppliers and intermediaries performing better (or worse); pressure group endorsements or protests; employee disputes, turnover or productivity; interventions by regulatory bodies – and so on.

However, stakeholders are also capable of **expressing** their attitudes to, and level of satisfaction with, the organisation. The organisation needs to stimulate and gather this feedback. In other words, if in doubt about how stakeholders feel about you: ask!

The gathering of stakeholder feedback is important in:

- Giving the organisation **stakeholder-generated data** about their needs, expectations and perceptions, which can be used to fine-tune the marketing mix.

- Allowing stakeholders to **feel listened to and heard**: this may be an important part of the organisation's stakeholder management strategy (eg for voiceless or low power/high interest stakeholders, as discussed in Chapter 1).

- Establishing **on-going contact and two-way dialogue** with stakeholders, which supports relationship development.

Positive feedback (satisfied responses) is useful to confirm organisational plans and strategies. It is also helpful in internal marketing: reinforcing value-adding behaviours through recognition and appreciation. **Negative feedback** – dissatisfied responses – is, however, even more useful in defining what it is that the organisation needs to do (or do better) in order to engage stakeholders, retain customers, inspire loyalty and commitment and so on.

Jobber (2007, p879) suggests that three customer groups need to be surveyed to give a valid picture of customer satisfaction and marketing effectiveness.

- Current customers
- Lapsed customers (who bought from 'us' in the past, but no longer)
- Non-customers (who are in the market for the product, but haven't yet bought it from 'us')

5.4.1 Media monitoring

Organisations need continuously to scan the press and other media for references to them and feedback about them. (This is often provided by stakeholders, who are motivated to form opinions and share them with others.) This may be done by the marketing function or other 'environment scanners' in the organisation, or it may employee a media monitoring (or 'cuttings') agency to scan the press and collect items relating to the organisation or its industry.

Monitoring should cover press and publicity (editorial and news articles, in all media), published industry/market reports, public statements and press releases (eg by government agencies, regulatory bodies or pressure groups), and the internet. Increasingly, stakeholders share their views in virtual communities, via discussion boards, email news groups, web logs (blogs), user reviews (eg on Amazon.com or eBay) and content sharing (eg on YouTube and Myspace): organisations need to monitor this traffic to see what is being said about them. One tool to undertake this task is Google Alerts – check it out at http://www.google.co.uk/alerts.

5.4.2 Stakeholder satisfaction and attitude surveys

Stakeholder satisfaction and attitudes can be systematically researched using a range of tools.

- **Feedback forms** (such as the one at the back of this book), inviting stakeholders to rate and/or comment on the organisation, its performance (in areas relevant to the stakeholder) and the quality of the relationship between them (whether value is added for the stakeholder)

- **Survey questionnaires**, administered by post, telephone, personal interview or online. This method is often used for fairly large samples of stakeholders, as it gets answers to standard questions (so that results can be collated and compared) fairly cost-effectively. A powerful question to ask customers (Reichheld, 2001) is: 'Would you recommend Brand X to a friend or colleague?' This goes to the heart of customer relationships, and has been found to be a reasonable predictor of future purchase.

- **Attitude surveys** are often used in market research and also in employee relations (eg to gauge employee morale and attitudes to their work, and to monitor attitudes to particular planned changes). They are usually carried out by means of interview or questionnaire, using attitude scales which allow responses to be quantified.

- **Depth interviews or group discussions (focus groups),** facilitated by trained interviewers, using open-ended conversation rather than a standardised questionnaire, to allow more complex feedback gathering. Interviews can be conducted online, using web conferencing, for greater convenience (and/or to reach widely dispersed and international stakeholders). The purpose of this kind of qualitative research is to understand stakeholder perceptions, expectations, drivers and attitudes in more depth.

You will study such techniques in more detail in the *Marketing Information & Research* unit of your course.

5.4.3 Behavioural indicators

In the same way that sales are used as an indicator of marketing effectiveness, various behavioural measures may be used to infer customer loyalty. For example:

- **Relationship duration**: that is, how long customers (or other stakeholders) remain in relationship with the organisation

- **Retention rate**: that is, the percentage of customers (or other stakeholders) who remain after one year, two years and so on

- **Defection rate**: that is, the percentage of customers (or other stakeholders) who leave a supplier in a given period – sometimes described as the "churn rate".

You should be able to see the use of such measures for employee loyalty and retention, for example, as well as customer loyalty and retention.

5.4.4 Informal feedback gathering

In addition to the formal information-gathering methods discussed above, stakeholder-contacting staff members have extensive opportunities to gather informal direct and indirect feedback at all touch points and contacts with stakeholders. They can observe stakeholder behaviour, and talk to stakeholders: they need to listen intentionally for explicit or implied complaints or suggestions for improvement. Returned products, for example, should be interpreted as non-verbal feedback from consumers, as should returned promotional mailings. Similar examples should come to mind in everyday dealings with other internal and external stakeholder groups.

ACTIVITY 7.10

What might be the *internal* stakeholder equivalent of customer service staff gathering customer feedback?

Postma (1999) argues that the stated attitudes, preferences and intentions of customers and other stakeholders (as expressed in research surveys) are notoriously subjective and unreliable: there can be a considerable difference between the answers given and actual behaviour. Only **actual behaviour** can be depended on to give the true picture of what stakeholders perceive, want and expect from the organisation – and whether they are satisfied with what they are getting. Fortunately, as Postma argues, developments in technology support the organisation in gathering and analysing data about stakeholder behaviour (eg through Customer Relationship Management, Supplier Relationship Management and other similar systems).

5.5 Third party evaluation

One final possibility is to let others judge the quality of your marketing effort. For example:

- CIM and *Marketing Week* run Marketing Effectiveness Awards, and many other marketing journals and magazines also publish evaluations of current campaigns.

- The Institute of Practitioners in Advertising (IPA) run a bi-annual Advertising Effectiveness Awards competition and encourage entries from companies of all sorts and sizes.

- The Medinge Group, an international think-tank on branding and business, launched an annual 'Top Brands with a Conscience' list in 2004. The list features companies which adapt their marketing mix effectively to external stakeholder needs and Corporate Social Responsibility issues. (see The Real World example in Chapter 2).

- The importance of responding to stakeholder needs and drivers

- Involvement theory

- Perceived risk: cost/benefit analysis

- Attitudes

- Group influence and opinion leadership

- Personal buying behaviour: the decision-making unit (DMU), the decision-making process (DMP), influences

- Organisational buying behaviour: DMU, DMP and influences

- Differences between personal and organisational buying behaviour

- The marketing planning process

- SMART objectives

- A framework for a stakeholder marketing mix plan

- The importance of performance measurement

- Measuring promotional effectiveness: inquiry, recall and recognition tests

- Measuring relationships and results: internal diagnostics, sales and market share, tracking studies, financial analysis

- Measuring stakeholder satisfaction and attitudes: media monitoring, satisfaction and attitude surveys, behavioural measures, informal feedback gathering

FURTHER READING

Marketing planning

Jobber, D. (2007) *Principles & Practice of Marketing*. 5th edition. Maidenhead, McGraw-Hill Education. Chapter 2

Egan, G. (2004) *Relationship Marketing*. 2nd edition. Harlow, Pearson Education.
Chapter 11 – section on *The marketing plan*

General

Jobber, D. (2007) *Principles & Practice of Marketing*. 5th edition. Maidenhead, McGraw-Hill Education. Chapters 4 and 5

Check the websites of some of the third-party evaluators mentioned in the text; browse through the judging criteria for their awards, and the descriptions of award winners.

Marketing Week: http://www.marketingweek.co.uk/

The IPA: http://www.ipa.co.uk

The Medinge Group: http://medinge.org/

Dibb, S. and Simkin, L. (1996) *The Marketing Planning Workbook*. International Thomson Business Press.

Egan, J. (2004) *Relationship Marketing: Exploring Relational Strategies in Marketing*. 2nd edition. Harlow, Essex, Pearson Education.

Experian Marketing Services (2011) *Changing attitudes in a changing financial world*, White Paper.

Ford, D. *et al* (2003) *Managing Business Relationships*. 2nd edition. Chichester, John Wiley & Sons.

Jobber, D. (2007) *Principles and Practice of Marketing*. 5th edition. Maidenhead, Berks, McGraw Hill Education.

Gummesson, E. (2002) *Total Relationship Marketing.* Elsevier Butterworth-Heimann, Oxford

Kotler, P. *et al* (1999) *Marketing: An Introduction*. Sydney, Prentice Hall Australia.

Maslow, A. (1954) *Motivation and Personality*. New York, Harper & Row.

Postma, P. (1999) *The New Marketing Era*. New York, McGraw Hill.

Powers, T. L. (1991) *Modern Business Marketing: A strategic planning approach to business and industrial markets*. Saint Paul, MN, West Pub Co.

Reichheld, F. F. (2001) *The Loyalty Effect*. Boston, Harvard Business School.

Smithson, R. (2005) Sowing the Seeds for Success, *AdNews*.

Varey, R.J. (2002) *Marketing Communications: Principles & Practice*. Abingdon, Oxon, Routledge.

Webster, F. E. and Wind, Y. (1972) *Organisational Buying Behaviour*. New Jersey, Englewood Cliffs, Prentice Hall.

QUICK QUIZ

1   List Maslow's categories of needs.

2   What are (a) involvement and (b) attitudes?

3   How do decisions makers calculate perceived risk?

4   How can marketers change attitudes, if they need to do so?

5   What is opinion leadership?

6   List (a) the roles in a typical consumer DMU and (b) the stages in a consumer decision-making process (DMP).

7   In what ways is B2B marketing different from B2C marketing?

8   What does the acronym SMARTER stand for in objective setting?

9   Explain the use of (a) inquiry tests, (b) recall tests and (c) sales analysis in measuring marketing performance.

10   How can stakeholder satisfaction and attitudes be measured?

The Chartered
Institute of Marketing

Activity 7.1

Some of the implications of a high-involvement stakeholder decision for the marketer may be as follows.

- Need to provide substantial information to aid the other party in evaluation of the decision

- Need to emphasise positive outcomes and benefits of the decision

- May need to build up trust to reduce the risk of the decision (eg through product samples, or trial or pilot projects with other stakeholders)

- The other party is motivated to seek information: repetitive messages (eg advertising) are not needed, but there may be a need for own-time scrutiny of information (eg use of print media) and/or personal discussion for explanations, Q & A etc.

- May need to appeal to a range of factors in the decision: cost/benefit, perceptions and emotions, influence groups (See the following sections of the chapter.)

Activity 7.2

This is very personal to you, and will depend on your age, lifestyle and other personal factors. Do think through the question on what kinds of marketing you respond to: this is the kind of thinking you will need to do as a marketer – and for the assignment.

Activity 7.3

Figure 7.5 Flow chart

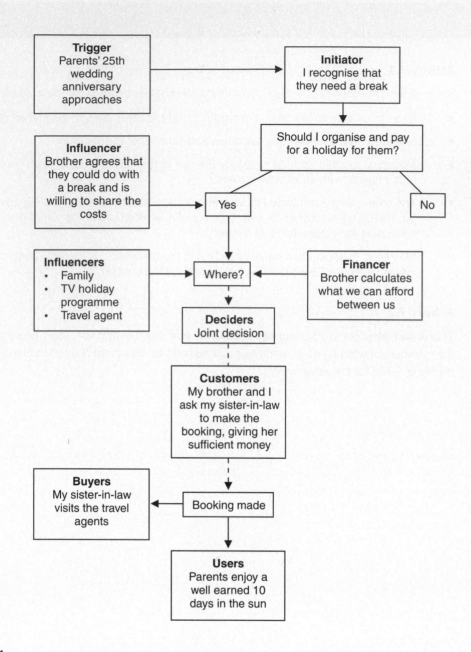

Activity 7.4

Gatekeepers/initiators/deciders/buyers: traditionally, the male head of household. Other members of the family are likely to be influencers/users. So wide reach: TV advertising. Also a high-value, well-researched purchase: target specialist media (What Car? Magazine, auto section of newspapers, Motor Show). Message: focus on the family: spacious, good fuel economy, family fun outings and/or school transport.

Activity 7.5

Give some additional thought to whether you performed this process independently, or whether others were involved: what DMU roles did they perform, and how did they contribute to each stage of your decision-making process?

Activity 7.6

To be discussed with colleagues or your own research.

Activity 7.7

Purchasing decisions may be influenced by:

- Employers or managers in operational departments: requisition or recommend purchase of suppliers/equipment/services (initiators, influencers)

- Purchasing or buying managers: recommending, authorising or implementing purchases (influencers, deciders, buyers)

- Engineers and other technical staff: providing technical specifications or recommendations for component/equipment purchases (gatekeepers, influencers)

- Accounts: set a limit on the price the organisation will pay (influencers, financers)

- The directors and perhaps also shareholders: authorise large items of capital expenditure (deciders, financers)

Activity 7.8

Some general objectives or KPIs for relationship marketing include: increased sales, increased stakeholder or customer awareness and recognition of the brand, customer retention (perhaps expressed in terms of cross-selling or up-selling), increased supplier reliability, increased stock taken by intermediaries, increased systems integration with suppliers or intermediaries, or reduced incidence of bad publicity (or increased generation of positive word-of-mouth).

Activity 7.9

Your own research. Note that this may be very useful preparation for your assignment.

Activity 7.10

Internal feedback may come from: team leaders informally asking staff opinions; team meetings; suggestion schemes; staff appraisal interviews; staff attitude surveys by questionnaire (perhaps on the company Intranet). The marketing department could ask staff, for example, whether they feel they have enough information about the marketing plan to service customers effectively, or how effectively promotional messages reflect how they feel about the product/organisation.

1   Maslow's need categories are: physiological, safety/security, social, esteem and self-actualisation needs.

2   Involvement is the degree of perceived relevance and importance of a brand choice, or other decision. Attitudes are a learned tendency to respond to something in a consistently positive or negative way.

3   Decision makers calculate the benefits or value expected to accrue from the decision, how *likely* they are to accrue and how *important* they are to them. They then weigh this against the costs, sacrifices or other downsides that may have to be endured to secure the benefits, and their likelihood. The net result is risk: the perceived probability of losing out through the decision.

4   Attitudes can be changed by: providing powerful contrary information, especially from a respected or influential source; or getting people to change their behaviour (on the grounds that attitude change will often follow) eg by trialling, explaining or championing products.

5   Opinion leaders are people within a reference group who, because of special skills, knowledge, personality traits or other characteristics, exert influence on others in regard to a decision.

6   A typical consumer DMU consists of: gatekeeper, indicator/initiator, influencer, decider, buyer, financer and user. The stages in a consumer DMP are: need recognition, information search, evaluation of alternatives, purchase decision and post-purchase evaluation.

7   See section 3.4 for a full answer.

8   SMARTER stands for: specific, measurable, attainable, relevant, time-bounded, evaluated and responsible (or relational).

9   Inquiry tests compare the number of inquiries generated by particular campaigns or media and the cost per inquiry. Recall tests measure how much of the content of marketing messages members of the target audience remember, both unprompted and prompted. Sales analysis compares actual sales revenue with forecast or target sales revenue, to highlight any shortfalls that may need investigation and adjustment.

10   Stakeholder satisfaction and attitudes be measured via media monitoring, various forms of surveys and questionnaires (feedback forms, research surveys, attitude surveys), depth interviews or focus group discussions, behavioural analysis (relationship duration, retention rate and defection rate) and informal feedback gathering during contacts with staff.

CHAPTER 8
Stakeholder communications

Introduction

This chapter explores the promotion (or marketing communications) mix, introduced as one of the 4Ps in Chapter 6. As we saw in that chapter, it may not always be possible to adapt product/service, price or place to the needs and interests of different stakeholder groups – but it will almost always be possible to address them as distinct audiences, selecting media and developing messages to match.

In Chapter 6, we gave a brief overview of the marketing communications mix and suggested how stakeholder groups could be viewed as target audiences. We will add some detail to that overview in section 1 of this chapter.

In sections 2 – 7 we explore the nature, aims and applications of the key promotional tools, and how they can contribute to long-term sustainable stakeholder relationships. We include advertising, sales promotion (both consumer and trade), direct marketing, personal selling, branding (with particular emphasis on its contribution to corporate social responsibility goals), and public relations (including a range of audiences, plus related areas such as exhibitions, sponsorship and hospitality).

The focus throughout will be not just on communicating with customers, but also with the broader range of internal and external stakeholders.

In section 8 of this chapter, we focus again on the need to co-ordinate elements of the marketing communications mix – as with the marketing mix as a whole – and introduce the concept of Integrated Marketing Communications.

Internal stakeholder (employee) communications are discussed separately in Chapter 9, together with the distinctive challenges of marketing communications in an international environment. Similarly, the 'new-technology' promotional mix is discussed separately in Chapter 10. Chapter 11 will complete our exploration by looking at how marketing communications are planned, budgeted and evaluated.

Topic list

The marketing communications mix	1
Advertising	2
Sales promotion	3
Personal selling	4
Direct marketing	5
Branding	6
Public relations	7
Integrated marketing communications	8

4.1	Evaluate the extensive range of marketing communications mix tools and explain how they can be co-coordinated to contribute towards developing long-term sustainable stakeholder relationships:
	■ Advertising
	■ Public Relations
	■ New media
	■ Sponsorship and hospitality
	■ Personal selling
	■ Direct marketing
	■ Sales promotion

1 The marketing communications mix

1.1 The role of communications in relationship marketing

We have already seen, in Chapters 3 and 4 of this text, that communications are essential to support stakeholder relationship marketing.

■ The organisation needs to use extensive contact, interaction and feedback to **learn about (and from) stakeholders**, with the aim of continually adding value. 'In order to leverage relationship marketing, marketers need to move from monologue to dialogue with customers [and other stakeholders].' (Allen *et al*, 2001).

■ The organisation needs to maintain **direct and regular stakeholder communication**, through multiple points of contact and across a range of reasons for contact, in order to develop relationship ties with stakeholders.

■ The organisation needs to maintain multiple exchanges with a number of stakeholders (**network relationships**) rather than a single focus on customers, in order to manage all links in the customer value delivery chain.

■ Dialogue and developing trust provide a basis for the **customisation and personalisation** of contacts, messages and value-propositions, which further deepen stakeholder relationships.

■ Communication is part of the **relationship value** offered to stakeholders: keeping them informed in areas of their interest or concern, guiding and supporting them through changes in the organisation's plans, communicating support for their causes and agendas and so on.

1.2 Stakeholders as target audiences

Promotion is the process of communication by a seller to a market. As we have seen, however, this market or target audience may be:

■ A **consumer audience**: purchasers of the product/service
■ A **channel audience**: suppliers and intermediaries
■ An **all-stakeholder audience**: all the publics who have an interest in the organisation's activities.

Targeting the communications mix for stakeholders means identifying and using:

■ Appropriate **communication media and tools** to target relevant groups, to suit their needs and characteristics, and to attract them to the message

■ Appropriate **modes of communication** to express the message in a way that reflects their interests, motives and objectives – and in a way that establishes and maintains constructive, sustainable relationships with them.

1.3 The promotion (marketing communication) mix

The **promotion** mix is the total marketing communications programme of the organisation, consisting of a specific combination or blend of promotional tools used to reach the target audience for a given marketing task. The full range of tools that can be used to secure favourable responses from, and build sustainable relationships with, stakeholder audiences is shown in Figure 8.1. Not all tools will be included in the promotion mix for a given task – but you need to be aware that a wide range of tools is available.

Figure 8.1   Marketing communications tools

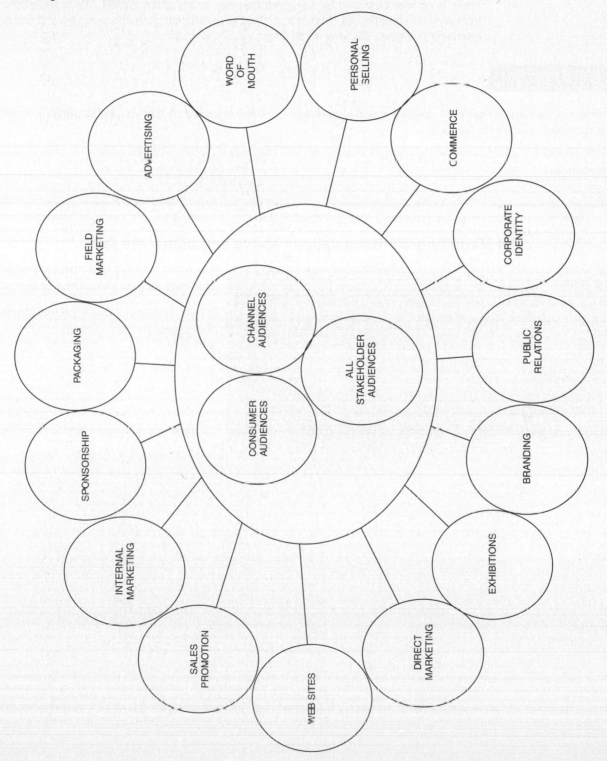

If the sheer range of tools available seems a bit intimidating, we have bad news – and good news.

- **The range of promotional tools and media continues to grow.** The variety of media has increased (or been fragmented) in many ways. There are more print media (publications aimed at more and more highly defined niche segments) and more broadcast media (with developments in satellite, cable and digital TV, DVD, Webcasting and Podcasting and so on). Marketing messages are being put on more and more surfaces, from buildings to tabletops to Post-it Notes – and even people! Technological developments have (as we will see in Chapter 10) created new one-to-one marketing tools such as the internet, mobile phone text messaging and database marketing.

- **There is no 'one best mix' for any given message in any given market.** While some communication tools may be identified as more or less effective in different contexts, selecting and combining promotional tools is still very much an art – *not* a science!

ACTIVITY 8.1

Which of the tools in Figure 8.1 does your work organisation, or other organisation that you are studying, use? What audience(s) is each tool designed to address?

Which tools are particularly used to address shareholder, supplier, intermediary, pressure group and wider community audiences?

1.4 Marketing communications above and below the line

> **Key term**
>
> **Above-the-line promotion** is advertising placed in paid-for media, such as print media (newspapers and magazines), radio, TV, cinema and outdoor/transport poster sites. (The 'line' is one in an advertising agency's accounts, *above* which are shown its earnings on a commission basis from the buying of media space for clients.)
>
> **Below-the-line promotion** is a blanket term for a range of non-commissionable marketing communication activities. (Agencies' earnings on a *fee* basis are shown *below* the 'line' in their accounts.) More specifically, it refers to activities such as public relations, direct marketing, sales promotions, sponsorship and exhibitions.

It is worth knowing that marketing communications are often classified as above-the-line and below-the-line.

Let's now look at each of the major marketing communication tools in turn.

2 Advertising

▶ **Key term**

Advertising is 'any **paid** form of **non-personal** presentation and promotion of ideas, goods or services by an **identifiable** sponsor.' (American Marketing Association)

2.1 Purposes of advertising

Advertising can be effective for a range of purposes, usually directed at a fairly large target audience.

- **To promote sales (or other desired responses from stakeholders)**

  Advertising is particularly good at raising awareness, informing and persuading. It can be used to stimulate primary demand for a product (eg in the introduction of a new product) and selective demand for a particular brand (eg in competition with other brands). This works in intermediary markets (eg selling in to retailers) as well as consumer markets, effectively 'introducing' the product in advance of a sales call. One example of a different sort of response is recruitment advertising: promoting the organisation and the job within the recruitment market, in order to secure applications from the best potential recruits. The same kind of approach may be used to advertise for suppliers (eg by putting a contract out to tender).

- **To create an image or to promote an organisation or idea**

  Institutional advertising is used by companies to improve their public image, and by not-for-profit and public sector organisations to promote their programmes (eg persuading people not to drink and drive, to support a pressure group or donate to a charity). Marketing organisations often use advertising to promote their corporate social responsibility credentials to the wider stakeholder audience.

- **To support other promotional tools**

  Advertising can support personal selling, for example, by raising customer (consumer or intermediary) awareness of the product/service, motivating them to contact sales representatives. The company's sales promotions, presence at exhibitions, website and other communication channels can also be brought to the target audience's attention by advertising.

- **To offset competing or contrary messages**

  Companies often attempt to defend their market share by responding aggressively to competitors' advertising campaigns. Advertisements may also be used to counter negative public relations messages and alter public opinion (eg correcting negative impressions given by critical incidents such as a product recall, or countering negative pressure group statements)

- **To remind and reassure**

  Advertising reinforces the purchase decision and repeat purchase, by reminding consumers that the product continues to be available – and offers benefits – and reassuring them that they have made the right choice. In industrial markets, advertising may add credibility to sales visits by demonstrating professionalism and expenditure.

2.2 Advertising media

Major advertising media include television, cinema, radio, newspapers, magazines and outdoor media (poster sites, bus stops, buildings and so on). In addition, opportunities are emerging in interactive advertising through electronic media such as the internet, direct response television, mobile telephone text messaging, enhanced CD and CD-ROM, websites and so on.

Media are selected according to:

- **The size of the audience that regularly uses the medium.** Mass media (such as television, radio and national newspapers) have large exposure. Reader/viewer numbers (newspaper circulation, programme ratings) are closely monitored, helping the media planner to assess the reach of the advertisement.

- **The type of audience targeted by the medium.** There is a trade-off between the size and relevance of the available audience. Segmentation (for example, placing an ad in special-interest sections of a newspaper) and targeting (in local or regional media, specialist magazines and journals and so on) may be possible. If the organisation wants to reach suppliers and intermediaries, for example, it may advertise in specialist trade/industry publications. If it wants to appeal to 'green' consumers, it may advertise in special-interest publications or in the breaks in nature programmes on TV, say.

- **The suitability of the medium for the message.** Print ads, for example, allow high volumes of information to be taken in and kept, with response mechanisms (eg coupons) added if desired. Television and cinema have a high impact on awareness and retention because of the potential for creativity, and sound/moving-image combinations. Radio has a highly trusted interpersonal quality, but as a sound-only medium has limited potential for information retention.

- **The cost of the medium in relation to all the above.** Cinema and TV have very high space and production costs. Newspapers and magazines are priced according to the size and quality of their circulation, which may or may not include a high proportion of the advertiser's target audience.

The Chartered
Institute of Marketing

In February 2011, Adobe announced it is to launch a multi-million pound marketing campaign in the UK using a wide range of media

Figure 8.2   Adobe

'The software company will launch the campaign on 27 February to showcase what it can do for brands, publishers and creatives in this increasing digital environment. It will be focusing on its most recent offering, Adobe SocialAnalytics, by launching with the theme "Adobe & social".

The campaign will run on several channels including online, print, mobile, tablet and across national and industry-specific media, as well as social platforms. The main creative is based around Adobe's iconic red ampersand.

Speaking about the campaign, Emma Chalwin, brand director, EMEA at Adobe said, "This is our first brand campaign in the UK to raise awareness of the breadth of Adobe's business, notably in the digital media and digital marketing space."

"The campaign is about more than us just telling our customers how we can help them; it is about giving them real life examples of how Adobe is transforming digital experiences. The creative does a fantastic job of bringing this to life, with the iconic red ampersand demonstrating the connection between Adobe the brand and its innovations and customer experiences."

Notice the clear reference to the different target audiences for the advertisements – how suitable do you think the media chosen are for these audiences?

(B2B Marketing, 2012)

Find examples of advertisements in newspapers of magazines, which illustrate:

- Business-to-business (B2B) or trade advertising

- Business-to-consumer (B2C) advertising, selling a product: try to find one example of a minor or everyday purchase, and one of a major long-term purchase.

- Business-to-consumer (B2C) advertising, selling a service

- Government-to-consumer (G2C) advertising (eg notices about tax time, or elections, or public service announcements)

- Not-for-profit or voluntary sector advertising (eg by a charity or religious organisation)

- Pressure group advertising: try to find one example of an awareness campaign and one fundraising campaign

- Recruitment advertising.

What differences in tone or style do you notice – and how do these suit the aims/purposes and target audiences of each advertiser in each case?

Media planning, buying and scheduling, and the origination and production of highly designed and technically demanding advertising formats, are generally undertaken by specialist **agencies**, which form a multi-billion dollar global industry. The main tasks of the marketer in the client organisation will be to brief the agency and liaise with account executives to monitor, co-ordinate and approve plans at each stage of the process. (For some organisations their advertising agency may be an important stakeholder with whom a close relationship should be developed!)

2.3 New media

Digital technology has increased the number and variety of media channels and the services they can offer to audiences. We will look at technology-based communication tools in Chapter 10, but you should be aware of the following advertising media.

- **Digital television** has been developing over the past decade (in the UK, for example, all terrestrial television will be digital by the end of 2012). Transmitting programmes by digital signal increases the number of services that can be delivered to audiences. It also allows viewers greater choice over how and when they watch, allowing them to interact with programmes and to select their own programme content: another manifestation of the trend towards adding value through customisation.

  - Broadcasters are able to offer additional programmes, information, sound and graphics to complement what is being shown on the main channel. This allows marketers to add viewer-selected information, promotional offers and competitions relating to programme content and so on.

  - The proliferation of TV channels caters for an increasing number of niche audiences, presenting targeting opportunities for marketers.

- **Interactive television** refers to the possibility of the audience's controlling and responding to transmitted programmes.

  - **Teletext** is a limited but popular form of interactivity, by which users can search information pages using standard remote control devices.

  - **Direct response television (DRTV)** may also be a relatively low-tech approach: standard television commercials and infomercials urge immediate response via a call centre or website.

The Chartered
Institute of Marketing

- More genuinely **interactive TV** is provided via TV/telecom links provided by a set-top box. 'Pop up' messages on Sky TV, for example, offer the option to interact, by being switched across to the Sky 'Open...' channel and a branded location: here, there are instructions for accessing more information and placing orders.

- **Interactive catalogues and newsletters** can be emailed, downloaded or viewed online, to convey information to target audiences on topics of interest to them (new products, industry developments, exhibitions, sales promotions, training opportunities for employees and so on) with links to related website pages if stakeholders want to follow up on particular items. These approaches allow complex data to be made available to stakeholders, with the element of choice reinforcing their interest and motivation at the follow-up stage.

- **SMS text messaging** is a huge advertising growth area, and the integration of digital mobile phone networks with the internet has also facilitated a range of m-commerce (mobile commerce) applications. SMS is low-cost, easy-to-use and highly personal and compelling (especially in the always-connected youth market). It is used for relational marketing by brands including Cadbury, Smirnoff, Avon, British Airways, Nestlé, Pepsi, Haagen-Daaz and even Liverpool FC.

- **Web advertising**. The internet is a major advertising medium, through dedicated corporate and brand websites; pop-up and banner/button advertising (giving a click-through link to a website); and ranking on internet search engines (to increase site exposure). The forecast global penetration of the internet over the next few years would give it a significantly larger (international, 24/7) audience than any of the TV networks, print media outlets or other advertising vehicles. Studies have shown that brand awareness increases some five percent after using banner advertising. The other plus point for web advertising is the ability to monitor traffic, gathering information on users' interests and browsing habits, and placing 'cookies' on their computers to enable customisation of future contacts.

- **Apps**. The term 'apps' has been used to mean 'application' in the IT world for a long time. However, it has now become popular in referring to applications for mobile devices such as smartphones and tablets as well as gaming devices and smart TVs. Many UK retailers for example have launched apps for the iPhone which allow users to browse catalogues and also to receive messages from the retailer about special offers. (See the Honda The Real World example below.)

- **QR codes**. Short for Quick Response codes, these two dimensional barcodes can be printed on brochures and business cards or in press advertisements – anyone with a smartphone with the necessary app (see above) can then scan the code when they will be directed to the website page whose address was embedded in the code. This enables the creator of the code to track responses to the code. This technology is still in its infancy at the time of writing, but you should keep an eye open for further developments in this area.

THE REAL WORLD

Honda trials use of apps

Honda is trialing the use of apps for its new Civic model. It has launched pilot apps for Samsung Smart TVs and Xbox 360 game machines which will feature video content from the car manufacturer. New video material has been created for the apps featuring the new Civic, and other car video content is planned to follow later on. The company launched the app for the iPhone on 16 March 2012 – see details on iTunes at http://itunes.apple.com/gb/app/honda-civic-uk/id476374565?mt=8#.

2.4 Evaluation of advertising for stakeholder marketing

As a stakeholder marketing tool, advertising has the following advantages and limitations.

- Media advertising is best suited to **large non-individualised stakeholder audiences**, as it is overly expensive and insufficiently personalised for addressing small groups of known stakeholders. (Web and direct mail advertising can be individually addressed and personalised, however.)

- Advertising is **highly versatile** in terms of the messages it can be used to convey, and therefore suits all audiences and communication scenarios – whether launching a brand, notifying customers of a product

recall, putting supply contracts up for tender, recruiting employees, announcing industry awards, highlighting corporate support for the environment/community/local business, or informing the general public of issues and causes.

- Advertising is **essentially one-directional**. While it is excellent for conveying information and arousing interest, added elements may be needed to secure engagement. Response mechanisms (coupons, contact details and so on) can be used to engage stakeholders and to capture their contact details, supporting direct on-going contact to build a relationship. Web advertising is particularly effective in initiating a relationship, through its interactivity: facilitating membership of virtual networks and communities, direct two-way communication and so on.

- Advertising is a major part of the promotion mix in **consumer markets**, especially branded FMCG markets. It is less prominent in the mix for **B2B marketing**, where more collaborative relationships and complex offerings favour personal selling. Similarly, there are likely to be more direct communications with employee and supply chain stakeholders, government, media and so on.

- There are **ethical issues** in advertising, mainly around its truthfulness; its potential for misleading or manipulating (particularly if targeted to children); its potential to persuade people to buy products which are harmful or not beneficial; and its potential to encourage over-consumption. On the other hand, advertising can also be used to raise awareness of philanthropic, environmental and ethical issues and causes, and to stimulate action (such as recycling, green consumption or donations, say).

---

3 Sales promotion

Sales promotion activity is aimed at the customer (intermediary or consumer) market, typically in order to **increase short-term sales volume**, by encouraging first time, repeat or multiple purchase within a stated time frame ('offer closes on such-and-such a date'). It seeks to do this by **adding value** to the product or service: customers are offered something extra – or the chance to obtain something extra – if they purchase, purchase more or purchase again.

The objectives of sales promotion, stated in broad terms, may be:

- To increase **awareness and interest** among target audiences: the incentive or added value element may increase engagement, and competition-style promotions may require customers to research the product to provide answers, say

- To **motivate** customers to try a product or switch from competing brands

- To **smooth seasonal fluctuations** in demand, via incentives to purchase in off-peak periods, say

- To **foster customer retention**, by encouraging repeat or multiple purchase; offering opportunities to try related products (supporting cross-selling); and capturing customer data (supporting relationship marketing).

3.1 Techniques of sales promotion

Consumer sales promotion techniques include:

- **Price promotions:** eg discounted selling price or additional product on *current* purchase, or coupons (on packs or advertisements) offering discounts on *next* purchase

- **'Gift with purchase' or 'premium' promotions**: the consumer receives a bonus, gift or refund on purchase or repeat purchase, or on sending in tokens or proofs of multiple purchases

- **Competitions and prizes**: eg entry in prize draws or 'lucky purchase' prizes, often used both to stimulate purchase (more chances to win) and to capture customer data

- **Frequent user (loyalty) incentives**: eg air miles programmes or points-for-prizes reward cards.

THE REAL WORLD

Supermarket chain **Morrisons** launched a campaign in the UK in February 2012 offering customers 15p per litre off the price of petrol when they spent £60 or more in store. The campaign was supported by press advertising. The campaign followed similar promotions by rivals Tesco and Sainsbury's but the discount offered was higher.

As an example of how promotional offerings can be tailored for synergy with the brand, consider cereal maker **Kelloggs**. Its Special K brand, aimed mainly at 18-35 year old women who care about health and fitness, did a promotion offering a free hour with a personal trainer, and a pedometer. Sugar Puffs, on the other hand, are marketed to children, so the offer was a free swim voucher.

At the other end of the scale, the most notorious cautionary tale in sales promotion is provided by the experience of **Hoover**. In 1992, Hoover and Your Leisure offered two free flights (to Europe and the US) to any customer who spent a minimum of £100 on Hoover products. Spot the mistake! Leonard Hadley, Chairman of Hoover's US parent company, Maytag, had to admit that the offer was like 'a bad accident… You can't determine what was in the driver's mind.' The promotion attracted more than double the anticipated applications, leading to the dismissal of three senior managers and a £19 million provision to cover the costs. The promotion had not been insured against unforeseen demand. The bargain was just too good. And the second-hand vacuum cleaner market would take a long time to recover from the over-supply!

3.2 Trade promotion

Trade promotions are directed at trade customers (intermediaries), to encourage them to stock or sell more of a product or service (sometimes called a 'push' marketing strategy). Techniques include:

- **Monetary incentives** such as increased trade discounts, extended credit or 'baker's dozen' packs (13 items/packs for the price of 12)

- **Collaborative advertising and promotion**: sharing costs with the dealer or retailer to promote both the brand and the stockist

- **Point-of-sale support**: supplying display materials, information and merchandising

- **Competitions and awards** for the most successful dealers or sales people

- **Business gifts**: linked to sales or purely relational (eg diaries, calendars and other Christmas gifts – although these may be subject to ethical guidelines)

- **Consumer promotions** demonstrating an aggressive 'pull' strategy which offers the intermediary good sales.

ACTIVITY 8.3

What forms of sales promotion (consumer or trade) are used by your organisation? What are their aims? Find out, if you can, how *effective* some of the specific sales promotion campaigns were.

3.3 Point-of-sale display and product packaging

Two-thirds of purchases are estimated to result from in-store decisions: attractive and informative in-store displays and promotional materials are a key part of sales promotion.

Point-of-sale display materials include product housing or display casing (such as racks and carousels), posters and leaflet dispensers. Their purpose is to attract the attention of buyers; stimulate purchase in preference to rival brands; increase available display and promotion space for the product; and motivate retailers to stock the product (because they add to store appeal).

Product packaging is also a promotional aid.

- The **design** can be used to attract attention, convey brand identity and promote brand recognition. (Most people come to recognise their favourite brands on the shelf – even from a distance – by the packing colour and design.)

- **Printable surfaces** can be used for product labelling and information (some of which is required by law) and also promotional messages, sales promotions and coupons.

- **Values** integral **to the packaging itself** (size, environment-friendliness, convenience, attractiveness, protection of product quality/safety) are part of the overall benefit and image bundle of the product. They may also be used for wider stakeholder marketing: eg emphasising 'green' values (less packaging, recyclability) or awareness of social needs (family economy sizes, convenience).

3.4 Evaluation of sales promotion for stakeholder marketing

Sales promotion is limited in its scope, aims and target audiences (intermediary and consumer customers). For these uses, its advantages and disadvantages can be summarised as follows.

Table 8.1   Advantages and disadvantages of sales promotion

Advantages	Disadvantages
Short-term measurable boost in sales	May pose fulfilment challenges (if over-subscribed)
Push tactic to gain distributor and POS support	May suggest incentive required for purchase to be worthwhile
Flexible for collaborative promotions and creative synergy	Does not necessarily create brand loyalty (if consumers switch from promotion to promotion)
Potential source of customer data (eg through competition entry)	Product given away or discounted: impact on bottom-line profit

> ▶ **Assessment tip**
>
> It is worth being aware of the potential for confusion between the terms '**promotion**' (used as another way of saying 'marketing communications' in general) and '**sales promotion**' (which is a specialist term reserved for the techniques described here). If the word promotion comes up in an assignment brief, remember to check the context carefully – and to answer the requirement set.

4 Personal selling

▶ Key term

Personal selling is 'the presentation of products and associated persuasive communication to potential clients, by sales representatives employed by the supplying organisation. It is the most direct and longest established means of promotion within the promotional mix.' (Baron *et al*, 1991)

4.1 Activities of personal selling

Kotler *et al* (1999) identify a number of activities that the sales force might perform.

Table 8.2   Sales force activities

Prospecting	Gathering leads and referrals for other potential customers
Communicating	Communicating information to existing and potential customers about the company's products and services
Selling	Establishing rapport with the customer, defining the need/problem, persuasively presenting product benefits, dealing with resistance and objections, negotiating terms (if required) and closing the sale
Servicing	Providing services to the customer, such as giving technical assistance, monitoring and replenishing stock, arranging finance or expediting delivery
Information gathering	Acting as a key source of marketing and competitor intelligence and feedback to the company, as the main direct link to the customer

If the organisation relies on consumer advertising to draw customers into stores to ask for its brands, the role of the sales force may primarily be **servicing**: ensuring that retailers carry sufficient stock, negotiating adequate shelf space and so on. In high-value consumer goods/services markets (such as car or insurance sales), where personal information and persuasion may be required to close the sale, the **selling** role may be paramount. In B2B markets, the relationship between client and sales representative (or account handler) is more complex, important and on-going.

4.2 Personal selling within the promotional mix

Personal selling is part of the co-ordinated promotional mix. It will need to be supported by a range of other marketing communication activities:

- **Product advertising, public relations and sales promotion**, drawing consumer attention and interest to the product and its sources *and* motivating retailers to stock and sell the product.

- **'Leads'** (interested prospective customers) generated by contacts and enquiries made through exhibitions, promotional competitions, enquiry coupons and other methods.

- **Informational tools** such as brochures and presentation kits. These can add interest and variety to sales presentations, and leave customers with helpful reminders and information.

- **Sales support information**: customer/segment profiling; competitor intelligence; access to customer contact/transaction histories and product data and so on. (This is an important aspect of Customer Relationship Management, enabling field sales teams to facilitate immediate response and transactions – without time-lags to obtain the information required.)

What do you think are the advantages and disadvantages of personal selling, compared to other promotional tools discussed so far?

4.3 Evaluation of personal selling for stakeholder marketing

Personal selling is an effective tool for relationship development, since it fosters '**actor bonds**': that is, repeated and deepening personal contacts between individual sellers and buyers. It is highly **interactive and flexible**, enabling the salesperson to customise the message to the audience's immediate and individual interests, needs and concerns. The two-way nature of the process allows dialogue, question-and-answer and feedback. Personal selling enables more of a **collaborative approach** to defining and creating customer value, and is therefore most appropriate for high-value consumer purchases, and for business-to-business (B2B) relationships.

The main disadvantage is that this is labour intensive, and therefore **costly**. A salesperson can only interact with one customer at a time. The organisation will have to make a value judgement between the effectiveness of relationship development and persuasion – and the relative expense.

Personal selling is often appropriate in **B2B markets**, where there are fewer, higher-value customers who are looking for a more complex total offering tailored to a more specific set of requirements. Personal selling allows a partnership relationship to be established which:

- Adds value by allowing customer needs to be met more flexibly

- Allows sales force effort to be targeted at high-return relationships; and

- Reinforces the 'inertia' of industrial markets, making it hard for buyers to switch suppliers, and creating loyalty and inter-dependency over time.

It should also be noted that although 'selling' will not be relevant to all stakeholder relationships, there may be elements of **negotiation** and/or **persuasion** involved in forming relationships and exercising influence in relation to non-customer stakeholder groups. A **one-to-one discussion approach**, similar to personal selling, may be used for:

- **Clarification and discussion of issues** eg with representatives of pressure groups

- **Supplier relationships**: eg negotiation of requirements and terms, contract and relationship management, or dispute resolution. (This is really personal selling seen from the customer's side.)

- **Internal marketing**: eg one-to-one interviews with employees or their representatives, for motivation, consultation, briefings, change management, conflict resolution and so on.

 The Chartered Institute of Marketing

5 Direct marketing

These definitions highlight some key aspects of direct marketing (DM) for stakeholders:

Table 8.3   Direct marketing definitions

Interactivity	Direct marketing is a two-way direct dialogue between buyer and seller.
Response	It is about getting people to respond: to send in coupons, or make telephone calls, or visit the website, in response to invitations and offers.
Recording and analysis	Response data are collected and analysed so that customer needs and wants can be more effectively and efficiently targeted.
Relationship marketing	This allows the supplier to make appropriately targeted, customised or personalised offerings to the customer on an on-going basis.

Direct marketing helps to create and develop **direct one-to-one relationships** between the company and its key prospects or customers. It may also be a form of **direct supply**, because it removes all channel intermediaries apart from the advertising medium and the delivery medium: there are no resellers. This allows the company to retain control over where and how its products are promoted, to develop business contacts efficiently – and to deepen relationships over time.

5.1 Tools of direct marketing

Direct marketing is the fastest growing sector of promotional activity. It now embraces a range of techniques, some traditional – and some new-technology based.

- **Direct mail**: a personally addressed 'written offering' (letter and/or sales literature) with some form of response mechanisms, sent to existing customers from an in-house database (or commercially obtained) mailing list.

- **E-mail**: messages sent via the internet from an e-mail database of customers. E-mails can offer routine information, updates, information about new products and so on, with links to the company's website for response. E-mail is very versatile and can be used as a covering letter for a range of attachments: feedback or attitude surveys, brochures and catalogues, newsletters, vouchers and so on. Addresses can be gathered via enquiries and contact permissions at the company's website.

- **Mobile phone text messaging**. 'SMS combines mobility, intimacy, immediacy and the ability to push a simple powerful message to a receptive audience. There is nothing else like it. For marketing purposes SMS allows customer services, alerts, CRM, two-way direct responses, brand bonding, event ticketing: the possibilities are still being explored.' (Mullin, 2002)

- **Direct response advertising**. This may be traditional advertising in a newspaper or magazine with a cut out (or stuck on) response coupon; loose inserts with response coupons or reply cards; direct-response

TV or radio advertisements, giving a call centre number or website address to contact. QR (Quick Response) codes are increasingly being used in print ads to enable readers to connect directly to the advertiser's website through a smartphone.

- **Mail order**. Mail order brochures typically contain a selection of items which are also available in a shop or trade outlet, but which can be ordered direct via an order form included with the brochure and delivered to the customer. (BPP Learning Media Study Texts are one example.) Mail order extends the reach of a retail business to more, and more geographically wide-spread, customers.

- **Catalogue marketing** is similar to mail order, but involves a complete catalogue of the products of the firm, which typically would not have retail outlets at all. Electronic catalogues can also be downloaded on the internet, with the option of transferring to the website for transaction processing, or on CD-ROM.

- **Call centres and tele-marketing**. A call centre is a telephone service (in-house or outsourced) responding to, or making, sales or service calls. This is a cost-effective way of providing a professionally trained response to customer callers and enquirers. It may also be used, eg by government agencies, as a contact point for enquiries and information in the event of an emergency, for example.

- **Web marketing**. A website acts as a form of direct response advertising, enabling users to make queries, enquiries and (if the site is set up for transactions) purchase orders and payments, in response to product/service information. It can also be used for customer service (eg providing information, searchable databases, Frequently Asked Questions and Contact Us links). It may even be a focus for direct distribution (eg for information or booking/ticketing services, and downloadable products such as music, podcasts and images). It also enables the company to gather customer information such as contact details, buying/browsing history and preferences and so on. We will discuss this further in Chapter 10.

THE REAL WORLD

National Geographic Society (a non-profit scientific and educational institution, with a for-profit subsidiary funding its activities).

'The first issue of the National Geographic Society's magazine was provided to 265 member subscribers as a journal. Today, some 9 million people receive the magazine in 17 languages. Furthermore, 60 million members in 62 countries receive the National Geographic TV channels via BSkyB, NBC and Fox. Some 147 book titles are published, and a thriving video, CD-ROM and DVD business operates internationally... Online delivery provides members with not only super-fast distribution, but further added-value from special editorial content.

To bring the corporation up to contemporary performance, membership is being re-emphasized over subscriptions. The **relationship-marketing** programme has been developed to manage expectations, in terms of fulfilling member needs and keeping promises. New products are being developed to diversify the business into additional markets. This has been managed through partnerships based on licenses, affinities and some joint ventures.

National Geographic is sold to new members through **direct-marketing** activities of direct mail, door-to-door, direct-response TV and radio, and affinity programmes. Some press and TV advertising and sales promotion support this effort. Customers are retained through emphasis on efficient and friendly service, a number of added-value benefits, and a recently enhanced renewal management strategy.

Partnering with other providers enables National Geographic to capitalize on local market expertise and to build huge databases that provide the information that enhances knowledge about interests and values.'

(Varey, 2002)

5.2 Evaluation of direct marketing for stakeholder marketing

Direct marketing was developed specifically as a way of securing sales responses from **customers**, both in B2B and consumer markets. For this purpose, its advantages and disadvantages can be summarised as follows.

Table 8.4   Advantages and disadvantages of direct marketing

Advantages	Disadvantages
Establishes direct contact and gathers customer data, supporting on-going relationship marketing	Possible negative perceptions of intrusion, volume of contact, 'hard' sell. Remember: not all customers want (or are worth the cost of) more contact!
Potential for audience targeting and personalisation	Challenges and costs of fulfilment, especially to distant (international?) customers
Relatively short lead-time for campaign development and delivery: can be used to respond to competitor action, changes, crises (eg product recalls)	Costs of customer data processing

Again, direct marketing should be seen as part of a **co-ordinated promotional mix**. In relationship marketing, it will be one of several points of direct contact with the customer. It will also have to be supported by the whole marketing mix: it's all very well allowing customers to respond instantly to successful promotional messages – but if the delivery infrastructure isn't up to the job, and the product takes weeks to reach them (negative service encounter!), the relational potential of the approach will be wasted.

ACTIVITY 8.5

How could a direct marketing approach be extended beyond customers to non-customer stakeholder groups?

6 Branding

We explained the concept of branding in Chapter 5, and discussed how it could be used to engage and enhance customer loyalty.

Branding is now apparent in just about all markets. Not long ago – and this is still the case in less developed countries – most products were sold unbranded. Today, even salt, oranges, nuts and screws are branded. There has been a limited return recently to 'generics': cheap products packaged plainly and not heavily advertised. This apparent lack of branding may, however, been seen as simply another branding strategy: creating 'No Frills' brands.

6.1 Branding within the promotion mix

Branding supports other marketing effort in various ways.

- It aids **product differentiation**, conveying a lot of information very quickly and concisely. This helps customers readily to identify the goods or services and thereby helps to create a customer loyalty to the brand.

- It maximises the impact of **advertising** for product identification and recognition. The more similar a product is to competing goods, the more branding is necessary to create a distinctive product identity.

- Branding leads to readier acceptance by **intermediaries**.

- It supports **market segmentation**, since different brands of similar products may be developed to meet specific needs of categories of customers.

- It eases the task of **personal selling**, by enhancing product recognition.

It is worth noting, however, that branding is not equally relevant to all products. The cost of intensive brand advertising to project a brand image nationally or internationally may be prohibitively high. Goods which are sold in large numbers, on the other hand, may promote a brand name just by their existence and circulation!

6.2 Evaluation of branding for stakeholder marketing

As we saw in Chapter 5, branding is a very general term covering brand names, designs, trademarks, symbols, jingles and the like. In addition, of course, a brand shares the attributes of a **product or service**: it is a bundle of tangible and intangible benefits which delivers customer value.

More importantly in the context of the wider stakeholder audience, perhaps, a brand is often associated with a set of **values and characteristics** that position it in the public's perception. This positioning can be proactively managed by the organisation to send messages not just to customers but to the wider stakeholder audience, to engage their interest and support. In Chapter 2, for example, we highlighted examples of ethical branding (eg The Body Shop) and the repositioning of brands to enhance their corporate social responsibility image (eg Nike's supplier ethics policies and McDonald's new healthier menus).

Brands can be associated with **positive CSR and ethical values** in a number of ways:

- **Brand name** eg Fairtrade brands

- **Marketing mix** eg safe products, recyclable packaging, fair pricing – and promotions emphasising all of these aspects

- **Endorsement** by relevant pressure groups and opinion leaders: eg cosmetics endorsed as cruelty-free by the RSPCA

- **Sponsorship** of community, cultural and sporting events.

- **Promotional messages** specifically focused on CSR and corporate citizenship. Examples include:

    - Branded toy company Mattel advertising its child welfare activities – especially in the wake of a major 2007 PR crisis with toys withdrawn due to contamination with toxic lead paint

    - McDonald's promoting its Ronald McDonald charitable initiatives

    - Banks advertising their support for local businesses. (A recent ANZ Bank TV campaign in Australia features a very short message by a branch employee – followed by a lengthy spoof voice-over stating: 'Tony is dressed by…, eats lunch at…, works out at…. Flowers provided by…' and so on, as the names and addresses of the local businesses scroll across the screen. The final line is: 'Support local businesses: we do.')

    - Car companies promoting low fuel consumption and other environmental benefits of their models

    - Unilever's Dove brand promoting the 'Campaign for Real Beauty', embracing age and figure diversity and realistic body image. The advertising is supported by other activities, such as debate forum, workshops to help young women with body-related low self-esteem, a touring photography exhibition showcasing diverse images of beauty, and a comprehensive website.

7 Public relations

This is an important discipline for stakeholder marketing, because although it may not directly stimulate sales, the organisation's image and reputation are important factors in whether it attracts and retains employees, whether the community supports or resists its presence and activities, and whether the media reports positively on its operations. Public relations activity sees all these stakeholders as potential audiences for its messages.

An organisation can be either reactive or proactive in its management of relationships with its publics or stakeholder audiences.

- **Reactive PR** is primarily concerned with the communication of what has happened and responding to factors affecting the organisation. It is primarily defensive.
- **Proactive PR** practitioners have a much wider role and thus have a far greater influence on overall marketing strategy. The scope of the PR function is much wider, encompassing a range of communications and image management activities.

THE REAL WORLD

An example of reactive PR going badly wrong followed the Deepwater Horizon oil rig explosion in the Gulf of Mexico in 2010. BP, the owner of the rig, failed to treat the problem seriously enough in the media with a resulting dramatic fall in the company's share price and the forced resignation of its Chief Executive.

Read a summary of the story here: http://www.time.com/time/business/article/0,8599,2004701,00.html.

7.1 Audiences and tools of public relations

The scope of PR is very broad, but some frequently used techniques are as follows.

Table 8.5   PR techniques

Consumer marketing support	- Publicity: generating editorial coverage in the press
	- Consumer and trade press releases (to secure coverage)
	- Sending product samples for media (or consumer) trial and review
	- Product placement (in TV, movies)
	- Product/service literature (including brochures, video and CD-ROM)
	- Special events (eg celebrity store openings, product launch events, in-store competitions)
	- Consumer exhibitions and shows
	- Customer magazines, e-zines, newsletters, blogs
	- Sport, arts and community sponsorship
	- Publicity 'stunts' (attention-grabbing events to gain media coverage)
B2B communication	- Corporate identity (logos, liveries, house style of communications)
	- Corporate literature, website, videos
	- Trade exhibitions and conferences
	- Trade and general press relations
	- Corporate hospitality and gifts
Internal/employee communication	- In-house magazines, employee newsletters and corporate intranet (internal-access website)
	- Recruitment exhibitions and conferences
	- Direct employee communications: briefings, consultation meetings, works councils and so on
Corporate, external and public affairs	- Corporate literature and website
	- Corporate social responsibility and community involvement programmes: liaison with pressure groups, community representatives, local chamber of commerce
	- Sponsorship of arts, sporting and community organisations and events (often as part of a CSR profile)
	- Media relations: networking and image management through trade, local, national (and possibly international) press
	- Offering spokespeople and 'experts' for media interviews, consultation or authorship of articles

	▪ Local/central government and industry/trade lobbying, to protect or promote corporate/industry interests
	▪ Crisis and issues management: minimising the negative impacts of problems and bad publicity by managing media and public relations
Financial public relations	▪ Financial media relations
	▪ Design of annual and interim financial reports for shareholders
	▪ Facility visits for analysts, brokers, fund managers etc
	▪ Shareholder meetings and communications

ACTIVITY 8.6

Start collecting examples of:

▪ Editorial articles (or radio/TV segments) which quote representatives of a named commercial organisation: what impression is created by the attribution of the quoted statement, or the presence of the corporate representative?

▪ Named or visibly identifiable brands (watches, cars, soft drinks) in movies and TV programmes: this is called 'product placement'. How noticeable are they, and what effect does their presence have?

▪ Letters, notices or statements from spokespersons apologising for mistakes or errors (in advertising or customer service, or on larger issues of public concern such as a product recall, environmental disaster or other damaging revelations): how effectively do they minimise potential negative feelings on the part of stakeholders?

7.2 Sponsorship

> ▶ **Key term**
>
> **Sponsorship** involves supporting an event or activity by providing money (or some other value, such as product prizes for a competition), usually in return for naming rights, advertising or acknowledgement at the event and in any publicity connected with the event.

Sponsorship is often sought for sporting events, artistic events, education providers and charity/community programmes. A relatively new field in the UK is TV/radio programme sponsorship, which is more a form of advertising (getting the brand mentioned and/or shown) but with potential for affinity marketing (by association with a popular or 'worthwhile' programme).

Sponsorship is often seen as part of a company's socially-responsible and community-friendly public relations profile: it has the benefit of positive association with the sponsored cause or event. The profile gained (for example, in the case of TV coverage of a sporting event) can be cost-effective compared to TV advertising. However, it relies heavily on awareness and association: unless additional advertising space or 'air time' is part of the deal, not much information may be conveyed to stakeholders simply by naming rights or logo displays.

Marketers may sponsor local area or school groups and events – all the way up to national and international sporting and cultural events and organisations. Sponsorship has offered marketing avenues for organisations which are restricted in their advertising (such as alcohol and tobacco companies) or which wish to widen their awareness base among wider stakeholder audiences.

▪ There is wide corporate involvement in **mass-support sports** such as football and cricket.

▪ **Arts** sponsorship (of galleries, orchestra, theatrical productions and so on) tends to be taken up by financial institutions and prestige marketing organisations – although this depends on the target audience: youth arts events are more likely to be sponsored by music, clothing and soft drink brands, for example.

▪ **Community event** sponsorship (supporting local environment 'clean up' days, tree planting days, charity fun-runs, books for schools programmes and so on) is often used to associate companies with particular values (eg environmental concern, education) or with socially responsible community involvement.

 The Chartered Institute of Marketing

Arts sponsorship by Coutts

Coutts is a London bank offering private banking facilities to high net-worth individuals including clients from the arts and entertainment industries.

It sponsors a number of theatres including the Royal Court and the Young Vic in London. On its website, it explains 'From the earliest days, we have supported the performing arts and looked after the financial affairs of many influential figures connected with the arts such as Bram Stoker, Charles Dickens, Chopin and Berlioz.'

This sponsorship thus reflects its brand positioning effectively and in turn helps the theatres it sponsors to communicate with the bank's other clients who may be potential theatre-goers.

(Coutts, 2012)

7.2.1 Purposes of sponsorship

The objective of the organisation **soliciting sponsorship** (ie asking for sponsors) is most often financial support – or some other form of contribution, such as prizes for a competition, or a prestige name to be associated with the event to attract media coverage and consumer awareness. In return, it will need to offer potential sponsors satisfaction of *their* objectives.

▶ **Assessment tip**

It is worth remembering that the organisation you focus on in your assignment may want to consider *getting* sponsorship, as part of its promotion mix, rather than *offering sponsorship*. Both are tools of stakeholder marketing.

The objectives of the **sponsor** may be:

- **Awareness creation** in the target audience of the sponsored event (where it coincides with the target audience of the sponsor)

- **Media coverage** generated by the sponsored event (especially if direct advertising is regulated, as for tobacco companies)

- Opportunities for **corporate hospitality** at sponsored events

- **Association** with prestigious or popular events, or particular causes or values

- Creation of a **positive image** among employees or the wider community, through a reputation for corporate social responsibility profile or corporate citizenship

- Securing **potential employees** (eg by sponsoring vocational/tertiary education)

- **Cost-effective** achievement of the above (compared to, say, TV advertising).

Heineken sponsors Vietnam New Year

In Vietnam Christmas is increasingly perceived as a family event. To take advantage of this, Heineken turned to New Year's Eve 2010 as an opportunity to use sponsorship to raise its brand profile in the country. It launched a big outdoor party in Ho Chi Minh City, attended by over 200,000 people. The event was also broadcast via a live telecast with over a million viewers. In 2011, the pressure was on to create an even larger event – this was achieved by holding parties in both Ho Chi Minh City and Hanoi.

The brand has now gained approval from the Government and People's Committee to organise these events annually throughout Vietnam. Heineken now plans to use the New Year's Eve sponsorship to act as the focus of its brand platform in Vietnam for the next ten years. You can watch part of the 2012 celebrations on YouTube: http://www.youtube.com/watch?v=G3lTEhm2iFY.

(Warc, 2012)

7.3 Exhibitions

Consumer exhibitions (such as the Ideal Home Show) and B2B or trade fairs (such as the Frankfurt Book Fair) vary in the opportunities they offer for public relations, selling and networking. However, they are generally regarded as useful forums for:

- **Public relations**: both direct to visitors/attendees and via media coverage of the event, taking advantage of the interest generated by the exhibition organisers.

- **Promoting and selling** to a wide audience of pre-targeted, self-selected potential customers, suppliers, intermediaries, allies or employees – depending on the nature of the exhibition. Exhibitions are particularly useful where demonstrations (eg of technical innovations) or visual inspection (eg clothes or motor cars) are likely to influence buyers. Sales leads and contacts can be collected for later follow-up.

- **Networking** within the industry and with existing clients, and/or making supply and distribution chain contacts. Exhibitions may be a cost-effective opportunity for face-to-face meetings with overseas contacts, for example.

- **Testing the response** to new products and marketing messages.

- **Researching competitors**, their products and promotions, if they are also present.

Open-access exhibitions may attract a wide range of stakeholders.

7.4 Hospitality

Corporate hospitality involves entertaining members of key organisational stakeholders at corporate or public events. It is used for:

- Building or cementing relationships with key clients, supply chain partners, allies, media contacts, pressure groups and so on

- Rewarding and motivating key suppliers, intermediaries and/or employees

- Wooing potential employees in competitive labour markets

- Encouraging networking with representatives of other organisations, to establish contacts and build relationships

- Showing a presence at major events, to maintain public and industry profile and/or association with a cause or event values.

Large-scale corporate entertaining at sporting and cultural events is often handled by agencies, which purchase a block of tickets and sell them on to companies as part of a **hospitality package** including a marquee, box or hospitality room, refreshments and even programmes. Larger companies may own – or secure sponsor rights to – a permanent box or block of seats at stadiums and theatres. For a small company with no particular status requirements, ordinary ticket purchase and on-site catering may be sufficient. Organisations may also organise their own catered events, sports days, launch parties, award ceremonies and so on.

The **return on investment** on such entertaining is not always readily quantifiable, since there are many other factors in stakeholder loyalty – but there may well be industry norms and expectations to live up to. On the other hand, corporate ethical guidelines often place **restrictions** on the hospitality that can be accepted by employees, in order to maintain the appearance of objectivity in business decisions: principles such as transparency (openness) and mutuality (not accepting hospitality unless it can be reciprocated) may be observed.

7.5 Evaluation of PR for stakeholder marketing

Unlike other elements of the promotion mix, PR explicitly acknowledges a wide range of stakeholder publics or audiences – and the need to manage on-going contacts and relationships with them. It is therefore directly applicable to the full range of stakeholder groups, with established channels and tools of communication for each.

ACTIVITY 8.7

What do you think are the advantages and disadvantages of PR as a promotional tool for stakeholder marketing?

THE REAL WORLD

In 2011 Europcar, one of the biggest car hire companies both in and outside the UK, faced a market in which customers have little brand loyalty and are driven by price. After conducting research into views of motorway service station food, it was decided to partner with the Guild of Food Writers (the professional association of food writers and broadcasters in the UK) to produce the *Europcar Roadside Gastro Guide* which highlighted Britain's best-hidden motorway restaurants.

The guide was made available for free download from the Europcar website, discussion in social media stimulated by a Twitter feed and radio interviews with food writers offered to radio stations and newspapers.

The results were reported in thedrum.co.uk in September 2011:

- 55 pieces of quality branded coverage, including a seven minute piece on BBC Breakfast as well as 20 regional radio interviews, 6 national newspaper articles including the Sun and the Guardian

- ROI was 1:43, with 20,435 people reached for every £1 spent

- 25% increase in Twitter users during campaign

- 3,779 downloads in the first week – beating sales of that week's bestselling hardback

- 6,499 visits to the Gastro Guide page on the Europcar site.

(The Drum, 2011)

---

8 Integrated marketing communications

We will discuss the planning of the promotions mix in Chapter 11. However, you should be aware that this mix – like the marketing mix as a whole – needs to be **co-ordinated** so that:

- **Available resources** are appropriately spread across the mix, maximising its reach and impact.

- All promotional tools **convey the core message** of the organisation or brand, in line with marketing plans. So, for example, if you wished to position yourself as an exclusive, luxury perfume house, you might use stylish photographic images in *Vogue* and discreet personal selling in up-market department stores, rather than a 'win a body spray' competition in *Woman's Own* or discount offers at Tesco.

- All promotion tools **work in harmony** (avoiding giving contradictory or confusing messages) and therefore **reinforce each other** (cumulatively adding messages which consistently repeat and develop the core message). So, for example, you would not want to use the stylish photographic images in *Vogue* AND the discount offers at Tesco…

Stakeholders receive and assimilate product data from a wide range of sources and media. (This range is increasing all the time, as we have seen.) From the stakeholder's point of view, tools such as advertising, public relations and sales promotion aren't experienced as 'separate disciplines' or 'separate functions in the organisation': they comprise a **total experience** of an organisation and its brands and service. The stakeholder doesn't (and shouldn't) care that the person who published a sales promotion leaflet is not in the same department or location as the salesperson who doesn't know anything about the special offer: what the stakeholder sees is an organisation whose left hand doesn't know what its right hand is doing!

8.1 Integrated Marketing Communications (IMC)

> ▶ **Key term**
>
> **Integrated Marketing Communications (IMC)** is 'A concept of marketing communications planning that recognises the added value of a comprehensive plan that evaluates the strategic roles of a variety of communications disciplines and combines them to provide clarity, consistency and maximum communications impact through the seamless integration of discrete messages.' (American Association of Advertising Agencies)

The total marketing communication model can be shown as follows.

Figure 8.3   Integrated marketing communications

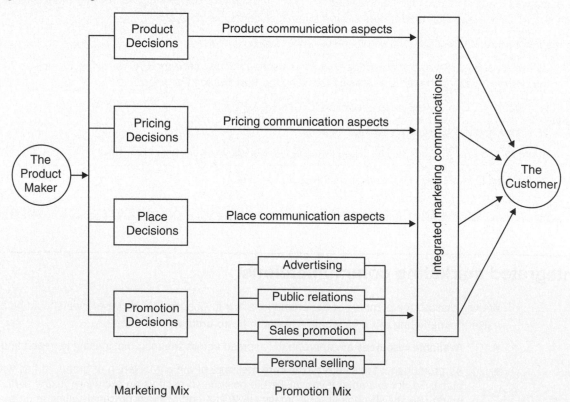

The Chartered Institute of Marketing

The **benefits** of co-ordinating or integrating marketing communications include the following.

- Greater direction, efficiency and accountability in marketing management

- Competitive advantage through more co-ordinated brand development

- More effective response to the increasing proliferation of media and audiences

- More effective response to the increasing information needs (and rights) of customers and other stakeholders – while minimising the tendency towards information overload and 'clutter'

- Support for relationship marketing: co-ordinating multiple (consistent) contacts with stakeholders to develop on-going dialogue and relationship

- Increased effectiveness of promotions, through consistency and reinforcement of core messages.

8.2 Integration and internal stakeholder communication

Communication within the marketing organisation will be an essential part of an effective IMC approach, ensuring that:

- All units of the organisation who deal with customers (directly or indirectly) are aware of the messages being communicated by themselves and others

- All units understand the desired core messages of the organisation/brand, and the need for consistency in getting that core message across

- Promises made by one customer contact are delivered by subsequent customer contacts!

ACTIVITY 8.8

You are an officer of the Health Education Council, a government-supported body, and you have been asked to develop a campaign to reduce alcohol consumption among young adults. In a memorandum to your manager, state what relative emphasis you would place on each element of the promotion mix. Also set out how you would seek to integrate the campaign.

- The range of tools of the marketing communications (promotional) mix

- Stakeholders as target audiences

- Above- and below-the-line promotion

- Advertising

- Sales promotion (consumer and trade)

- Direct marketing

- Personal selling

- Branding

- Public relations: publicity sponsorship, exhibitions, corporate hospitality

- Integrated marketing communications (IMC)

- Consistency, coherence and co-operation

- Selecting the promotional mix

FURTHER READING

Browse through advertising industry magazines, which have examples and evaluations of up-to-date campaigns, tools and techniques. Many are online and some addresses are given here.

Campaign Magazine: http://www.campaignlive.co.uk

Direct marketing ideas and campaigns

Direct Marketing News: http://www.dmnews.com/

There are useful articles posted on the website of the BDS Sponsorship consultancy.

http://www.sponsorship.co.uk

Public relations

PR Week: http://www.prweek.com

REFERENCES

Allen, C. *et al* (2001) *One to One Web Marketing.* 2nd edition. New York, Wiley.

Anon (2011) P. R. success: Europecar Roadside Gastro Guide is a winner, thanks to 'hidden gems'. The Drum. http://www.thedrum.co.uk/news/2011/09/06/pr-success-europcar-roadside-gastro-guide-winner-thanks-hidden-gems [Accessed 24 June 2012].

B2B Marketing (2012) Branding News: Adobe launches multi-million pound brand campaign. http://www.b2bmarketing.net/news/archive/branding-news-adobe-launches-multi-million-pound-brand-campaign [Accessed 24 June 2012].

Baron S. (ed) (1991) *Macmillan Dictionary of Retailing.* Palgrave Macmillan.

Coutts (2012) http://www.coutts.com/about-us/sponsorship/. [Accessed 24 June 2012].

Davies, J. (2012) Honda kicks off connected TV and console content trials. New Media Age. http://www.nma.co.uk/news/honda-kicks-off-connected-tv-and-console-content-trials/4000315.article [Accessed 24 June 2012].

Kotler, P. *et al* (1999) *Marketing: An Introduction.* Sydney, Prentice Hall Australia.

Mullins, R. (2002) *Direct Marketing.* London, Kogan Page.

Smith, P. R. *et al* (1997*) Strategic Marketing Communications: New Ways to Guild and Integrate Communications.* London, Kogan Page.

Varey, R. J. (2002) *Marketing Communications: Principles & Practice.* Abingdon, Oxon, Routledge.

Warc (2011) http://www.warc.com/Content/Documents/A95170_Heineken_Creating_a_national_phenomenon_in_Vietnam.content?CID=A95170&ID=2d65dd13-b5dd-40ff-a7a3-564a270932fc&q=&qr= [Accessed on 18 June 2012].

QUICK QUIZ

1 Distinguish between above- and below-the-line promotion.

2 What criteria can be used to select advertising media?

3 Give three examples of 'new media' in advertising.

4 List three techniques of (a) sales promotion and (b) trade promotion.

5 Identify four activities involved in personal selling.

6 Give three examples of direct marketing tools.

7 Define (a) public relations and (b) sponsorship.

8 What is 'financial PR' and what activities might it consist of?

9 List three uses of corporate hospitality.

10 Why is it important to co-ordinate or integrate the promotional mix?

Activity 8.1

Your own research. This is just intended as a 'warm-up' exercise to get you thinking.

Activity 8.2

Your own research. If you can include ads by your own work organisation, or another organisation you are focusing on, this may be useful groundwork for your assignment.

Activity 8.3

You own research.

Activity 8.4

The advantages and disadvantages of personal selling can be summarised as follows.

Advantages	Disadvantages
Relatively high level of customer attention, because of face-to-face factor	Costly, because labour intensive
Enables the salesperson to customise the message to the customer	Can only reach one or a few customers at a time
Two-way: immediate feedback	Unsuitable for many consumer purchases
Can convey large amounts of technical and complex information	Requires sales force recruitment, training, management, motivation and so on
Ability to demonstrate the product	
Frequent contact and interaction develops long-term, collaborative relationship	

Activity 8.5

As with personal selling, it is worth noting that DM can be extended to non-customer stakeholders as well. Many companies, for example, send periodical surveys, newsletters, briefings and reports to their shareholders, supplier and business networks, and employees. These may be designed purely to maintain contact and communication, as part of a relational marketing strategy – but they may also elicit direct responses (feedback, contact, suggestions, attendance at a meeting or conference and so on).

Activity 8.6

Your own research. Again, if you can include examples from your own work organisation, this would be useful preparation for an assignment.

Activity 8.7

The advantages and disadvantages of PR as a promotional tool can be summarised as follows.

Advantages	Disadvantages
Raises awareness of wider audiences	The organisation can't control editorial content or guarantee coverage when desired (unlike advertising)
Builds corporate identity, supporting relationship with stakeholders (internal and external)	Media have their own agenda (circulation/ratings, public information) which may not always support positive publicity for the organisation
Relatively low cost (no media costs)	Difficult to measure effectiveness/impact
Can add legitimacy (implication of endorsement or recommendation), word-of-mouth promotion and goodwill (support in times of difficulty)	There is a risk of poor publicity and negative associations – as well as positive ones. (Yes, there is such a thing as bad publicity!)
Supports advertising, sales promotion and personal selling	

Activity 8.8

Our full specimen answer is as follows. The details of your answer will differ, but note some of the elements we have included.

Memorandum

To: Chief Executive
From: Information Officer
Date: [today]
Subject: Reduction in alcohol consumption

In response to your request I set out my recommendations for the relative emphasis to be placed on each element of the marketing communications mix in the first year of our campaign.

(a)   **Overall intention**

We should concentrate in the first instance on medium to heavy users. In this way we will avoid a head-on clash with committed users and alcoholics, yet ensure that there is overspill from our work into both the light and heavy user segments.

We should target the influential members of our target audience rather than attempt a widespread campaign that would dissipate our budget and minimise the effect.

The whole campaign should be co-ordinated around a positioning statement to ensure that we have consonance throughout.

(b)   **Advertising (40% emphasis)**

The role of advertising is to inform, to persuade. It is necessary to target our campaign very carefully so as to hit the target audience, those with influence within the medium to heavy consumers of alcohol.

The trade press should be used to remind vendors of their legal obligations. More profit can be made from certain alternatives to alcohol, and this fact should be stressed.

Media advertising should focus not on the dangers of alcohol, but on the pleasure to be derived from the alternatives.

There should be a strong congratulatory element within the advertising (avoiding smugness) to reinforce the non-users and, in particular, those who have given up, or reduced their consumption.

(c) **Public relations (40% emphasis)**

PR should be our main weapon at this stage. We should endeavour to encourage prominent non-users of alcohol to mention the fact whenever possible without becoming strident nor appearing to preach.

Parliament should be lobbied to introduce legislation. Both government and opposition parties should be targeted, and individual MPs supportive of the cause recruited and supported.

Public media of regard, and particularly individuals who have an affinity with certain target segments, should be provided with case histories, and pertinent information in easy-to-use press packs.

Evidence of success in similar campaigns across the world should be compiled and used as appropriate in our briefings and press packs.

Non-alcohol events should be encouraged, and sponsorship such as the Milk Race should be supported.

Local pressure groups should be formed, and encouraged to be self-supportive within our overall promotional policy.

(d) **Packaging (Longer term emphasis)**

We cannot use packaging, since this is the province of the manufacturers. It is, however, a major target for our parliamentary lobby since we should endeavour to enforce government health warnings following the pattern established in the tobacco market.

(e) **Sales promotion (10% emphasis)**

We should develop sales promotion and point-of-purchase materials which will encourage moderation in consumption especially at critical periods such as Christmas and New Year.

(f) **Contingency (10% emphasis)**

We should hold 10% of the budget as reserve to counter the expected reaction from the powerful alcohol industry and its established lobby. This budget should not be committed until six months into our campaign when we have assessed preliminary achievement and can decide where best to focus our effort.

(g) **Integration**

It is vital that we plan the above elements into an integrated campaign. We will use the same creative designs in all elements in a cost-effective manner. We will need to plan each stage so that they reinforce each other in a logical manner.

(h) **Summary**

This will be a prolonged campaign that must be sustained against great odds over a considerable period of time. To judge from the ASH campaign against smoking it may take ten years for the first effects to show in any marked way. However, the ASH curve of success was exponential. This is to be expected as attitude shift gains momentum, but we should not be too optimistic about immediate marked success. There are, after all, more committed users of alcohol than there are smokers, and the secondary effects of alcohol are less pronounced. It is nevertheless a campaign that must be undertaken, and one to which great numbers of the public will subscribe as it gains credibility.

1   Above-the-line promotion involves advertising in paid-for media (such as print media, radio and TV). Below-the-line promotion is other activities, such as PR, direct marketing and sales promotion.

2   Criteria used to select advertising media include: size of audience, type and targeting of audience, suitability of the medium for the message, and cost.

3   See section 2.3 for a full list to choose from.

4   Sales promotion techniques include: price promotions, gift with purchase (or premium) promotions, competitions and frequent user (loyalty) incentives. Trade promotion techniques include: trade discounts, baker's dozen packs, collaborative promotion, point of sale support, competitions and awards for sales, and business gifts.

5   Personal selling involves communicating, selling, servicing and information gathering.

6   See section 5.1 for a full list to choose from.

7   Public relations is the planned and sustained effort to establish and maintain goodwill and mutual understanding between an organisation and its publics. Sponsorship involves supporting an event or activity by providing money or some other value, in return for naming rights, advertising or other form of association with the event.

8   Financial public relations is PR activity directed at shareholders, the financial press and financial markets. It may include financial media relations, shareholder reports, facility visits, and shareholder meetings and communications.

9   Corporate hospitality may be used for building or cementing relationships with stakeholders; rewarding or motivating suppliers, intermediaries or staff; wooing potential employees; encouraging networking; or showing a presence at events.

10 It is important to co-ordinate the promotional mix in order to maximise the use of resources; maintain coherence and clarity of messages, and maintain consistency of messages.

CHAPTER 9

Internal stakeholder communications

Introduction

This chapter explores one particular context in which stakeholder marketing communications take place: the internal stakeholder environment.

Whereas traditional marketing has focused exclusively on the external customer, relationship marketing, as we have seen, embraces a wider range of stakeholder markets – including the **internal market** of employees and inter-departmental relations.

In section 1, we explain the nature of the internal market and the 'internal customer concept' which underpins much of the thinking on internal marketing.

In sections 2 to 5, we look at some key areas of internal marketing: internal communications; employee retention, loyalty and commitment (highlighted by the syllabus); employee involvement and empowerment; and cross-functional co-operation. We consider why each is important, and what tools can be used to encourage them.

Topic list

Internal stakeholders	1
Internal communications	2
Employee retention, loyalty and commitment	3
Employee empowerment and involvement	4
Cross-functional co-operation	5

4.2	Identify and evaluate the range of tools available to support the communications relating to internal customer loyalty, ie, employee support, engagement and retention within the organisation:
	■ Email
	■ Intranet
	■ Training – staff enrichment programmes
	■ Support – technical, management
	■ Flexible working
	– Secondments
	– Gap years
	■ Team meetings

1 Internal stakeholders

We have already mentioned internal stakeholders several times in the course of our coverage so far – and it should be fairly obvious why.

- Organisations are made up of people (often referred to, these days, as the **human resources** of a business). When we talk about 'organisations' marketing to external customers/stakeholders, or establishing relationships with them, what we are really talking about is *employees of the organisation* implementing these activities.

- Employees and their employing organisations are mutually dependent. Employees need work and its financial rewards in order to live – and organisations need employees to implement their plans and carry out their activities. Employees are therefore **key stakeholders** in the organisation, with both high interest and high (collective) power.

Peck *et al* (1999) identify the **internal market** as a key component of their Six Markets Model. It includes employees in all parts of an organisation with potential to contribute towards marketing effectiveness.

'There are two key aspects to internal marketing. The first is concerned with how **staff work together across functional boundaries** so that their work is attuned to the company's mission, strategy and goals. The second involves the idea of the **internal customer**. That is, every person working within an organisation is both a supplier and a customer.' (*ibid* p 302)

Gummesson (2002, p198) similarly suggests that:

'The objective of internal marketing within Relationship Marketing is to **create relationships between management and employees, and between functions**. The personnel can be viewed as an **internal market**, and this market must be reached efficiently in order to prepare the personnel for external contacts: efficient internal marketing becomes an antecedent to efficient external marketing'.

We will explore both these aspects in this chapter.

1.1 The internal customer concept

As the term suggests, the internal customer concept implies the following ideas.

- Any unit of the organisation whose task contributes to the task of other units (whether as part of a process or in an advisory or service relationship) can be regarded as a supplier of a product/service. In other words, there is an **internal supply chain** – and the 'next person to handle your work' is your internal customer.

- The objective of each unit and individual thus becomes the 'efficient and effective **identification and satisfaction of the needs, wants and expectations of customers**' (one definition of marketing) *within* the internal value chain – as well as outside it.

- Any given unit of the organisation must 'create, build and maintain **mutually beneficial exchanges and relationships**' (another definition of marketing) *within* the organisation, as well as outside it.

ACTIVITY 9.1

Who are the internal customers of the marketing function in your organisation, or any organisation? What are their key needs and expectations?

1.2 Internal marketing

> ▶ **Key term**
>
> **Internal marketing** may be defined as a variety of approaches and techniques by which an organisation acquires, motivates, equips and retains customer-conscious employees (George & Grönroos, 1989), in order to help retain customers through achieving high quality service delivery and increased customer satisfaction.
>
> Berry and Parasuraman (1991) define it as: 'attracting, developing, motivating and retaining qualified employees through job products that satisfy their needs' – which relates it clearly to the conventional concept of the marketing exchange.

Internal marketing has been well summarised by Peck *et al* (*op cit*, p313):

'Internal marketing is concerned with creating, developing and maintaining an **internal service culture and orientation**, which in turn assists and supports the organisation in the achievement of its goals. The internal service culture has a vital impact on how service-oriented and customer-oriented employees are, and, thus, how well they perform their tasks... The development and maintenance of a customer-oriented culture is a critical determinant of long-term success in relationship marketing...

The basic premise behind the development of internal marketing is the acknowledgement of the **impact of employee behaviour and attitudes** on the relationship between staff and external customers. This is particularly true where employees occupy boundary-spanning positions in the organisation... The skills and customer orientation of these employees are, therefore, critical to the customers' perception of the organisation and their future loyalty to the organisation.'

In other words, it is through internal marketing that all employees can develop an understanding of how their tasks, and the way they perform them, create and deliver customer value and build relationship.

THE REAL WORLD

LL Bean (US catalogue retailer)

To inspire its employees to practise the marketing concept, LL Bean has for decades displayed posters around its office that proclaim the following:

'What is a customer? A customer is the most important person ever in this company, in person or by mail. A customer is not dependent on us, we are dependent on him. A customer is not an interruption of our work, he is the purpose of it. We are not doing a favour by serving him, he is doing us a favour by giving us the opportunity to do so. A customer is not someone to argue or match wits with, nobody ever won an argument with a customer. A customer is a person who brings us his wants; it is our job to handle them profitably to him and to ourselves.'

Peck *et al* (1999, p324) identify the following range of inter-related activities thought to be critical in implementing internal marketing.

- **Organisational design**: eg drawing key employees together in cross-functional customer service or quality teams

- **Regular staff surveys**: assessing the internal service culture and attitudes

- **Internal customer segmentation**: adapting the internal marketing mix to different employee groups

- **Personal development and training**: focused on core competencies for internal marketing

- **Empowerment and involvement**: enabling staff, within defined parameters, to use their discretion to deliver better service to customers

- **Recognition and rewards**: based on employees' contribution to service excellence

- **Internal communications**: ensuring information flows to support cross-functional co-ordination, and all-employee awareness of their role and contribution to service

- **Performance measures**: evaluating each individual's and department's contribution to marketing objectives

- **Building supportive working relationships**: creating a climate of consideration, trust and support, within which internal communications and service delivery can be continuously encouraged and improved.

▶ **Assessment tip**

You will find a variety of terms used to describe internal stakeholder relations, including 'internal partnerships', 'internal relationships', 'internal marketing', and 'internal customer loyalty' (the phrase used by the syllabus). They are broadly interchangeable, so don't be worried if you see them in your assignment brief. Egan (2004, p153) suggests a helpful way of distinguishing between them if you need to: '*Internal marketing* can be seen as the process towards the development of *internal partnerships*' (which in turn, you might say, are aimed at creating *internal customer loyalty*).

1.3 The internal marketing mix

Jobber (2007, p864) directly relates the elements of the **marketing mix** to internal customers as follows.

Table 9.1   The internal marketing mix

Product	The **marketing plan** and strategies that are being proposed to employees or other functions, together with the values, attitudes and actions needed to make the plan successful (eg marketing budgets, extra staff).
Price	What internal customers are being asked to **pay or sacrifice** as a result of accepting the marketing plan (eg lost resources, lower status, new ways of working or harder work).
Promotion (or communications)	The communications **media and messages** used to inform, persuade and gain the support of internal customers for the marketing plan. The message and language will have to be adapted to the needs, concerns and understanding of the target audience (eg eliminating marketing jargon).
Place	How the product (plan) and communications are **delivered** to internal customers: eg via meetings, committees, seminars, informal conversations and so on. This may be direct or via intermediaries (eg consultants).

1.3.1 Segmenting the internal market

The internal marketing mix (like the external marketing mix) will need to be adapted to the needs and drivers of the target audience. The internal market can (like the external market) be **segmented** to allow targeting to the distinctive needs of each group.

Jobber (2007) suggests segmentation of internal customers into:

- **Supporters**: those who are likely to gain from the change or plan, or are already committed to it
- **Neutrals**: those who are likely to experience both gains and losses from the change or plan
- **Opposers**: those who are likely to lose from the change or plan, or are traditional opponents.

The product (plan) and price may have to be modified to gain acceptance from opponents. Place decisions will be used to reach each group most effectively (eg high-involvement approaches such as consultation meetings for supporters and neutrals). Promotional objectives will also differ according to the target group, because of their different positions on issues.

ACTIVITY 9.2

From your knowledge of Egan's stakeholders in change (Chapter 1), recommend promotional strategies for internal supporters, neutrals and opposers.

Christopher *et al* (2002, p109) suggest an alternative way of segmenting internal customers, according to **how close they are to external customers**:

- **Contactors** have frequent or regular customer contact and are typically heavily involved with conventional marketing activities (eg sales or customer service roles). They need to be well-versed in the firm's marketing strategies, and trained, prepared and motivated to service customers on a day-to-day basis in a responsive manner.

- **Modifiers** are not directly involved with conventional marketing activities, but still have frequent contact with customers (eg receptionists, switchboard, the credit department). These people need a clear view of the organisation's marketing strategy and the importance of being responsive to customers' needs.

- **Influencers** are involved with the traditional elements of marketing, but have little or no direct customer contact (eg in product development or market research). Companies must ensure that these people develop a sense of customer responsiveness, as they influence the total value offering to the customer.

- **Isolateds** are support functions that have neither direct customer contact nor marketing input – but whose activities nevertheless affect the organisation's performance (eg purchasing, HR and data processing). Such staff need to be sensitive to the needs of *internal* customers as well as their role in the chain that delivers value to customers. Gummesson (*op cit*) uses the term 'part-time marketers' to describe such employees.

ACTIVITY 9.3

- Draw up Christopher *et al's* internal market segments as a two-dimensional matrix (like the power/interest matrix, say), using the two dimensions mentioned i.e. customer contact and marketing involvement.

- List examples of specific departments or job roles in your own organisation that correspond to each segment, building on the examples we have already given.

2 Internal communications

2.1 The importance of internal customer communications

Information and communication are the foundation of all organisational activity. From a marketing point of view, internal communications may be particularly important in the following areas.

Table 9.2   Areas that may benefit from internal communications

Employer branding	The organisation's image, mediated by communication, creates an employer brand: the organisation's image or identity as an employer in the market in which it competes for quality labour.
	Recruitment communications (job ads, application handling, interviews and so on) are public relations and marketing exercises. They must reflect the organisation's values and make an attractive offering to potential employees.
Employee communication and involvement	In many countries, there are **legal requirements** for communication and consultation with employees on matters that affect them.
	The sharing of marketing information encourages employees to **identify with the organisation**, its products/ services and its customers and other stakeholders: the marketing function effectively 'sells' quality- and customer-focused values.
	Information sharing also supports **task performance** (keeping employees informed about new products and marketing plans, and equipping them to make a competent contribution) and **decision making** (eg by supplying market information or customer feedback to managers in other departments).
	Internal communications (eg through meetings, presentations, newsletters, intranet sites or suggestion schemes) can be used to improve **information flow** in all directions through the organisation. This may be particularly helpful where it encourages information- and ideas-sharing between management and front-line customer-facing staff, and between different organisational functions.
Employee relations	Armstrong (2000) describes the aims of employee relations as:
	▪ Building **stable and co-operative relationships** with employees and minimising conflict
	▪ Achieving **commitment** through employee involvement and communications processes
	▪ Developing **mutuality**: a common interest in achieving the organisation's goals, through the development of a culture of shared values.
	Co-operative employee relations depend on direct and open communication with employees, and giving employees a voice on matters that concern them (including customer care and corporate social responsibility).

ACTIVITY 9.4

▪ Identify each of the elements of the marketing mix (four Ps) in relation to the recruitment of new employees. What are the product, price, promotion and place in this process?

▪ Get hold of the Report and Accounts of your work organisation and/or any other that interests you, or browse its website. What attitudes and values towards employees and the employment relationship do these statements express? What are the internal and external marketing effects of these kinds of statements?

If relevant, you may like to draft some recommendations for how these statements might be improved, as a marketing message to (a) employees and (b) potential employees of the organisation.

2.2 Challenges for internal communication

Jones & Cheeseman (2005) argue that it is growing more *difficult* for organisations to maintain communication with staff, while other pressures contribute to increasing staff diversity and isolation – making such communications even more *necessary* for integration and involvement. Some of the challenges they identify include:

▪ Flatter management structures, meaning that managers have more people reporting to them (a wider 'span of control')

The Chartered Institute of Marketing

- Downsizing, creating workload pressures that may hinder communication and networking
- A trend towards tele-working and 'virtual' organisation, so that staff may be geographically remote from the office, manager and each other
- Globalisation, creating increasingly diverse workforces and culturally distinctive units within the organisation, which pose barriers to 'mass' communication.

Jobber (2007) cites the example of software giant **Microsoft**.

'It is very easy for senior management to decide upon a set of values that represent a company's ethos, but much harder to **engage employees' attention**. This was the problem Microsoft faced when trying to **communicate its identity** as a company internally. It expressed its company values in terms of six attributes: passion, respect, accountability, integrity, self-criticism and eagerness.

Its **internal marketing strategy** was to ensure this ethos was communicated to employees in three stages. First, there was a campaign across the UK to generate positive feelings about the project. Second, a series of road-shows was held around the firm's UK offices to discuss the core values in depth. Third, a compulsory education programme was launched to ensure all staff understood the proposition.

The creative element of the programme was centred on the well-known David Brent character from the BBC series The Office. Actor Ricky Gervais, who played this character, became involved and a special 15-minute video in the style of the programme was filmed, adding humour to the project and raising its appeal to staff.

The result was that the project achieved high recognition levels for the main message of the campaign among employees, national press coverage and an award for the best internal marketing campaign from the magazine *Marketing*.'

2.3 Tools of internal communication

A very wide variety of communication media is used in formal internal communications, including: company reports, brochures and newsletters; corporate intranet (staff website); video- and web-conferencing; video and CD-ROM presentations; team meetings, briefings, presentations and conferences; one-to-one interviews; negotiating and consultative meetings (eg with employee representatives); letters, e-mail, memoranda and notices; and so on.

The syllabus highlights three internal communication tools: e-mail, intranet and team meetings.

2.3.1 Email

The term 'electronic mail' or e-mail is used to describe various systems for sending messages electronically via a telecom or data network. E-mail has to a large extent replaced letters, memos, faxes, documents and even telephone calls – combining many of the advantages of each medium with new advantages of speed, cost and convenience.

E-mail offers many advantages for internal customer communication.

- Messages can be sent and received very quickly (allowing real-time message dialogue)
- E-mail is economical, especially for international communication: no postage or similar costs are involved
- All parties can print out a 'hard copy' of the message, for detailed perusal and repeated reference
- Messages can be sent worldwide at any time: email is 24-7, regardless of time zones and office hours
- The user can attach complex documents (spreadsheets, graphics, photos) where added data or impact are required

- E-mail message management software (such as Microsoft Outlook) has convenient features such as: message copying (to multiple recipients); integration with an 'address book' (database of contacts); corporate stationery options; and facilities for mail organisation and filing.

ACTIVITY 9.5

- From your knowledge of e-mail, what might be some of the *disadvantages* of e-mail for internal communication with colleagues in your own department or other departments?

- How is e-mail used in your work organisation, and what rules and guidelines are given for its use?

- What other communication tools are commonly used in your organisation for internal communication (i) on a one-to-one basis and (ii) within a department and (iii) for 'mass' communication with all staff?

2.3.2 Intranet

An intranet is an internal, mini version of the internet, using a combination of networked computers and web technology.

'Inter' means 'between' and 'intra' means 'within'. This may be a useful reminder. The **internet** is used to disseminate and exchange information among the public at large, and between organisations. An **intranet** is used to disseminate and exchange information within an organisation: only employees are able to access this information.

The corporate intranet may be used for:

- **Performance data**: linked to sales, inventory, job progress and other database and reporting systems, enabling employees to process and analyse data to fulfil their work objectives

- **Employment information**: online policy and procedures manuals (health and safety, equal opportunity, disciplinary rules, customer service values and so on), training and induction material, internal contacts for help and information

- **Employee support/information**: advice on first aid, healthy working at computer terminals, training courses offered and so on

- **Notice boards** for the posting of messages to and from employees: notice of meetings, events, trade union activities and so on

- **Departmental home pages**: information and news about each department's personnel and activities, to aid cross-functional understanding

- **Bulletins or newsletters**: details of product launches and marketing campaigns, staff moves, changes in company policy – or whatever might be communicated through the print equivalent, plus links to relevant pages for details

- **E-mail facilities** for the exchange of messages, memos and reports between employees in different locations

- **Upward communication**: suggestion schemes, feedback questionnaires, employee attitude surveys

- **Individual personnel files**, to which employees can upload their training materials, references, certificates, appraisals, goal plans and so on.

Advantages cited for the use of intranets include the following.

- **Cost savings** from the elimination of storage, printing and distribution of documents that can instead be exchanged electronically or be made available online

- **More frequent use** made of online documents than printed reference resources (eg procedures manuals) and more flexible and efficient searching and updating of data

- **Wider access to corporate information**. This facilitates multi-directional communication and co-ordination (particularly for multi-site working). It is also a mechanism of internal marketing and corporate culture

- **Virtual team working**. The term 'virtual team' has been coined to describe how ICT can link people in structures which simulate the dynamics of team working (sense of belonging, joint goals, information sharing and collaboration) despite the geographical dispersion of team members in different locations or constantly on the move.

THE REAL WORLD

The importance of company intranets in supporting internal marketing is reflected in the fact that there is now an annual award for the best intranets! The Nielsen Norman Group (a US-based consulting and research firm, specialising in user experience and usability of websites) publishes a report each year reviewing the design and usability of the world's top ten intranets.

Its 2012 report highlighted two UK companies in the top ten – Logica, a business and technology service company, and Everything Everywhere, the joint venture between Orange and T-Mobile in the UK.

(*Communicate* magazine, 2012)

2.3.3 Team meetings

Meetings play an important part in the life of any organisation.

- **Formal discussions** are used for information exchange, problem solving and decision making: for example, negotiations with suppliers, meetings to give or receive product/idea presentations or 'pitches', and employee interviews

- **Informal discussions** may be called regularly, or on an ad hoc basis, for communication and consultation on matters of interest or concern: for example, informal briefings and marketing or project team meetings.

Despite the relative inconvenience (compared to group emails, say) of gathering people together in a physical location, team meetings are an excellent tool of internal communication and marketing. Face-to-face discussion is particularly effective in exchanging information *and* developing relationships.

Table 9.3   Advantages of team meetings

Advantages	Examples
Encourages **ideas generation:** participants encouraging and prompting each other	Brainstorming meeting for promotion planning or customer care improvement
Encourages **problem solving** and **conflict resolution:** allows exchange, supportive communication and sensitivity to personal factors	Customer complaint handling, or team conflict resolution
Improves **decision making:** adds different viewpoints and information in real time	Team meetings to decide plans or allocate roles and tasks
Facilitates **persuasion:** use of personal charisma, logic, sensitivity to feedback	Sales negotiations, pitching ideas to internal customers, promoting service values
Encourages **co-operation:** information sharing and all-member participation	Cross-functional team meetings, briefings, project meetings
Shows the **human face** of an organisation and encourages identification with it	Personal internal/external customer service, internal marketing

- What disadvantages can you see in the use of team meetings for internal marketing? (Think about the meetings you have participated in.)

- How are team meetings used in your work organisation, and how effectively are they managed and led to achieve their intended purposes?

2.3.4 Informal communication channels

In addition to formal attempts by the organisation to communicate with its employees, there are informal communication channels such as the 'grapevine': friends, colleagues and contacts developing internal networks, sharing news, information and gossip. This is a fast and effective way of transmitting information: unfortunately, it is often inaccurate, subjective – and difficult for management to control. Marketers should feed plenty of information into informal networks, to avoid inaccurate speculation. They should also tap into these networks themselves, so that they know what is being said!

3 Employee retention, loyalty and commitment

3.1 The value of employee loyalty and retention

The basic argument for employee retention is that a long-term, stable and experienced work force delivers higher service quality at lower cost – which in turn may lead to higher customer retention and higher profitability.

The advantages of retaining employees, or reducing employee turnover, may be summarised as follows.

- Long-term employees have had time to adjust to the organisation's processes and systems, and to undergo necessary learning. High labour turnover means that there is a higher proportion of new employees facing adjustment issues and a steep learning curve before they can achieve consistent high-quality performance.

- Employee retention (like customer retention) is more profitable than replacing lost employees through recruitment. Retained employees save on the costs of recruitment advertising and procedures, and on-going costs of initial under-performance (while learning), training, instruction and supervision until they get up to speed.

- Long-term employees are often able to form personal relationships with customers, through repeated contact. This interpersonal contact, and the building of trust, may be a factor in customer loyalty.

- When employee turnover is reduced, service values and norms are more consistent, and are transmitted to incoming employees without frequent, costly interventions by management.

In addition, retention policies are often what make an organisation 'good to work for' – and this not only enhances existing employee retention, but makes the organisation an 'employer of choice' in the recruitment market. Retention policies enhance the organisation's employer brand, making it easier to attract quality labour.

3.2 The value of employee commitment

Compliance means performing according to set rules and standards, according to what you are expected and asked to do (but not necessarily more than that). **Commitment**, on the other hand, has been defined as: 'The relative strength of an individual's identification with, and involvement in, a particular organisation.' (Mowdray *et al*, 1982). It is characterised by at least three factors:

- A strong belief in, and acceptance of, an organisation's goals and values
- A willingness to exert considerable effort on behalf of the organisation
- A strong desire to maintain membership of the organisation.

Commitment-based management is said to be most effective in environments where customer demands and technologies are varied and changing, and employees are required to be flexible, creative and positive in contributing to the organisation's goals. They contribute because they *want* to – and often contribute more (and more flexibly) than they would under compliance-based management, which tends to invite performance at the set standard but no more, since there is little incentive or space for creative or exceptional input or effort. In other words, committed employees add more value.

3.3 The value of employee satisfaction

We have already discussed how the **service profit cycle** and Reichheld's loyalty-based cycle of growth trace a clear relationship between employee satisfaction/ loyalty and external customer satisfaction/loyalty.

- Investment in employee satisfaction leads to employee retention (improving customer service over time, through familiarity, contacts and learning) and commitment (improving customer service through greater effort, productivity, flexibility and identification with the organisation's customer care values).

- Improved customer service creates more satisfied and loyal customers. This is satisfying for employees (if only because it results in less hassles and complaints!). It also makes marketing more cost-effective, because customer retention is more profitable than customer acquisition – and the resulting profits can partly be reinvested in enhanced employee rewards and retention policies. And so on, round the cycle.

You should recognise many of the elements from earlier chapters, but notice how external customer service is underpinned by:

- **Leadership, vision and values** (organisation culture) which 'sell' the idea of customer focus and organisation-wide marketing responsibility.

- **Internal customer relations**. The satisfaction of *external* customers is the result of a range of satisfying *internal* relationships and transactions between colleagues and departments. Encouraging staff to consider the needs of their internal customers ('the next person to handle your work') helps to foster quality and service at the interface with external customers. Key factors in managing the quality of internal service operations include:

    - The recruitment of skilled customer-facing people
    - The supply of appropriate (and generous) training
    - The empowerment of staff to take decisions that will attract and keep customers
    - The reward and recognition of staff who deliver outstanding service.

As a would-be marketing communicator, you should recognise the importance of getting production staff excited about an upcoming launch (which might soften the blow of the production deadlines!), say, or encouraging brand managers and sales staff to feel energised by your marketing support for their efforts.

THE REAL WORLD

The **Great Place to Work Institute** conducts an annual survey identifying the best workplaces in Europe and around the world. The following are the top UK and worldwide firms in the 2011 survey.

Baringa Partners: UK management consultancy Best Workplace in the UK for the second consecutive year.

'Creating an environment that forms a supportive and enjoyable place to work is of paramount importance to us. Attracting, developing and retaining the best people allows us to work with the best clients in our industries on their most important programmes of change. Working with the best clients on exciting programmes allows us to attract, develop and retain the best people. This virtuous circle is the cornerstone of our business model.' (Bariga, 2012)

3.4 Tools of employee retention, loyalty and commitment

Retention may not be the same thing as loyalty and commitment. Like customers buying repeatedly because they do not have other options, employees may stay with an organisation simply because jobs are scarce. This doesn't necessarily mean that they are loyal and committed to the organisation in such a way as to enhance their attitudes, motivation or performance!

One approach to retention is to investigate the cause of unusually or undesirably high labour turnover: why don't staff stay long in customer service jobs, for example? This may be done using **exit interviews** with leaving staff, or **employee attitude surveys** to gauge the general feeling of staff about their jobs. The specific causes of labour turnover can then be addressed, where it is practical and cost-effective to do so: eg by changing leadership style, giving better induction training to new staff, solving problems with working conditions, or reviewing pay levels in the light of competitor rates.

Some organisations, however, see themselves as already having invested heavily in acquiring and training staff. They therefore focus on retention through developing greater employee skill, loyalty and commitment, to maximise the return on their investment – and the potential for customer value.

3.4.1 Motivation and rewards

This is a huge subject in its own right, and is usually the responsibility of the Human Resources function and individual department managers, rather than marketing. However, you should be aware that:

- People expect to be adequately rewarded or compensated for their contribution to the organisation: pay, benefits, recognition and other forms of reward should reflect this, in order to keep employees motivated and committed – particularly if there are better rewards available elsewhere.

- The marketing department can use rewards and incentives to foster a service culture: for example, by offering customer service bonuses or 'service employee/team of the month' awards.

- Monetary rewards and incentives are not the only motivators: recognition, praise/acknowledgement, added interest and responsibility in the job, positive leadership and greater participation in decision making are all regarded as motivating factors.

- Organisational culture is also a key motivating (or de-motivating) factor. Marketing has a key role in promoting positive, energising, shared values, with which people can identify: quality, customer focus, all-member contribution, beating the competition and so on. (Coca Cola's expressed corporate mission statement at one time was simply: 'Beat Pepsi'.)

ACTIVITY 9.7

How are customer service values built into (a) the employee selection criteria, (b) performance appraisal criteria, (c) training programmes and (d) rewards and recognition systems of your work organisation, or other organisation you have been studying?

Does this apply only to marketing or customer service staff, or is it organisation-wide?

The Chartered
Institute of Marketing

3.4.2 Job satisfaction

Frederick Herzberg (1966) developed an influential theory of motivation called **'two factor theory'**, which argued that people have two basic needs at work:

- **The need to avoid unpleasantness.** This need is satisfied by what Herzberg called 'hygiene' factors: fair pay, fair management, good working conditions and so on. Such factors minimise dissatisfaction and poor job performance, but don't really give positive satisfaction or motivate people to higher-level performance: after a while, they get taken for granted and become a source of dissatisfaction again.

- **The need for personal growth.** These needs are satisfied by what Herzberg called 'motivator' factors in the job itself: recognition, added responsibility, challenge, interest and achievement. Such factors create positive job satisfaction, and motivate people to higher levels of committed performance.

Herzberg argued that: 'Dissatisfaction arises from environment factors: **satisfaction can only arise from the job**'. This influential theory has focused managers' attention on methods of motivation and retention which built satisfaction into people's jobs: offering intrinsic (or internal) rewards rather than just extrinsic (or external) rewards.

Job enrichment was the method recommended by Herzberg. It is 'the planned process of up-grading the responsibility, challenge and content of the work' to offer greater satisfaction. Staff enrichment programmes may involve adding:

- **Skill variety:** making job descriptions wider or more flexible, giving employees the opportunity to exercise different skills and perform different tasks

- **Task identity and significance**: allowing employees to perform 'whole' tasks, or meaningful segments of a task (rather than just their small bit of the task, as on an assembly line), and emphasising how their job contributes to the whole operation and the organisation's objectives. This gives a sense of purpose and value to the work

- **Autonomy**: increasing opportunities to exercise discretion or self-management (eg in areas such as target-setting and work methods)

- **Feedback**: offering performance and results feedback (so people can assess their progress and celebrate successful contribution) and asking for feedback in return (giving employees a voice)

- **Training and development**: offering individuals and teams opportunities to develop their personal and job-related skills and competences. This is, of course, a 'win-win': the organisation reaps the benefits of a trained, more competent and confident workforce, while employees reap the benefits of greater satisfaction, reward/promotion opportunities and employability.

Training and development, or informal learning activities, will be particularly important in fostering organisation-wide **customer awareness** and **service competence**. As we saw earlier, some staff may not be aware that their jobs are really 'customer service' jobs; many will assume that 'marketing' is just something done by the marketing department; and technically-skilled individuals may never have had training in inter-personal or relationship-building skills.

3.4.3 Technical and managerial support

Employees must be supported in doing their work effectively, otherwise there will be a mismatch between what they are expected to do and what they are able to do: this is a major source of frustration and stress – as well as under-performance. Staff should be given:

- **Technical support**. That is, they should be equipped with the tools, systems, training and other resources (such as budget, information and help from other staff) needed to perform their work. They should have access to expert instruction, advice and help (eg from an IT support or legal team) when required.

- **Managerial support**. That is, they should be given adequate instruction, guidelines (policies, procedures, goals and standards), encouragement, feedback, supervision (if necessary) and authority/discretion by their managers, so that they can carry out their work and, where possible, grow and develop in the job.

- **Personal support.** Support from managers or colleagues may also be required to help team members who are struggling with their workload, particular work problems, or non-work issues affecting their attitude and performance. This is often the purpose of coaching (helping staff to do their jobs better), mentoring (helping staff to manage their personal and career development) and workplace counselling programmes (helping staff to work through personal problems affecting their work or welfare).

- **Support through change.** Change often causes insecurity, as it brings uncertainty and the loss of competence and confidence, and may be perceived as threatening. Managers should support staff in understanding, accepting and coping with organisational changes, such as the introduction of new systems or work methods.

3.4.4 Ethical and responsible employment practices

In order to retain and motivate employees, the employer will need to treat them fairly and well – usually, over and above minimum standards set by employment law. ('The law is a floor': it provides for basic standards of ethical and humane treatment, but is not intended to reflect best practice.) Responsible employment policies should address matters such as:

- Fair pay for the work and contribution given

- Safe and healthy working conditions

- Learning and development opportunities

- Commitment to equal opportunity (non-discrimination) and workforce diversity

- Fair and humane management of disciplinary and grievance situations, dismissals, redundancies and so on

- Willingness to inform and consult employee representatives (unionised or otherwise)

- Support for employee welfare (benefits, compassionate leave, flexible working options, employee counselling and so on, where required).

ACTIVITY 9.8

What forms of technical, managerial and personal support are you given in your work role? What help is available if you have: (a) a work problem or (b) a personal problem affecting your work? How might this support be improved?

What categories of staff in your organisation do you think are most in need of technical, managerial and/or personal support?

3.4.5 Flexible working

Flexible working is a 'hot topic' in human resource management at the moment, supported by the UK Government's commitment to encouraging '**work-life balance**': that is, a balance between the demands of the job and the demands of home, family and personal life.

Despite the desire to increase productivity, many companies are realising that increasing workloads and working hours is in fact counter-productive, potentially encouraging absenteeism, ill-health, accidents and poor-quality customer service.

A work-life balance programme may include **awareness training and skills training**: in time management, delegation, work organisation or relaxation techniques, say. However, the main thrust of European legislation and social policy in this area has been to introduce **family-friendly policies** on flexible working, designed to give employees options in regard to their hours and/or locations of work. The UK Employment Act 2002, for example, gives parents of children under the age of six (or disabled children under the age of 18) the right to request flexible working arrangements.

Flexible working arrangements may involve:

The Chartered
Institute of Marketing

- **Part-time working or job sharing**: two people share a single job, working part-time.

- **Tele-working or home-working**: working from home, or elsewhere, linked to the office by computers, the internet, phone and mobile phone.

- **Annualised and term-time contracts**: agreeing a number of hours' work per year, rather than per week or month. Intensive hours can be called on during peak periods, but employees can then take time off or work flexible hours in periods of low demand. Term-time contracts allow parents to maximise work hours during school terms, giving them time off during school holidays.

- **Flexi-time systems**: employees are required to be at their job during 'core time', but time at the beginning and end of the day can be scheduled at their discretion. The total working week or month must add up to a set number of hours.

- **Gap years, sabbaticals or long-service leave:** enabling employees to take substantial time off (say, every 10 years) to pursue their own interests, study, attend to family or personal demands – or simply have a refreshing break from work. Such opportunities are often used as a retention tool, as employees need to stay with the organisation in order to earn them.

- **Secondments:** employees may be offered the opportunity to be seconded to other functions, units or locations within the firm (or even with other, allied firms), as a way of broadening their outlook, developing new competences and enhancing their careers. This may also be used as a form of training: for example, giving product managers experience in production or marketing, or giving marketers experience of international branches.

3.4.6 Organisation culture

> **▶ Key term**
>
> **Organisation culture** may be defined as:
>
> - 'The collection of traditions, values, policies, beliefs and attitudes that constitute a pervasive context for everything we do and think in an organisation' (Mullins, 1999)
> - 'A pattern of beliefs and expectations shared by the organisation's members, and which produce norms which powerfully shape the behaviour of individuals and groups in the organisation' (Schwartz & Davies 1981)
> - 'The way we do things around here'. (Deal & Kennedy, 1982)

Organisation culture is transmitted by, and reflected in, a number of different elements of organisational life:

- **Beliefs and values**: eg customer focus, team working, co-operation or competition. These may be communicated by senior management, team leaders, mottos and slogans ('the customer is always right'), or just taken for granted within the organisation.

- **Behaviour**: norms of personal and interpersonal behaviour; customs and rules about behaviours that are acceptable or unacceptable. Examples include (formal or informal) dress codes and familiarity or formality in addressing managers.

- **Artefacts**: concrete expressions such as office space and décor, logos and brand identity

- **Symbols**: objects which take on special meanings within the organisation, such as status symbols and corporate 'myths and legends'

- **Rituals:** patterns of collective behaviour which have traditional or symbolic value, such as greeting styles, business formalities, awards ceremonies and so on

- **HR systems**: the desired values and norms of the organisation are communicated and reinforced by employee selection, appraisal, reward, promotion and training.

Taken together, these elements form a strong **style and identity** for the organisation. This may be a climate that is satisfying and enjoyable to work in – or not. In addition to retention and loyalty, organisational culture defines **values** about customer service, employee involvement and empowerment, the desirability of cross-functional co-operation and team working and so on. It is a key underpinning tool of internal marketing.

ACTIVITY 9.9

- Prepare a brief portrait of your organisation's culture, using the elements listed above as a checklist.

- Prepare a similar portrait of the culture of (a) the marketing department and (b) one other function in the organisation. (You may need to use your networking and stakeholder communication skills to get information from a member of that function.)

- What differences can you identify between the cultures of the two functions – and what might be the implications for (a) internal communication and co-ordination and (b) the service culture of the organisation as a whole?

4 Employee empowerment and involvement

4.1 Employee empowerment

Another key internal marketing activity is the empowerment of staff to enable them to use their discretion, judgement, experience and skills to deliver a better quality of service to their customers.

There are various levels of empowerment, from the ability to make suggestions (low level of involvement) to the latitude to do whatever is necessary to satisfy the customer in a given set of circumstances (high level of involvement and empowerment).

> 'Empowerment means that the company must create the right culture and climate for employees to operate in. This includes four empowerment criteria: providing employees with information about the organisation's performance; providing rewards based on the organisation's performance; providing employees with knowledge that enables them to understand and contribute to organisational performance; and giving them power to take decisions that influence organisational direction and performance'. (Bowen & Lawler, 1992, cited Peck et al, p322).

Advantages claimed for employee empowerment include:

- Faster and more flexible response to customers' needs (because staff are better informed and more confident)

- Improved employee job satisfaction, motivation and commitment (because empowerment offers a high degree of challenge, interest, responsibility and trust)

- Improved upward communication (from employees to management), which helps keep the organisation sensitive to stakeholder demands and environmental changes

- Improved ability to learn and adapt to change (because employees are more flexible in their attitudes and behaviours, and more confident in their coping skills).

Of course, these benefits must be balanced with the increased costs of training, development, reward and retention of empowered employees (they will still expect to be paid for the extra contribution they are making!) – and the risk of their sometimes getting it wrong. There is also an issue of ensuring service consistency, as individual discretion may lead to wide variations (which may be perceived and resented by some customers).

ACTIVITY 9.10

What practical ways can you think of to empower front-line staff to maintain customer care and service quality?

The Chartered
Institute of Marketing

'**Virgin Atlantic** has long recognised the critical role internal marketing plays in its success. One of the secrets of the airline's success has been enthusiastic empowered, motivated employees. Sir Richard Branson has said: "I want employees in the airline to feel that it is *they* who can make the difference, and influence what passengers get. "

"We aren't interested in having just happy employees. We want employees who feel involved and prepared to express dissatisfaction when necessary. In fact, we think that the constructively dissatisfied employee is an asset we should encourage and we need an organisation that allows us to do this – and that encourages employees to take responsibility, since I don't believe it is enough for us simply to give it."

Virgin Atlantic's philosophy has been to stimulate the individual, to encourage staff to take initiatives and to empower them to do so.'

(Christopher *et al*, 2002, p111)

Virgin Atlantic's website explains more about how it values its employees, the expectations it has of them, and the values it tries to encourage in them.

'Our commitment to our people is something that's ingrained in the very fabric of our business. We've always treated our employees as the single most important part of Virgin Atlantic. And that's a pledge that goes all the way to the top, as Richard Branson explains:

"The people who make up Virgin Atlantic make Virgin Atlantic. This isn't a company that just talks about putting employees first or glibly claims that our people are our greatest asset. This is a company that simply wouldn't exist without the energy, the determination, the wit and the wisdom of our people." (Virgin Atlantic, 2012)

Visit http://www.virgin-atlantic.com/en/gb/index.jsp. Follow the Careers link to the dedicated recruitment site and click on 'Working for Us'.

4.2 Employee involvement

The concept of '**employee voice**' embraces 'a whole variety of processes and structures which enable, and sometimes empower employees, directly and indirectly, to contribute to decision making in the firm' (Boxall & Purcell, 2003). Armstrong (2003) summarises it as 'the say employees have in matters of concern to them in their organisation'. The term has come to embrace a wide range of mechanisms for:

- **Employee involvement:** informing and consulting employees about aspects of decision making. This is sometimes called 'upward problem solving': two-way communication; the use of staff feedback, suggestion schemes and employee intranet discussion groups; or project teams, which bring staff and management together to solve problems, discuss issues or generate ideas (eg quality circles or customer care task forces).

- **Employee participation:** involving employees (often via their elected representatives) in the decision-making machinery of the organisation. This is sometimes called 'representative participation': collective negotiations and conflict resolution via trade unions, formal consultative meetings with worker representatives, or formal partnership agreements.

Marchington *et al* (2001) argue that paying attention to employee voice offers:

- The ability for individual employees to express dissatisfaction, solve problems within management and preserve working relationships

- The ability for employees collectively to express their needs and wishes in matters that affect them, providing a counterbalance to managerial power

- The ability for employees to contribute to management decisions, allowing the organisation to harness the expertise and commitment of workers to improve quality, productivity and work organisation

- The ability for employers and employees to demonstrate their intention to focus on shared goals, mutual interests and co-operative working relations, for the long-term benefit of the organisation and its people.

5 Cross-functional co-operation

5.1 The value of cross-functional co-operation

> ▶ **Key term**
>
> **Co-ordination** is planning, or taking action to improve, the inter-relationships (especially of timing and methods of communication) between a number of various activities, which contribute to the achievement of a single objective, so that they do not conflict and the objective is achieved with a minimal expenditure of time and effort.

One of the main purposes of internal communication is co-ordination, co-operation or integration between different functions and units of the organisation.

The marketing department needs to ensure that other departments that depend on its work, or on which its work depends, are kept informed. At the most basic, information should include: plans and schedules, any *changes* to plans and schedules, and any feedback on the results of plans and schedules.

This may seem like common sense. It should be obvious that you should check with the design or production team before you advertise product specifications, and inform them of the planned date of a new product launch, and monitor their readiness as the date approaches. However, failure to do these things presents common problems, sources of conflict – and even chaos!

5.1.1 Potential for conflict in interdepartmental relations

'In principle, business functions should mesh harmoniously to achieve the overall objectives of the firm. In practice, departmental interfaces are often characterised by deep rivalries and misunderstandings... Some inter-departmental conflict stems from differences of opinion about what lies in the best interests of the firm; some from real trade-offs between departmental well-being and company well-being; and some from unfortunate departmental stereotypes and prejudices.' (Kotler, 2002)

Kotler summarises the potential for conflict as follows.

Table 9.4   Potential for conflict in interdepartmental relations

Other functions	Their emphasis	Marketing's emphasis
Research & Development (R & D)	Basic research	Applied (customer) research
	Intrinsic quality	Perceivable quality
	Functional features	Sales features
Purchasing	Narrow product line	Broad product line
	Price of materials	Quality of materials
	Economical lot size	Large lot size to avoid stock-out
	Infrequent batch purchase	Immediate purchase on demand
Manufacturing	Long product lead time	Short production lead time
	Long runs with few models	Short runs with many models
	No model changes	Frequent model changes
	Standard orders	Custom orders
	Ease of fabrication	Aesthetic appearance, features
	Average quality control	Zero-defects quality control

Other functions	Their emphasis	Marketing's emphasis
Finance and accounting	Strict rationale for spending	Intuitive arguments for spending
	Fixed budgets	Flexible budgets
	Pricing to cover costs	Pricing for demand, competition
	Standard transactions	Special terms and discounts
	Tough credit terms and debt collection	Easy credit terms and debt collection

A relationship marketing orientation, as we have seen, is designed to foster a deeper appreciation by all functions and departments of the need to add customer value and build relationships. 'Internal marketing is seen as a way of **integrating various functions** to enable staff to work together across functional boundaries, and aligning those cross-functional teams with **internal and external customer needs** and expectations, so that their work is attuned to the company's **mission, strategy and goals**.' (Peck et al, 1999, p315).

5.1.2 Whole-organisation marketing

Egan (2004) argues that one of the key causes of customer service problems is poor teamwork. Different functions in the organisation often operate as isolated towers or 'silos': unconnected to each other, acting independently and with little co-ordination or sense of shared goals. This causes problems because activities in the value chain are interrelated.

Customers experience the organisation '**horizontally**': that is, they deal in sequence with marketing, sales, order processing, accounts, deliveries, after-sales service – being passed from one department to another. Customers want this experience to be seamless: they don't want to come up against 'vertical' barriers or gaps between the units and functions of the organisation, where one department isn't talking to another, or has different systems and policies, or gives completely different messages.

Effective marketing and customer service therefore depends on cross-functional sharing of goals, values and information. It also requires all employees to see themselves as 'part-time marketers': as direct or indirect contributors to customer relations, customer satisfaction and customer value.

5.2 Tools of inter-departmental relations

5.2.1 Formal communication and co-ordination mechanisms

Formal mechanisms for improving cross-functional relationships include the following.

- **Communication channels and flows**: using available channels and tools of communication (conferences, team/project meetings, email, intranet, newsletters and briefings, forms and reports, plans and schedules, shared access to a central database) to share and exchange information with other functions.

- **Communication and liaison positions**. Dedicated communications or liaison officers may be appointed to act as a 'hub' for cross-functional communication. Managers may also act as a 'cross-over' point for communication, where they have responsibility for two or more departments.

- **Cross-functional project teams, task-forces or committees**. Cross-functional teams include representatives from different functions and departments. Joint planning and on-going collaboration require them to share and exchange information on a regular, task-focused basis. This builds 'bridges' and interpersonal networks between functions.

- **Matrix organisation**: cross-functional working which is permanently embedded in the organisation structure. This often takes the form of **customer or product management**: staff in different functions report to their departmental managers in regard to the routine activities of the function – but also report to a customer or product manager, in regard to activities performed in relation to a particular customer account or product. While this can cause difficulties because of the dual authority, it means that customer or product managers act as hubs for communication between members of their teams who otherwise work in different functions.

5.2.2 Networking

The more marketers have contact with other departments, learn what they do and show that they appreciate their problems and capabilities, the more likely they are to develop co-operative relationships. Cross-functional networking, or informal communications, are very important in internal marketing. Marketers may:

- Attend organisation-wide and inter-departmental meetings and events

- Join quality circles or other multi-disciplinary teams and committees that focus on shared objectives

- Use contacts in other departments to arrange visits and briefings to learn about each other's objectives, culture and issues.

▶ **Assessment tip**

It is worth bearing the internal marketing dimension in mind if you are asked to make proposals for external customer (or other stakeholder) marketing in your assignment. What will be the internal market implications of your proposal? What internal human resources will be required? What training and communication will they need to adapt to the change or perform the task? What sources of resistance might there be – and how can these be changed into support and commitment? This may not be a major (or even explicit) part of the assignment brief, but by considering the internal marketing implications, you will be demonstrating your grasp of the syllabus, and of the interconnected nature of stakeholder marketing.

- The recruitment market and the internal market

- The internal customer concept

- The importance of internal communication

- The value of employee retention: labour turnover

- The value of employee loyalty and commitment: commitment versus compliance; the service profit chain and loyalty cycle

- Inter-departmental relations: potential for dis-integration

- Organisation culture and RM success

- Employee communications: communication tools, intranet, briefings, team meetings, formal consultation

- Employee retention: motivation and rewards, flexible working, technical and management support, training and development

- Employee involvement: industrial relations and employee relations; empowerment

- Inter-departmental relations: communication, culture, cross-functional teams, networking

FURTHER READING

Browse through *People Management*, the journal of the Chartered Institute of Personnel and Development (CIPD).

http://www.peoplemanagement.co.uk/pm

Internal marketing

Egan, G. (2004) *Relationship Marketing*. 2nd edition. Harlow, Pearson Education. Chapter 7.

Gummesson, E. (2002) *Total Relationship Marketing*. 2nd edition. Oxford, Elsevier Butterworth-Heinemann. See Relationship 27: Internal marketing – relationships with the 'employee market'.

Jobber, D. (2007) *Principles & Practice of Marketing.* 5th edition. Maidenhead, McGraw-Hill Education. Chapter 22
Focuses on wider issues of overcoming resistance to the implementation of marketing changes and plans in the organisation

Peck, H. *et al* (1999) *Relationship Marketing: Strategy & Implementation.* Oxford, Elsevier Butterworth-Heinemann. Chapter 5

Anon (2012) Two UK intranets in the global top 10. Communicate.
http://communicatemagazine.co.uk/news/3336--two-uk-intranets-in-the-global-top-10. [Accessed 27 June 2012].

Armstrong, M. (2000) *Strategic Human Resource Management*. 2nd edition. London, Kogan Page.

Armstrong, M. (2003) *A Handbook of Human Resource Management Practice*. 9th edition. London, Kogan Page.

Baringa (2012). Great place to work. http://www.baringa.com/our_company/great_place_to_work/. [Accessed 24 June 2012].

Berry, L..L and Parasuraman, A (1991) *Marketing Services: competing through quality*. New York, Free Press.

Boddy, D. (2005) *Management: An Introduction* 3rd edition. Harlow, Essex, FT Prentice Hall.

Bowen, D.E. and Lawler, E.E. (1992). *The empowerment of service workers: what, why, how and when in Sloan Management Review*, Spring, pp31-39.

Boxall, B.F. and Purcell, J (2003) *Strategy and Human Resource Management*. Basingstoke, Palgrave Macmillan.

Christopher M. G. et al (2002) *Relationship Marketing: Creating Stakeholder Value*. Oxford, Butterworth-Heinemann.

Deal, T. E. and Kennedy, A.A. (1982) *Corporate Culture: the rites and rituals of corporate life*. Reading, Ma, Addison-Wesley.

Egan, J. (2004) *Relationship Marketing: Exploring Relational Strategies in Marketing*. 2nd edition. Harlow, Essex, Pearson Education.

George, W.R. and Grönroos, C (1989) Developing customer-conscious employees at every level – internal marketing in Congram, CA & Friedman, ML (eds) *Handbook of Services Marketing*. New York, AMACOM.

Gummesson, E. (2002). *Total Relationship Marketing* (2002) Oxford, Elsevier Butterworth-Heinemann.

Herzberg, F. W. (1966) *Work and the Nature of Man*. NY, Staples.

Jobber, D. (2007) *Principles & Practice of Marketing*. 5th edition. Maidenhead, Berks, McGraw Hill Education. p865.

Jones, M. and Cheeseman, A. (2005) *Customer Communications*. Oxford, Elsevier Butterworth-Heinemann.

Kotler, P. (2002) *Marketing Management*. 11th edition. Pearson.

Marchington, M. et al (2001) *Management Choice and Employee Voice*. London, CIPD.

Microsoft (2005). Company Information.
http://www.microsoft.com/about/companyinformation/en/us/default.aspx [Accessed 24 June 2012].

Mowdray, R. et al (1982) *Employee-Organisation Linkages*. London, Academic Press.

Mullins, L. (1999) *Management and Organisational Behaviour*. 5th edition. Harlow, Essex, Pearson Education.

Peck, H.L. et al (1999) *Relationship Marketing: Strategy and Implementation*. Oxford, Elsevier Butterworth-Heinemann.

Schwartz, H. and Davies, S.M. (1981) Matching Corporate Culture and Business Strategy in *Organisational Dynamics*, Summer (1981).

The Chartered Institute of Marketing

Virgin Atlantic (2012) Careers. http://www.virgin-atlantic.com/en/gb/careers/index.jsp. [Accessed 24 June 2012].

QUICK QUIZ

1   Define internal marketing.

2   Give five examples of activities that contribute to internal marketing.

3   Suggest two ways in which the internal market can be segmented.

4   What is (a) an intranet and (b) a virtual team?

5   Why should an organisation want to retain employees, as part of an internal marketing approach?

6   How does internal customer relations impact on external customer relations?

7   Explain Herzberg's two factor theory of motivation and its significance?

8   What are the elements or manifestations of organisation culture?

9   Define 'employee voice'.

10   What are some potential sources of conflict between the marketing function and the manufacturing or operations function?

ACTIVITY DEBRIEFS

Activity 9.1

Internal customers of the marketing function include:

- Senior management and shareholders, who expect the strategic objectives of the organisation to be met through effective and efficient marketing activity.

- The product/operations function, which expects to be given practicable product specifications and production schedules, and expects its efforts to be justified by the success of the product in the market place – to feel that its output is being effectively 'sold'.

- The finance/accounts/admin function, which expects clear and accurate budgets, forecasts and records of expenditure, sales and so on, for the required financial control, reporting and record-keeping systems.

- The members of the organisation as a whole, who expect to be given information – and particularly 'good news' – to be able to feel pride in the organisation's image to the outside world, to identify with it and to feel that the marketing function is 'getting it right' on their behalf.

Activity 9.2

With supporters, existing positive attitudes should be reinforced, and support (especially from key influencers) mobilised.

With neutrals, rewards and benefits should be emphasised, and downsides de-emphasised. Supporters may be used to 'win over' neutrals.

With opposers, promotion may be used to counter their objections, discredit or marginalise their position (if this can be done without causing negative relationship effects), or negotiate/bargain to lower resistance.

Activity 9.3

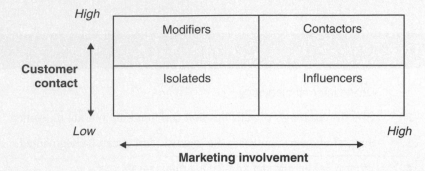

It is a useful skill to be able to format information concisely, analytically and visually like this. Such a diagram would be helpful in illustrating points in an assignment report or appendix, for example.

Activity 9.4

(a) In recruitment, the product would be the package (bundle of benefits) of the job role, the organisation (whether it is good to work for etc) and the rewards and benefits offered. The price would be the requirement for work and loyalty; perhaps sacrifices of relocation, commuting, less leisure time; perhaps unpleasant or risky working conditions. Place would be how the job information reaches the audience: advertising media, careers centre, work-of-mouth referral, website etc. Promotion would be the communication of the product benefits: corporate identity, job information, the persuasive tone of the ad and so on.

(b) Your own research.

Activity 9.5

The disadvantages of e-mail include:

- Their legal effect: firms can be sued for libellous, offensive or misleading remarks made in e-mail.

- E-mail can be used excessively, to the exclusion of other tools that might be more appropriate – or simply creating time-wasting information/message overload. Excessive personal use (or abuse) is also an issue for many organisations (as it has been with the telephone).

- E-mail is not private, and remains on the server. There are thus risks in using it to send confidential messages.

- E-mail is impersonal: it is often difficult to get the 'tone' right for sensitive interpersonal messages.

Activity 9.6

Disadvantages of meetings include:

- Slowing down the process of decision making (where face-to-face discussion is involved). Meetings are often felt to be a 'waste of time'.

- Allowing the personal charisma of one or more participants to dominate others (an advantage in persuasion, but not in collaborative problem solving or perspective sharing)

- Making it difficult to conceal or distort information (a disadvantage if you are the person who wishes to do so: eg if you are in a weak negotiating position, or wish to put a positive 'spin' on a PR problem)

- Not allowing preparation and polishing of messages (verbal and non-verbal) prior to communication

- Lacking concreteness: 'just talk' unless something is done or put in writing.

Some issues you may have encountered in the leadership of meetings include: lack of a discussion plan or agenda for the meeting; lack of information to hand when required; poor or pointless use of visual aids; lack of leadership to ensure that everyone gets to contribute; lack of leadership to ensure that the discussion stays on track; no clear process for reaching decisions (eg by vote, summary/consensus or decision by the leader); no record or minutes of what was decided; no plan or accountability for follow-up action.

Activity 9.7

Your own research. Note that such Human Resources systems are a key tool of culture creation and reinforcement.

Activity 9.8

Your own knowledge and research.

Activity 9.9

Your own research. Note that this is potentially very useful preparation for an assignment task.

Activity 9.10

Some ideas you may have come up with:

- Provide front-line staff with information required to serve customers effectively: contact details, product/service information, briefing on marketing plans, brochures and newsletters etc

- Train staff in interpersonal and communication skills

- Develop tools for feedback gathering (eg feedback forms, complaint and enquiry logs)

- Facilitate communication between departments

- Communicate, reward and recognise positive customer care values and attitudes

- Giving front-line staff delegated authority (within clear boundaries) to take action to solve customer problems

- Providing appropriate facilities (eg interview rooms) where staff can safely and effectively deal with customers, especially in sensitive situations.

1   Internal marketing is a variety of approaches and techniques by which an organisation acquires, motivates, equips and retains customer-conscious employees.

2   Activities that contribute to internal marketing include: organisational design, staff surveys, internal customer segmentation, personal development and training, empowerment and involvement, recognition and rewards, internal communications, performance measures and building supportive working relationships.

3   The internal market can be segmented by position on the marketing plan (supporters, neutrals, opposers) or by closeness to external customers (contactors, modifiers, influencers and isolateds).

4   An intranet is an internal computer network allowing data sharing via internal-access web pages. A virtual team is a group of individuals who collaborate, share data and have a sense of team identity – but are linked mainly or solely via computer and telecom links.

5   See section 3.1 for a full justification of employee retention.

6   See section 3.4 for a full explanation of the link between employee satisfaction and customer satisfaction.

7   Herzberg argued that people have two basic needs: avoiding unpleasantness (satisfied by extrinsic rewards such as pay and conditions) and personal growth (satisfied by intrinsic rewards in the job itself: that is, job satisfaction). Employees are only positive motivated by job satisfaction, so managers need to pay attention to factors such as the interest, challenge and responsibility of the job.

8   The elements of organisation culture include: beliefs and values, behavioural norms, artefacts symbols, rituals and HR systems.

9   Employee voice is 'a whole variety of processes and structures which enable, and sometimes empower employees, directly and indirectly, to contribute to decision making in the firm'.

10 See the table in section 5.1.1 for a range of potentially-conflicting emphases.

CHAPTER 10

International and technology-based communications

Introduction

This chapter introduces two key contexts in which stakeholder communications take place.

The first is the **international stakeholder environment**. In section 1, we give a brief overview of the international market, explaining how organisational activity is increasingly globalised – and how this process creates international stakeholders. This should build on your studies for Unit 2: *Assessing the Marketing Environment*, which also had an international dimension.

In section 2, we focus on the challenges of communicating with stakeholders in international markets, as specified by the syllabus. Other international marketing and supply issues, such as international market entry methods or global sourcing and logistics, are beyond the scope of this syllabus. Remember: our focus here is still on marketing communications.

In section 3, we turn to the **technological environment**, describing some of the recent and on-going changes that characterise Information and Communication Technology (ICT).

In section 4, we briefly outline the impact of new technologies on the marketing mix as a whole, suggesting how ICT can be applied to product, price, place, promotion and service. We then go on, in section 5, to discuss technological innovations in communications, which can be used in stakeholder relationship marketing.

Finally, in section 6, we discuss how all these developments can contribute to the economic and environmental sustainability of stakeholder relationships.

Topic list

The international stakeholder environment (1)

Challenges of international stakeholder communication (2)

The technological environment (3)

Technology and the marketing mix (4)

Technology for stakeholder communication (5)

Technology's contribution to sustainable relationships (6)

4.3	Explain the challenges in communicating with stakeholders in international markets:
	■ Adaptation versus standardisation
	■ Culture – influence of religion, cultural norms and protocols
	■ Language and symbols
	■ Availability of technology
	■ Ensuring consistency of key messages
	■ Availability of media
4.4	Identify and evaluate the continuously evolving impact of new technologies and their contribution to economic and environmental sustainability on stakeholder relationships:
	■ Tele kits
	■ Virtual conferencing
	■ SMS
	■ Voice over internet protocol (VOIP)
	■ Economic – reduction in overheads
	■ Environmental – CSR, carbon footprint

1 The international stakeholder environment

1.1 Globalisation

> ▶ **Key term**
>
> **Globalisation** is 'the increasing integration of internationally dispersed economic activities' (Boddy, 2005).

Markets are becoming increasingly global, due to factors such as:

- Developments in **media and travel**, which allow people to experience each other's cultures, creating a 'convergence' in cultural values and consumer tasks – and hence the potential for more global brands

- Developments in **transport**, creating the 'shrinking' of distances for the purposes of logistics

- **Trade agreements and de-regulation** to facilitate cross-border trading (eg within the EU, and between North and South America)

- Developments in **information and communication technology** or ICT (especially the internet), enabling communication and transactions between widely dispersed parties: e-commerce, strategic alliances and 'virtual' organisations (with workers and call centres all over the world)

- Political changes creating **new markets** (eg Eastern European countries joining the EU, and the opening up of commerce in China)

- The power of **multi-national organisations and global brands**, lobbying governments and working through the World Trade Organisation to foster conditions conducive to international trade

- The **business benefits of international marketing**: larger markets; economies of scale; outsourcing to low-cost-labour countries; moving out of saturated or intensively competitive domestic markets; extending product life cycles by introducing products to new markets etc.

However, international markets have different languages, different cultures, different legal systems, different demographic profiles and so on. Geographical distance is also a problem when it comes to exchanging physical objects (such as products) or getting people together (eg for meetings). Marketers who want to do business with other countries, and manage overseas stakeholders, must expect to make minor (and sometimes major) adjustments to the marketing mix!

The Chartered Institute of Marketing

All the aspects of stakeholder marketing discussed so far in this book may be relevant to the practice of international marketing. There are some particular challenges, however, which are highlighted by the syllabus.

1.1.1 Types of globalisation

For any given organisation, globalisation may manifest itself in:

- **International markets**. In the 1980s, it was thought that with worldwide access to media, travel and communications, there was a convergence of consumer needs and wants: major brands (such as Coca Cola and McDonald's) could be sold worldwide, without much modification for particular geographic markets. This approach lost ground in the 1990s, however, as global brands lost market share against locally-adapted brands which catered to specific national and regional cultures, tastes and conditions.

- **International production**. Since the 1960s, firms in developed countries have faced the problem of high domestic labour costs, enabling intense competition from cheaper imports originating in countries with lower-cost labour. This has stimulated the growth of off-shoring and outsourcing, as companies moved their manufacturing (and service) operations to countries such as China, Taiwan, South Korea and India. The media is now full of examples of companies off-shoring administrative and call centre services (eg major banks) and product assembly (eg Dyson, Hitachi, Compaq, Mattel toys).

This means that organisations may have a wide variety of international stakeholders: customers and intermediaries; suppliers; network allies; foreign government and regulatory bodies; foreign pressure groups (and domestic pressure groups opposed to globalisation); foreign advertising and news media; and, increasingly, foreign employees and wider communities affected by globalisation.

ACTIVITY 10.1

What are the international activities and dimensions of your own organisation, or the organisation that you are studying?

Identify the organisation's international stakeholder groups (including secondary stakeholders) and plot them on a Mendelow power/interest matrix.

1.1.2 CSR issues of globalisation

It is worth being aware that globalisation itself is increasingly regarded as an issue of corporate social responsibility, which might arouse the interest of external stakeholders.

A number of CSR arguments can be put forward for and against globalisation – as you may be aware from the publicity surrounding violent protests outside World Trade Organisation meetings, for example!

Table 10.1   Arguments for and against globalisation

Arguments for globalisation	Arguments against globalisation
International trade stimulates local economic activity, helping to create employment, prosperity, educational development and so on.	It encourages the exploitation of labour in developing nations for lower-cost production, often with poor wages and working conditions.
The siting of operations in developing countries may bring investment in technology, infrastructure, skills etc.	It 'exports' pollution, deforestation, urbanisation and other environmental damage to developing nations.
There may be improvements in human rights and labour conditions, where foreign companies operate ethical/CSR policies and monitoring.	It encourages the exploitation of local markets, using them as dumping grounds for poor-quality or obsolete goods, and leading to increased foreign debt.
Global consumers benefit from more product/service choice and lower prices.	It creates job losses in developed nations where labour costs are higher.
International trade can support positive international relations and deter conflict.	It squeezes small, local businesses out of markets, with negative effects on communities and local cultures.

THE REAL WORLD

World Trade Organisation

Globalisation has been encouraged by the development of free trade between nations around the world. The World Trade Organisation (WTO) is a body run by its member governments (of whom there were 155 in May 2012 including all the major trading nations around the world).

On its web site, the WTO explains its role as:

'Simply put the World Trade Organisation (WTO) deals with the rules of trade between nations at a global or near-global level.'

'At its heart are the WTO agreements, negotiated and signed by the bulk of the world's trading nations. These documents provide the legal ground-rules for international commerce. They are essentially contracts, binding governments to keep their trade policies within agreed limits. Although negotiated and signed by governments, the goal is to help producers of goods and services, exporters, and importers conduct their business, while allowing governments to meet social and environmental objectives.'

Much of the trade between nations that we take for granted today would arguably not have developed without these agreements brokered by the WTO which was formed in 1995. Find out more about this important organisation on its web site at http://www.wto.org/english/thewto_e/whatis_e/whatis_e.htm.

1.2 The international marketing mix

The syllabus focuses on international stakeholder communication, but it is worth noting that international issues affect the entire marketing mix.

- **Product and brand decisions** may have to be adapted to local market needs and values. McDonald's, for example, offers regional dishes (eg 'croque monsieur' in France, 'Aussie' burgers in Australia and a spiced chicken 'Maharajah Mac' in India) and uses local produce in different countries. Levi Strauss jeans are positioned as work clothes in the US, as a fashion garment in the UK, and as an American icon in Japan. Coca Cola varies its recipes from market to market, according to different tastes in sweetness and carbonation, and different legal regulations on the use of artificial sweeteners.

- **Price** is complicated by exchange rates and different economic environments. For instance, average income in the exporting country may be much higher than in the target country, so a straight conversion of the home currency price into the local currency at the prevailing exchange rate might not achieve marketing objectives. It might turn what is a basic commodity at home into a luxury product in the

foreign market! In each country, the factors influencing pricing will differ, so a different pricing policy may be appropriate.

- **Place**. Distribution channels are a key issue for entrants to global markets. The usual channel decisions may be complicated by the difficulties of gathering information about intermediaries and buyer preferences, and by the fact that the marketer may be unknown to local intermediaries. E-distribution faces significant challenges because ordering is instant – but physical delivery to distant markets isn't! In addition, there are strategic decisions to be made as to how products will get to the international market:

  - Exporting goods manufactured locally to the target country (either direct or via an agent or distributor): this is sometimes called **export entry** to the market.

  - Licensing or franchising arrangements, where goods are manufactured in the target country using the designs, technology and/or business model of the exporter: **contractual entry** to the market.

  - Transferring manufacturing and marketing activity to the target country, through wholly-owned off-shore or joint venture businesses: **investment entry**.

- **Promotion**. International marketers would wish to use the same communications in as many different countries as possible to keep costs down – but this is rarely possible, due to the extent of language, cultural and infrastructure differences. We will discuss these issues in more detail below.

2 Challenges of international stakeholder communication

2.1 Adaptation or standardisation

International stakeholder communication (and product) strategy may be approached in one of two ways – or some mixture of the two.

- Using the same messages and products for all countries (**standardisation**) is possible when they are not culture-sensitive, and when potential economies of scale (from mass communication or production) are significant. Such an approach assumes that consumer needs and perceptions are very similar everywhere.

- Adjusting the message and product to local conditions (**adaptation**), in order to appeal more directly to the needs, values and perceptions of the local market. This helps to overcome some of the challenges created by different languages, cultural norms and values and so on (which are discussed below).

A marketing communications mix, or product, developed and used successfully within one country cannot necessarily be moved 'as is' into another market without problems!

2.1.1 Think global?

Arguments for standardisation include the following.

- **Economies of scale**. Cost savings may result from locating production in one country, rather than duplicating or splitting production capacity across different plants. There may also be savings on local market research and stakeholder consultation. Communications which can use the same images and themes in advertising are more cost-effective, cutting down on creative costs.

- **Consumer mobility**. Stakeholders may find it reassuring to encounter familiar, consistent products and brand messages wherever they are in the world.

- **Reduced risk**. Standardising marketing communications allows the organisation to control and develop a consistent brand and corporate image.

2.1.2 Act local?

Arguments in favour of adaptation include the following.

- **More effective marketing**, through targeting customer/stakeholder needs more accurately. This may be particularly important for **relationship marketing**, where stakeholders value and expect some form of personalisation or customisation of messages, rather than mass marketing which may be largely inappropriate for their culture or needs.

- **Differences in local audiences**. There may be very wide differences in language, literacy levels and media consumption (affecting the accessibility of the message); different social and religious values (affecting the congeniality of the message); and different government policies and regulatory regimes (eg affecting use of media, privacy, data protection and so on). We will discuss some of the key differences below.

Many international corporations find these arguments so compelling that they attempt to 'Think global, act local'. That is, they develop supply and customer markets globally – but are aware of the need to adapt to the needs and motivations of local stakeholders.

ACTIVITY 10.2

Does your work organisation, or another organisation that you are studying, standardise or adapt its products and services for international markets?

Compare and contrast any *one* product or service offered by the organisation, in any *two* markets (domestic and foreign), using the following template.

Product/Service/Brand:

	Domestic market:	Foreign market:	Reason for difference:
Product			
Price			
Place			
Promotion			
Process			
People			
Physical			

2.2 Cultural and linguistic differences

For stakeholder communications, language barriers are perhaps the most obvious challenge – but there may also be a number of other cultural factors to take into account.

2.2.1 Language barriers

Language may be a significant barrier to communication. Global corporations need to develop linguistic skills, or use local managers, marketers and translators. The potential for misunderstanding arising from the mistranslation of words – or the non-translatability of ideas – into foreign languages is very great. This applies not just to verbal language, but also to visual symbols used in branding and stakeholder messages: different meanings may attach to images, colours and symbols in one culture than in another.

Classic Communication *faux pas*

Language differences have caused innumerable problems for international marketers, and can provide a barrier to foreign market entry...

Here are some classic examples of translations that have gone wrong.

- A Thai dry cleaners: 'Drop your trousers here for best results'
- A sign in Hong Kong tailors: 'Ladies may have a fit upstairs'
- 'Come alive with Pepsi': 'Rise from the grave with Pepsi' (German)
- 'Cleans the really dirty parts of your wash': 'Cleans your private parts' (French)
- Tomato paste: 'Tomato glue' (Arabic)

Brand names have also caused problems:

- GM car model called 'Nova': means 'doesn't go' in Spanish

- Toyota model 'MR2' is pronounced 'merde' in French – which translates to 'excrement'. (A similar problem might be faced by the French drink brand 'Pschitt'. if it tried to market in English-speaking nations...)

- Nissan's model 'Moco' means 'mucus' in Spanish

Language differences also create **power issues**, to which both external and internal stakeholders may be sensitive, particularly in situations such as negotiations and consultations. The language being spoken in the meeting may not be the first language of all participants, putting them at a disadvantage and preventing them from adding their input. This may be considered an ethical issue in some settings, and interviews or discussion facilitators will need to take steps to ensure equitable participation, for example by providing translation, or just being aware of the need to speak more clearly and simply.

2.2.2 Cultural differences

Different countries (and even regions, ethnic and religious sub-groups) may have widely different cultural norms, values and assumptions which influence what they buy, how they do business, and how they manage people in organisations.

Distinctive national features may be a source of **competitive advantage** in domestic and international markets (because of, for example, 'fashions' for the products or management techniques of particular cultures). However, they may also be a source of difficulties in cross-cultural stakeholder communication, business relationships, people management and marketing (because of failure to understand differences in underlying needs and expectations).

Cultural differences may significantly affect stakeholders' responses to products, communications, business dealings and management styles. The following are just some general examples.

- **Religious values**. In some Islamic countries, for example, women are not allowed to be shown in advertising unless they are 'properly attired'. Religious norms may also govern when business can be conducted (eg on holy days, Sabbaths or religious holidays) or what hospitality can be given (eg fast days or alcohol prohibitions).

- **Time values**. Latin cultures do not have as strict a sense of deadlines and appointment times as Anglo cultures: the style is more relaxed. The imposition of deadlines may even be perceived as an insult eg in some Middle Eastern countries. Stakeholder meetings and supply/sale negotiations may have to be adapted accordingly.

- **Business norms and customs**. In some cultures, hospitality is regarded as separate from business: a Westerner's attempt to 'get down to business' over a meal would be insulting. In Japan, the exchange of business cards is an important ritual. In some cultures, business gifts are regarded as an important

relationship-building and business-facilitating tool – while in the West, they are regarded as unethical attempts to influence the objectivity of decisions. Similarly, some cultures regard a person's word as a binding contract, and may be insulted by a request for a written contract, which is the norm in Western cultures.

- **Negotiating, conflict-handling and decision-making styles**. Some cultures (eg the Japanese) favour a low-key, respectful, consensus-seeking approach. In Germany, negotiating success is associated with a 'hard sell' approach, while in France it is associated with common ground between negotiators. Different cultures tend to have different norms and preferences with regard to the appropriateness of assertiveness, criticism or argument, and the need to compromise, reach consensus and save 'face' for the other party. Some cultures prefer to raise issues or ideas one-to-one rather than in a group. Some have a problem with questioning or offering ideas to people in positions of respect or authority.

- **Gender roles**. Some cultures value equal opportunities for women, while others (such as Middle Eastern and less-developed Latin cultures) limit the involvement of women in business dealings and employment. Gender roles will also need to be reflected in promotional messages and the targeting of communications, for example.

- **Status differences**. Some cultures are highly status conscious, and prefer to work in well-defined hierarchical power relationships: let managers be managers, and workers be workers. Anglo work cultures, in contrast, tend to be more participative and egalitarian: employees will expect to be empowered and involved, and the style of communication between managers and workers will be much less formal and respectful.

- **Team working**. 'Collective' working styles (such as team working and group decision making) may be more congenial to some cultures than to more individualistic, competitive cultures. Differences in social and business customs and communication styles, identified above, may initially get in the way of co-operative working in any culturally diverse stakeholder team or meeting.

ACTIVITY 10.3

There are several TV programmes that show award-winning TV ads from across the world. Try to catch a programme of that type next time you get the chance, and watch out for differences in culture and customs, as captured in advertising.

An alternative would be to buy a foreign language magazine or newspaper containing lots of advertisements. Look out for images distinctive to that culture. Also look out for advertising by familiar global brands: do you recognise the brand and advertising messages – or has the message been adapted to the new culture?

2.3 Infrastructure differences

Different countries may not be 'set up' to facilitate stakeholder communication in the same way, or to the same extent.

- **Technology** may, or may not, be available to facilitate communication. For example, undeveloped areas may not have television coverage, telephone coverage or internet access. This severely restricts the channels of communication available to the international marketer, buyer or employer.

- **Time zones** may be an issue for communication in 'real time': the local office's working day may be in the middle of the night for international stakeholders (and *vice versa*). Although the internet and e-mail have reduced this problem, it may still be an issue for urgent communications.

- **Media** variations will also have to be taken into account.

  - Media may, or may not, be available for promotional messages. Undeveloped areas may not have television or radio coverage, or reliable delivery of print media (newspapers and magazines).

  - The effectiveness and reach of media may differ from the home country: for example, cinema is highly significant in India, and radio in the USA.

- Media may be controlled by the state, limiting the kinds of marketing messages that will be carried.

- There may be different regulations in regard to advertising messages: for example, wine cannot be advertised on TV in Denmark, or beer in France, or toys to children under 12 in Sweden. In some Islamic countries, there are regulations on dress and bodily display in advertising.

- Media may be relatively unsophisticated, creating challenges for advertising quality, targeting of market segments, and monitoring of circulation and responses.

- Media costs may be difficult to estimate in some countries, since negotiation and the influence of intermediaries are likely to be much greater.

- There may be lack of effective information on the characteristics of the target market or stakeholder groups.

- **Transport** infrastructure – and the sheer distance to the foreign market – may limit the potential for face-to-face stakeholder communication, which may be important in developing supplier, client or network partnerships, for example. Technology may fill this gap – for example, by allowing video- or web-conferencing – but again, the infrastructure may not be available for such methods.

2.4 Overcoming communication barriers

Schneider & Barsoux (1997) argued that: 'Rather than knowing what to do in Country X, or whether national or functional cultures are more important in multi-cultural teams, what is necessary is **to know how to assess the potential impact** of culture, national or otherwise, on performance'.

At the organisational level, there should be a plan to evaluate the potential impact of cultural and infrastructure differences on stakeholder communications, and to implement programmes to encourage awareness of areas of cultural difference and sensitivities, behavioural flexibility and constructive communication, conflict resolution and problem solving.

- **Marketers' cross-cultural competence** can be enhanced through: encouraging diversified work experience in international or multi-cultural settings; undertaking training exercises (eg language learning or cultural briefings); networking with colleagues and contacts from other cultures and using them as consultants; and seeking to learn through all cross-cultural stakeholder interactions.

- Stakeholder-facing staff may be offered **awareness training** to understand the potential for problems arising from cultural assumptions: the need to recognise and move beyond cultural stereotypes; the need to listen and ask questions; etc.

- **Inter-cultural stakeholder communication** is the only way to bring cultural values and assumptions out into the open, in order to limit potential misunderstandings. This cannot be done by single cultural profiles or briefings: it requires on-going monitoring of messages, interpretations and areas of difference. Mechanisms for this kind of communication may include: cross-cultural teams; cross-cultural discussion, consultation and conflict resolution groups; cultural education and briefings; cross-cultural networking and forums (eg on the corporate intranet); etc.

- Marketers should also use appropriate **resources and relationships** to enhance their communication with international stakeholders. For example, the organisation may use an international advertising or communications agency local to the target market. It may use local distributors and retailers to mediate communication with consumers; appoint local managers for its international offices and factories; and exploit local business contacts and allies as consultants or as facilitators, communicating with local stakeholders on its behalf.

If your organisation has identifiable international stakeholders, select *one* nation or region from which they come, and do some research into the distinctive challenges of communicating with them. Prepare a 'cultural briefing' on the nation or region; include language, cultural and infrastructure issues.

3 The technological environment

3.1 Changing communication

In the last twenty years, the infrastructure and tools of communication have radically changed. The phone is swiftly being overtaken by e-mail as the most popular method of remote interpersonal communication. The internet has changed the way people access information. Even 'old' media like the TV and telephone are being transformed by new data transmission infrastructures and integration with computer systems.

Even a decade ago Ebbs (2001) summed it up as follows.

'The World Wide Web has truly changed communication. Those of us with a computer at work share jokes and yarns as if we are sitting around a campfire, do the sort of research that five years ago was restricted to major libraries, and write more letters to people than most of the literary giants we grew up studying...'

Given that discussion of technological innovations goes out of date almost as soon as it is printed, it might help to be aware of the general trends in ICT (information and communication technology) development.

3.1.1 Speed of communication

The development of 'facsimile transfer' (fax) was a breakthrough in its day, enabling documents that previously had to be mailed, to be transferred down a phone line. Now, messages can be transferred via a local computer network or the internet almost instantly, to the point where real time conversations can be held using online messaging, chat rooms and Voice Over Internet Protocol (VoIP). Recent **infrastructure innovations** such as ISDN (Integrated Systems Digital Network), DSL (Digital Subscriber Lines), satellite transmission (for telephone and television signals), fibre optic cabling and increased 'band width' (allowing more data to pass through networks more swiftly) have supported this process.

3.1.2 Wider access to information

Over 15 years ago, Krol and Ferguson (1996) said, 'Once you're connected to the internet, you have instant access to an almost indescribable wealth of **information**...'.

In the years since that was written, the availability of information online has multiplied further and the impact of that trend is being felt in many fields – market research is one area which has been transformed with the availability of online information. It may even also allow you to study in a different way than in the past with the development of distance learning by many organisations.

3.1.3 24-7 global communication

ICT has enabled 24-hour 7-day global communication: across working or office hours, time zones and geographical distances. Fax and answer machines were a start in this direction – but they required (possibly delayed) human intervention to initiate a response. The internet allows users to access information/services and perform transactions at any time of any day. Nor is there any distinction between local and international sites,

in terms of speed or cost of access. (Physical delivery of products ordered will, as we have noted, re-erect some of the geographical barriers...)

3.1.4 Interactivity and multi-media

Interactivity is mutual responsiveness. Consumers are increasingly demanding, in terms of interactivity in accessing and responding to promotional messages. According to Postma (1999), true interactivity implies:

- Speed of dialogue/response (for example, the immediacy of telephone, e-mail and internet message exchanges)

- Up-to-dateness of the information provided at time of contact

- Flexibility and scope of response (for example, access information, get questions answered *and* submit detailed order requirements and payments).

Consumers are also increasingly demanding in terms of the **stimulation** provided by promotional messages. **Multi-media** communication implies the use of written, visual and audio elements to enhance a message's impact and interest. Postma (op cit) suggests that: 'there is nothing the human nervous system desires more than colour video pictures with sound'.

The internet and related technologies have made young people, in particular, very familiar with multi-media presentations, high-level animated/video-based graphics and interaction with material. Printed matter may seem relatively unstimulating in comparison. Some of the features of online and multi-media presentation are being added to traditional print communications: simulated 'links' and buttons, multi-directional graphics, opportunities for response/participation and so on.

3.1.5 Personalisation

Database, document generation and web technologies have improved the ease and sophistication of targeting and personalisation of contact between organisations and stakeholders. Examples include:

- Allowing users to customise web pages for their personal interests and tastes

- Making individually-targeted product offers and recommendations based on actual browsing/buying behaviour

- Sending personally addressed and targeted-content messages to stakeholders

- Encouraging stakeholders to form virtual communities: for example, using chat rooms, discussion boards and newsgroups, user weblogs ['blogs'], and, increasingly, social networking sites such as Facebook.

ACTIVITY 10.5

How might the marketing organisation exploit the 'virtual community' aspects of ICT for relationship marketing?

3.2 ICT and competitive advantage

Jobber (2007, p 736) identifies various ways in which ICT offers organisations opportunities for competitive advantage, and we have added some of our own.

- **Lower costs and lower prices**. ICT can make direct links between suppliers and customers without the cost of using intermediaries. It can also streamline administrative procedures for purchase and payment (some of which may be carried out electronically without human intervention). Some of these cost savings may be passed on to consumers eg via discounts for online bookings/purchases.

- **Improved service quality**. ICT can make the 'process' part of the extended marketing mix faster and less variable, giving fast, 24 7 access to information and transactions, and empowering customers for self-service (eg entertainment and travel bookings) and control over service (eg tracking of deliveries). At the

same time, it improves staff access to stakeholder and product information, enabling them to provide a more personal, informed service.

- **Greater product choice**. Retail stores have limited space to store and display items; 'virtual' stores can offer an unlimited range of goods (as long as they can back them up by supplying physical goods in response to orders!)

- **Product/service customisation**. The gathering of data on web users' browsing and purchasing patterns and preferences can be used to customise messages and offerings to individual stakeholders: one-to-one marketing. ICT links between organisations and their suppliers also makes possible the late customisation of products to customers' specification: we have used the example of Dell Computers elsewhere in this text.

- **Virtual organisation**. ICT links enable an organisation to co-opt the services of quality workers, advisers and collaborators as part of their organisation or network – regardless of where they are located in the world.

- **Innovation and learning**. ICT gives access to global information, enabling the organisation to learn about global best practice and competitor activity, for benchmarking and imitation.

- **Relationship management**. ICT can be used to develop loyal, mutually beneficial stakeholder relationships, by:

  - Giving wider stakeholders access to information about the organisation and its CSR and stakeholder policies

  - Allowing transaction processing, delivery tracking and other value-adding service elements

  - Supporting the customisation of products/services and the personalisation of contacts for stakeholder relationship management

  - Creating knowledge communities – sharing information with allies and partners via extranets, for example

  - Facilitating the co-ordination of collaborative activities with partners, encouraging activity links and integration of systems, which fosters mutual dependency.

▶ **Assessment tip**

You are unlikely to need to have detailed *technical* knowledge of how ICT systems and tools operate – but you should cultivate some awareness of their uses and implications for marketing practice and stakeholder communications. If in doubt, ask yourself: what does this technology *do* for the organisation, and for its internal and external stakeholders? How might it contribute to building and sustaining relationships between them? How does it save money and/or contribute to environmental sustainability? Are there ethical issues in its use? We will explore some of these questions later.

---

4 Technology and the marketing mix

Although the syllabus focuses on marketing communications, you should be aware that technological developments have had, and will continue to have, a significant influence on all aspects of the marketing mix.

Peppers and Rogers (1997) argued that the traditional 4Ps marketing mix is inadequate in the internet age, and suggested a replacement approach to maximise the potential of ICT: the **5Is**. (We have replaced the word 'customers' with 'stakeholders'. because the principles are equally valid for all markets.)

- **Identification**: learn about the specific preferences of specific [stakeholders]
- **Individualisation**: tailored products, services and messages to develop relationships for lifetime value
- **Interaction**: engage in two-way dialogue to learn about [stakeholders'] needs
- **Integration**: share knowledge about [stakeholders] throughout the organisation (internal marketing)
- **Integrity**: develop trust, through non-intrusive use of communications tools (eg permission marketing).

The Chartered Institute of Marketing

4.1 ICT and product

ICT may itself, increasingly, represent a product or service.

- **Technology components, tools and services** are sold in both consumer and B2B markets: think of PCs, mobile phones, digital cameras, iPods (and their accessories), internet services and cafés, software packages, IT consultancy and so on.

- ICT enables **information** to be sold as a product/service: think of subscriptions to online databases, publications and news services, for example.

- ICT enables **service provision**: think of online banking, travel reservations, e-learning education services, dating/connection services, 'apps' for smartphones etc.

ICT is also now used to **add value** to conventional products and services. For example, if you send a parcel by international courier you can track its progress online. If you study by distance education, you can use e-learning to enhance the group learning and interactivity of the experience. Even a tin of baked beans is enhanced – as a total package of benefits – by its packaging being electronically bar-coded: providing information to the retailer and supplier (on sales values/frequency etc) and to the consumer (recording special offers, use-by-dates and so on).

4.2 ICT and price

ICT may impact directly or indirectly on price in various ways.

- It gives the marketer more sophisticated tools for **analysing costs**, and for analysing **market responses to price changes**.

- Stakeholders have greater access to **price information** too: marketers could view the many online price comparison sites as a threat, especially if their product or retail outlet comes out as the most expensive!

- On-line catalogues and auctions empower customers to **define price parameters**. For example, catalogue shoppers can specify a price range and be given a menu of options in that range. eBay members effectively decide the price they are willing to pay for goods – and the same is possible in a large-scale B2B environment through the use of commercial e-auctions for supply contracts.

- The use of ICT may enable suppliers to **pass on to consumers** the cost savings obtained by streamlined administration and 'self-service' marketing.

4.3 ICT and place

ICT has enabled direct marketing of products and services to consumers and business users, cutting short distribution channels by:

- **Facilitating conventional direct sales**: sales force information linked to central databases (Customer Relationship Management), personalised direct mail, online mail order catalogues etc.

- **Empowering customers to purchase direct**: eg from virtual stores and auctions. Online shopping (e-commerce) and its B2B equivalent (e-procurement) via the internet has exploded in many sectors in recent years, especially in markets such as music and books, clothing, travel products, banking services, groceries and niche goods (arts and crafts).

- **Facilitating home delivery of goods**, eg by allowing remote ordering, payment and delivery tracking – and 'virtual' supply (eg by downloading information, software, books or music direct from the internet).

ACTIVITY 10.6

Based on your own experience of internet shopping, identify how ICT is applied to the 3Ps of the service mix (Process, People and Physicals) in the case of a consumer online purchase.

It is important for marketers to be aware of what ICT *can't* do. It may enable instant, global ordering of physical goods – but it can't get them delivered to far-flung locations any faster! Because of the promotional strengths of the internet, and the illusion of virtual supply, there is great potential for disappointment if the product does not live up to the sophistication of the promises – or if it cannot be delivered in a reasonable condition or within a reasonable period of time.

4.4 ICT and promotion

ICT can add impact, speed, interactivity and fun to the full range of promotional methods and tools. This has a relationship marketing aspect, because it provides incentives for stakeholders to keep consuming promotional media and messages.

Table 10.2   ICT and promotion

Promotion activity	Impact/opportunity	Examples of supporting technology
Advertising	▪ Publicising sponsorships ▪ Publicising exhibition attendance ▪ Up-to-date information for sales force & call centre staff	▪ Web site ▪ Web site/e-mail for clients ▪ Access to product/stock and customer database
Sales promotion	▪ Staff access to information relevant to their jobs ▪ Co-ordination of dispersed offices and off-site staff	▪ Intranet newsletters, bulletins, policy info ▪ E-mail, tele- and video-conferencing
Direct marketing	▪ Supplier/client access to information relevant to business relationship	▪ Extranet: access to selected information ▪ Electronic Data Interchange (EDI): linked computer systems for direct data sharing and communication
Public relation & publicity	▪ Publicising sponsorships ▪ Publicising exhibition attendance ▪ Up-to-date information for sales force & call centre staff	▪ Web site ▪ Web site/e-mail for clients ▪ Access to product/stock and customer database
Marketing/sales support	▪ Publicising sponsorships ▪ Publicising exhibition attendance ▪ Up-to-date information for sales force & call centre staff	▪ Web site ▪ Web site/e-mail for clients ▪ Access to product/stock and customer database
Internal marketing	▪ Staff access to information relevant to their jobs ▪ Co-ordination of dispersed offices and off-site staff	▪ Intranet newsletters, bulletins, policy info ▪ E-mail, tele- and video-conferencing
Network marketing	▪ Supplier/client access to information relevant to business relationship	▪ Extranet: access to selected information ▪ Electronic Data Interchange (EDI): linked computer systems for direct data sharing and communication

ICT has also offered significant new media for marketing communications purposes: we discussed a range of these in Chapter 8.

Mobile phone companies appear to be particularly good at making use of Facebook pages to build relationships with their customers. Not only do they use them to advertise their products, but also to gain feedback from customers.

For example, **Sony Ericson** recently showed different colours that they were considering for an accessory for the Xperia phone on their Facebook page – within one hour of posting, they had over 3,500 responses from people choosing their preferences.

Nokia meanwhile has used its Facebook page to showcase videos shot by customers on their Nokia phones – thus both demonstrating the capabilities of the phones to other users and also making customers feel part of the brand, ie building relationships with them.

Check out what these two companies are up to at present on Facebook:

- http://www.facebook.com/sonymobile
- http://www.facebook.com/nokia

ACTIVITY 10.7

Identify the key features of the ICT marketing mix for your own organisation, or another organisation you are studying, using our coverage to give you ideas of what to look for. You may like to use the following template.

Mix element	ICT tools used	Impact of ICT
Product		
Price		
Place		
Promotion		

4.5 The internet

The internet is not explicitly mentioned in the syllabus – but it has clearly been relevant to a great deal of our coverage of relationship marketing. In fact, it has had such a pervasive and powerful influence on marketing, and specifically on relationship marketing, that we thought it was worth giving it separate attention here.

4.5.1 The internet as a promotional tool

The internet can be used across the promotion mix.

Table 10.3   The internet as a promotional tool

Advertising	• Dedicated corporate web sites, banner/button advertising, ranking on internet search engines (to increase site exposure) • The forecast global penetration of the internet over the next few years would give it a significantly larger audience than any of the television networks, print media outlets or other advertising vehicles
Direct marketing	• E-mail messages sent to targeted mailing lists (rented, or developed by the marketing organisation itself) • 'Permission marketing' (targeting consumers who have opted to receive commercial mailings)
Direct response advertising	• Immediate contact (information/transaction facilities) to follow up customer responses to TV/radio/print advertising
Sales promotion	• Online prize draws and competitions • Online discounts (offset by lower transaction costs)

	■ Downloadable or e-mailed discount vouchers
Customer loyalty programmes	■ Value-added benefits that enhance the internet buying experience ■ User home page customisation ■ Virtual communities (chat rooms etc) ■ Free e-cards/SMS messages
Media/press relations	■ Online media/press kits ■ E-mailed media releases ■ 'About us' and 'contacts' pages ■ Technical briefings and articles on key issues
Public relations	■ 'About us' and 'FAQ' (frequently asked question) features ■ News bulletins (eg for crisis or issues management) ■ Publicity/information for sponsorships, exhibitions and events ■ Sponsorship of popular/ useful information sites
Relationship marketing	■ Customisation of web pages and targeting of offers/promotions ■ E-mail follow-up of contacts ■ E-zines: special interest newsletters published on the web, or distributed by e-mail direct to subscribers and mailing lists ■ Web-casts and podcasts enabling virtual meetings, conferences, classes/lectures and so on ■ Social networking sites such as Facebook
Grass roots and viral marketing	■ Generating word-of-mouth promotion and recommendation among customers ■ Participating in user-driven content sites or Consumer Generated Media (CGM) eg posting ad clips on YouTube or Myspace ■ Online chat or message board forums and 'blogs' (weblogs), where users (and producers eg authors and film-makers on Amazon.com) share their views and experiences online ■ 'Viral marketing' (so called because it simulates the way a virus works!): giving visitors communication tools which they send to others, requiring them to visit the site: eg electronic postcards, greeting cards and links ('Send this page to a friend'), shared online games and so on
Direct distribution	■ Of products (through online shopping) and services (including access to information databases) ■ Products can be ordered via the internet ■ Some can also be delivered via the internet, by downloading direct to the purchaser's PC: examples include music, computer software, photographs, product catalogues and instruction manuals
Customer service and technical support	■ E-mail contact ■ FAQs (frequently asked questions) ■ Access to databased information ■ Online messaging or voice interruption for interactive support
Market/stakeholder research	■ Gathering information on customers and visitors for the purposes of market segmentation, personalisation/customisation of future contacts ■ Site monitoring ■ Online or e-mailed feedback questionnaires and surveys

The Chartered Institute of Marketing

4.5.2 Advantages of internet marketing

Rich (1999) suggests a number of reasons why the internet is attractive to marketing organisations of all sizes in virtually all industries.

- The **initial costs** for creating a basic internet presence are relatively low.

- The internet has a potential **reach** of millions of consumers and other stakeholders.

- The internet can also be used for targeted **niche marketing**, since the technology facilitates reaching small (even individual) audiences according to specifically defined criteria.

- The internet is active **24-7** across a **global** stakeholder marketplace.

- The internet is **highly interactive**, presenting opportunities for dialogue, and creating an entertaining, ever-changing experience which can draw users to a web site again and again over time.

- Online contacts can be **accurately monitored and evaluated**: who is visiting the site, when, for how long, what information is sought, what products are ordered. This feedback can be used to adjust the marketing and communications mix.

- Web sites are highly **versatile** (as shown in their communications mix applications listed above).

ACTIVITY 10.8

Identify the purposes for which your organisation, or another organisation you are studying, uses its web site(s).

Which target stakeholder audiences are specifically addressed by the site?

How effectively does the site (a) meet stakeholders' information needs, (b) create the desired impression of the organisation and its values, (c) give users an incentive to visit the site repeatedly and (d) support other relationship marketing approaches?

4.6 Overview of the ICT marketing mix

The new marketing mix can be summarised as follows (based on Jobber, *op cit*, p727).

Figure 10.1   The ICT marketing mix

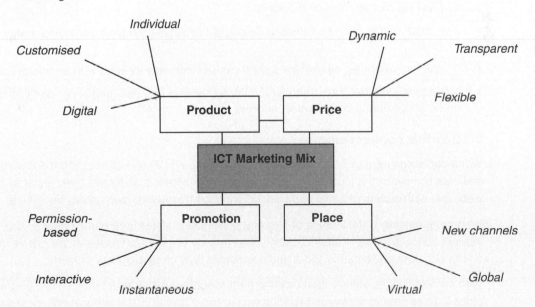

5 Technology for stakeholder communication

ICT-enabled communication tools are developing at a very rapid rate. We cover some of the current tools here, but be aware that, as you read this, other tools will be available that will have been developed since this text was written!

5.1 Telecommunications infrastructure

Developments in the telecommunications infrastructure (means of connecting A to B) are generally allowing more data to be carried more swiftly.

- **ISDN (Integrated Systems Digital Network)** is a digital telecom network. It is a faster alternative to analogue services, supporting high-speed access to the internet, shorter connection times (for cost savings), and use of more than one service over the link at the same time (eg internet and telephone).

- **Digital mobile telecommunications networks** (such as GSM – Group Special Mobile – a pan-European digital cellular network) provide increasingly wide mobile phone coverage and services, including internet access for a range of m-commerce and data management applications.

5.2 Computer-telephony integration

Telephony (the use of telephones) can be integrated with IT (computer) systems in various ways.

5.2.1 VoIP (Voice Over Internet Protocol)

> ▶ **Key term**
>
> **VoIP** is a system protocol that allows a person to use an internet connection to make voice calls to another party with either an internet connection *or* a telephone. It is also referred to as 'internet telephony', 'voice over broadband' or 'broadband telephony'.

The **benefits** claimed for VoIP include:

- Low-cost telephone calls: some VoIP-to-VoIP calls are free.

- The ability to transmit more than one call over the same broadband connection: an easy way to add an extra phone line to a home or office.

- A full range of telecom features and services (conference calls, call forwarding, caller ID and so on) provided by most service providers.

- A more secure phone connection, since digitisation is already in place, and makes data encryption easier.

- Mobility: users (eg call centre agents) can call from any location with an internet connection.

- Integration of telephony with other internet services eg video- and audio-conferencing, data/message exchange during conversation, address books and so on.

5.2.2 Virtual conferencing

Video-conferencing was first used commercially in the 1970s and at one time there were thousands of dedicated conferencing studios in use worldwide. These have now largely been replaced by the potential for **web-** and **pod-casting** of audio and video information from users' own homes and offices.

Web-conferencing is the sharing of files and presentation slides from participants' PCs or laptops, over an internet connection. More sophisticated tools allow participants to engage in interactive messaging or 'chat'. and to annotate presentation slides and documents 'live' on participants' screens.

Web conferencing enables virtual meeting participants to share presentation slides, diagrams, documents and other files, as well as seeing and hearing each other. This has many applications for presentations, training sessions and meetings where participants are geographically dispersed (eg overseas clients or suppliers). It also enables very large groups to participate: the Oprah Winfrey TV show, for example, recently set up the world's largest interactive 'classroom discussion' for its book club.

These tools are likely to have a significant impact on contacts with internal and external stakeholders.

- Given that a high proportion of interpersonal communication is non-verbal, virtual face-to-face communication enhances possibilities for more 'personal' service, better understanding, complaint handling, negotiation etc.

- At the same time, large amounts of complex data can be shared and manipulated, as in a face-to-face meeting.

- Widely dispersed external stakeholders and internal teams can be brought together without the cost and inconvenience of having to be in the same location. This dramatically improves the organisation's ability to communicate with international stakeholders – without the cost and carbon footprint of international travel.

5.2.3 Automated telephony

Automated call handling is a system whereby a computerised or recorded voice asks telephone callers to select from a menu of options by pressing buttons on their telephone. This can be used:

- To route calls through a switchboard, by specifying connection choices (nature of call, target department and extension, if known) and putting the caller through.

- To complete entire transactions (eg booking cinema tickets and paying bills by credit card) and information searches (eg transport timetables, cinema film times)

- Without intervention by a human operators (although there is usually the option to switch to a human operator in case of difficulty)

Interactive voice response (IVR) systems involve a similar approach, but selections are made from the menu options by voice response: that is, responding verbally by answering questions with selected words ('yes'. 'no'. numbers and key terms) which can be recognised by the receiving software. This is extensively used in the booking of taxis, for example: the caller responds to questions by saying 'yes' or 'no' ('Are we picking you up from this address?'. 'Are you ready now?'), numbers ('How many passengers?') and other recognisable words ('What is the destination area?').

ACTIVITY 10.9

From your own experience of such systems, what do you think are the advantages and disadvantages of automated call handling systems for stakeholder relationship management?

5.2.4 Computer-Telephony Integration (CTI) systems

▶ **Key term**

Computer Telephony Integration (CTI) systems link the telephone systems of an organisation (or its call centre) to computerised databases of information about callers and/or products, so that staff members have real-time access to information for handling the call.

Information gathered from stakeholders in the course of telephone calls and transactions can be input to a database and called up and sent to the screen of the person handling subsequent calls.

- Service staff dealing with hundreds of calls every day can give the impression of **recognising** individual callers personally and knowing in advance what information they are likely to need. Order and enquiry forms with key details already entered can be displayed on operators' screens automatically, **saving time** for both parties.

- Relevant information on products or other databased information can be called up in response to stakeholder questions, during the call. A financial planner, for example, might use CTI to call up changes in share prices or details of investment products relevant to a customer's enquiry.

- Similarly, calls from suppliers and intermediaries can be handled with all relevant details readily to hand, in order to answer questions in real time.

5.3 Mobile telecommunications

Mobile phone networks started up in the late 1980s and have boomed in developed countries ever since. This means that a salesperson or other stakeholder contact on the road, say, can send or receive phone calls and a variety of other message types (including e-mails, faxes and downloaded content via an internet connection). The development of smartphones such as the Blackberry or iPhone and "tablet computers" such as the iPad have accelerated this process. In theory it is now possible to do any kind of 'office' communication activity outside the office and on the move – although limitations in battery power (a technology so far lagging behind others described in this chapter) impose some restrictions.

However, the mobile phone is no longer just a means of speaking to stakeholders on the way to meetings, or taking calls when out of the office. The services available to users are increasing all the time, making the mobile phone a tool of promotion and e-commerce as well as interpersonal communication.

5.3.1 SMS text messaging

We mentioned SMS text messaging as one of the 'hot' new advertising and direct marketing media, in Chapter 8. However, it is also a common tool of quick messaging in a variety of communication contexts. It is quicker and less intrusive than a phone call (since it does not need to be accepted or returned immediately), and enables mobile messaging for those without immediate access to e-mail (although SMS messages can also be sent from phones to computers and *vice versa).*

5.4 E-mail

We have already discussed the use of e-mail for internal stakeholder communication (in Chapter 9). However, it is equally commonly used – and with the same advantages – in communication with external stakeholders.

- **Cost-effectiveness**. E-mail is one of the least expensive ways to reach people in a highly targeted, personalised manner – whether one person in the office across the hall or millions of people all over the world.

- **Speed of delivery/response**. Apart from instant transmission (unlike postal direct mail packages), most e-mail campaigns are said to elicit 5% of their responses within 24 hours and 15% of their responses within 72 hours.

- **Targeting**. E-mail messages can be written for the interests of a highly targeted audience, using integrated address books and databased information to personalise content for individual recipients.

- **Acceptability**. 'People look forward to receiving e-mail from friends, relatives and co-workers. This means that their attitude is more open and accepting than in more advertising-oriented communications.' (Allen *et al*, 2001)

ACTIVITY 10.10

(a) From your own experience, can you suggest some potential *barriers* to using e-mail marketing to stakeholders?

(b) What steps could you take to ensure that e-mail communications campaigns overcome stakeholder resistance to 'spam'? Write a concise set of guidelines for staff.

The advantages of e-mail outlined above have led to considerable use of this medium to send regular newsletters to customers and other stakeholders. Online services such as ConstantContact (http://www.constantcontact.com) and MailChimp (http://mailchimp.com/) enable users to send targeted e-mails to contacts and be able to track whether the e-mails were opened by the recipients, whether any links in the e-mails were clicked on, and many other statistics, thus providing not only an economical method of communicating with stakeholders but also being able to monitor the success of these communications.

5.5 Intranet and extranet

We have already discussed the **internet** (earlier in this chapter) and **intranets** (in Chapter 9). An **extranet** is the equivalent network used to communicate with selected stakeholders external to the organisation. ('inter' means between; 'intra' means within; 'extra' means outside.)

An extranet, like an intranet, excludes access by the general public, but **selected outside users** are given passwords to enable them to access particular areas or levels of the system. Since information will not be available to the public in general, it can be used as part of a relationship marketing strategy. Examples include the member-only pages of the web sites of professional bodies (and their student equivalents), which make information and downloads available only to registered members. You might like to refresh your memory of the CIM site, for example, both internet (general access) and extranet (member/student areas) at http://www.cim.co.uk.

Extranets are particularly useful tools for **supply chain partners** and **network allies**. An extranet may be used to:

- Provide a 'pooled' service which a number of business partners can access
- Exchange news which is of use to partner companies and clients
- Share training or development resources
- Put contracts up for tender to a pool of pre-qualified suppliers
- Publicise loyalty schemes, sponsorships, exhibition attendance information and other promotional tools
- Exchange potentially large volumes of inventory, transaction and delivery data efficiently
- Provide online presentations to business partners and prospects (and *not* to competitors!).

5.6 e-Procurement

You shouldn't be required to have a detailed awareness of electronic sourcing and purchasing systems, but be aware that there are such things and that they are an increasing feature of organisations' relationships with their suppliers.

e-Sourcing may take a number of forms, at different levels of buyer-seller interaction.

> **Key term**
>
> **e-Sourcing** is 'using the internet to make decisions and form strategies regarding how and where services or products are obtained' (Chartered Institute of Purchasing & Supply, CIPS).
>
> **e-Procurement** is 'using the internet to operate the transactional aspects of requisitioning, authoring, ordering, receipting and payment processes for the required services or products' (CIPS).

- **Electronic (or e-) catalogues**: suppliers exhibit their products in electronic catalogues and buyers work with those details to purchase materials and services.

- **e-auctions** (where a seller offers goods for sale, buyers bid competitively for them and the highest bid wins) and reverse auctions (where a buyer specifies its needs, suppliers submit quotes competitively, and the lowest bid wins).

- **Market exchanges**: electronic marketplaces where multiple buyers and sellers 'meet' to buy, sell and exchange goods.

e-Procurement may also take a number of forms:

- **Electronic Data Interchange (EDI)**: exchange of documents in standardised electronic form, directly from a computer application in one organisation to an application in another

- **Online track-and-trace systems**: using global positioning systems (GPS) and barcodes or radio frequency identification (RFID) tags to follow deliveries or movements of inventory

- **Payment**: eg automated invoicing, electronic funds transfer (EFT), or use of purchasing cards

- **Electronic point-of-sale (EPOS) systems**: enabling retailers to gather and share sales data with suppliers, to support collaborative stock replenishment, marketing planning etc

- **Contract management systems**: e-contracts, automatic updating for changes, and reporting by exception on performance discrepancies (eg late deliveries or payments).

It should be noted that data links only add value if they are used! Optimum use of ICT in supplier relationships still requires trust, deepening collaboration, relationship management and long-term mutual benefit and commitment (to make the investment in relationship technology worthwhile).

▶ **Assessment tip**

You may or may not be asked explicitly to discuss the impact of ICT developments on the marketing mix or stakeholder relationships in your assignment. However, it will still be worthwhile bearing them in mind, and showing your coverage of this learning objective by including ICT aspects when you analyse the marketing mix, discuss relationship-building tools, or make recommendations.

5.7 Other relationship marketing tools

We have already highlighted a number of other ICT-based tools specifically designed for relationship marketing, in our coverage in Chapter 4. To remind you...

5.7.1 Database marketing

Database marketing uses gathered stakeholder data to target, customise and personalise communications with stakeholders, to add value and enhance relationships.

- **Targeting** of communications, so that they reach the right people and have greater relevance to the recipients. For example, this may mean targeting customers in particular geographic areas with information relevant to their location, targeting customers with offers tailored to their past buying preferences, or targeting other stakeholder groups with media and messages relevant to their interests, concerns and characteristics.

- **Personalising** of communications, so that they have a greater relevance and sense of recognition for the stakeholder. For example, this may mean personally addressed communications, individual stakeholder information made available in real time to call centre staff, or relational use of personal information (eg birthday cards to key contacts).

Postma (1999) suggests that such techniques:

- **Build relationship**: 'Reacting to the personal behaviour of [stakeholders] by responding to their interests with an electronic message, a letter, a brochure or an offer actually fosters [their] feeling that you are becoming acquainted with their tastes and preferences and are taking them into consideration.'

- **Reinforce loyalty**. 'Loyal customers [and other stakeholders] will value being recognised as such and receiving direct communications'.

- **Out-perform human beings**! 'An assistant in a fashion store may very well recognise a client's face after half a year, but will not instantly remember the client's measurements and tastes. A database, on the other hand, has no problem whatsoever retaining these facts or other information about the customer's average expenditure, quality standards or preferred brand. We won't even mention the fact that the employee who served the customer last time has moved on to a different job and been replaced.'

5.7.2 Customer Relationship Management (CRM)

CRM (and its equivalents for supplier and other stakeholder relationship management) is 'a comprehensive approach that provides seamless co-ordination between sales, customer service, marketing, field support and other customer-touching functions. CRM integrates people, process and technology to maximise relationships with all your customers including eCustomers, distribution channel members, internal customers and suppliers.' (www.ismguide.com)

The term '**e-CRM**' has been coined to describe a web-centric approach to synchronising customer relationships across communication channels, business functions and audiences. Each time a customer contacts a company with an effective CRM system – whether by telephone, in a retail outlet or online – the customer should be recognised and should receive appropriate information and attention on that basis. CRM software also provides advanced personalisation and customised solutions to customer demands, giving customer care staff a range of information about each customer which can be applied to the contact or transaction.

As we saw in Chapter 9, traditional vertical organisation structures have tended to create stand alone systems developed for distinct functions or department, which were responsible for the four main types of interaction with a customer: marketing, sales, fulfilment and after-sales service. For relationship marketing, these systems need to be integrated into a central database, with facilities for data to be accessed from, and fed into, the system from other departments and applications (including the web site), so that all stakeholder information can be kept up to date – and shared.

Figure 10.2   CRM system

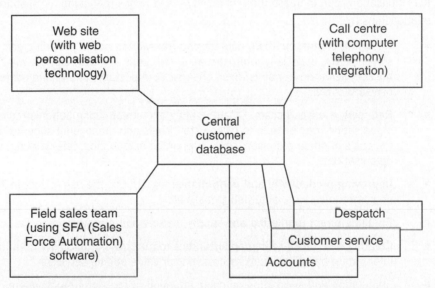

CRM software is produced by a wide variety of providers, including Oracle, Surf Aid (used by IBM and Hilton Hotels), Blue Martini (used by Levi Strauss), Netperceptions and NeuralWare.

6 Technology's contribution to sustainable relationships

6.1 ICT contribution to stakeholder relationship marketing

ICT applications in stakeholder relationship marketing management include:

- The use of **databases**, to improve marketing planning, personalisation of stakeholder contacts, and provision of 'real-time' information to stakeholders (in conjunction with systems such as computer-telephony integration).

- The use of **multiple communication channels** for stakeholder contacts, including e-mail, web site, mobile phones, SMS text messaging etc.

- The use of web sites to **increase voluntary contact** by stakeholders: providing value-adding features (eg communities and discussion boards, database searches, online-only discounts and special offers) and changing content to stimulate repeat visits.

- The use of database, web and computer technology to **personalise contacts**: from personally addressed letters and postcards to caller 'recognition' by customer service staff (using computer-telephony integration) to customised web experiences (using cookies to 'remember' user preferences).

- The use of ICT to **add value to contacts and customer service**: e-mail speeding up response to queries; FAQs on web sites allowing self-service information; automated voice systems allowing self-service telephony; e-commerce empowering customers (online shopping, internet banking) etc.

- The use of online **monitoring and feedback** to gather stakeholder preference data, enabling further contacts and offerings to be better tailored to their needs.

- **Creative applications** aimed at stakeholder 'delight' and loyalty – eg sending birthday cards/e-mails to loyal customers, key suppliers or journalists.

- Using ICT tools for **loyalty schemes**: swipe card points systems, online vouchers etc.

- Creating **stakeholder communities** as an incentive to identify with the organisation or brand, eg membership of customer/user clubs, online discussion boards, user-generated content (such as blogs, reviews and recommendations).

6.2 ICT and economic sustainability

ICT applications can increase the profitability – and hence the economic sustainability – of stakeholder relationships by:

- **Reducing communication, contact and transaction costs**, providing cost-effective ways of reaching stakeholders, especially internationally. VoIP calls, for example, are much cheaper than conventional telecom services; e-mail is much cheaper than postage; and online conferencing is much cheaper than overseas travel.

- **Reducing overhead costs**. By automating and streamlining administrative and service tasks, the organisation may be able to reduce staff levels and managerial supervision. It may also be able to reduce the costs of office premises, eg by supporting outsourcing, tele-working, virtual team-working and virtual organisation.

- **Improving productivity and performance**: eg through the use of Just-in-Time supply systems, speeding up communications, automating tasks etc.

- **Enabling direct marketing and supply**, cutting out intermediary costs.

- **Creating new cross-selling opportunities** to maximise profitability from loyal customers: eg for ICT- or information-based products, accessories or value-adding services.

- Stimulating and supporting on-going attention to the recruitment, retention and development of **high-quality, technologically-skilled employees** – which will have long-term advantages for organisational competitiveness and profitability.

- **Supporting access to markets** for small buyers and suppliers. Small players might otherwise be disadvantaged in competition with large multinational corporations, so the businesses themselves might be economically unsustainable. Supporting small suppliers ultimately supports business sustainability, as it helps to preserve diverse and competitive supply markets for the future.

- **Supporting access to employment** for people in remote areas, the less mobile (eg disabled) or people with heavy home/family responsibilities.

- Creating low-cost or cost-effective marketing options for **micro enterprises and small-medium enterprises (SMEs)** which might otherwise not be able to afford much in the way of media advertising or public relations activity.

'An excellent example of e-commerce productivity is provided by **Dell Corporation,** the world's largest computer direct marketing operation. Customers visiting the Dell web site are provided not just with an effective ordering system but, in addition, a multitude of tools for answering technical questions and for configuring their own personalised computer design. If customers hit a problem at the click of a button they will be put in telephone contact with a highly trained Dell service employee who can offer an appropriate solution. Once an order is placed, the Dell automated procurement, manufacturing and distribution system ensures that logistics productivity is at a standard that is the envy of the competition.'

(Jobber, 2007)

ACTIVITY 10.11

Can you see any ways in which the kinds of economic benefits listed above could *damage* the sustainability of an organisation's relationships with particular stakeholder groups?

6.3 ICT and environmental sustainability

ICT solutions are environmentally friendly, in comparison to:

- **Production and packaging methods** that involve the use of non-renewable material resources and create physical wastes. (Compare the supply of downloadable music files with the supply of a fully-packaged CD, for example.)

- **Delivery methods** that involve physical transportation of goods and messages, which damage the environment through traffic congestion, carbon emissions, noise, use of non-renewable fuel resources etc.

- **Documentary communication and transaction methods** that involve paper documentation and its waste products (which are not always effectively recycled).

- **Face-to-face and interactive communication methods** (such as international meetings and conferences) that require road or air travel, a major source of carbon emissions.

ICT can also support reverse logistics for the safe disposal and recycling of waste or obsolete products: eg by aiding reverse delivery planning, informing customers about returns and recycling etc.

6.4 CSR and ethical issues in ICT

Jobber (2007, p753) identifies the following ethical issues in the increasing adoption of digital technologies in marketing.

- **Inequality of access**. Despite rapid penetration, there remains a divide between technology 'haves' and 'have nots'. Lack of infrastructure, financial restrictions and lack of education/skilling may deprive some citizens – even in developed nations – of internet access. Rural internet users are typically stuck with slow and unreliable connections in comparison with urban users, for example.

- **Social exclusion**. There is a fear of social exclusion for members of society who cannot afford a computer, broadband connection or 3G phone – and therefore cannot benefit from the information, products or services available. Some companies (eg in the financial services market) are criticised for offering internet-only access to services, cutting themselves off from mainstream customers in the interest of customer leverage and profitability. Others, however, are proactively positioning themselves as access supporters, for example, by providing computers to schools.

- Conversely, ICT can also *reduce* social exclusion: eg mobile phones helping homeless people access employment, and SMS text messaging aiding the hearing impaired.

- **Privacy issues**. ICT systems may be perceived to invade consumer privacy in various ways, such as electronically recording details of user's buying/browsing habits (using cookies) or sending unsolicited emails (spam), mass faxes and automatic-dialled telesales calls. (We might also add illegal fraud mechanisms, such as fake emails and web links requesting bank details – although these obviously have legal and ethical implications beyond privacy.)

- Conversely, again, ICT can *protect* privacy: eg sending confidential messages (such as medical test results) to password-protected SMS numbers or email addresses, rather than more readily interceptable phone or postal messages.

- **Marketing to children**. The internet is very popular with children and teens, and there may be ethical issues in merging advertising and editorial content, soliciting information from them, or offering access to age-inappropriate content.

- **Intellectual property**. Many customer-generated content and content sharing web services are accused of infringing copyright law eg by encouraging the downloading or sharing of copyrighted music, text and images (which robs the copyright owners of the royalties they would earn from sales).

In addition, there may be socio-economic impacts from the potential for:

- **Downsizing**, where ICT tools and processes replace workers (and where they cannot be retrained or redeployed)

- **Outsourcing and off-shoring** of business activities, supported by ICT links, which may cause local unemployment or supplier failure.

Conversely, again, ICT has also *created* employment opportunities and a strong demand for ICT-related skills.

▶ **Assessment tip**

Everything in the world of telecommunications, IT and the internet is changing at the speed of light! New technologies are introduced every day; companies and brands emerge and disappear seemingly overnight; and projections for the on-going penetration of e-commerce vary widely.

If you get a question on new technologies in your assignment, you will be expected to show an awareness of the dynamic nature of change in this area – and to keep abreast of developments. You should supplement your reading of this Study Text – and other books – with a regular diet of browsing in the quality press, appropriate marketing magazines and their web equivalents (as well as drawing on your own experience of e-marketing and e-commerce as a consumer).

The Chartered
Institute of Marketing

- Globalisation: drivers of globalisation; types of international operation; CSR issues of globalisation
- The international marketing mix
- Adaptation v standardisation
- Cultural and linguistic differences
- Infrastructure challenges: technology, media, transport
- The pace and impact of technological change
- From four Ps to five Is (Peppers & Rogers)
- Impact on the marketing mix: new products, distribution channels, price competition, promotional media/tools, people issues and processes
- Impact on communications: infrastructure development; computer-telephony integration (including VoIP); mobile telecommunications (including SMS); email; relational tools (including database marketing and CRM systems); e-sourcing and e-procurement
- ICT contribution to relationship marketing
- Economic sustainability
- Environmental sustainability
- CSR and ethical issues

FURTHER READING

International marketing

Jobber, D. (2007) *Principles & Practice of Marketing*. 5th edition. Maidenhead, McGraw-Hill Education Chapter 23.

Bear in mind that much of this coverage is beyond the direct scope of your syllabus, however. You might like to focus on the section International marketing mix decisions.

Impact of technology on the marketing mix

Jobber, D. (2007) *Principles & Practice of Marketing*. 5th edition. Maidenhead, McGraw-Hill Education. Chapter 18.

The application of technology to relationship marketing

Egan, G. (2004) *Relationship Marketing*. 2nd edition. Harlow, Pearson Education. Chapter 10.

REFERENCES

Allen, C. *et al* (2001) *One to One Web Marketing*. 2nd edition. New York, Wiley, New York.

Boddy, D. (2005) *Management: An Introduction* 3rd edition, Harlow, Essex, FT Prentice Hall.

Ebbs, G. (2001) *Living on the Web for Dummies*. Sydney, Australian edition IDG Books.

Jobber, D. (2007) *Principles & Practice of Marketing*. 5th edition. Berks, McGraw Hill Education. pp753.

Krol, E. and Ferguson, P. (1996) *The Whole Internet*. Australian edition. Sydney, O'Reilly & Assoc.

Peppers, D. & Rogers, M. (1997) *The One to One Future: Building Relationships One Customer at a Time*. New York, Doubleday.

Postma, P. (1999) *The New Marketing Era*. New York, McGraw Hill.

Rich, J. R. (1999) *Unofficial Guide to Marketing Your Business On-line*. Foster City, Ca, IDG Books.

Schneider, S. and Barsoux, J. (1997) *Managing Across Cultures*. Harlow, Essex, FT Prentice Hall.

Nestlé (2012) Taking IT Global (2012). http://www.nestle.com. [Accessed 24 June 2012].

Taking IT Global (2012) http://issues.tigweb.org/csr. [Accessed 24 June 2012].

WTO (2012) http://www.wto.org/english/thewto_e/whatis_e/whatis_e.htm. [Accessed 24 June 2012].

QUICK QUIZ

1   List three factors driving increasing globalisation.

2   Identify three forms of 'market entry' to an international market.

3   Give three examples of (a) cultural and (b) media differences presenting a challenge for international stakeholder communications.

4   How does ICT support (a) interactivity and (b) personalisation of communications.

5   What are the five Is of the ICT marketing mix?

6   How does ICT impact on (a) product and (b) price?

7   What are (a) consumer-generated media and (b) viral marketing?

8   List the benefits of (a) VoIP and (b) web-conferencing for stakeholder communication.

9   Define (a) extranet, (b) e-sourcing and (c) e-CRM.

10 Give two examples of ICT's contribution to (a) economic and (b) environmental sustainability.

 The Chartered Institute of Marketing

Activity 10.1

Your own research. Mendelow's power/interest matrix was covered in Chapter 1: your power/interest matrix here may be useful preparation for any assignment task in relation to international stakeholders.

Activity 10.2

Your own research. The format of the template may be useful groundwork for the assignment – and for demonstrating systematic data gathering and analysis.

Activity 10.3

Your own research. You may like to undertake these activities in a group with fellow students, and discuss your findings, to get the value of analyses of different cultures.

Activity 10.4

Your own research.

Activity 10.5

Virtual communities can be used to:

- Underpin the personalisation of relationship marketing messages.

- Enhance stakeholder relations (and the stickiness of web sites) by offering opportunities for users to see online shopping and information search as a social activity (eg free e-cards, chat rooms, discussion boards and so on).

- Facilitate the contracting-out of marketing services (especially to overseas facilities), since in cyberspace, it does not matter where messages originate.

- Gather stakeholder information by inviting subscription to email discussion lists etc.

- Gather customer feedback through forums and blogs.

- Encourage stakeholders in 'self-service'. mutual support and information sharing. eg parents groups in schools, self-help groups (for example supplementing the work of government agencies and charities), supplier consortia (small suppliers getting together to put together a better tender), student discussion groups etc.

Activity 10.6

Increasingly, the online shopping experience is simulating physical service, with familiar **processes** (eg 'shopping carts' and 'checkouts'), access to people (eg e-mail contact or voice/phone options) and **physical evidence** (perhaps in the form of downloadable/printable order confirmations, vouchers and brochures).

Activity 10.7

Your own research. Again, the format may be a useful example of presentation for an assignment report appendix.

Activity 10.8

Your own research. Think broadly about how a web site attracts repeat (or lengthier) visits: regularly updated content, virtual community interaction, interesting/fun content (games etc), ease/speed of navigation and use, attractive design etc.

Activity 10.9

Some of the advantages and disadvantages of automated telephony are as follows.

Table 10.4   The advantages and disadvantages of automated telephony

Advantages	Disadvantages
Callers can leave messages after hours	If not carefully structured, callers can be 'trapped' in a never-ending loop of menus
Customers can place orders and perform other transaction (for example, bill paying) 24-7	Callers may be frustrated or uncomfortable not being able to talk to a human being
Stakeholders do not have the frustration of unanswered calls	Stakeholders may not be able to identify the service or department they require and be put through to the wrong person
Stakeholders are able to access information (eg transport timetables, cinema times) at any time	
Calls can be swiftly routed to the department they require	

Activity 10.10

The main barrier to email marketing is the use of 'spam' (unsolicited, untargeted mass email broadcasts), market opposition to it, legal regulations restricting it and software designed to filter it out. A high percentage of users simply delete untargeted emails without reading the message – and a significant percentage actively retaliate against the spammer. 'Spam makes you look cheap and sleazy in the eyes of many people online... Regardless of how targeted, relevant or informative you think your message is, unless the recipient specifically agreed to receive the information, you risk alienating a portion of your audience.'

GUIDELINES FOR STAFF

E-MAIL MARKETING – NOT SPAM!

- Use e-mail sparingly

- Develop a message that caters directly to the interests of the intended recipients

- Beware campaigns that will be perceived as a scam: if you make an offer, make sure you follow through

- Make sure the subject line and introductory sentences are short, catchy and to the point (grabbing interest before the message goes in the recycling bin...)

- Be transparent: clearly disclose the sender and consider putting the word 'advertisement' in the subject line of the e-mail

- Format your message so that it is easy to read on the computer screen (using different reading programs) and in printout

- Either make your message short and to the point, or supply worthwhile editorial content (as in an electronic newsletter or e-zine)

- Personalise the e-mail where possible

- Don't include attachments: this is one of the most common ways computer viruses are spread, and files with attachments are often blocked

- Emphasise that you will not be selling or distributing your e-mail list to other companies – and follow through on all privacy promises

- Give recipients the option to have their name deleted from your mailing list (both for their sake and yours) and make the opt-out easy (via a hyperlink or clear instructions)

- Pre-test the campaign on a sample list

The Chartered
Institute of Marketing

Activity 10.11

Technology may impair the economic sustainability of stakeholder relationships in various ways.

- Direct supply to consumers via the internet, for example, competes with **intermediaries** and may cut them out altogether. This impacts on the economic sustainability of the supplier's relationship with dealers, distributors and retailers: the relationship may no longer be profitable, compared to direct supply – and the intermediary may even be squeezed out of business.

- Similarly, e-sourcing methods may disadvantage **small suppliers** who are unable to compete on price. The investment required to develop and integrate systems (eg for just-in-time supply or e-procurement) may be too costly for some suppliers – and for either party, the risks of technological inter-dependency may be too high to sustain the relationship.

- ICT's potential to streamline processes and staffing has an impact on **internal stakeholder** relationships. It may be argued that organisational downsizing, outsourcing and off-shoring, supported by ICT, are ultimately unsustainable because of their costs to the organisation (redundancy costs, increased management costs, loss of morale in 'surviving' staff, reputational damage, loss of distinctive knowledge and expertise) and/or their wider socio-economic costs (unemployment, community decline).

1   See section 1.1 for a full list of drivers.

2   Forms of 'market entry' include: export entry, contractual entry (licensing or franchising) and investment entry (off-shore subsidiaries or joint ventures)

3   See section 2.2.2 for an extensive list of cultural differences, and paragraph 2.3 for a list of media variations.

4   ICT supports interactivity by increasing the speed of transmission and response (eg instant messaging), allowing access to up-dated information and increasing options for interacting with information. It supports personalisation through gathering and applying user information (eg for personally-addressed media), allowing customisation of web pages and applications (eg individually targeted offers based on past behaviour) and encouraging virtual community.

5   The five Is are: Identification, Individualisation, Interaction, Integration and Integrity.

6   See sections 4.1 and 4.2 for a variety of ideas.

7   Consumer-generated media are web sites where the content is driven and provided by users (eg YouTube or Myspace). Viral marketing simulates the way a virus works through 'infection': eg giving web site users communication tools which they send to others requiring them to also visit the site, or providing content (eg mobile ring tones, video/music clips) which users spread to their own networks.

8   See sections 5.2.1 and 5.2.2 for a range of advantages.

9   An extranet is a web-based network which gives access to selected external users (such as business partners or suppliers). e-Sourcing comprises internet-based techniques for finding and evaluating suppliers and entering into purchase contracts (ie pre-purchase: e-procurement is the internet-based purchase-to-pay cycle). e-CRM is a web-centric approach to synchronising customer relationships across communication channels, business functions and audiences.

10 See sections 6.2 and 6.3 for a full answer to each question.

CHAPTER 11

Managing marketing communications activity

Introduction

This chapter introduces various concepts in the organisation, planning and control of marketing communications activity at the tactical level.

Section 1 looks briefly at how marketing communications activities and tasks can be grouped and allocated as part of the organisation structure, including the key issue of whether management is centralised (vested in one group or location) or decentralised (devolved to different units or departments of the organisation).

Section 2 picks up on our discussion of the co-ordinated marketing communications mix in Chapter 8, by outlining how such a mix can be planned: what are the factors in deciding which communications tools to use? Since you may be asked to prepare a basic marketing communications plan for one or more stakeholder groups, as part of your assignment, we also provide an outline for such a plan.

In section 3, we look at methods of budgeting, or allocating resources, for the marketing communications mix, focusing on explaining and evaluating the various approaches that may be used.

Finally, in section 4, we explain methods available for measuring the success of marketing communications activities. You may recognise some of these concepts from *Unit 1: Marketing Essentials*: they also develop some of the ideas already introduced in Chapter 7 on the measurement of the marketing mix as a whole.

Topic list

Organising for marketing communications   (1)

Planning marketing communications   (2)

Allocating and controlling resources   (3)

Measuring and evaluating marketing communications activity   (4)

4.5	Explain approaches to managing budget resource for tactical communication activities:
	■ Marginal analysis
	■ Arbitrary
	■ Affordable
	■ Objective and task
	■ Percentage of sales
	■ Competitive parity
	■ Share of Voice (SOV)
	■ Centralised or decentralised management
4.6	Explain the methods available for measuring the success of coordinated marketing communications activities:
	■ Media exposure measurement
	■ Campaign measurement
	■ Increased sales
	■ Response rates
	■ Conversion rates
	■ Order values
	■ Repeat orders

1 Organising for marketing communications

There are various ways in which the marketing function can be organised to implement marketing communications plans most effectively.

1.1 Departmentalisation

▶ **Key term**

Departmentalisation refers to the way tasks and activities are grouped together and allocated to different departments or sections of the organisation.

Departmentalisation can be carried out in a number of ways:

■ **By function**

A marketing department organised by function (Figure 11.1) allocates responsibility to managers according to their specialist areas, across all products, markets or stakeholder groups. This approach allows individuals and teams to develop **specialist** knowledge and expertise. It also allows the marketing director to **co-ordinate** plans and budgets to ensure the development of a coherent marketing and communications mix across the product and stakeholder range.

The Chartered Institute of Marketing

Figure 11.1   Functional organisation of marketing activity

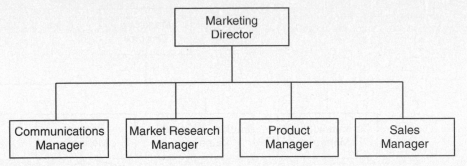

- **By geography**

  A marketing department organised by geography (Figure 11.2) makes managers responsible for all activities (or functional activities) within a given 'territory' or geographical area. This type of organisation would be suitable for firms operating **internationally**: you might have a communications manager for each country or region of operation, say, in order to capitalise on local knowledge and relationships. (We saw in Chapter 10 how important it is to adapt communications to different cultural, linguistic and infrastructure factors in different countries.) It is also typically used to organise **sales** departments, enabling sales people to concentrate their knowledge (and travel) on particular territories or areas.

Figure 11.2   Geographical organisation of marketing activity

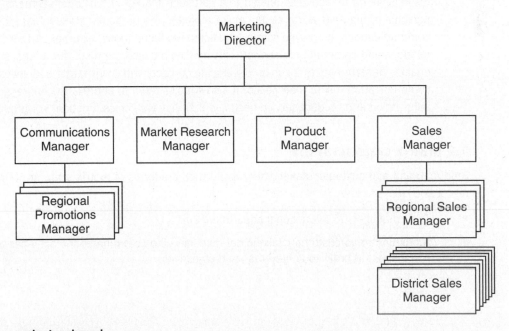

- **By product or brand**

  A marketing department organised by product or brand (Figure 11.3) adds an extra tier of management which co-ordinates the activities of different functions. Product or brand managers take responsibility for all activities in relation to their product or brand, and for its competitiveness and profitability. This approach is likely to be particularly appropriate for organisations with a diverse range of products and/or strong brand identities, since they may need to be communicated quite differently.

Figure 11.3   Product/brand organisation of marketing activity

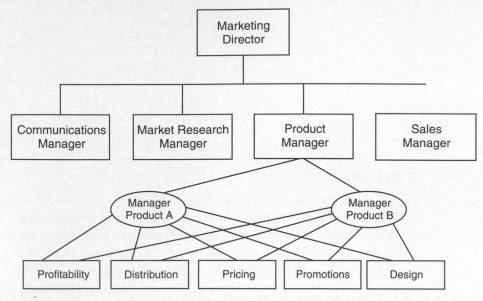

- **By customer segment or stakeholder group**

    Marketing communications activity organised by customer or stakeholder group makes managers responsible for all activities related to a particular market or customer segment (eg the corporate, personal or high-net-worth customers of a bank), or a particular stakeholder group (eg customer communications, employee communications, media relations, external partnership relations, supplier relations and community relations). This may be a useful approach for relationship marketing, since it enables departments to focus on developing contacts with their target audiences, and to adapt the communication mix to their needs. It also enables them to address the full range of the target group's information and product/service needs, which may well cross functional or product boundaries.

1.2 Matrix organisation

Product/brand and customer/stakeholder organisation are forms of **matrix structure** (Figure 11.4), where people report *both* to:

- Their managers in a functional department *and*

- A product/brand/customer/stakeholder manager who co-ordinates the activities of staff across functional boundaries, in order to achieved shared objectives.

Figure 11.4   Matrix organisation

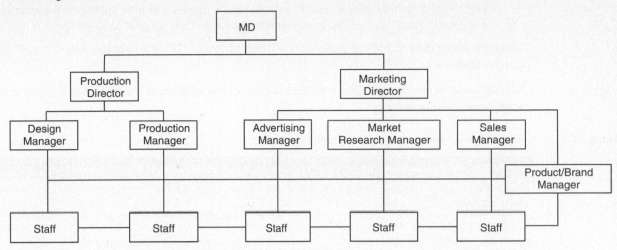

Project management (which might be used to put together a product 'pitch' to a client, say, or to develop a collaboration with an external ally, or to implement a CSR or customer care programme among employees) is another example of multi-disciplinary team working under the authority of a co-ordinating manager.

Tom Peters (1994) called this a form of **horizontal structure** (which facilitates the flow of work and information across department/functional boundaries), overlaid on the **vertical structure** (represented by the organisation hierarchy, functional specialism and formal communication channels). Horizontal structures are important in service delivery and the co-ordination of stakeholder communications, Peters argues, because they are essentially horizontal processes: value and information need to flow through the internal supply chain to the external customer. (We discussed this in connection with the importance of cross-functional co-operation in Chapter 9.)

ACTIVITY 11.1

What can you see as the potential benefits and problems of adopting a matrix management approach to stakeholder marketing?

1.3 Centralised and decentralised management

> ▶ **Key term**
>
> **Centralised management** means that authority is concentrated in one place, while **decentralisation** means that it is dispersed more widely.

'Centralised or decentralised management' is mentioned in the indicative content of the syllabus in the context of budgeting, but it is really a wider organisational issue.

We can look at this in two ways.

- **Concentration**. Activities may be centralised in a single department or location, or decentralised to (dispersed among) different offices, departments or locations.

  - So, for example, there may be a centralised marketing communications **department** for the whole organisation *or* each unit or division of the organisation may carry out its own decentralised marketing communications, as relevant to its own activities, geographical region and stakeholders.

  - Similarly, centralised **resource budgets** may be set by head office (on the basis that resources will be more fairly allocated among different units and activities), or decentralised budgeting may be carried out by individual units (on the basis that they carry out the activities and are better aware of local opportunities and costs).

- **Authority**. Centralisation also refers to the extent to which authority is held at the top of the organisation, so that people have to refer decisions upwards to their superiors. Decentralisation therefore implies increased delegation, empowerment and autonomy for staff at lower levels of the organisation.

There are advantages to both centralisation and decentralisation for the management of marketing communications.

'Management' is mentioned in the indicative content of the syllabus in the context of budgeting, but it is really a wider organisational issue.

Table 11.1 Advantages of centralisation and decentralisation

Advantages of centralisation	Advantages of decentralisation
Decisions and plans are made at one point and so are easier to co-ordinate	Allows activity beyond the limitations of managers
Enables a broader view of organisational objectives, issues, trade-offs, resource constraints etc.	Improves the motivation, loyalty and commitment of junior staff who are empowered
Balances the interests of different units and stakeholder groups: eg in allocating resource budgets across the range	Greater awareness of 'local' stakeholder needs, issues, preferences etc. (eg decentralisation by stakeholder regions, different stakeholder groups or different brands with distinct stakeholder issues)
Quality of decisions is (theoretically) higher due to senior managers' experience, and the concentration of specialist skills and resources	Greater speed of decision making, and flexible response to stakeholder needs, since no need to refer decisions upwards
Avoids duplication of management, skills, resources etc if dispersed in different units	Helps develop the communication and decision-making skills of junior staff
There is authority to take crisis decisions more quickly	Separate spheres of responsibility can be identified for budgeting, performance measurement and accountability

The trend appears to be towards the decentralisation of decision making at the tactical level, while retaining strategic decision making centrally. **Co-ordinated decentralisation** supports greater sensitivity and responsiveness to stakeholders' needs. It also helps to foster a service orientation. Rather than having lots of layers of management, which distance the decision makers at the top from the front line of contact with customers and other stakeholders, service-focused organisations tend to be **flatter**, as responsibility for customer-service and stakeholder relationship management is decentralised to lower-level staff.

Daffy (2001) argues that an organisation structure that is totally customer-focused would have just two layers: Figure 11.5.

Figure 11.5 A decentralised, service-focused structure

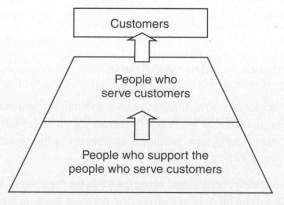

Note that the traditional organisational structure has also been turned **upside down** in this model. Instead of putting management at the top and front-line workers at the bottom (organising factor: managerial power and

The Chartered
Institute of Marketing

authority), a service-focused structure puts front-line workers at the top and sees the task of management as supporting them in doing their jobs (organising factor: support for customer service).

ACTIVITY 11.2

How is the marketing communications function organised in your organisation?

Draw an organisation chart (such as one of those shown earlier in this section) to show how it fits within the marketing function – and how the marketing function fits within the whole organisation structure.

What are the advantages and disadvantages of this structure for carrying out effective stakeholder communications?

2 Planning marketing communications

Choosing the correct tools for a particular marketing communication task is not easy – although new technology is making it somewhat more scientific: computers can match databased stakeholder and media profiles to formulate an optimal mix, and communications budgets can be modelled on spreadsheets for a variety of different mixes.

At a basic level, however, communications planning can be seen as a typical decision sequence: Figure 11.6.

Figure 11.6 The marketing communications planning process

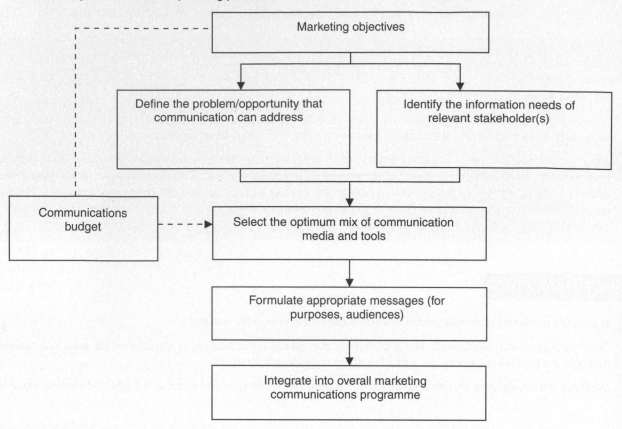

▶ **Assessment tip**

In an assignment you may be asked to recommend improvements to the communications mix of your chosen organisation. Presenting your recommendations as part of a communications plan will enable you to justify the recommendations by demonstrating to examiners that you have fully understood the context within which your recommendations apply. So it is worth paying attention to some practical aspects here.

ACTIVITY 11.3

Do some research into the following two organisations.

■   Coca Cola Enterprises Inc
■   Amnesty International (or any charity or pressure group that interests you).

How do their marketing communications reflect their overall organisational and marketing objectives?

Coca Cola has two sites: its corporate Coca Cola Enterprises Inc site (http://www.cokecce.com) and its consumer-facing site (http://www.coca-cola.com). Visit both and consider what the different communication objectives of each site may be, and how they support the company's overall objectives.

Amnesty International: http://www.amnesty.org/en

The Chartered Institute of Marketing

2.1 Selecting the communications mix

Perhaps the main challenge is to select the optimum mix of the communication media and tools discussed in Chapter 8.

The relative emphasis placed on different tools and approaches will differ according to a number of factors.

2.1.1 Media consumption and influence

This may involve researching factors such as:

- Which media and tools are **most used** by, and most **influential for**, a given stakeholder group, and therefore most effective in reaching them.

    Suppliers and intermediaries, for example, are more likely to be reached via trade journals, exhibitions and personal selling. Employees may, nowadays, be reached more effectively by email than by notices affixed to office noticeboards or posted on the company intranet. Different consumer segments may use and pay attention to different media, according to their habits and interests. And so on.

- The most appropriate tools for the **specific information needs** of stakeholders, bearing in mind factors such as the need for privacy or shared mass communication; the need for interactivity (eg Q & A); the volume and detail of information required; the need for a hard copy for reference (or legal evidence) and so on.

- In communicating with parents, for example, a school might issues reports to convey pupils' performance; personal letters or interviews to discuss disciplinary issues; parents' meetings to give information about changes of policy; and SMS messages or calls to a mobile phone for urgent messages (eg about an injury, sickness or non-attendance).

- The most **cost-effective** media and tools for fulfilling these criteria for the organisation. What tools are the organisation good at using and set up to use? What is the cost per contact of each tool? Do the benefits of using the tool outweigh the costs?

ACTIVITY 11.4

Select any one stakeholder group of your work organisation or other organisation you have been studying.

- What media and communication tools are most used by, and influential for, this target audience.
- What are the information and communication needs of this target audience?
- Which media and tools might be most appropriate for each information need?
- You may like to use the following format for your analysis.

Stakeholder:		
Key media/tools		
Information need	**Suitable medium/tool**	**Justification/comment**

2.1.2 Direct and indirect communication strategies

> ▶ **Key terms**
>
> A **'push' communication strategy** involves 'pushing' the product into distribution channels, eg through personal selling, trade advertising and promotion, trade exhibitions and sales force incentives.
>
> A **'pull' communication strategy** involves 'pulling' the product into and through distribution channels by stimulating consumer demand, eg through advertising, sales promotion, public relations and in-store merchandising.

The target audience for a product/service promotion may be primarily channel members (intermediaries) or consumers.

Similar decisions may be made in wider stakeholder marketing: for example, whether the organisation wants to reach 'green' consumers **direct** (eg through advertising, public relations or sponsorship of environmental causes) or whether it decides to communicate **via intermediaries or influencers** (eg persuading an environmental pressure group to endorse the product or enter into an alliance, which will require more focused personal negotiation and incentives).

2.1.3 Product/market or stakeholder type

As we saw in Chapter 7, consumer (B2C) and business (B2B) markets behave differently. **Business stakeholders** are generally less susceptible to mass communications and prefer to negotiate and develop ongoing business terms and relationships through personal selling (supported by trade promotion). **Consumer markets** tend to favour advertising (supported by sales promotion).

2.1.4 The awareness, knowledge and engagement of the audience

Different communication tools are effective at generating awareness (eg advertising and PR); knowledge (direct marketing or information); preference and conviction (personal selling, sales promotion); and engagement, commitment and loyalty (relationship marketing techniques).

More costly techniques, such as one-to-one discussion, negotiation or sales, may only be worthwhile for high-value transactions (eg in B2B sales or conflict resolution with influential pressure groups) or where stakeholders are approaching readiness to engage (eg in alliance negotiation).

ACTIVITY 11.5

What items of information would you, as a relationship marketer, want your sales force to have on a regular basis? (You may consider this question in the light of a particular product, service or market sector if you wish.) How would you go about disseminating the required information?

2.1.5 Product life cycle stage

You may remember the concept of the product life cycle (PLC) from your studies in Unit 1: *Marketing Essentials.* The organisation may have different communication aims at each stage of the life cycle, and this will influence the kinds of tools that will be required in the mix.

Table 11.2   Product life cycle stages

Stage	Aim of communications activity	Communication tools
Introduction	Produce high awareness Induce early trial Sell in to intermediaries	Advertising, PR Sales promotion Personal selling
Growth	Broaden awareness Fewer incentives needed?	Maintain advertising, PR Reduce sales promotion?

The Chartered Institute of Marketing

Stage	Aim of communications activity	Communication tools
Maturity	Reminders, loyalty building Maximise sales levels/profit	Maintain activity, RM tools Sales promotion
Decline	Maintain profitability Secure last available sales	Reduce activity Final sales promotions

You might similarly apply a life cycle model to **messages** (such as promoting the organisation's CSR credentials, say) and **issues** (such as stakeholder concern about global warming). In the case of a positive message:

■ While the message or issues is new, you will need to focus on raising awareness (advertising, PR and publicity)

■ Once it is established, you can focus on reminders and engagement (eg by sponsorship or alliances)

■ Once it has ceased to engage attention, you can reduce activity – or renew interest with a new 'take' on the issue and start the cycle again.

If the issue has negative PR potential, on the other hand, you may want to *suppress* the growth stage and *hasten* the decline stage: communicating clearly and comprehensively and then letting interest fade away (or giving stakeholders something else of interest to distract them)...

2.2 Outline marketing communications plan

As with our outline marketing mix plans in Chapter 7, the following is not a standard or compulsory model: it is just a suggested framework for thinking about the issues. (We have, for example, left out more detailed implementation aspects such as media scheduling, budgeting, agency briefings and so on, which should not be required at this level.)

You should feel free to use whatever other templates you are used to from your work, or prefer from your wider reading or study course.

Table 11.3   Example marketing communications plan

MARKETING COMMUNICATIONS PLAN FOR [IDENTIFIED STAKEHOLDER if relevant]		
1	**Communications objectives**	■ What problem/need the communication plan is designed to address ■ What the communications plan is intended to achieve (SMART objectives if possible) ■ Co-ordinating marketing mix strategies within which the plan has been developed
2	**Target audience**	■ Stakeholder group targeted by the plan ■ Key needs, concerns, interests and drivers of the group ■ Information needs of the group (either in general or in relation to the specific problem/situation) ■ Media and communication tools most used by and influential for the stakeholder group
3	**Core message(s)**	■ Purpose of the message: desired stakeholder response ■ Content: key points of the message, and how best conveyed (eg text, multi-media) ■ Style: informative, persuasive, personal etc. ■ How the message fits within the co-ordinated marketing mix: consistency, synergy.
4	**Communication media and tools**	Which media and tools will be used (with brief explanation/justification of each, if required): ■ Advertising ■ Direct Marketing ■ Public Relations And so on...
5	**Timetable**	■ Period over which communication will be required ■ Timescales for review and measurement

	MARKETING COMMUNICATIONS PLAN FOR [IDENTIFIED STAKEHOLDER if relevant]	
6	**Resource allocation**	Estimated expenditure (or basis on which budget should be set: see section 3 of this chapter)
7	**Monitoring and control**	How progress and results will be monitored, reviewed and measured against objectives (see section 4 of this chapter)

Alternatively, you could merge sections 3 and 4 of this plan under the heading **Communication Action Plans** and either:

- Outline the use of each **selected promotional tool** in turn, discussing the content and style of messages to be conveyed by each.

- Outline **specific communication plans** based on the information needs of the stakeholder group and your purposes for communicating. This is more flexible, whether or not your communication plan uses promotional media. For example:

  - Consumer promotion: TV advertising to convey message A (with a focus on image/awareness); print advertising to convey message B (giving more information); data capture and direct email or telesales follow-up to convey message C (offer of added value through relationship).

  - Specific employee communication scenario: e-mail to all staff to notify of staff meeting; meeting to brief staff on changes; follow-up team briefings to enable more detailed discussion; phone or personal interviews with team leaders to gather feedback.

THE REAL WORLD

The following is part of an advertising agency plan for a campaign to promote a new MP3 player (the 'mStick'), presented as part of a 2006 competition in *AdNews* (Australia).

OVERVIEW

		JUN	JUL	AUG	SEPT	OCT	NOV	DEC	COST
									$
Television	*Australian Idol*								300,000
	Video Hits								
Radio	Mstar Competition								235,000
	Spots								
Newspaper	Teasers								30,772
	Strips								
Magazine	*Cosmopolitan*								110,280
Internet	Viral e-mails								80,000
	Banners & mailing lists								
Cinema	Stunts								35,000
Outdoor	Buses								170,240
Evaluation									35,000
TOTAL									996,292

Pre-launch   Launch   Maintenance

(AdNews, 2006)

The Chartered Institute of Marketing

From the Marketing Plan you drafted in Chapter 7, expand the Promotion section of the plan into a full Marketing Communications Plan using the outline plan template provided above.

If you didn't prepare the Marketing Plan, feel free to start fresh with any specific stakeholder communication task – or a more general plan to communicate with a specific stakeholder group.

Just have a go!

3 Allocating and controlling resources

3.1 Budgets

> **Key term**
>
> A **budget** is a statement of desired performance expressed in financial terms: expenditure, revenue, profit and so on.

If you are planning or proposing a marketing communications activity, you need to be aware that there will inevitably be resource constraints, arising from expenditure limits and budgets which have already been set – and from the general facts that (a) there is competition for limited financial, material and human resources; (b) business activities are expected to show a profit (that is, they must earn more than they spend); and (c) organisations are accountable for how they spend their investors' money!

As we have noted elsewhere, it is important for marketing resources to be **co-ordinated**: allocated across a range of tasks and objectives, so that available (often scarce) resources are utilised and leveraged to the greatest effect. (You wouldn't want to spend your entire communications budget on one television advertisement during the FA Cup Final, for example, when you could use the same resources for a whole programme of stakeholder communication.)

There are various types of budget planning, depending on how the organisation is managed.

- **Top-down planning** involves the setting of goals for lower management by higher management (ie centralised budgeting).

- **Bottom-up planning** involves employees in setting their own goals and submitting them to higher management for approval (ie decentralised budgeting).

- **'Goals down, plans up'** planning is a mixture of the two styles, whereby top management sets overall goals and lower-level employees then set plans for achieving those goals. This approach is well suited to the formulation of sales and marketing communications budgets.

How are budgets set in your work organisation, or another organisation you are studying (if it is possible to find out: remember that there may be confidentiality issues around organisations disclosing their budgets and policies…)

- Who sets the budget for marketing communications?

- Are there separate budgets for different communications activities or target audiences?

- What kinds of expenditure are included in the budgets (eg staff salaries, media costs, creative and print costs, agency fees, contingency sums)?

See if you can get hold of a copy of a tactical level marketing budget – just to see what it looks like (if you don't regularly have access to such things).

3.2 Approaches to setting marketing communications budgets

There are a number of ways of setting expenditure budgets for tactical marketing communications activity:

- Arbitrary estimation
- Affordability
- Competitive parity
- Percentage of sales
- Objective and task

We will look at each method in turn.

> **▶ Assessment tip**
>
> You will not have to prepare budgets for your assignment at this level. The syllabus and CIM tutor guidance focus on your being able to explain what approaches are available; to evaluate them (that is, to discuss their advantages and disadvantages or limitations); to identify which approach is being used by your own organisation; and perhaps to recommend a suitable approach, or more suitable approach.

3.2.1 Arbitrary budgeting

This is the least scientific method, based more or less on pulling a figure out of a hat – although it may be based on the budgeter's experience of past expenditures and communications activity, and knowledge of cost trends, organisational profitability and so on.

Arbitrary estimation has the advantage of being quick and easy: it does not incur any costs of research or the budgeter's time. It may offer a useful 'ballpark' figure for initial brainstorming on a possible communications activity, or for allocating contingency ('just in case') sums as part of a more systematic budgeting exercise. However, you should be able to see that this is an unscientific and risky method.

ACTIVITY 11.8

See if you can identify the disadvantages of arbitrary budgeting, both for the fulfilment of marketing communications tasks and for *internal* marketing.

3.2.2 Affordability budgeting

In this method, communications expenditure is based on what the organisation can afford, in the judgement of the budgeter. In other words: 'How much do we available have to spend?'

Resource availability will inevitably influence the type of communications activities that can be carried out. Some activities, for example, will simply be too expensive, while others may offer better reach and frequency for the same cost. This is likely to be an important factor for **micro- and small-medium enterprises** and **non-profit organisations**: resources for marketing may be severely limited.

Affordability therefore certainly needs to be taken into account. However, it has disadvantages as a sole criterion for setting the budget.

- The organisation may not *need* to spend up to the amount that it could afford, in order to meet its objectives. Affordability budgeting creates a temptation and pressure to 'spend up' to the budget (if only to avoid its being cut back next year because it hasn't been spent) – and this may be a waste of resources.

- It does not encourage the formulation of specific communication objectives, or cultivate awareness of market opportunities to grow sales and profits (Jobber, 2007, p513)

3.2.3 Competitive parity budgeting

Competitive parity means setting communications budgets based on matching the spending (or percentage of sales spent, or year-on-year increase in spending) of competitors.

This may be advantageous in ensuring that the organisation matches the communication activity of competitors, and hence maintains its competitive position. It may also be advantageous in preventing potentially costly advertising and promotion wars, as it prevents the organisation from simply trying to *outspend* the competition.

However, it is still an unsatisfactory approach.

- It assumes that the competitor has made good budgeting decisions or arrived at a 'correct' level of spending – which may not be the case. Competitive parity may be a case of the blind leading the blind!

- It is reactive and lacks direction: it does not take account of specific marketing objectives, stakeholder drivers or opportunities. (There may be an opportunity to build market share by additional expenditure, say, or to harvest profits from a declining product by reducing expenditure.)

- Like affordability, it may create pressure to 'spend up' to competitor levels, when the organisation doesn't need to do so – or when, if given the incentive, it could find opportunities to achieve the same marketing effect for less.

- It may also create pressure to 'spend down' to competitor levels, reducing the organisation's ability to exploit opportunities to grow sales and profits by higher-level communications expenditure.

And, of course, it may not be possible to determine what competitors are spending in the first place!

3.2.4 Percentage of sales budgeting

This method bases communication expenditure on a specified percentage of current or budgeted sales revenue for the year. This may be done to secure a predictable level of profitability, or it may be based on company or industry tradition, or research into the returns that can be (statistically) expected from different percentage expenditure.

Again, this method is quick and easy to apply. It depends less on the subjective judgement of the budgeter than the arbitrary or affordability method, and makes less assumptions than the competitive parity method. It preserves a minimum level of profitability, by ensuring that expenditure is matched to revenue. It may also help to avoid costly advertising wars with competitors, if everybody observes their standard percentages year on year.

However, this is still a rule-of-thumb, unscientific method.

- It still doesn't take account of specific marketing objectives and opportunities to increase sales or profits by increasing or reducing communications spending.

- It doesn't provide any means of determining the 'correct' percentage to use. There is no reason why communication costs should relate directly to total turnover, since other factors may also be responsible for boosts or reductions in sales.

- It may have a detrimental effect on sales. If sales decline, for any reason, communication budgets also decline – when additional promotion may be exactly what is required for sales recovery! Less promotional spending may only cause further decline in sales, in a vicious circle...

3.2.5 Objective and task budgeting

This method is based on a systematic calculation of the expenditure required to fulfil communications objectives and to carry out the specific communications tasks planned to achieve them. If the objective is to increase awareness of a brand name by 10%, say, the planned communication campaign will be broken down into its component tasks and elements, and estimated (or known) costs will be allocated to each: promotional media, staff time, agency fees, merchandising costs and so on. The total estimated cost of all such campaigns

(perhaps with an added contingency sum for emergencies and opportunities) will comprise the communication budget.

This method has several advantages.

- It is relatively scientific and systematic, and can be based fairly closely on known costs (eg media rate cards and known discount rates, agreed agency fees, quoted print costs and so on).
- It can be performed for each communications activity, at a detailed level, building up to the total communications budget.
- It focuses managerial attention on objectives, tasks, opportunities and the effects of expenditure on outcomes (return on communications investment).
- It can be readily justified to internal and external stakeholders, as a sound and results-focused method.

Objective and task is regarded as the most effective method among those available. However, it should be noted that it still has limitations. The amount of effort and activity required to achieve communications objectives may not be easy to estimate – particularly if those objectives are long-range or qualitative in nature (such as increased stakeholder engagement or customer loyalty). Contingency sums will still have to be built in to take account of unforeseen tasks (such as crisis communication or countering competitor campaigns) and opportunities (such as newly available communication media or reduced-cost media space).

ACTIVITY 11.9

Formulate the advantages and disadvantages discussed for arbitrary, affordability, competitive parity, percentage of sales and objective-and-task budgeting into a concise and easy-to-use table.

THE REAL WORLD

Bellwether Report

The Institute of Practitioners in Advertising (IPA) in the UK publishes a quarterly report known as the Bellwether Report. This surveys companies to determine their level of optimism for the future and their marketing spending plans.

Here is an extract from the report for the final quarter of 2011:

'The latest IPA Bellwether survey reveals that marketing budgets were revised up in Q4 for a second successive quarter, as companies sought to protect market share against competitors.

Yet business optimism is falling further in the face of economic uncertainty, to levels seen prior to the onset of the 08/09 financial crisis. Marketing executives' confidence for the industries in which they operate has fallen to an 11-quarter low.'

Despite that, the survey indicated that marketing communications budgets for 2012 looked set to rise relative to 2011 actual spend.

Analysing the data in more detail, it became clear that companies are becoming reluctant to invest in traditional media such as TV and press media. Instead money is increasingly being diverted towards the internet and direct marketing.

The report comments that it is encouraging to see that companies plan to raise their marketing spend in 2012 despite seeing their financial prospects for the next three months falling. It appears that many companies may be deciding to combat the prospects of a challenging year ahead with increased promotional activity. (IPA, 2012)

Question: Do you think that raising marketing budgets during an economic downturn is the right thing to do?

The Chartered Institute of Marketing

3.3 Internal marketing and budget-setting

It is worth noting that budget-setting is usually a **collaborative** and **political** process, involving negotiation between marketers, general management and the finance function – particularly since marketing budgets are only one part of the overall co-ordinated budget of the organisation. Different functions compete for resource allocations. Accountants and financial managers usually seek to reduce expenditure – while marketing managers are likely to argue that the greater the marketing expenditure, the better for the long-term profitability of the brand and the business.

Robust internal marketing and negotiation will be required to strengthen marketing's claim to a share of resources. Marketers will need to make a sound 'business case' for their plans, demonstrating that they are in the interests of the organisation as a whole (contributing to profitability, brand strength and so on).

3.4 Budgetary control

Once the plan has been implemented, the task of marketing communications management is to **control** the use of resources.

- Compare actual communications costs against budgeted levels (measuring the effectiveness of cost control).

- Compare communications costs against sales, responses and other results/benefits (measuring cost-effectiveness).

4 Measuring and evaluating marketing communications activity

We have already covered some aspects of this in Chapter 7, when we discussed measurement of the marketing mix, including some promotional measures.

Here, we will look at each of the measurement methods listed in the syllabus, as well as suggesting how each of the main marketing communications activities can be measured.

> ▶ **Assessment tip**
>
> As with budgeting, you are very unlikely to have to actually measure the marketing communications activity of your organisation for your assignment – although you may be asked to appraise it in a general way. The syllabus and CIM tutor guidance focuses on your being able to explain what approaches to measurement are available; to evaluate them (that is, to discuss their advantages and disadvantages or limitations); perhaps to identify which approaches are used by your own organisation; and perhaps to recommend suitable approaches. For example, a recent assignment asked candidates to: '**Identify and evaluate a range of relevant methods** for measuring the success of your communications mix.'

4.1 Media exposure measurement

Media exposure refers to the amount, duration and frequency with which the organisation, brand or marketing message is featured across all communications media (or particular media segments): in other words, how much 'air time' the message or brand is getting. This may be measured by:

- The organisation's **media schedule**: that is, the amount of TV, cinema and radio advertising 'spots', pages of print advertising and poster sites the organisation has purchased over a period (or for a particular campaign). An advertising agency should provide this information, together with published **reach data**: viewer figures or ratings (for TV), listener figures (for radio), audited circulation and estimated number of readers per publication (for print media).

- Number of **mentions** in the news and information media, online discussion boards, blogs, promotion of sponsored events, and other essentially uncontrolled communications. This is usually monitored by specialist media monitoring agencies.

4.1.1 Share of Voice (SOV)

Share of Voice is a term now used for a brand's **total communications presence** or 'advertising weight', measured as a percentage of a defined total market or market segment in a given time period.

Communications presence or advertising weight may be expressed as communications expenditure, circulation or audience ratings of media, the amount of media exposure (number of pages, radio spots, posters), and the number of mentions in editorial media, online discussion boards and the 'blogosphere' (on-line web logs). Online share of voice measuring agency 'Go Global!' explains the concept and importance of online SOV as follows.

'It's the exact number of online mentions, total impressions, and percentage of impressions your brand receives when people search for and read articles about you and your competitor's products or services. Knowing it is key to understanding the effectiveness of your advertising, public relations (PR), and overall online marketing efforts in generating coverage, mindshare, and the attributes you want your target to associate with your brand. Most importantly, it's about driving awareness and sales.' (www.goglobalinteractive.com/share-of-voice).

SOV is included under budgeting in the syllabus: we would argue that it is more properly a marketing communications objective or performance measure. However, the budgeter could include SOV as an objective for objective and task budgeting. It represents a global measure which should ensure that resources are well spread across different communications activities, and which focuses flexibly on results (stakeholder awareness) rather than just on activities and inputs.

4.1.2 Evaluating media exposure as a performance measure

Media exposure is an effective method for evaluating the effectiveness of your media buying, public relations and publicity activity, in the sense that it measures how far your message is getting 'out there': how much of your target audience it is (theoretically) reaching, and how frequently.

However, it is impossible to measure exposure with any degree of accuracy, other than for highly controlled media such as a web site, where you can electronically monitor the number, duration, frequency and focus of visits to the site. It also doesn't measure other important factors, such as whether a significant proportion of your target audience are actually consuming the media, and whether they are noticing, understanding, being attracted to or being influenced by your message. These factors may have to be researched via recall and recognition tests, customer media analysis ('where did you hear about us?'), and results-based measures such as responses, enquiries and sales.

4.2 Campaign measurement

The success of a particular marketing communications campaign can be fairly scientifically measured by pre-campaign and post-campaign testing: the differences in the two sets of results should (theoretically) be attributable to the campaign.

Pre-and post-testing may use a variety of quantitative and qualitative techniques, including:

- **Results**: increases in sales (or donations, say); increases in enquiries, responses or web site visits; increase in repeat orders or order value; and so on. (We discuss these measures below.)

- **Survey questionnaires or depth (one-to-one) or focus group interviews** (as discussed in Chapter 7). These methods can direct questions to more complex information about the impact of the campaign on the target audience: awareness of the campaign/brand; recall and recognition of the campaign/brand; what messages were understood from the campaign; the congeniality (likeableness) of the campaign/brand; perceptions and attitudes to the campaign/brand and so on.

Wilmshurst (1999) argues that clearly quantified objectives should be set for all marketing communications activities, even in qualitative areas such as awareness, recall and recognition. For example:

- 'To increase the number of people who have knowledge of specific features of the product or company from 15% of the target audience to 25%'.

- 'To achieve a situation where at least 60% of the target audience can 'recall' an advertisement, unprompted, up to two weeks after it has appeared'.

THE REAL WORLD

Jobber (2007, p539) offers the case study of charity **Christian Aid**, and its national 'Christian Aid Week' fundraising campaign in 2005. This shows the depth of information that can be gathered on the success of a particular campaign.

'Every year NOP carries out before (pre-) and after (post-) research on the effectiveness of Christian Aid Week using a UK representative sample and a street-based questionnaire…

Detailed results included:

- Significant shift in awareness of Christian Aid achieved by the 2005 campaign (pre-campaign compared to post-campaign): 8% increase in spontaneous awareness, 13% increase in total awareness.

- Awareness of Christian Aid advertising in 2005 higher than in 2004: 13% increase in spontaneous awareness; 6% increase in total awareness.

- The advertising in 2005 was seen as interesting and increased positive perceptions of Christian Aid: it made 4 out of 10 respondents laugh; it wasn't the sort of advertising expected from Christian Aid; it was seen as different from other charity advertising.

- Recall of advertising content was very encouraging.

- 70% of those who responded directly to Christian Aid Week advertising were new contacts.

- The main messages were communicated well. Respondents understood the message as: giving a poor family a chicken is better than giving them an omelette (30%); Christian Aid invests in things that multiply (19%); Christian Aid helps people to help themselves (18%); Christian Aid helps people in the third world stand on their own two feet (14%).

- Overall, Christian Aid Week donations were higher in 2005: the house-to-house envelope collection broke the £15 million (€21 million) for the first time and £100,000 (€140,000) was raised online.'

4.2.1 Evaluating campaign measurement as a performance measure

A campaign measurement approach generates some very useful information for campaign evaluation and future planning. It addresses both qualitative or subjective issues in the perceptions and recall of the target audience (what they thought of the campaign; what awareness, interest and intention it created in them) and quantitative results (what they actually *did* about it).

However, it has some limitations. The more qualitative data is sought, the more expensive it is to gather and analyse. On-line survey questionnaires cut down on the cost of having people administer the survey, but often incur costs in providing incentives for respondents to complete them – and still require expert human analysis (other than for basic attitude-scale type responses).

This means that surveys – and particularly interviews and focus groups – typically use a very small sample of the total target audience. It is difficult to get a truly representative sample, and even then, with a small statistical sample, there is a risk that the results will not reflect the responses or attitudes of the target audience as a whole. (It is all very well saying that '8 out of 10 people' recalled your message – but if the interview was only 10 people, you can't necessarily extrapolate those results as a proportion of the whole stakeholder audience.

4.3 Results-based measurement

As we noted in Chapter 7, exposure, recall and recognition are all very well – but if the target audience doesn't *do* anything, or do anything *different*, as a result of marketing communications, you know that *something* about the communication mix isn't working.

The success of the marketing communications activity can be measured by its effects, in relation to specific results-focused objectives.

4.3.1 Increased sales

You might, for example, set as your campaign objective 'To produce direct sales of £X,000': that is, orders are to be received from people replying directly to the advertisement totalling this amount or more.

In order to attribute sales directly to marketing communications, you need to identify what prompted a person to make a purchase: this can be done with direct response order forms or coupons (identifying media, date, campaign and so on), or by sales staff asking 'Where did you hear about us?' type questions.

Pre- and post-campaign sales data may also be used, but this is less reliable, as other factors may have intervened to boost or depress sales: a competitor may have dropped out of the market during the campaign period, say, or the product may have increased in price.

4.3.2 Response rates

You might, for example, set as your campaign objective: 'To produce enquiries from genuinely interested potential customers at a cost of not more than £X per enquiry'.

Response rates can be most easily measured by using direct response advertising: dedicated telephone numbers, e-mail addresses or web site entry points may be advertised for different campaigns, or in different media, so that responses can be directly attributed to them. In other cases, however, it may be difficult to gather data on exactly what people are responding to.

It may also be difficult to define what a 'genuinely interested potential customer' is: that is, whether the response constitutes an engaged, qualified prospect or 'lead' – or just a casual enquiry that will not result in a sale. The organisation will want to *discourage* high response rates from people who are unlikely to convert into sales (unprofitable contacts), by targeting its marketing communications so that they self-select more effectively.

ACTIVITY 11.10

Response rates are also a useful measure for non-selling messages to wider stakeholders. See if you can come up with some examples.

4.3.3 Conversion rates

Conversion rates refer to how many responders, enquirers, prospects or sales leads actually become customers by committing to a purchase. This measure usefully recognises the unprofitability of generating responses/enquiries which do not convert into sales.

It is, however, a short-term measure. Consumers may be engaging in extensive product search and evaluation (as we discussed in Chapter 7) for complex, high-involvement purchases: a marketing communications campaign, and enquiries generated by it, may only bear fruit some time later.

The recruitment advertising equivalent of conversion would be the number of offers made (or new recruits actually taken on).

The Chartered Institute of Marketing

4.3.4 Repeat orders

As we saw in Chapter 3, one of the aspirations of relationship marketing is to move customers up the relationship ladder of loyalty to the status of 'clients' or repeat purchasers. Repeat purchase is a useful measure of the effectiveness of relationship marketing communications and loyalty programmes.

As we noted in our discussion of such schemes, however, it cannot be assumed that repeat purchasers are necessarily loyal, committed or ready for more intensive relationship marketing: they may simply be buying repeatedly because no better product or offer is available.

4.3.5 Order value

Another of the aspirations of relationship marketing is to improve the profitability of loyal customers, which comes not just from repeat orders but from orders of increasing size and value. Order value is a useful measure of the effectiveness of cross-selling and up-selling activity, and of relationship marketing communications in general: higher-value orders may reflect the development of trust in the relationship, in both consumer and B2B markets.

4.3.6 Evaluating results-focused performance measures

Results-focused approaches are highly practical and can be used to present a sound business case for marketing communications expenditure. However, it should be noted that not all results can be directly attributed to marketing communications – nor to a specific marketing communications campaign or promotional tool (since they are intentionally co-ordinated with one another).

Nor can it be concluded that marketing communications are not worthwhile or necessary if they fail to make measurable contributions in such specific, short-term ways. What short-term financial value can be put on the development of stakeholder trust, engagement and advocacy over time, for example – or on the *avoidance* of bad publicity, negative perceptions and relationship barriers (eg through issues management)? Such efforts represent a short-term quantifiable cost, but may only reap long-term non-quantifiable returns.

4.4 Evaluating different marketing communications tools

As a final round-up, here are some sample measures for evaluating the effectiveness of particular marketing communications tools and campaigns. (Not intended to be comprehensive: just some ideas.)

Table 11.4   Measures for evaluating marketing tool effectiveness

Advertising and direct mail	Awareness, recall and recognition testing
	Congeniality (likeability) to the target audience
	Attitude surveys
	Media exposure: viewer/listener/circulation figures
	Cost per 1,000 target audience reached
	Cost per direct sale, inquiry or response generated
	Pre- and post-measurement of sales, enquiries, order value etc
	Advertising industry/media awards
	User comment on, or sharing of, ad content (eg on YouTube)
	Monitoring hits on web advertising, banner ad clicks etc.
Sales promotion	Increased consumer sales during the promotion period
	Increased intermediary sales during trade promotion period
	First-time intermediary sales from the trade promotion
	Number of coupons, vouchers, competition entries received
	Quality customer data gathered and input to database
	Cost per sale or response generated

Public relations	Media exposure
	Research/testing of audience awareness of key messages
	Research/testing of audience attitudes and perceptions
	Sales recovery after crisis communication
	Specific audience measures eg:
	▪ Focus group awareness of a publicity campaign
	▪ Reduction in employee turnover
	▪ Positive coverage in financial and other media
	▪ Increased trade in shares
	▪ Endorsement (or less opposition) from pressure groups
	▪ Change in government policy in line with lobbying
Exhibitions	Awareness of brand in industry, trade press
	Media exposure at or related to the exhibition
	Number of visitors to the stand
	Number of new qualified leads generated
	Contacts later converted to sales, supply contracts or alliances
	(An Exhibition Industry Federation survey found that the average time to convert an exhibition lead to a sale was seven months, and in some cases, two years or more...)
	Cost per sales (or other value) generated
Sponsorship	Awareness of sponsorship and brand
	Direct sales and enquiries (if attributable to the sponsorship)
	Media exposure arising from the sponsorship
	Cost per sale or response generated
Relationship marketing	Repeat sales
	Increased order value and up-selling
	Take up and use of loyalty programmes
	Percentage of leads from customer recommendations/referrals
	Customer/supplier/intermediary/employee relationship duration
	Customer/supplier/intermediary/employee retention and defection rates
	Value added through collaboration, relationship leverage

THE REAL WORLD

Vodafone's sponsorship deal with **Manchester United** cost Vodafone £30 million over a four-year period. Vodafone clearly had to evaluate the effectiveness of this partnership in terms of its own marketing objectives. It did so in four ways:

▪ General awareness was measured through consumer research. For example, consumers were asked questions such as: 'Did you know that Vodafone sponsors Manchester United?'

▪ The impact on the performance of Vodafone's phones and accessories was measured by charting on-going improvements in sales.

▪ The success of value added services such as ManUmobile was monitored in terms of the number of people registered and usage of the service.

▪ Media evaluation: Vodafone monitored TV and press coverage to measure the exposure of the Vodafone brand resulting from the sponsorship.

Keeping check in this way enabled Vodafone to assess whether or not it had made a wise strategic move in teaming up with Manchester United. Evidence strongly suggests that it did.

The Chartered Institute of Marketing

CHAPTER ROUNDUP

- Marketing organisation: departmentalisation, matrix organisation

- Centralised and decentralised management

- Horizontal and up-side-down management for service delivery

- Factors in marketing communications mix decisions: stakeholder groups, push or pull approaches, audience readiness, product life cycle stage

- A framework marketing communications plan

- Budgets and budgetary control

- Methods of setting expenditure budgets: arbitrary, affordable, competitive parity, percentage of sales, objective/task

- Marginal analysis

- Media exposure, share of voice (SOV), campaign measurement and results-related measures

- Measuring different elements of the marketing communications mix

FURTHER READING

Marketing communications campaign planning and control

Jobber, D. (2007) *Principles & Practice of Marketing.* 5th edition. Maidenhead, McGraw-Hill Education
Case 25: Christian Aid.

REFERENCES

AdNews (2006) http://www.adnews.com.au [Accessed 21 June 2012].

Anon (2012) Q4 Bellwether: spend still up, confidence drops. *IPA*. http://www.ipa.co.uk/Content/Q4-Bellwether-spend-still-up-confidence-drops.

Daffy, C. (2001) *Once a Customer, Always a Customer.* 3rd edition. Oak Tree Press.

IPA (2012) IPA Bellwether Report. http://www.ipa.co.uk/page/IPA-Bellwether-Report [Accessed on 18 June 2012]

Jobber, D. (2007) *Principles & Practice of Marketing.* 5th edition. Maidenhead, Berks, McGraw Hill Education.

Peters, T. (1994) *Liberation Management.* New York, Pan.

Wilmshurst, J. (1999) *Fundamentals of Advertising.* 2nd edition. Oxford, Butterworth-Heinemann.

1   Distinguish between functional and brand departmentalisation.

2   Explain the advantages of decentralised management.

3   List five factors in selecting the communications mix.

4   What is the product life cycle and what communications tools are suitable for each stage of the cycle?

5   What are the advantages of (a) affordability and (b) competitive parity as approaches to setting marketing communications budgets?

6   What are the limitations of (a) percentage of sales and (b) objective and task budget-setting?

7   Explain the concept of the law of diminishing returns.

8   What is 'share of voice'?

9   What are the advantages and limitations of campaign measurement?

10   Identify five results-based performance measures for marketing communications.

ACTIVITY DEBRIEFS

Activity 11.1

The advantages and disadvantages of matrix organisation are as follows.

Advantages	Disadvantages
Greater employee flexibility: people and departments are geared to change	Higher managerial costs: extra layer of management
Greater flexibility of tasks/structure: the matrix can be short-term (eg for a project) and easily amended	Potential for conflict between functional and product/customer managers
Re-orientation towards responsiveness to customer needs, results	Stresses of dual authority (two bosses), dual responsibilities
Better managerial accountability for results	
Fosters cross-functional communication and co-operation	

Activity 11.2

Your own research.

Activity 11.3

Coca Cola is famous for its brand identity (logo style, bottle shape, 'real thing' slogan). One key strategy objective is to win the 'Cola Wars' against Pepsi. Communications pursue this end: eg through direct competitive advertising, culture-targeted advertising to build local markets, exclusivity deals in stocking school/office drinks machines.

Amnesty International is a non-commercial organisation with primarily ethical and political objectives. Communications pursue this end: eg through responsible (low-cost, non-discriminatory) publications, use of

PR/press relations and lobbying; direct contact selling of membership and subscription publications (involving the public rather than 'selling' to them, funds supporting causes, information on issues).

Activity 11.4

Your own research. Note that this is highly relevant to the kind of methodology and presentation that may be required for your assignment.

Activity 11.5

Examples of sales force information include: information about products and services (especially any changes or updates to the specifications); prices (especially any changes) and terms (eg discount policies); the content of advertising and other promotional activities; feedback from customers (complaints, comments); perhaps technical, industry and competitor developments (in markets where customers may want this sort of information or advice); information about the mission, values and policies of the organisation.

Activity 11.6

Your own research and development of a plan. Just have a go!

Activity 11.7

Your own research. This is just intended as a 'warm up' activity to give you a practical overview for the discussion that follows.

Activity 11.8

Arbitrary budgeting presents a crucial disadvantage of bearing no accurate or predictable relation to the levels of expenditure that may be affordable, profitable, or required to fulfil marketing objectives. This will be particularly critical if the budget is under-estimated, allocating inadequate funds to fulfil task objectives or to meet unexpected contingencies – or causing internal customer problems when marketing overspends the budget.

Arbitrary budgeting is poor internal marketing. It conveys the message that the marketing function has no awareness of the organisation's strategic objectives or resource constraints; that it always overestimates its budget needs (and can therefore have less resource allocated to it in future); or that it is careless with its expenditure.

Activity 11.9

We will leave you to do this, from the information given. Note that this kind of presentation is particularly useful for an assignment which asks you to 'compare and contrast' or 'evaluate': it allows you to put features or advantages and disadvantages clearly side by side – without taking up too much of your word count!

Activity 11.10

Response rates may be used to measure take-up of a public information service; donations or membership applications to a charity; or any specific response to a request or instruction given by the organisation (proxy votes returned by shareholders; tax returns submitted on time by taxpayers; overdue library books returned; attendance at meetings – and so on). Response rates are also a helpful measure of recruitment advertising: how many suitably qualified or minority group applicants responded to the ad?

1. Functional departmentalisation allocates tasks according to specialisation of skills or technology. Brand departmentalisation usually adds an extra tier of management, whereby brand managers co-ordinate the work of different functions on behalf of the brand.

2. See the table in section 1.3 for a selection of advantages.

3. Factors in selecting the communications mix include: media consumption and influence; push or pull communication strategy; product/market or stakeholder type; audience readiness; and product life cycle stage.

4. The product life cycle is a model of how a product performs over its lifetime in the market. See the table in section 2.1.5 for the stages and appropriate communication tools.

5. Affordability is highly relevant, since it takes account of resource availability. Competitive parity ensures matching of competitor activity, to preserve market share, and may prevent advertising/promotion wars with competitors.

6. Percentage of sales doesn't take account of marketing objectives and opportunities; doesn't provide a means of determining the 'correct' percentage to use; and may cause a vicious circle if sales decline. Objective and task budget-setting is only limited through the difficulty of estimating the costs of tasks, and particularly unforeseen contingencies and opportunities.

7. The law of diminishing returns says that the marginal return (in sales) from every £1 of extra communications expenditure will decline (because as more of the audience is reached, and more people already own the product, the difference made by the extra investment will not be as great). It will eventually reach the point where the marginal benefit no longer exceeds the marginal cost.

8. Share of voice is a brand's total communications presence or 'advertising weight', measured as a percentage of a defined total market or market segment in a given time period.

9. See section 4.2.1 for a full answer.

10. Results-based performance measures include: sales, response rates, conversion rates, repeat orders and order value.

Index

3OR model, 65
3Ps, 147
4 Ps, 135

Above-the-line promotion, **204**
Activity links, 59
Actor bonds, 59
ACURA, 109
Adaptation, 263
Added value, 16, 18, 88, 98, 106, 112, 113, 123, 150, 192
Advertising, 205
Alliance market, 64
Amazon.co.uk, 60
Amazon.com, 70
Attitudes, 173

Band width, 268
Below-the-line promotion, 204
Blogs, 274
Brand, 115
Branding, 217
Budget, 303
Business processes, 48
Buyer behaviour, 176

Causal pressure groups, 45
Cause-related marketing, 40
Centralised management, 295
Channels, 61
Classic market relationships, 66
Codes of Ethics, 36
Commitment, 91
Communications plan, 298, 301, 302, 303
Computer Telephony Integration, 277
Conflicting interests, 8
Connected stakeholders, 4, 17
Consumer buyer behaviour, 176
Consumerism, 32, 38
Contractual relationships, 7
Co-ordination, 250
Corporate citizens, 36
Corporate Social Responsibility (CSR), 36
Crisis communication, 44
Crisis management, 43
Customer loyalty, 95
Customer markets, 63
Customer Relationship Management (CRM), 74, **93**
Customer retention, 96
Customers, 6, 17
Customisation, 73

Data mining, **93**
Database marketing, 93
Decentralisation, 295
Decision making unit (DMU), 64
Decision-making process (DMP), 178
Dell Computers, 73
Departmentalisation, 292
Direct marketing, 215

Ebbs, 268
Employee loyalty, 242
Employees, 6, 16, 43
Employers associations, 46
Empowerment, 248
Environment, 38
Environmental issues, 41
Environmentalism, 38
E-Procurement, 279
E-relationships, 72
E-Sourcing, 279
Ethical consumption, 38
External stakeholders, 4, 18, 30
Externalities, 14
E-zines, 274

Fair trade marketing, **40**
Four Ps, 134
French and Raven, 10

Globalisation, **260**
Government, 31, 33
Green consumption, 41
Green marketing, 41
Gummesson, 42, 65

Hainsworth & Meng, 43

IBM, 70
Identity, 115
Indicators of power, 11
Influence market, 32
Influence, 8
Integrated Marketing Communications (IMC), 224
Interactivity, 269
Interest groups, 46
Internal customer relationships, 73
Internal market, 234
Internal marketing, 43, 64, **235**
Internal markets, 64
Internal stakeholders, 4, 16
International, 260
Issues life cycle, 43
Issues management, 43

The Chartered
Institute of Marketing

The Chartered
Institute of Marketing

The Chartered
Institute of Marketing

The Chartered
Institute of Marketing

The Chartered
Institute of Marketing

The Chartered
Institute of Marketing

Review form

Please help us to ensure that the CIM learning materials we produce remain as accurate and user-friendly as possible. We cannot promise to answer every submission we receive, but we do promise that it will be read and taken into account when we update this Study Text.

Name: _____   **Address:** _____

_____

_____

1. How have you used this Text?
(Tick one box only)

☐ Self study (book only)

☐ On a course: college_____

☐ Other _____

3. Why did you decide to purchase this Text?
(Tick one box only)

☐ Have used companion Assessment workbook

☐ Have used BPP Texts in the past

☐ Recommendation by friend/colleague

☐ Recommendation by a lecturer at college

☐ Saw advertising in journals

☐ Saw information on BPP website

☐ Other _____

2. During the past six months do you recall seeing/receiving any of the following?
(Tick as many boxes as are relevant)

☐ Our advertisement in *The Marketer*

☐ Our brochure with a letter through the post

☐ Our website www.bpp.com

4. Which (if any) aspects of our advertising do you find useful?
(Tick as many boxes as are relevant)

☐ Prices and publication dates of new editions

☐ Information on product content

☐ Facility to order books off-the-page

☐ None of the above

5. Have you used the companion Assessment Workbook?   Yes ☐   No ☐

6. Have you used the companion Passcards?   Yes ☐   No ☐

7. Your ratings, comments and suggestions would be appreciated on the following areas.

	Very useful	Useful	Not useful
Introductory section (How to use this text, study checklist, etc)	☐	☐	☐
Chapter introductions	☐	☐	☐
Syllabus learning outcomes	☐	☐	☐
Activities	☐	☐	☐
The Real World examples	☐	☐	☐
Quick quizzes	☐	☐	
Quality of explanations			
Index	☐	☐	☐
Structure and presentation	☐	☐	☐

	Excellent	Good	Adequate	Poor
Overall opinion of this Text	☐	☐	☐	☐

8. Do you intend to continue using BPP CIM products?   ☐ Yes   ☐ No

On the reverse of this page is space for you to write your comments about our Study Text. We welcome your feedback.

Please return to: CIM Publishing Manager, BPP Learning Media, FREEPOST, London, W12 8BR.

TELL US WHAT YOU THINK

Please note any further comments and suggestions/errors below. For example, was the text accurate, readable, concise, user-friendly and comprehensive?